ESSAYS IN
JURISPRUDENCE AND PHILOSOPHY

ESSAYS IN
JURISPRUDENCE
AND
PHILOSOPHY

by
H. L. A. HART

CLARENDON PRESS · OXFORD
1983

Oxford University Press, Walton Street, Oxford OX2 6DP

London Glasgow New York Toronto
Delhi Bombay Calcutta Madras Karachi
Kuala Lumpur Singapore Hong Kong Tokyo
Nairobi Dar es Salaam Cape Town
Melbourne Auckland

and associated companies in
Beirut Berlin Ibadan Mexico City Nicosia

Oxford is a trade mark of Oxford University Press

Published in the United States
by Oxford University Press, New York

British Library Cataloguing in Publication Data
Hart, H. L. A.
Essays in jurisprudence and philosophy.
1. Jurisprudence
I. Title
340'.1   K230
ISBN 0-19-825387-7
ISBN 0-19-825388-5 Pbk

Library of Congress Cataloging in Publication Data
Hart, H. L. A. (Herbert Lionel Adolphus), 1907–
Essays in jurisprudence and philosophy.
Includes index.
1. Jurisprudence — Addresses, essays, lectures.
2. Law — Philosophy — Addresses, essays, lectures.
I. Title.
K230.H365A2 1983   340'.1   83–4197
ISBN 0-19-825387-7
ISBN 0-19-825388-5 (pbk.)

Set by Hope Services, Abingdon
Printed in Great Britain
at the University Press, Oxford
by Eric Buckley,
Printer to the University

Contents

Acknowledgements

Essay 1. Reprinted from *Law Quarterly Review*, vol. 70 (Jan. 1954), by permission of Sweet & Maxwell Ltd.

Essay 2. Reprinted with permission from *Harvard Law Review*, vol. 71 (Feb. 1958). Copyright © 1958 Harvard Law Review Association, Cambridge, Mass.

Essay 3. Reprinted by permission of the publisher from the *Encyclopedia of Philosophy*, Paul Edwards, Editor in Chief, vol. 6, pp. 264-76. Copyright © 1967 by Macmillan, Inc.

Essay 4. This article was originally published in 11 *Georgia Law Review*, No. 5 and is reprinted by permission.

Essay 5. Reprinted by permission from 1776-1976, 51 *New York Law Review* 538 (1976).

Essay 6. Reprinted by permission of Cambridge University Press from *Cambridge Law Journal*, vol. 17 (1959), pp. 233-40.

Essay 7. Reprinted by permission of Norstedts, Stockholm, Sweden from *Festskrift till Karl Olivecrona*, pp. 307-16 (1964).

Essay 8. Reprinted by permission of the Tulane Law Review Association from *Tulane Law Review*, vol. 53, No. 3 (April 1979).

Essay 9. Copyright © 1983 by the Directors of the Columbia Law Review Association, Inc, all rights reserved. This article originally appeared at 79 *Col. L. Rev.* 828-46 (1979). Reprinted by permission.

Essay 10. Copyright © 1973 The University of Chicago Law Review. Reprinted with permission from 40 *U. Chi. L. Rev.* 534-55 (1973).

Essay 11. Copyright © 1967 The University of Chicago Law Review. Reprinted with permission from 35 *U. Chi. L. Rev.* 1-13 (1967).

Essay 12. Reprinted by permission of Vandenhoeck & Ruprecht Verlag. from *Jherings Erbe, Göttinger Symposium zur 150 Wiederkehr des Geburtstags von Rudolph von Ihering*, ed. F. Wieacker and Chr. Wollschläger (1970).

Essay 13. Reprinted with permission from *The New York Review of Books*. Copyright © 1963 Nyrev, Inc.

Essay 14. Reprinted with permission from *UCLA Law Review*, vol. 10 (1963), pp. 709-28. © 1963 The Regents of the University of California.

Essay 15. Reprinted from *Ethics and Social Justice*, edited by Howard E. Kiefer and Milton K. Munitz, by permission of the publisher. © 1968, 1970, State University of New York Press, Albany, New York. All rights reserved.

Essay 16. Reprinted with permission from *Harvard Law Review*, vol. 78 (1965), pp. 1281-96. Copyright © 1965 Harvard Law Review Association, Cambridge, Mass.

Essay 17. Reprinted by permission of the publisher from *Crime, Proof and Punishment: Essays in Memory of Sir Rupert Cross*, edited by Colin Tapper (Butterworth, 1981).

Introduction

I

The seventeen essays collected here were written over a period of twenty-eight years (1953–81) and cover a wide range of topics. I have arranged sixteen of them in more or less distinct groups, roughly labelled, as follows: I, General Theory; II, American Jurisprudence; III, Scandinavian Jurisprudence; IV, Liberty, Utility, and Rights; V, Four Legal Theorists. The last essay included here (Essay 17: The House of Lords on Attempting the Impossible) stands apart from the rest, since it deals not with any recognized philosophical or jurisprudential issue but with what was, until its elimination by statute in 1981, a particular doctrine of English Criminal Law. My justification for including it here is that it brings a distinction established in modern philosophical semantics to the solution — or dissolution — of a perplexity concerning the notion of an attempt which has long plagued lawyers on both sides of the Atlantic. I hope that my use of philosophy in this last essay supports the belief on which I have acted in most of my work, that if there is some philosophical point which can clarify or settle issues which non-philosophers have found problematic, it is always possible simultaneously to expound for them the philosophical point and to use it for that purpose.

In the course of the years during which these essays were written some of my views have changed. Though I still adhere to the central themes for which I argue in these essays, there are certainly points where I now think I was mistaken, others which I failed to relate to important wider issues or presented in an oversimplified or confused form. I have learned much during this period from my many critics, some of whom, including Professor Dworkin, Dr Raz and Dr Finnis, and the late Professor Lon Fuller,[1] have produced theories of their own in which my works are taken as a principal target.

I have also learnt much during the period covered by these

---

[1] See references to their works added to several of these essays.

essays from later developments in philosophy. Thus, to take one example, which I discuss further below, had I commanded at the time of writing Essay 1 in 1953 the seminal distinction between the 'meaning' and the 'force' of utterances, and the theory of 'speech acts' the foundations of which were laid by J. L. Austin, I should not have claimed that statements of legal rights and duties were not 'descriptive', or have suggested, as I did by calling them 'conclusions of law' and 'the tail ends of legal calculations', that such statements were always put forward as inferences drawn by their authors. I have, however, notwithstanding recognition of errors in these essays, left the text untouched while adding to most of them a postscript referring the reader to the most important criticisms which they have attracted, or to opposed views.

Perhaps the following observations (which I hope are not excessively autobiographical) will sufficiently indicate and explain the character and degree of error as I now retrospectively see it in these essays. In 1953 when I was elected to the Chair of Jurisprudence at Oxford my qualifications were unorthodox. I had no law degree, but for eight years before the war I had practised as a Chancery Barrister and for seven years after the war I had taught philosophy at Oxford. Those seven years fell within the period when the approach to philosophy which became known as 'linguistic philosophy' was at its most influential both in Oxford and Cambridge. There were important differences of emphasis and aim between the Oxford variant of this form of philosophy, where J. L. Austin was its leading exponent, and the Cambridge variant which flourished under Wittgenstein. None the less both were inspired by the recognition of the great variety of types of human discourse and meaningful communication, and with this recognition there went a conviction that longstanding philosophical perplexities could often be resolved not by the deployment of some general theory but by sensitive piecemeal discrimination and characterization of the different ways, some reflecting different forms of human life, in which human language is used. According to this conception of philosophy it had been a blinding error of much philosophy in the past, and most recently and notably of the Logical Positivism of the pre-war years, to assume that there are only a few forms of discourse (empirical 'fact-stating' discourse or statements of definitional or logically necessary truths) which are meaningful, and to dismiss as meaningless or as mere expressions of feeling all other uses of language which, as in the case of some metaphysical statements or moral judgements, could not be shown to be disguised or complex forms of the few favoured types of discourse.

Linguistic philosophy thus conceived as an elucidation of the multiple forms and diverse functions of language knew no boundaries of subject-matter: its insights and illumination were available for the clarification not only of the discourse of everyday life but of any discipline at the points where there were reasons for thinking that a failure to grasp the differences between one form of discourse and another, which were often concealed by identical grammatical forms, have produced perplexity or confusion. So in Essay 1, written under the powerful and exciting influence of these ideas, I attempted to demonstrate the relevance of this form of linguistic philosophy to the philosophy of law and jurisprudence. For it seemed to me (and still seems) that attention to the diverse and complex ways in which words work in conjunction with legal rules of different types would serve to dispel confusion, such as that which had helped to generate vague inconclusive and conflicting theories of the nature of corporate bodies and corporate personality, which had long haunted jurisprudence, or had led serious jurists to claim that statements of legal rights referred to imaginary or fictitious entities 'having nothing to do with reality', or, alternatively, were predictions of juridical action. It is true that legal nouns like 'right', 'duty', or the name of a limited company seem not to have obvious counterparts in the world for which they stand or which they mean, and this has been one persisting source of perplexity. As Bentham had seen, attempts to define such expressions per genus and species in abstraction from the sentences and context in which they normally function had proved fruitless. But, as I argued here, what was needed was a close examination of the way in which statements e.g. of legal rights or of the duties of a limited company relate to the world in conjunction with legal rules, and the important first step to take was to ask under what conditions statements of this kind have a truth value and are true.

In other essays (Essays 3 and 12) I draw attention to some

other specific themes of linguistic philosophy which are of particular relevance to jurisprudence. These include the identification of a 'performative' use of language, where words are used in conjunction with a background of rules or conventions to change the normative situation of individuals and so have normative consequences and not merely causal effects. Thus, as I briefly show, this use of language is involved not only in the enactment of legislation (too often mis-assimilated to the simpler notion of a command), but in various legal transactions or so-called acts-in-the-law. Attention to the various modalities of the performative use of language serves to clarify among other things the idea of legal powers, contracts, and conveyances, and serves to disentangle what is true in the longstanding, competing will-theories and objective theories of contract. It also makes evident the interesting connections between such important legal phenomena and less formal ways 'of doing things with words' such as a christening ceremony, vows, and (though this is still contro-versial) the making of a promise.

So too, as I attempt to show in Essays 3 and 12, philos-ophers' discussions of the 'open texture' of language and generally of the ways in which the classificatory terms of a natural language may prove indeterminate is relevant to the study of adjudication and legal reasoning. Similarly, their insistence that there is not just one form of justification (the possession of common qualities) for classifying particulars under the same general term serves to free speculation from a cramping prejudice which has complicated both general accounts of the nature of law and the exposition of particular legal concepts such as that of possession.

II

These and other insights of modern linguistic philosophy are I think of permanent value, and the analytical study of the law has been advanced by them, but I certainly see a number of defects in my deployment of these ideas in my early essays. Thus the concept of different 'uses of language' is not as simple as I suggested; it is itself in need of clarification, there being a number of different senses of 'use'. Hence, in Essay 1 I fail to allow for the important distinction between the

relatively constant meaning or sense of a sentence fixed by
the conventions of language and the varying 'force' or way in
which it is put forward by the writer or speaker on different
occasions. 'There is a bull in the field' has the same meaning
or content whether it is intended by the author as an answer
to requests for information or as a warning or hypothesis.
Neglect of this distinction, to which I later drew attention in
Essay 3, vitiates part of my account in Essay 1 of the meaning
of statements of legal rights or statements about corporations.
It was just wrong to say that such statements *are* the conclusions of inferences from legal rules, for such sentences have
the same meaning on different occasions of use whether or
not the speaker or writer puts them forward as inferences
which he has drawn. If he does put such a statement forward
as an inference, that is the force of the utterance on that
occasion, not part of the meaning of the sentence. What
compounds my error is that though I speak of such sentences
as capable of being true or false I deny that they are 'descriptive' as if this were excluded by the status which I wrongly
assign to them as conclusions of law, and my denial that
such sentences are 'descriptive' obscured the truth that for a
full understanding of them we must understand what it is
for a rule of conduct to require, prohibit, or permit an act.

A more general defect in my early invocation in jurisprudence of linguistic philosophy was a failure to make clear
that an understanding, however sophisticated or profound,
of the workings of language could only yield significant
results for jurisprudence where difficulties had arisen from
a failure to identify the way in which some particular use of
language deviated from some tacitly accepted paradigm, or
where radically different forms of expression were mistakenly
assimilated to some familiar form. Misleading jurisprudential
theories such as those designed to explain the concepts of a
corporate body or legal rights or legal transactions such as
contract had arisen in part in these ways, but I should have
emphasized that it is an important feature of those legal
concepts, which linguistic philosophy could help most to free
from misunderstanding or confusion, that they constituted
sources of perplexity even when their applications to particular
cases were uncontroversial, and even for those who had a
perfect mastery of these concepts within the field of their

day-to-day use. The methods of linguistic philosophy which are neutral between moral and political principles and silent about different points of view which might endow one feature rather than another of legal phenomena with significance were suitable for such cases. Hence they are not suitable for resolving or clarifying those controversies which arise, as many of the central problems of legal philosophy do, from the divergence between partly overlapping concepts reflecting a divergence of basic point of view or values or background theory, or which arise from conflict or incompleteness of legal rules. For such cases what is needed is first, the identification of the latent conflicting points of view which led to the choice or formation of divergent concepts, and secondly, reasoned argument directed to establishing the merits of conflicting theories, divergent concepts or rules, or to showing how these could be made compatible by some suitable restriction of their scope.

III

Essay 2, given as the Holmes Lecture at Harvard, contains the germ of many of the arguments which I used in defence of a form of legal positivism in the *Concept of Law*, published five years later. This has provoked a very large subsidiary literature, much of it critical of the two main themes of this essay: first, my denial that there are any important necessary connections between law and morality, and secondly, my insistence that in any modern legal system there must be many occasions where the settled law fails to dictate a decision either way, so that if courts have to decide such cases they must exercise a limited 'interstitial' law-making power, or 'discretion'.

I hope that I am not simply blinded by natural obstinacy or by age in still adhering to these now much criticized positions. But I certainly recognize that my treatment in this essay of both these issues is at some points over-simple and at others obscure. Thus in connection with the second of these issues it may seem from what I wrote in Essay 2 that I thought that judges, when they reach a point at which the existing settled law fails to determine a decision either way, simply push aside their law-books and start to legislate *de novo* for the case in hand without further reference to the law. In fact this has never been my view, and at various points in Essays 3 and 4 I show that among the features which distinguish the judicial from legislative law-making is the importance characteristically attached by courts, when deciding cases left unregulated by the existing law, to proceeding by analogy so as to ensure that the new law they make is in accordance with principles or under-pinning reasons which can be recognized as already having a footing in existing law. Very often in deciding such cases courts cite some general principle or general aim or purpose which a considerable area of the existing law can be understood as exemplifying or advancing, and which points towards a determinate answer for the instant case. But to admit this is not to admit the correctness of a general holistic theory of law as a gapless system of entitlements, such as Dworkin has advanced and which I argue in Essay 4 is 'a noble dream' as remote from the truth as the 'nightmare' belief that judges never find but always make the law which they apply in particular cases. For though the search for and use of principles underlying the law defers the moment, it cannot eliminate the need for judicial law-making, since in any hard case different principles supporting competing analogies may present themselves and the judge will have to choose between them, relying like a conscientious legislator on his sense of what is best and not on any already established order of priorities among principles already prescribed for him by the law. Only if for all such cases there was always to be found, as Dworkin's theory implies, implicit in the existing law some unique set of higher order principles assigning relative weights or priorities to competing lower order principles would the moment for judicial law-making be not merely deferred but eliminated.

But there is a more serious defect in my argument on this point, since it is one of substance, not merely of exposition. Essay 3 treats the indeterminacy of legal rules as if this was always a purely linguistic matter, that is, solely a function of the indeterminacy of the constituent words used in the formulation of a particular rule. In fact, as I came later to see and to say in Essay 4, the question whether a *rule* applies or does not apply to some particular situation of fact is not the same as the question whether according to the settled

conventions of language this is determined or left open by
the words of that rule. For a legal system often has other
resources besides the words used in the formulations of its
rules which serve to determine their content or meaning in
particular cases. Thus, as I say in Essay 3, the obvious or
agreed purpose of a rule may be used to render determinate
a rule whose application may be left open by the conventions
of language, and may serve to show that words in the context
of a legal rule may have a meaning different from that which
they have in other contexts. My failure to make this clear
amounts, as Fuller argued in his reply to Essay 2, to a defective theory of statutory interpretation, which I do something
to correct in my later discussion, in Essay 3, of what it is that
makes clear cases clear. Certainly my arguments need to
be both amplified and corrected on this point. But their
correction does nothing to support the claim that the law is
a gapless system never incomplete and containing within it an
answer to every question of law even in the hardest of hard
cases, so that judges never have to exercise a law-making
power in choosing between alternatives left open by the
existing law.

IV

My main concern however in Essay 3 was to defend the
wisdom of insisting, as Bentham and Austin had, on the
distinction between law as it is and law as morally it ought to
be, against various forms of the claim that there are conceptual
necessary connections, not merely contingent ones, between
law and morality. Though Bentham's and Austin's general
theory of law is unsatisfactory in other respects, which I
indicated in this essay, the attempt to show that the distinction that they continually stress between what the law is and
what it ought to be is misleading, itself rests on a confusion of
issues which I attempt to disentangle and in particular on the
misidentification of the 'purpose' or function which laws
may have with a moral aim or value. However, I certainly
failed to discuss adequately different forms of the claim that
there is a conceptual connection between law and morality
which are compatible with the distinction between law as it is
and law as it ought to be. These include theories such as that

advanced by Fuller (which I criticize in Essay 16), that standards for the moral evaluation of law are implicit in the concept of law itself ('the inner morality of law'), even if laws often fail to satisfy such standards. Again, there need to be considered theories asserting that even if the law falls so far short of what morally it ought to be that there is no moral obligation, all things considered, to conform to it, there is none the less always a prima facie moral reason for conforming to the law, even if this may be outweighed by the moral badness of a particular law. There is also to be considered the theory that the law always *claims* moral authority, so that when courts hold that individuals have legal obligations to act contrary to their interest such holdings necessarily constitute a form of moral judgment, even if it is mistaken or insincere. (Theories of this latter sort do not strictly assert a conceptual connection between law and morality, but rather between law and certain professed moral beliefs.)

Since some important varieties of such theories form part of new comprehensive theories of law which have been elaborated since I wrote Essay 2, they certainly deserve consideration at length, but here I can only briefly indicate my objections to them. Thus, Dworkin has argued for the superior adequacy of a concept of law which includes, besides the explicit settled law of a system, a set of implicit principles hierarchically structured ('the soundest theory of the law') which both explains the settled law and exhibits its best moral justification, and which will yield a determinate answer when the explicit law fails to provide one. In addition to other difficulties (some of which I briefly note in Essays 4 and 5) this theory of law, though claiming to be distinct from 'orthodox natural law theory', seems to me to run into insuperable difficulties in its attempt to explain how there can be, as Dworkin admits, morally wicked legal systems in which what is legally right so far diverges from what is morally right that a judge would have a moral duty to lie rather than say what the law really is.

Raz, on the other hand, whose theory is generally of a severely positivist cast (since it requires that the law in any system be identified without reference to any moral criterion or argument and rejects any general moral obligation to conform to law), none the less holds out an olive branch to those who claim that there is an important conceptual connection between law and morality. For he rejects what he terms the positivist semantic theory which claims that statements of rights, obligations, or duty have a different meaning in legal and moral contexts; his rejection, however, of this semantic thesis does not entail that statements of legal rights and duties etc. always constitute a moral judgment or moral endorsement of the law to which its author is committed. For such statements, according to Raz, may be 'detached', that is, made as if from the point of view of one who holds that there is a moral obligation to do what the law requires, yet made by one who does not share that point of view. Such detached statements explain the normative language used by lawyers and others to describe the content of law without committing them in any way to its moral endorsement. On this view the main conceptual connection between law and morality reduces to the fact that where a legal system is in force its judges claim moral authority for the law and make committed statements of legal rights and duties, and so must believe or at least pretend to believe that there is a moral obligation to conform to law. But since according to this theory there is no general moral obligation to conform to the law, this may seem to be a minimal form of conceptual connection between law and morality, and certainly offers no ground for denying the distinction between law as it is and law as it ought to be. Yet, minimal as it is, it seems to me to be unrealistic to suppose that judges in making statements of legal obligation *must* always either believe or pretend to believe in the false theory that there is always a moral obligation to conform to the law. It seems to me that such statements may be better construed as stating what may be properly *demanded* of their subjects by way of action according to the law which the judges accept as setting the correct standard of legal adjudication and law enforcement.

Finnis's flexible interpretation of natural law is in many respects complementary to rather than a rival of positivist legal theory. For it is mainly concerned to elaborate a conception of natural law as consisting of certain principles of 'practical reason' for the ordering of human life and society directed to the realization of certain allegedly self-evident objective values or forms of good, and then to show that for their realization an authoritative human law and respect for such authority are required. Failure on the part of human law to conform to such principles of practical reason render it defective or perverse in various degrees, but will not, as in some versions of natural law (which Finnis considers a distortion), deprive such laws of their legal status, though they may be considered 'less legal' on that account. On this view, which recognizes the distinction between law as it is and law as it ought to be, the chief conceptual tie between law and morality is that the conception of a system of law orientated to an objective common good and fully conforming to the requirements of practical reason not only furnishes the basic forms of criticism of actual legal systems but constitutes the most illuminating perspective for understanding their actual working, the forms of legal reasoning, and the normative force of descriptions of the law in terms of rights, duties, and obligations. This conception is said to be the 'focal' meaning and central case of law. None the less positive law has a relative autonomy or independence of this ideal conception, so that lawyers for the internal purposes of the legal system properly speak of law and its obligations as if these were insulated from the moral merits of the law with which the 'flow' of practical reason is concerned.

The chief and very great merit of this natural law approach is that it shows the need to study law in the context of other disciplines and fosters awareness of the way in which unspoken assumptions, common sense, and moral aims influence the law and enter into adjudication. But these valuable lessons can be taught in other ways, and my objection to their presentation in a revived form of natural law theory (apart from my disagreement with its underlying philosophy of self-evident objective values) is that its stress on an ideal form of law which satisfies the requirements of practical reason as the 'central case' or 'focal meaning' of law, and the treatment of morally bad law as 'less legal', will revive old confusions between law and the standards appropriate for the criticism of law. Thus, in order to defend classical natural law theories from the distortions of which Finnis considers positivist critics (including myself) have been guilty, it has to be elaborately explained how it is that famous phrases such as Aquinas's statement that 'law is nothing else than an ordinance of reason for the common good',[2] is quite compatible with his statement that 'laws framed by men are either just or unjust'.[3] It is so because while 'law' in the last of these two statements refers to positive law, in the first statement it refers to law satisfying all the requirements of practical reason and so morally binding. The identification of the 'central case' of law with law in its ideal form will, I fear, invite a return to these obfuscating complexities. The contrary positivist stress on the elucidation of the concept of law, without reference to the moral values which it may be used to promote, seems to me to offer better guarantees of clear thought. But apart from this, the identification of the central meaning of law with what is morally legitimate, because orientated towards the common good, seems to me in view of the hideous record of the evil use of law for oppression to be an unbalanced perspective, and as great a distortion as the opposite Marxist identification of the central case of law with the pursuit of the interests of a dominant economic class.

V

In Essay 6 I focus attention on some themes of modern Scandinavian jurisprudence descended from the work of Axel Hägerström. These are instructive and somewhat startling examples in the field of jurisprudence of the same failure on the part of philosophers of considerable power to appreciate the wide variety of forms of intelligible human discourse that led Logical Positivists to stigmatize as meaningless metaphysical statements and moral judgments. Hägerström himself had understood more clearly than his predecessors that certain uses of language within the law were anomalous compared with what was commonly assumed to be its normal function. For he saw that the verbal forms used both in ancient and modern legal systems to effect such legal transactions as the alienation of property, or the making of an

---

[2] *Summa Theol.* I–II, Q. 90, art. 4. 'Definitio legis nihil est aliud quam quaedam rationis ordinatio ad bonum commune ab eo qui curam communitatis habet promulgata.'

[3] Ibid., Q. 96, art. 5. 'Leges positae humanitus sunt vel justae vel injustae.'

offer, a will, or a contract, were not, as their indicative
grammatical form often suggested, mere reports of the
intention or the will of those entering into such transactions,
and the conventional juristic classification of such verbal
forms as 'declarations of intention' left unexplained their
dynamic role in changing the legal situation of the parties.[4]
But Hägerström's explanation of this phenomenon in terms
of beliefs in 'mystical bonds' and 'the magical' powers of
language to produce changes in a supernatural world of rights
and duties simply abandoned the task of serious analysis of
an important dimension of language, the use of which is not
confined to legal contexts, and led his followers into a
blind alley.

Thus in Alf Ross, the most acute and best-equipped
philosopher of this school, a narrow empiricist conception
of rational meaningful discourse had bred a readiness to see
'superstition', 'fiction', or 'meaningless metaphysics' 'raising
the law above the world of facts' as embodied in the normative concepts and modes of description customarily used by
lawyers in representing the law. So he claimed that the only
method of representation of the law fit to figure in a modern
rational science of law was one which shared the structure
and logic of statements of empirical science. In effect this
involves an interpretation of propositions of law such as
statements of legal validity or legal obligation or legal rights
as essentially predictions of judicial behaviour accompanied
by feelings of being bound by legal directives.

My main objection to this reduction of propositions of law
which suppresses their normative aspect is that it fails to mark
and explain the crucial distinction that there is between mere
regularities of human behaviour and rule-governed behaviour.
It thus jettisons something vital to the understanding not only
of law but of any form of normative social structure. For the
understanding of this the methodology of the empirical
sciences is useless; what is needed is a 'hermeneutic' method
which involves portraying rule-governed behaviour as it
appears to its participants, who see it as conforming or
failing to conform to certain shared standards. My explanation
of the distinction which I have here called crucial is in terms

[4] *An Inquiry into the Nature of Law and Morals* (Uppsala 1953), pp. 5 ff. and
ch. 5.

of the idea of the 'acceptance' of preferred patterns of conduct as guides and standards of criticism, and so of an attitude to conduct which I call an 'internal point of view'. In the *Concept of Law* these ideas are elaborated further, though not wholly to my own satisfaction or that of those of my critics who, while complaining of various detailed aspects of my exposition, have generally welcomed my introduction of these ideas into jurisprudence as constituting an appropriate hermeneutic approach.

However, in Essay 6, in explaining the important difference between 'mere feelings of being bound' which Ross includes in his analysis, and the internal point of view of one who accepts a rule, I said something misleading. I drew a distinction between internal statements which manifest their authors' acceptance of a rule and external statements which simply state or predict certain regularities of behaviour whether it is rule-governed or not. But I wrongly wrote as if the normative vocabulary of 'ought', 'must', 'obligation', 'duty' were only properly used in such internal statements. This is a mistake, because, of course, such terms are quite properly used in other forms of statement, and particularly in lawyers' statements of legal obligations or duties describing the contents of a legal system (whether it be their own or an alien system) whose rules they themselves in no way endorse or accept as standards of behaviour. In so doing, lawyers report in normative form the contents of a law from the point of view of those who do accept its rules without themselves sharing that point of view. In terms of Raz's distinction, already mentioned, such statements of legal obligation or duties are 'detached', whereas the same statements made by those who accept the relevant rule are 'committed'. Of course those who make such 'detached' statements must understand the point of view of one who accepts the rule, and so their point of view might well be called 'hermeneutic'. Such detached statements constitute a third kind of statement to add to the two (internal and external statements) which I distinguish. To have made all this clear I should have emphasized that as well as the distinction between mere regularities of behaviour and rule-governed behaviour we need a distinction between the acceptance of rules and the recognition of their acceptance by others.

The distinction between committed and detached normative statements and the clarification of the hermeneutic
point of view throws light on what for many has been an
obscurity in Kelsen's characterization of propositions of law
made by legal theorists in expounding the law as 'rules in a
descriptive sense'. I discuss in Essay 14 Kelsen's account of
'ought-statements', in which the theorist of law represents
the norms, as 'having merely a descriptive import', but
though I had some glimmer then of important distinctions
between committed and detached statements I did not see
clearly that it was this distinction which Kelsen in effect
was making.

In Essay 7 I confront another quite different case, where
Ross claims to discover in lawyers' thinking a belief in the
'magical'. He finds this in their recognition of 'self-referring'
provisions made by certain constitutional laws for their own
repeal or amendment as legally valid and effective. English
constitutional lawyers are familiar with such provisions when
used to 'entrench' basic constitutional laws against change
by ordinary methods. Ross, however, who apparently believed
that no proposition (in which he included propositions of
law) could logically or meaningfully refer to itself, claimed
that if for example, Article 5 of the United States Constitution, providing for the amendment of the Constitution,
were held by lawyers to apply to itself and be capable of being
amended by the procedure which it itself determined, this
view was simply 'a social psychological fact', and the belief in
its legal validity was simply 'the expression of ideas which
cannot be expressed rationally but only in magical terms'.

In countering this extraordinary claim I drew a distinction
between *purely* self-referring laws, which are indeed empty
for lack of other reference, and partly self-referring laws like
the constitutional provisions in question, which refer both to
other laws and to themselves, and I endeavoured to show
how these give rise not to a vicious infinite regress or any
other logical vice, but to an infinite series of possible applications. Since my competence as a formal logician is very
limited I was glad to see this distinction accepted and formalized by Mr John Mackie in his illuminating treatment of
logical paradoxes.[5] While I think my arguments successfully

---

[5] In *Truth, Probability, and Paradox* (Oxford, 1973), ch. vi, pp. 285 ff.

dispose of Ross's scepticism (and also of Kelsen's argument that Austin's claim that all laws must have a sanction provided by law commits him to a vicious infinite regress), there is one argument advanced by Ross which though mistaken does, as I now see, show that there was *something* to be explained in what Ross took to be problematic. He argued that where one law authorizes the creation of other laws the continuing validity of laws so created must logically depend on the continued existence of the parent law authorizing their creation. This is a mistake, though certainly in some jurisdictions (including at one time English Common Law) the repeal of an enactment empowering rule-making has been taken to abrogate all rules made thereunder. But this is not a matter of logical necessity, and the contrary principle is widely accepted. However, what is true (and may have been confused by Ross with his mistaken claim) is that if courts affirm the continued validity of subordinate laws after the repeal of the parent law, without invoking any specific legal provision requiring this, they must tacitly accept the general principle that laws validly created according to the law at the time of creation remain valid until they expire according to their terms, or are validly terminated according to the law at the date of purported termination. So the continuing validity of subordinate laws notwithstanding the repeal of their parent laws depends on this principle and not, as Ross thought, on the continuing existence of the parent law. Largely as the result of Finnis's discussion[6] of this topic, I now see that I should have referred to this principle in my answer in Essay 16 to Fuller's complaint that my theory of law left unexplained the survival after a revolution of a great mass of laws made before the revolutionary break.

VI

In Essays 8-11 I consider different forms of liberal individualism which have issued in theories of basic human rights or liberties, in assertions of the priority of liberty over other values, or in resistance to claims that the legal enforcement of a society's conventional morality may be required and

[6] In 'Revolutions and Continuity of Law', *Oxford Essays in Jurisprudence*, Second Series (1973), 61-5.

justified as a means of preserving society from 'disintegration'. My earliest foray into this general field was an article 'Are there any Natural Rights?' published in 1955, and though it attracted some attention I have not included it here, since its main argument seems to me to be mistaken and my errors not sufficiently illuminating to justify re-printing now. The only part of that article which seems to me still to merit some consideration is my invocation of what has since been called 'the principle of fair play' as one ground of political obligation. In Essay 3 I briefly summarize this principle and direct attention to the criticism which my original exposition of it has attracted.

In Essays 8, 9, and 10 I consider three different attempts to provide a foundation for basic individual rights or liberties. In the first of these I discuss John Stuart Mill's attempts to furnish such rights with a utilitarian foundation. I argue here (and more elaborately in a later essay on Bentham and Mill on natural rights)[7] that in fact 'general utility' plays no operative part in Mill's construction. Instead, his arguments point to the conclusion that a theory of basic individual rights must rest on a specific conception of the human person and of what is needed for the exercise and development of distinctive human powers. I think, too, that the same lesson is to be learned from the attempts made by Nozick and Dworkin, which I examine in Essay 9, to base a theory of rights on the relatively uncontroversial ideas of the mere distinctness of individual persons or their claim to equal respect. I am confirmed in this belief by the fact that when Professor Rawls came to reply[8] to my arguments in Essay 10, the modifications which he made in his original statement of his own theory to meet my objections appear both to identify the basic liberties for which he argues and their priority over other values by reference to a conception of a human person and of what is necessary for the exercise and development of what he calls the moral powers. In this version of his theory choice in the 'original position' seems to play a much diminished part in the determination of basic liberties.

---

[7] In *Essays on Bentham* (Oxford 1982), ch. IV.
[8] In 'The Basic Liberties and their Priority' in *Tanner Lectures on Human Values*, iii (1982), 1.

VII

Two of the five essays (12-16) devoted to individual legal theorists are concerned with Kelsen's work, which like others I have always found both fascinating and puzzling. I share with him the conviction that a central task of legal philosophy is to explain the normative force of propositions of law which figure both in academic legal writing and in the discourse of judges and lawyers. None the less the directions of our respective theories are quite different and my main effort in these two essays is to show that references to both psychological and social facts, which Kelsen's theory in its excessive purity would exclude, are in fact quite indispensable for the understanding of many different aspects of law. These include the concepts of legal wrong, legal obligation, legal sanctions, and legal system. No acceptable account of the existence of separate systems of law or the relations between municipal and international law can be given if such facts are excluded.

I hope that in what is a second exchange of friendly polemics between myself and Fuller (Essay 16) I have not been unfair in my criticisms of his conception of an inner morality of law; but I see now largely as the result of Professor Lyon's essay on Formal Justice[9] that an argument similar to mine against Fuller might be used to show that my claim made in Essay 2 and repeated in my *Concept of Law* that a minimal form of justice is inherent in the very notion of a general legal rule applied according to its tenor to all its instances is similarly mistaken. I am not sure that it is so, but I am clear that my claim requires considerable modification.

[9] *58 Cornell L. R.* 873 (1973).

PART I

GENERAL THEORY

Definition and Theory in Jurisprudence

I

In law as elsewhere, we can know and yet not understand. Shadows often obscure our knowledge, which not only vary in intensity but are cast by different obstacles to light. These cannot all be removed by the same methods, and till the precise character of our perplexity is determined we cannot tell what tools we shall need.

The perplexities I propose to discuss are voiced in those questions of analytical jurisprudence which are usually characterized as requests for definitions: What is law? What is a State? What is a right? What is possession? I choose this topic because it seems to me that the common mode of definition is ill adapted to the law and has complicated its exposition; its use has, I think, led at certain points to a divorce between jurisprudence and the study of the law at work, and has helped to create the impression that there are certain fundamental concepts that the lawyer cannot hope to elucidate without entering a forbidding jungle of philosophical argument. I wish to suggest that this is not so; that legal notions however fundamental can be elucidated by methods properly adapted to their special character. Such methods were glimpsed by our predecessors but have only been fully understood and developed in our own day.

Questions such as those I have mentioned, 'What is a State?', 'What is law?', 'What is a right?', have great ambiguity. The same form of words may be used to demand a definition or the cause or the purpose or the justification or the origin of a legal or political institution. But if, in the effort to free them from this risk of confusion with other questions, we rephrase these requests for definitions as 'What is the meaning of the word "State"?', 'What is the meaning of the word "right"?', those who ask are apt to feel uneasy, as if this had trivialized their question. For what they want cannot be got out of a dictionary, and this transformation of their question suggests it can. This uneasiness is the expression of an instinct which deserves respect: it emphasizes the fact that those who ask these questions are not asking to be taught how to use these words in the correct way. This they know and yet are still puzzled. Hence it is no answer to this type of question merely to tender examples of what are correctly called rights, laws, or corporate bodies, and to tell the questioner if he is still puzzled that he is free to abandon the public convention and use words as he pleases.[1] For the puzzle arises from the fact that though the common use of these words is known, it is not understood; and it is not understood because compared with most ordinary words these legal words are in different ways anomalous. Sometimes, as with the word 'law' itself, one anomaly is that the range of cases to which it is applied has a diversity which baffles the initial attempt to extract any principle behind the application, yet we have the conviction that even here there is some principle and not an arbitrary convention underlying the surface differences; so that whereas it would be patently absurd to ask for elucidation of the principle in accordance with which different men are called Tom, it is not felt absurd to ask why, within municipal law, the immense variety of different types of rules are called law, nor why municipal law and international law, in spite of striking differences, are so called.

---

[1] Professor Glanville Williams in his beneficial article on 'International Law and the Controversy concerning the word Law' (*British Year Book of International Law*, 1945, 148) advocates this short way with those who ask whether international law is law. But the way is really too short; for the puzzle is not generated always or only by the superstitions about words or essences, or the confusion of 'verbal' with factual questions which he attacks. Perplexity here arises from three factors: (i) the well-founded belief that the word 'law' when used of municipal and international law is not a mere homonym; (ii) the mistaken belief (false not only of complex legal and political expressions like 'law', 'State', 'nation', but of humbler ones like 'a game') that if a word is not a mere homonym then all the instances to which it is applied must possess either a single quality or a single set of qualities in common; (iii) an exaggeration of the difference between municipal and international law due to the failure to see that the 'command' of a sovereign is only one particular form of a general feature which is no doubt logically necessary in a legal system, viz. some general test or criterion whereby the rules of the system are identified. Of course proper attention to these three factors will only show (by revealing the complexity of the issue and exposing some prejudices) that to call international law 'law' in spite of its differences from municipal law is not arbitrary — just as to call patience a 'game' is not arbitrary in spite of its differences from, say, polo. But there is no conclusive answer to give to those who are very impressed by the differences — in either case.

But in this and other cases, we are puzzled by a different and more troubling anomaly. The first efforts to define words like 'corporation', 'right', or 'duty' reveal that these do not have the straightforward connection with counterparts in the world of fact which most ordinary words have and to which we appeal in our definition of ordinary words. There is nothing which simply 'corresponds' to these legal words, and when we try to define them we find that the expressions we tender in our definition specifying kinds of persons, things, qualities, events, and processes, material or psychological, are never precisely the equivalent of these legal words, though often connected with them in some way. This is most obvious in the case of expressions for corporate bodies, and is commonly put by saying that a corporation is not a series or aggregate of persons. But it is true of other legal words. Though one who has a right usually has some expectation or power, the expression 'a right' is not synonymous with words like 'expectation' or 'power' even if we add 'based on law' or 'guaranteed by law'. And so too, though we speak of men having duties to do or abstain from certain actions the word 'duty' does not stand for or describe anything as ordinary words do. It has an altogether different function which makes the stock form of definition, 'a duty is a . . .', seem quite inappropriate.

These are genuine difficulties and in part account for something remarkable: that out of these innocent requests for definitions of fundamental legal notions there should have arisen vast and irreconcilable theories, so that not merely whole books but whole schools of juristic thought may be characterized by the type of answer they give to questions like 'What is a right?', or 'What is a corporate body?'. This alone, I think, suggests that something is wrong with the approach to definition; can we really not elucidate the meaning of words which every developed legal system handles smoothly and alike without assuming this incubus of theory? And the suspicion that something is amiss is confirmed by certain characteristics that many such theorists have. In the first place they fall disquietingly often into a familiar triad.[2] Thus the American Realists striving to give us

[2] The general form of this recurrent triad may be summarily described as follows. Theories of one type tell us that a word stands for some unexpected

an answer in terms of plain fact tell us that a right is a term by which we describe the prophecies we make of the probable behaviour of courts or officials;[3] the Scandinavian jurists, after dealing the Realist theory blows that might well be thought fatal (if these matters were strictly judged), say that a right is nothing real at all but an ideal or fictitious or imaginary power,[4] and then join with their opponents to denigrate the older type of theory that a right is an 'objective reality' — an invisible entity existing apart from the behaviour of men. These theories are in form similar to the three great theories of corporate personality, each of which has dealt deadly blows to the other. There too we have been told by turn that the name of a coporate body like a limited company or an organization like the State is really just a collective name or abbreviation for some complex but still plain facts about ordinary persons, or alternatively that it is the name of a fictitious person, or that on the contrary it is the name of a real person existing with a real will and life, but not a body of its own. And this same triad of theories has haunted the jurist even when concerned with relatively minor notions. Look for example at Austin's discussion of status[5] and you

variant of the familiar — a complex fact where we expect something unified and simple, a future fact where we expect something present, a psychological fact where we expect something external; theories of the second type tell us that a word stands for what is in some sense a fiction; theories of a third (now unfashionable) type tell us the word stands for something different from other things just in that we cannot touch it, hear it, see it, feel it.

[3] W. W. Cook, *The Logical and Legal Basis of the Conflict of Laws* (Cambridge, Mass., 1949), 30: '"Right" "duty" ... are not names of objects or entities which have an existence apart from the behaviour of officials but terms by means of which we describe to each other the prophecies we make as to the probable occurrence of a certain sequence of events — the behaviour of officials ... we must therefore constantly resist the tendency ... to reify rights ...'

[4] Karl Olivecrona, *Law as Fact* (London, 1939), 90: 'We hit the mark when we define a right as a power of some kind but this power does not exist in the real world ... it is not identical with the actual control ... exercised by the owner nor with his actual ability to set the legal machinery in motion. It is a fictitious power, an ideal or imaginary power.' See also A. Hägerström, *Inquiries into the Nature of Law and Morals* (ed. Broad, Stockholm, 1953), 4: 'The insuperable difficulty in finding the facts which correspond to our ideas of rights forces us to suppose that there are no such facts and that we are here concerned with ideas that have nothing to do with reality.' On p. 6: 'Thus it is shown that the notions we question cannot be reduced to anything in reality. The reason is that they have their roots in traditional ideas of mystical forces or bonds.'

[5] *Lectures on Jurisprudence* (5th edn., London, 1881), ii. 609-700.

will find that the choice lies for him between saying that it is a mere collective name for a set of special rights and duties, or that it is an 'ideal' or 'fictitious' basis for these rights and duties, or that it is an 'occult quality' in the person who has the status, distinguishable both from the rights and duties and from the facts engendering them.

Secondly, though these theories spring from the effort to define notions actually involved in the practice of a legal system, they rarely throw light on the precise work they do there. They seem to the lawyer to stand apart with their heads at least in the clouds; and hence it is that very often the use of such terms in a legal system is neutral between competing theories. For that use 'can be reconciled with any theory, but is authority for none'.[6]

Thirdly, in many of these theories there is often an amalgam of issues that should be distinguished. It is of course clear that the assertion that corporate bodies are real persons and the counter-assertion that they are fictions of the law were often not the battle-cries of analytical jurists. They were ways of asserting or denying the claims of organized groups to recognition by the State. But such claims have always been confused with the baffling analytical question, 'What is a corporate body?', so that the classification of such theories as Fiction or Realist or Concessionist is a criss-cross between logical and political criteria. So too the American Realist theories have much to tell us of value about the judicial process and how small a part deduction from predetermined premises may play in it, but the lesson is blurred when it is presented as a matter of definition of 'law' or 'a right'; not only analytical jurisprudence but every sort of jurisprudence suffers by this confusion of aim.

Hence, though theory is to be welcomed, the growth of theory on the back of definition is not. Theories so grown, indeed, represent valuable efforts to account for many puzzling things in law; and among these is the great anomaly of legal language — our inability to define its crucial words in terms of ordinary factual counterparts.[7] But here I think

[6] P. W. Duff, *Personality in Roman Private Law* (Cambridge, 1938), 215.

[7] See Olivecrona, op. cit. n. 4 *supra*, 88–9. 'It is impossible to find any facts that correspond to the idea of a right. The right eludes every attempt to pin it down and place it among the facts of social life. Though connected with the facts . . . the right is in essence something different from all facts.'

they largely fail because their method of attack commits them all, in spite of their mutual hostility, to a form of answer that can only distort the distinctive characteristics of legal language.

II

Long ago Bentham issued a warning that legal words demanded a special method of elucidation, and he enunciated a principle that is the beginning of wisdom in this matter, though it is not the end. He said we must never take these words alone, but consider whole sentences in which they play their characteristic role. We must take not the *word* 'right' but the sentence 'You have a right', not the *word* 'State', but the sentence 'He is a member or an official of the State.'[8] His warning has largely been disregarded and jurists have continued to hammer away at single words. This may be because he hid the product of his logical insight behind technical terms of his own invention 'Archetypation', 'Phraseoplerosis', and the rest; it may also be because his further suggestions were not well adapted to the peculiarities of legal language which as part of the works of 'Judge & Co.' was perhaps distasteful to him. But in fact the language involved in the enunciation and application of rules constitutes a special segment of human discourse with special features which lead to confusion if neglected. Of this type of discourse the law is one very complex example, and sometimes to see its features we need to look away from the law to simpler cases which in spite of many differences share these features. The economist or the scientist often uses a simple model with which to

---

[8] See *A Fragment on Government*, ch. V, notes to section vi: § (5) 'For expounding the words duty, right, title, and those other terms of the same stamp that abound so much in ethics and jurisprudence either I am much deceived or the only method by which any instruction can be conveyed is that which is here exemplified. An exposition framed after this method I would term paraphrase. § (6) A word may be said to be expounded by paraphrases when not that word alone is translated into other words but some whole sentence of which it forms part is translated into another sentence. § (7) The common method of defining — the method *per genus et differentiam* as logicians calls it, will in many cases not at all answer the purpose.' Cf. also Bentham, *An Introduction to the Principles of Morals and Legislation*, ch. XVI, para 25; *Of Laws in General*, Appendix C, para. 17; *Chrestomathia* in *Works*, viii. 126 n. (Bowring edn., 1838–43); *Essay on Logic* in *Works*, viii. 246–81.

understand the complex; and this can be done for the law. So in what follows I shall use as a simple analogy the rules of a game which at many vital points have the same puzzling logical structure as rules of law. And I shall describe four distinctive features which show, I think, the method of elucidation we should apply to the law and why the common mode of definition fails.

1. First, let us take words like 'right' or 'duty' or the names of corporations, not alone but in examples of typical contexts where these words are at work. Consider them when used in statements made on a particular occasion by a judge or an ordinary lawyer. They will be statements such as 'A has a right to be paid £10 by B.'; 'A is under a duty to fence off his machinery.'; 'A & Company, Ltd. have a contract with B.' It is obvious that the use of these sentences silently assumes a special and very complicated setting, namely the existence of a legal system with all that this implies by way of general obedience, the operation of the sanctions of the system, and the general likelihood that this will continue. But though this complex situation is assumed in the use of these statements of rights or duties they do not *state* that it exists. There is a parallel situation in a game. 'He is out' said in the course of a game of cricket has as its proper context the playing of the game, with all that this implies by way of general compliance by both the players and the officials of the game in the past, present, and future. Yet one who says 'He is out' does not *state* that a game is being played or that the players and officials will comply with the rules. 'He is out' is an expression used to appeal to rules, to make claims, or give decisions under them; it is not a statement *about* the rules to the effect that they will be enforced or acted on in a given case, nor any other kind of statement *about* them. The analysis of statements of rights and duties as predictions ignores this distinction, yet it is just as erroneous to say that 'A has a right' is a prediction that a court or official will treat A in a certain way as to say that 'He is out' is a prediction that the umpire is likely to order the batsman off the field or the scorer to mark him out. No doubt, when someone has a legal right a corresponding prediction will normally be justified, but this should not lead us to identify two quite different forms of statement.

2. If we take 'A has a right to be paid £10 by B' as an example, we can see what the distinctive function of this form of statement is. For it is clear that as well as presupposing the existence of a legal system, the use of this statement has also a special connection with a particular rule of the system. This would be made explicit if we asked 'Why has A this right?' For the appropriate answer could only consist of two things: first, the statement of some rule or rules of law (say those of Contract), under which given certain facts certain legal consequences follow; and secondly, a statement that these facts were here the case. But again it is important to see that one who says that 'A has a right' does not *state* the relevant rule of law; and that though, given certain facts, it is correct to say 'A has a right', one who says this does not state or describe those facts. He has done something different from either of these two things: he has drawn a conclusion from the relevant but unstated rule, and from the relevant but unstated facts of the case. 'A has a right', like 'He is out', is therefore the tail-end of a simple legal calculation: it records a result and may be well called a conclusion of law. It is not therefore used to predict the future, as the American Realists say; it refers to the present, as their opponents claim, but unlike ordinary statements does not do this by describing present or continuing facts. This it is — this matter of principle — and not the existence of stray exceptions for lunatics or infants — that frustrates the definition of a right in factual terms such as expectations or powers. A paralysed man watching the thief's hand close over his gold watch is properly said to have a right to retain it as against the thief, though he has neither expectation nor power in any ordinary sense of these words. This is possible just because the expression 'a right' in this case does not describe or stand for any expectation, or power, or indeed anything else, but has meaning only as part of a sentence the function of which as a whole is to draw a conclusion of law from a specific kind of legal rule.

3. A third peculiarity is this: the assertion 'Smith has a right to be paid £10' said by a judge in deciding the case has a different status from the utterance of it out of court, where it may be used to make a claim, or an admission and in many other ways. The judge's utterance is official, authoritative,

and, let us assume, final; the other is none of these things, yet in spite of these differences the sentences are of the same sort: they are both conclusions of law. We can compare this similarity in spite of difference with 'He is out' said by the umpire in giving his decision and said by a player to make a claim. Now of course the unofficial utterance may have to be withdrawn in the light of a later official utterance, but this is not a sufficient reason for treating the first as a prophecy of the last, for plainly not all mistakes are mistaken predictions. Nor surely need the finality of a judge's decision either be confused with infallibility or tempt us to *define* laws in terms of what courts do, even though there are many laws which the courts must first interpret before they can apply them. We can acknowledge that what the scorer says is final; yet we can still abstain from defining the notion of a score as what the scorer says. And we can admit that the umpire may be wrong in his decision though the rules give us no remedy if he is and though there may be doubtful cases which he has to decide with but little help from the rules.

4. In any system, legal or not, rules may for excellent practical reasons attach identical consequences to any one of a set of very different facts. The rule of cricket attaches the same consèquence to the batsman's being bowled, stumped, or caught. And the word 'out' is used in giving decisions or making claims under the rule, and in other verbal applications of it. It is easy to see here that no one of these different ways of being out is more essentially what the word means than the others, and that there need be nothing common to all these ways of being out other than their falling under the same rule, though there *may* be some similarity or analogy between them.[9] But it is less easy to see this in those important

[9] Yet neglect of just these features of the language of rules has complicated the exposition of the concept of possession. Here the word is, of course, ambiguous as between (i) certain legal consequences attached to certain kinds of fact and (ii) those kinds of fact. But when we come to define the word in the second of these uses we are liable to assume that there is something which really or essentially is 'possession in fact' independent of any legal system, and that there is something *illogical* in the terminology of a legal system if it does not confine its use of the word 'possession' to this (see Paton, *Jurisprudence*, 2nd edn., 461). But the only meaning of 'possession' which is independent of the rules of a legal system is the vague meaning in common non-legal usage, and there is no logical vice in disregarding this. Or again we may assume that there *must* be some single factor common to all the diverse cases which are treated alike by the rules. This will

cases where rules treat a *sequence* of different actions or states of affairs in a way which unifies them. In a game a rule may simply attach a single consequence to the successive actions of a set of different men — as when a team is said to have won a game. A more complex rule may prescribe that what is to be done at one point in a sequence shall depend on what was done or occurred earlier; and it may be indifferent to the identity of the persons concerned in the sequence so long as they fall under certain defining conditions. An example of this is when a team permitted by the rules of a tournament to have a varying membership is penalized only in the third round — when the membership has changed — for what was done in the first round. In all such cases a sequence of action or states of affairs is unified simply by falling under certain rules; they *may* be otherwise as different as you please. Here can be seen the essential elements of the language of legal corporations. For in law, the lives of ten men that overlap but do not coincide may fall under separate rules under which they have separate rights and duties, and then they are a collection of individuals for the law; but their actions may fall under rules of a different kind which make what is to be done by any one or more of them depend in complex ways on what was done or occurred earlier. And then we may speak in appropriately unified ways of the sequence so unified, using a terminology like that of corporation law which will show that it is *this* sort of rule we are applying to the facts. But here the unity of the rule may mislead us when we come to define this terminology. It may cast a shadow: we may look for an identical continuing thing or person or quality *in* the sequence. We may find it — in 'corporate spirit'. This is real enough; but it is a secret of success not a criterion of identity.

---

lead us either, as the classical theories do, to select one predominant case as a paradigm and to degrade the rest to the level of 'exceptions', or to obscure the real diversity of the facts with expository devices ('constructive' or 'fictitious' possession). Preoccupation with the search for some common feature is apt in either case to divert us from the important inquiries, which are (1) what for any given legal system are the conditions under which possessory rights are acquired and lost; (2) what general features of the given system and what practical reasons lead to diverse cases being treated alike in this respect. Cf. Kocourek, *Jural Relations* (Indianapolis, 1927), ch. XX, *passim*, on 'continuing possession' and 'legal possession'.

III

These four general characteristics of legal language explain both why definition of words like 'right', 'duty', and 'corporation' is baffled by the absence of some counterpart to 'correspond' to these words, and also why the unobvious counterparts which have been so ingeniously contrived — the future facts, the complex facts, or the psychological facts — turn out not to be something in terms of which we can define these words, although to be connected with them in complex or indirect ways. The fundamental point is that the primary function of these words[10] is not to stand for or describe anything but a distinct function; this makes it vital to attend to Bentham's warning that we should not, as does the traditional method of definition, abstract words like 'right' and 'duty', 'State', or 'corporation' from the sentences in which alone their full function can be seen, and then demand of them so abstracted their genus and differentia.

Let us see what the use of this traditional method of definition presupposes and what the limits of its efficacy are, and why it may be misleading. It is of course the simplest form of definition, and also a peculiarly satisfying form because it gives us a set of words which can always be substituted for the word defined whenever it is used; it gives us a comprehensible synonym or translation for the word which puzzles us. It is peculiarly appropriate where the words have the straightforward function of standing for some kind of thing, or quality, person, process, or event, for here we are not mystified or puzzled about the general characteristics of our subject-matter, but we ask for a definition simply to locate within this familiar general kind or class some special subordinate kind or class.[11] Thus since we are not puzzled

---

[10] Lawyers might best understand the distinctive function of such expressions as 'He has a right' and others which I discuss here, by comparing them to the *operative* words of a conveyance as distinct from the *descriptive* words of the recitals. The point of similarity is that 'He has a right', like 'X hereby conveys', is used to *operate with* legal rules and not to state or describe facts. Of course there are great differences: one who says 'He has a right' operates with a rule by drawing a conclusion from it, whereas one who uses operative words in a conveyance does something to which the rule attaches legal consequences.

[11] Bentham's reason for rejecting the common method of defining legal words was that 'among such abstract terms we soon come to such as have no superior genus. A definition *per genus et differentiam* when applied to these it is manifest

about the general notions of furniture or animals we can take a word like 'chair' or 'cat' and give the principle of its use by first specifying the general class to which what it is used to describe belongs, and then going on to define the specific differences that mark it off from other species of the same general kind. And of course if we are *not* puzzled about the general notion of a corporate body, but only wish to know how one species (say a college) differs from another (say a limited company), we can use this form of definition of single words perfectly well. But just because the method is appropriate at this level of inquiry, it cannot help us when our perplexities are deeper. For if our question arises, as it does with fundamental legal notions, because we are puzzled about the general category to which something belongs and how some general type of expression relates to fact, and not merely about the place within that category, then until the puzzle is cleared up this form of definition is at the best unilluminating and at the worst profoundly misleading. It is unilluminating because a mode of definition designed to locate some subordinate species within some familiar category cannot elucidate the characteristics of some anomalous category; and it is misleading because it will suggest that what is in fact an anomalous category is after all some species of the familiar. Hence if applied to legal words like 'right', 'duty', 'State', or 'corporation' the common mode of definition suggests that these words, like ordinary words, stand for or describe some thing, person, quality, process, or event; when the difficulty of finding these becomes apparent, different contrivances varying with tastes are used to explain or explain away the anomaly. Some say the difference is that the things for which these legal words stand are real but not sensory; others that they are fictitious entities; others that these words stand for plain fact but of a complex, future, or psychological variety. So this standard mode of definition forces our familiar triad of theories into existence as a confused way of accounting for the anomalous character of legal words.

can make no advance ... As well in short were it to define in this manner a preposition or a conjunction ... a *through* is a ... a *because* is a ... and so go on defining them.' *A Fragment on Government*, ch. V, n. 6, § § 7–8.

How then shall we define such words? If definition is the provision of a synonym which will not equally puzzle us, these words cannot be defined. But I think there is a method of elucidation of quite general application and which we can call definition, if we wish. Bentham and others practised it, though they did not preach it. But before applying it to the highly complex legal cases, I shall illustrate it from the simple case of a game. Take the notion of a trick in a game of cards. Somebody says 'What is a trick?', and you reply 'I will explain: when you have a game and among its rules is one providing that when each of our players has played a card then the player who has put down the highest card scores a point, in these circumstances that player is said to have "taken a trick".' This natural explanation has not taken the form of a definition of the single word 'trick': no synonym has been offered for it. Instead we have taken a sentence in which the word 'trick' plays its characteristic role and explained it first by specifying the conditions under which the whole sentence is true, and secondly by showing how it is used in drawing a conclusion from the rules in a particular case. Suppose now that after such an explanation your questioner presses on: 'That is all very well, that explains "taking a trick"; but I still want to know what the word "trick" means just by itself. I want a definition of "trick"; I want something which can be substituted for it whenever it is used.' If we yield to this demand for a single-word definition we might reply: 'The trick is just a collective name for the four cards.' But someone may object: 'The trick is not just a name for the four cards because these four cards will not always constitute a trick. It must therefore be some entity to which the four cards belong.' A third might say: 'No, the trick is a fictitious entity which the players pretend exists and to which by a fiction which is part of the game they ascribe the cards.' But in so simple a case we would not tolerate these theories, fraught as they are with mystery and empty of any guidance as to the use made of the word within the game: we would stand by the original two-fold explanation; for this surely gave us all we needed when it explained the conditions under which the statement 'He has taken a trick' is true and showed us how it was used in drawing a conclusion from the rules in a particular case.

If we turn back to Bentham we shall find that when his explanation of legal notions is illuminating, as it very often is, it conforms to this method, though only loosely. Yet curiously what he tells us to do is something different: it is to take a word like 'right' or 'duty' or 'State'; to embody it in a sentence such as 'you have a right' where it plays a characteristic role, and then to find a *translation* of it into what we should call factual terms.[12] This he called the method of paraphrase — giving phrase for phrase, not word for word. Now this method is applicable to many cases and has shed much light; but it distorts many legal words like 'right' or 'duty' whose characteristic role is not played in statements of fact but in conclusions of law. A paraphrase of these in factual terms is not possible, and when Bentham proffers such a paraphrase it turns out not to be one at all.

But more often and much to our profit he does not claim to paraphrase: but he makes a different kind of remark, in order to elucidate these words — remarks such as these: 'What you have a right to have me made do, is that which I am liable according to law upon a requisition made on your behalf to be punished for not doing',[13] or 'To know how to expound a right carry your eye to the act which in the circumstances in question would be a violation of that right; the law creates the right by forbidding that act'.[14] These, though defective, are on the right lines. They are not paraphrases but they specify some of the conditions necessary for the truth of a sentence of the form 'You have a right'. Bentham shows us how these conditions include the existence of a law imposing a duty on some other person; and moreover, that it must be a law which provides that the breach of the duty shall be visited with a sanction if you or someone on your behalf so choose. This has many virtues. By refusing to identify the meaning of the word 'right' with any psychological or physical fact it correctly leaves open the question whether on any given occasion a person who has a right has

[12] Actually he made the more stringent requirement that the translations should be in terms calculated to raise images of 'substances' or 'perceptions'. This was in accord with Bentham's form of empiricism, but the utility of the method of paraphrases (which is identical with the modern 'definition in use') is independent of this requirement.

[13] *A Fragment on Government, ubi sup.*

[14] *Introduction to the Principles of Morals and Legislation*, ch. XVI, para. 25.

in fact any expectation or power; and so it leaves us free to
treat men's expectations or powers as what in general men
will have if there is a system of rights, and as part of what
a system of rights is generally intended to secure. Some of
the improvements which should be made on Bentham's
efforts are obvious. Instead of characterizing a right in terms
of punishment many would do so in terms of the remedy.
But I would prefer to show the special position of one who
has a right by mentioning not the remedy but the choice
which is open to one who has a right as to whether the
corresponding duty shall be performed or not. For it is, I
think, characteristic of those laws that confer rights (as
distinguished from those that only impose obligations) that
the obligation to perform the corresponding duty is made
by law to depend on the choice of the individual who is said
to have the right or the choice of some person authorized
to act on his behalf.

I would, therefore, tender the following as an elucidation
of the expression 'a legal right': (1) A statement of the form
'X has a right' is true if the following conditions are satisfied:

(a) There is in existence a legal system.

(b) Under a rule or rules of the system some other person
Y is, in the events which have happened, obliged to do or
abstain from some action.

(c) This obligation is made by law dependent on the choice
either of X or some other person authorized to act on his
behalf so that either Y is bound to do or abstain from some
action only if X (or some authorized person) so chooses or
alternatively only until X (or such person) chooses otherwise.

(2) A statement of the form 'X has a right' is used to draw
a conclusion of law in a particular case which falls under
such rules.[15]

[15] This deals only with a right in the first sense (correlative to duty) distinguished
by Hohfeld. But the same form of elucidation can be used for the cases of 'liberty',
'power', and 'immunity', and will I think show what is usually left unexplained,
viz. why these four varieties in spite of differences are referred to as 'rights'. The
unifying element seems to be this: in all four cases the law specifically recognizes
the *choice* of an individual either negatively by not impeding or obstructing it
(liberty and immunity) or affirmatively by giving legal effect to it (claim and
power). In the negative cases there is no law to interfere if the individual chooses
to do or abstain from some action (liberty) or to retain his legal position unchanged
(immunity); in the affirmative cases the law gives legal effect to the choice of an
individual that some other person shall do or shall abstain from some action

IV

It is said by many that the juristic controversy over the
nature of corporate personality is dead. If so we have a
corpse, and the opportunity to learn from its anatomy. Let
us imagine an intelligent lawyer innocent of theories of
corporate personality because he was educated in a legal
Arcadia where rights and duties were ascribed only to
individuals and all legal theory is banned. He is then introduced to our own and other systems and learns how in
practice rights and duties are ascribed to bodies like the
University of Oxford, to the State, to idols, to the *hereditas
jacens* and also to the one-man tax-dodging company. He
would learn with us that forms of statement were in daily
use by which rights were ascribed to Smith & Co. Ltd. in
circumstances and with consequences partly similar and
partly different from those in which they were ascribed
to Smith. He would see that the analogy was often thin,
but that, given the circumstances specified in the Companies
Acts and the general law, 'Smith & Co. Ltd. owes White £10'
applied as directly to the facts after its own fashion as
'Smith owes White £10.' Gradually he would discover that
many ordinary words when used of a limited company were
used in a special manner. For he would early learn that even
if all the members and servants of the company are dead
there are yet conditions under which it is true to say that the
company still exists; if he was here in 1936 he would have
learnt that it can be correctly said of a foreign corporation
that though dissolved it still exists; and if he stayed till
1944 he would have learned that given certain circumstances
it is true that a company has intended to deceive. On his
return to Arcadia he would tell of the extension to corporate
bodies of rules worked out for individuals and of the analogies
followed and the adjustment of ordinary words involved in
this extension. All this he would have to do and could do
without mentioning fiction, collective names, abbreviations,

or that the legal position of some other person shall be altered. Of course when
we say in any of these four senses that a person has a right we are not referring to
any *actual* choice that he has made, but either the relevant rules of law are such
that *if* he chooses certain consequences follow, or there are no rules to impede
his choice *if* he makes it. If there are legal rights which cannot be waived these
would need special treatment.

or brackets, or the *Gesammtperson* and the *Gesammtwille* of
Realist theory. Would he not have said all there was to say
about the legal personality of corporation? At what point
then would the need be felt for a theory? Would it not be
when someone asked 'When it is true that Smith owes Black
£10, here is the name "Smith" and there is the man Smith,
but when Smith & Co. Ltd. owes £10 to Black what is there
that corresponds to "Smith & Co. Ltd." as the man Smith
corresponds to the name "Smith"? What *is* Smith & Co. Ltd.?
What is *it*, which has the right? Surely it can only be a
collection of individuals or a real individual or a fictitious
individual.' In other words we could make the simple Arcadian
feel the theorists' agonies only by inducing him to ask 'What
is Smith & Co. Ltd.?', and not to admit in answer a description of how, and under what conditions, the names of
corporate bodies are used in practice, but instead to start
the search for what it is that the name taken alone describes,
for what *it* stands, for what *it* means.[16]

That the presentation of the question in this way has been
crucial in the growth of theory could be proved from many
famous passages in the literature. Let me take one example.
Maitland in his greatness indeed sensed that the choice did
not necessarily lie, as it seemed, between the traditional
theories, and that ultimately some mode of analysis might
supply a different answer. I do not understand why he is
called a Realist[17] or thought to have accepted the doctrine
of Gierke that he expounded, for though he was certain
that fiction and collective-name theories 'denatured the
facts', he left the matter with a final question to which he
then saw no answer. But observe the significant form that
question took: he imagined a sovereign State and, inventing
the Latin for Never-never land, called it Nusquamia. Of this
he said:

Like many other sovereign States, it owes money, and I will suppose
that you are one of its creditors . . .

---

[16] 'It is highly improbable that they [early Roman lawyers] ever asked or were
asked the question.' Duff, op. cit. n. 6 *supra*, 134. But the question is mistaken
with regard to the form of answer that it suggests, and it is important to see this.
[17] Cf. Duff, op. cit., 209 and 216 n. 3. See, for a discussion of the precise point
where Maitland diverged from Gierke's *Genossenschafttheorie* J. A. Mack, 'Group-
Personality: Footnote to Maitland', *Philosophical Quarterly*, ii (1952), 249.

Now the question that I want to raise is this: Who is it that really owes you money? Nusquamia? Granted, but can you convert the proposition that Nusquamia owes you money into a series of propositions imposing duties on certain human beings that are now in existence? The task will not be easy. Clearly you do not think that every Nusquamian owes you some aliquot share of the debt. No one thinks in that way. The debt of Venezuela is not owed by Fulano y Zutano and the rest of them. Nor, I think, shall we get much good out of the word 'collectively', which is the smudgiest word in the English language, for the largest 'collection' of zeros is only zero. I do not wish to say that I have suggested an impossible task, and that the right-and-duty-bearing group must be for the philosopher an ultimate and unanalysable moral unit . . . Only if that task can be performed, I think that in the interests of jurisprudence and of moral philosophy it is eminently worthy of circumspect performance.[18]

Such was Maitland's question: when Nusquamia owes you money who owes you this? How should it be answered? Surely only by ceasing to batter our heads against the single word 'Nusquamia'. Pressing the question 'Who or what when Nusquamia owes you £1,000 is it which owes you this?' is like demanding desperately: 'When you lost that game what was it that you lost?' To the question so pressed the only answer is to repeat 'a game', as to the other the only answer is to repeat 'Nusquamia'. This, of course, tells us precisely nothing, but is at least neither mystifying nor false. To elucidate it we must obey Bentham's first injunction: we must take the whole statement 'Nusquamia owes you £1,000' and describe its use perhaps as follows:

1. Here in the territory of Nusquamia there is a legal system in force; under the laws of this system certain persons on complying with certain conditions are authorized for certain purposes to receive sums of money and to do other actions analogous to those required to make a contract of loan between private individuals.

2. When such persons do such acts certain consequences, analogous to those attached to the similar actions of private individuals, follow, including the liability of persons defined by law to repay the sums of money out of funds defined by law.

3. The expression 'Nusquamia owes you £1,000' does not state the existence of these rules nor of these circumstances,

---

[18] 'Moral Personality and Legal Personality', *Collected Papers* (Cambridge, 1911), iii. 318–19.

but is true in a particular case when they exist, and is used in drawing a conclusion of law from these rules in a particular case.

How much detail should be given depends on the degree to which the questioner is puzzled. If all that he is puzzled by is his inability to say who or what Nusquamia is and the inadequacies of theories to explain this, he may be content with what has been done. But of course he may be puzzled by the notion of one and the same legal system existing throughout the lives of different men in terms of which this elucidation of 'Nusquamia' has been offered.[19] If so, this in its turn must be elucidated, as it can be in the same manner.

There is of course nothing in this method to prevent its application to the ephemeral technical one-man company which Realists regarded as a difficulty for their theory.[20] To explain what a limited company is we must refer to the relevant legal rules, which determine the conditions under which a characteristic sentence like 'Smith & Co. owes White £10' is true. Then we must show how the name of a limited company functions as part of a conclusion of law which is used to apply both special company rules and also rules such as those of contract which were originally worked out for individuals. It will, of course, be necessary to stress that under the special conditions defined by the special rules, other rules are applied to the conduct of individuals in a manner radically different from though still analogous to that in which such rules apply to individuals apart from such special conditions. This we could express by restating the familiar principle of our company law, 'A company is a distinct entity from its members', as 'The name of a limited company is used in conclusions of law which apply legal rules in special circumstances in a manner distinct from though analogous to those in which such rules are applied to individuals apart from such circumstances.' This restatement would show that we have to do not with anomalous or fictitious entities, but with a new and extended

---

[19] That is, we must elucidate the expression 'the same legal system' by showing what are conditions sufficient for the truth of statements on the form. 'The same legal system is in force in England now as in 1900'. The fundamental question here is the elucidation of the expression 'the same rule'.

[20] See Wolff, 'On the Nature of Legal Persons', 54 *Law Quarterly Review*, 494 at 504; Duff, op. cit. n. 6 *supra*, 218.

though analogous use of legal rules and of the expressions involved in them.

V

If we look now at the type of theory so attractive to common sense which asserts that statements referring to corporations are 'abbreviations' and so can be reduced or translated into statements referring only to individuals, we can see now in precisely what way they failed. Their mistake was that of seeking a paraphrase or translation into other terms of statements referring to corporations instead of specifying the conditions under which such statements are true and the manner in which they are used. But in assessing these common-sense theories it is important to notice one very general feature of the language involved in the application of legal rules which the attempt to paraphrase always obscures. If we take a very simple legal statement like 'Smith has made a contract with Y', we must distinguish the meaning of this conclusion of law from two things: from (1) a statement of the facts required for its truth, e.g. that the parties have signed a written agreement, and also from (2) the statement of the legal consequences of it being true, e.g. that Y is bound to do certain things under the agreement. There is here at first sight something puzzling; it seems as if there is something intermediate between the facts, which make the conclusion of law true, and the legal consequences. But if we refer to the simple case of a game we can see what this is. When 'He is out' is said of a batsman (whether by a player, or by the umpire) this neither makes the factual statement that the ball has struck the wicket nor states that he is bound to leave the wicket; it is an utterance the function of which is to draw a conclusion from a specific rule under which, in circumstances such as these, consequences of this sort arise, and we should obviously neglect something vital in its meaning if, in the attempt to give a paraphrase, we said it meant the facts alone or the consequences alone or even the combination of these two. The combined statement 'The ball has struck the wicket and he must leave the wicket' fails to give the whole meaning of 'He is out' because it does not reproduce the distinctive manner in which the original statement is used to draw a conclusion from a specific but unstated rule under which such a consequence follows on such conditions. And no paraphrase can both elucidate the original and reproduce this feature.

I dwell on this point because it is here that the common-sense theories of corporate personality fail.[21] The theory that statements referring to corporations are disguised abbreviations for statements about the rights and duties of individuals was usually expounded with such crudity as not to deserve consideration. It is easy to see that a statement about the rights of a limited company is not equivalent to the statement that its members have those same rights. A conveyance by Smith & Co. Ltd. to the sole shareholder Smith is of course not a conveyance by Smith to Smith. But a few theorists, among them Hohfeld, have stated this type of theory with a requisite degree of subtlety. Hohfeld saw that to say that Smith & Co. Ltd. has a contract with Y was, of course, not to say the same thing about the members of the company: he thought it was to say something different and very complicated about the way in which the capacities, rights, powers, privileges, and liabilities of the natural persons concerned in the company had been affected. Though more formidable in this guise, the theory fails because, although it gives us the legal consequences upon the individuals of the original statement, it does not give us the force and meaning of that statement itself. The alleged paraphrase is less than the original statement 'Smith & Co. Ltd. has a contract with Y' because it gives no hint of what the original statement is used to do, namely, to draw a conclusion of law from special rules relating to companies and from rules extended by analogy from the case of individuals. So the paraphrase, complex and ingenious as it is, gives us too little; but it also gives us too much. It dissipates the unity of the simple statement 'Smith & Co. has a contract with Y', and substitutes a statement of the myriad legal rights, duties, powers, etc., of numerous individuals of whom we never have thought

---

[21] It is also the explanation of the sense of a *tertium quid* between the 'facts' and the 'legal consequences' which troubles the analysis of many legal notions, e.g. status. The status of a slave is not (*pace* Austin) just a collective name for his special rights and duties: there is a sense in which these are the 'consequences' of his status; it is the sense in which the obligation to leave the wicket is a consequence of being 'out'.

nor could have thought in making the original statement.[22] Hence it is that those who are attracted to this common-sense form of analysis feel cheated when they look at it more closely. And they *are* cheated; only they should not in despair clutch at the Realist or Fiction theories. For the elements which they miss in the translation, the analogy with individuals, the unity of the original statement, and its direct application to fact cannot be given them in these theories nor in any translation of the original; it can only be given in a detailed description of the conditions under which a statement of this form is true and of the distinctive manner in which it is used to draw a conclusion from specific rules in a particular case.

I have of course dealt only with the *legal* personality of corporations. I have argued that if we characterize adequately the distinctive manner in which expressions for corporate bodies are used in a legal system, then there is no residual question of the form 'What is a corporation?'. There only *seems* to be one if we insist on a form of definition or eluci-dation which is inappropriate. Theories of the traditional form can only give a distorted account of the meaning of expressions for corporate bodies because they all, in spite of their mutual hostility, make the common assumption that these expressions must stand for or describe something, and then give separate and incompatible accounts of its peculiarity as a complex or recondite or a fictitious entity; whereas the peculiarity lies not here but in the distinctive characteristics of expressions used in the enunciation and application of rules. But of course it is not the legal personality but the

---

[22] See Hohfeld, *Fundamental Legal Conceptions* (New Haven, 1923), 198–200, 220 ff. Though Hohfeld writes at times as if his complex statements of rights, duties, capacities, etc., were synonymous with the original statement about companies ['we mean nothing more than what can be explained by describing the capacities etc. ... of the natural persons concerned'] I think he also saw that statements concerning companies cannot be 'reduced' to statements con-cerning individuals, but are as he says 'sui generis' (198), and that this is why fictionist, realist, and collective-name theories all distort the concept of a corporate body. What he does not see is that in using these special forms of expressions we are not (my italics) '*describing* ... the peculiar process by which the burdens and benefits of the corporate members are worked out' (199), but drawing a conclu-sion of law from special rules. What is ignored here is the distinction (see 27, *supra*), between the statement *about* a legal rule and a statement which *applies* a legal rule by drawing a conclusion from it. To ignore this obscures the analysis of the notion of a corporate body as much as that of a right.

'moral' personality of organized groups that perplexes most; these exist apart from legal rules (one confusing sense of 'not fiction' is just to assert this fact), and no collective-name or abbreviation theory seems to be adequate; so we are tempted to ask, 'What *is* a Church, a Nation, a School?'; 'What is any association or organized group?'. But here too we should substitute for this ever-baffling form of question[23] the following: 'Under what conditions do we refer to numbers and sequences of men as aggregates of individuals and under what conditions do we adopt instead unifying phrases extended by analogy from individuals?' If we ask this and investigate the conditions of use of characteristic sentences ('The Nation suffered for fifty years', 'The University expressed its gratitude', 'The crowd was angry') we shall cease to talk about group personality (and indeed individual personality) as if it were a single quality or set of qualities. For we shall find that there are many varieties of widely different conditions (psychological and others) under which we talk in this unifying personal way. Some of these conditions will be shown to be significant for legal or political purposes; others will not. It was surely one of the sentimentalities of *Genossenschafttheorie* that unity just *as* unity was made to appear significant or worthy of respect, as compared with the vulgar plurality of persons strolling in the street. After all mere unity is not very much, though it is far more various than it appears to be.

VI

If we put aside the question 'What is a corporation?', and ask instead 'Under what types of conditions does the law ascribe liabilities to corporations?', this is likely to clarify the actual working of a legal system and bring out the precise issues at stake when judges, who are supposed not to legislate, make some new extension to corporate bodies of rules worked out for individuals. Take for example the recent extension to corporations of liability for crimes involving knowledge and

[23] Baffling, that is, so long as we are puzzled about fundamentals, though not if we are concerned only with some particular species of organized group and its differences from others. See 31-2 *supra*.

intention, or some other mental element[24] which are such that a natural person would not be criminally responsible if his servant with the requisite knowledge and intention committed the *actus reus* in the course of his employment. There are two ways, one illuminating and the other misleading, of representing the issues at stake here: two ways, that is, of interpreting the word 'can' in the question 'can a limited company commit a crime involving knowledge and intention?' The illuminating way would be to exhibit the obstacle to such an extension as consisting in the type of analogy that has been followed in fitting corporate bodies into the general structure of our law. It is, of course, predominantly the analogy with the case of an individual held liable for what his servant does in the course of employment. It is by use of this analogy that the liabilities of corporations were extended from contract to ordinary torts and then to torts involving malice; and the whole vocabulary of the law of principal and agent has been adapted to the case of the limited companies. But for crimes of the type under consideration this analogy is useless and the fundamental question is: is this the only analogy available to the courts? Is the law closed on this matter, or are there other criteria for the application to companies of rules originally applied to individuals? In fact judges have felt that they were not restricted in this way, and of course it has often been pointed out that it is possible in English law to find authority for imputing to a company the actions and mental states of those who are substantially carrying on its work. How far this alternative source of analogy can or should be utilized is of course a debatable legal issue, but the important thing is to see that this legal issue, and not some logical issue, is the character of the question. Here then is the force of the word 'can' in 'can a company be liable for a crime involving intention to deceive?'.[25] By contrast, the confusing way of stating the issue is to bring in definitions of what a company is and to

[24] *DPP* v. *Kent and Sussex Contractors Ltd.* [1944] K.B. 146: ('with intent to deceive made use of a document which was false in a material particular' and 'made a statement which they knew to be false in a material particular'). *Moore* v. *Bresler, Ltd.* [1944] K.B. 551: ('with intent to deceive made use of a document false in a material particular').

[25] And surely it is in this way also that the still-debated question 'can a company be liable for an *ultra vires* tort?' should be considered.

deduce from them answers to the question in hand. 'A company is a mere abstraction, a fiction, a metaphysical entity.' 'A company has no mind and therefore cannot intend.' These statements confuse the issue because they look like eternal truths about the nature of corporations given us by definitions; so it is made to appear that all legal statements about corporations *must* square with these if they are not to be logically inconsistent. It seems therefore that there is something over and above the analogies which are actually used in the legal system for the application to corporations of rules worked out for individuals, and that this limits or controls that application. And of course a Fiction theory taken seriously can impose irrelevant barriers just as much as a Realist theory: for just as a Realist theory appears to tell us that a company 'cannot' be bound by an agreement empowering another company to direct its business and appoint its personnel because this would be 'to degrade to the position of a tool' a person with a real will,[26] so a Fiction theory appears to say that a company 'cannot' be guilty of certain crimes because it has no mind.

Indeed the *suggestio falsi* in the use of the notion of 'fiction' in the exposition of this branch of the law merits our consideration. Its peculiar vice is to conceal that when words used normally of individuals are applied to companies as well as the analogy involved, there is also involved a radical difference in the mode in which such expressions are now used and so a shift in meaning. Even in the simplest case of all when we say 'X is a servant of Y & Company' the facts which justify the use of the words 'X is a servant' are not *just* the same as the facts which support 'Smith is a servant of Brown.' Hence any ordinary words or phrases when conjoined with the names of corporations take on a special legal use, for the words are now correlated with the facts, not solely by the rules of ordinary English, but also by the rules of English law, much as when we extend words like 'take' or 'lose' by using them of tricks in a game they become correlated with facts by the rules of that game. Now if we talk here of 'fiction' we cannot do justice to this radical difference in use of ordinary expressions when conjoined with the names

[26] See Wolff, op. cit. n. 20 *supra*, 54 *Law Quarterly Review* at 501, citing a decision of the German Supreme Court.

of corporations; we can only distort it. For when, for example, we say of a company that it resides in England even though its members and servants were killed last night by a bomb, the meaning of these words is to be found only by examining the legal rules which prescribe in what conditions such a statement is correct. But if we talk of 'fiction' we suggest that we are using words in their ordinary sense and are merely pretending that something exists to which they apply. In novels — real fiction — we *do* preserve the ordinary meanings of words and pretend that there are persons of whom they are true in their ordinary sense. This is just what we do *not* do when we talk of corporations in law. Yet one of the most curious pieces of logic that ever threatened to obstruct the path of legal development owes, I think, its origin to the confusion of such a shift in meaning with fiction.[27] It was once said that a corporation has no real will but a fictitious will imputed by law, and that since such a will so imputed could effect only lawful ends, we cannot, if we are logically consistent, say that it could commit a crime, or even perhaps a tort. Of course this use of the fiction theory does conjure up an allegorical picture: Law breathing into the nostrils of a Limited Company a Will Fictitious but, like that of its Creator, Good. But the picture is more misleading than even an allegory should be, because it conceals the fact that the word 'will' shifts its meaning when we use it of a company: the sense in which a company has a will is not that it wants to do legal or illegal actions but that certain expressions used to describe the voluntary actions of individuals may be used of it under conditions prescribed by legal rules. And from the bare fact that the law does prescribe such conditions for a wide range of expressions (which is all that imputing a will to a company can mean) it cannot be deduced that these conditions do not include the commission of a criminal or tortious act. Analogy with a living person and shift of meaning are therefore of the essence of the mode of legal statement which refers to corporate bodies. But these are just what they are. Analogy is not identity, so though we can now (as lawyers) say that a company has intended to

---

[27] On account of the standing possibility of this confusion I would abandon the use of the word 'fiction' in the exposition of this branch of the law, though Dr Wolff (op. cit. 505) was prepared to retain it 'as a formula'.

deceive, this has no theoretical consequences; and shift in meaning is not fiction, so the need for logical consistency with an irrelevant notion of a law-created pure Will need not have been added to the difficulties of judges who, in a case-law system, have to decide how far the analogies latent in the law permit them to extend to corporations rules worked out for individuals when justice seems to demand it.

This post-mortem has lasted long. I will add only this. It would of course be the merest provincialism to think of the history of jurisprudence in this matter of definition as a record of errors — even of illuminating errors. It is on the contrary full of invaluable hints as to what should be done to cater for the idiosyncrasies of legal language and the elucidation of its special concepts. Besides the precepts and practice of Bentham, there is the practice of Austin at his best; there is Bryce's pregnant observation[28] that fundamental legal notions could perhaps not be defined, only described, and much in Pollock and Maitland[29] to show how the inter-play of remedy with right has generated a special use of words. There is much, too, of value in Kocourek and Kelsen. Would it, I wonder, be folly to see in the Digest title *De acquirenda vel de amittenda possessione* with its evasion of the fruitless question 'What is possession?' an instinctive recognition of the cardinal principle that legal words can only be elucidated by considering the conditions under which statements in which they have their characteristic use are true? But though the subject of legal definition has this history, it is only since the beneficial turn of philosophical attention towards language that the general features have emerged of that whole style of human thought and discourse which is concerned with rules and their application to con-duct. I at least could not see how much of this was visible in the works of our predecessors until I was taught how to look by my contemporaries.

---

[28] *Studies in History and Jurisprudence* (Oxford, 1901), ii. 181. 'He [Austin] did not perceive how deep some of the difficulties of legal theory lie nor that there are some conceptions which it is safer to describe than to attempt to define.' But cf. Austin *Lectures on Jurisprudence*, 5th edn., ii. 1076: 'In truth some of these terms will not admit of definition in the formal or regular manner . . .' And as to the rest to define them in that manner is utterly useless.'

[29] *History of English Law* (Cambridge, 1895), ii. 31 ff.

POSTSCRIPT

See for criticisms and comments:

1. L. J. Cohen, 'Theory and Definition in Jurisprudence' *Proc. Aristot. Soc. Suppl.* xxix (1955), 213; and my reply thereto, ibid., 238.
2. P. M. Hacker, 'Definition in Jurisprudence' *Philosophical Quarterly*, xix (1969), 343.
3. J. Horwitz, *Law and Logic* (Springer Verlag 1972), 156.
4. J. Ross, *Portraying Analogy* (Cambridge 1981), 202-7.

Essay 2

Positivism and the Separation
of Law and Morals

In this article I shall discuss and attempt to defend a view
which Mr Justice Holmes, among others, held, and for which
he and they have been much criticized. But I wish first to say
why I think that Holmes, whatever the vicissitudes of his
American reputation may be, will always remain for Englishmen a heroic figure in jurisprudence. This will be so because
he magically combined two qualities: one of them is imaginative power, which English legal thinking has often lacked;
the other is clarity, which English legal thinking usually
possesses. The English lawyer who turns to read Holmes is
made to see that what he had taken to be settled and stable
is really always on the move. To make this discovery with
Holmes is to be with a guide whose words may leave you un-
convinced, sometimes even repelled, but never mystified. Like
our own Austin, with whom Holmes shared many ideals and
thoughts, Holmes was sometimes clearly wrong; but again
like Austin, when this was so he was always wrong clearly.
This surely is a sovereign virtue in jurisprudence. Clarity I
know is said not to be enough; this may be true, but there are
still questions in jurisprudence where the issues are confused
because they are discussed in a style which Holmes would
have spurned for its obscurity. Perhaps this is inevitable: jurisprudence trembles so uncertainly on the margin of many
subjects that there will always be a need for someone, in
Bentham's phrase, 'to pluck the mask of Mystery' from its
face.[1] This is true, to a pre-eminent degree, of the subject of
this article. Contemporary voices tell us we must recognize
something obscured by the legal 'positivists' whose day is now
over: that there is a 'point of intersection between law and
morals',[2] or that what *is* and what *ought* to be are somehow

---

[1] Bentham, *A Fragment on Government*, in I *Works* 221, 235 (Bowring edn.
1838–43) (preface, 41st para.). All references hereafter to Bentham's *Works* are
to this edition.

[2] D'Entrèves, *Natural Law* 116 (2nd edn. 1952).

indissolubly fused or inseparable,[3] though the positivists denied it. What do these phrases mean? Or rather which of the many things that they *could* mean, *do* they mean? Which of them do 'positivists' deny and why is it wrong to do so?

I

I shall present the subject as part of the history of an idea. At the close of the eighteenth century and the beginning of the nineteenth the most earnest thinkers in England about legal and social problems and the architects of great reforms were the great Utilitarians. Two of them, Bentham and Austin, constantly insisted on the need to distinguish, firmly and with the maximum of clarity, law as it is from law as it ought to be. This theme haunts their work, and they condemned the natural-law thinkers precisely because they had blurred this apparently simple but vital distinction. By contrast, at the present time in this country and to a lesser extent in England, this separation between law and morals is held to be superficial and wrong. Some critics have thought that it blinds men to the true nature of law and its roots in social life.[4] Others have thought it not only intellectually misleading but corrupting in practice, at its worst apt to weaken resistance to state tyranny or absolutism,[5] and at its best apt to bring law into disrespect. The now pejorative name 'Legal Positivism',

[3] Fuller, *The Law in Quest of Itself* 12 (1940); Brech, 'The Myth of Is and Ought', 54 *Harv. L. Rev.* 811 (1941), Fuller, 'Human Purpose and Natural Law', 53 *J. Philos.* 697 (1953).
[4] See Friedmann, *Legal Theory* 154, 294–95 (3rd edn. 1953). Friedmann also says of Austin that 'by his sharp distinction between the science of legislation and the science of law', he 'inaugurated an era of legal positivism and self-sufficiency which enabled the rising national State to assert its authority undisturbed by juristic doubts'. Ibid. at 416. Yet, 'the existence of a highly organised State which claimed sovereignty and unconditional obedience of the citizen' is said to be 'the political condition which makes analytical positivism possible'. Ibid. at 163. There is therefore some difficulty in determining which, in this account, is to be hen and which egg (analytical positivism or political condition). Apart from this there seems to be little evidence that any national State rising in or after 1832 (when the *Province of Jurisprudence Determined* was first published) was enabled to assert its authority by Austin's work or 'the era of legal positivism' which he 'inaugurated'.
[5] See Radbruch, 'Die Erneuerung des Rechts', 2 *Die Wandlung* 8 (Germany 1947);Radbruch,'Gesetzliches Unrecht und Übergesetzliches Recht', I *Süddeutsche Juristen-Zeitung* 105 (Germany 1946) (reprinted in Radbruch, *Rechtsphilosophie* 347 (4th edn. 1950)). Radbruch's views are discussed at 72–8 below.

like most terms which are used as missiles in intellectual
battles, has come to stand for a baffling multitude of different sins. One of them is the sin, real or alleged, of insisting, as
Austin and Bentham did, on the separation of law as it is and
law as it ought to be.

How then has this reversal of the wheel come about? What
are the theoretical errors in this distinction? Have the practical consequences of stressing the distinction, as Bentham and
Austin did, been bad? Should we now reject it or keep it? In
considering these questions we should recall the social philosophy which went along with the Utilitarians' insistence on
this distinction. They stood firmly but on their own utilitarian
ground for all the principles of liberalism in law and government. No one has ever combined, with such even-minded
sanity as the Utilitarians, the passion for reform with respect
for law together with due recognition of the need to control
the abuse of power even when power is in the hands of reformers. One by one in Bentham's works you can identify the
elements of the *Rechtsstaat* and all the principles for the
defence of which the terminology of natural law has in our
day been received. Here are liberty of speech, and of press,
the right of association,[6] the need that laws should be published and made widely known before they are enforced,[7]
the need to control administrative agencies,[8] the insistence
that there should be no criminal liability without fault,[9] and
the importance of the principle of legality, *nulla poena sine
lege.*[10] Some, I know, find the political and moral insight of
the Utilitarians a very simple one, but we should not mistake
this simplicity for superficiality, nor forget how favourably
their simplicities compare with the profundities of other
thinkers. Take only one example: Bentham on slavery. He
says the question at issue is not whether those who are held

[6] Bentham, *A Fragment on Government*, in I *Works* 221, 230 (preface, 16th
para.); Bentham, *Principles of Penal Law*, in I *Works* 365, 574-5, 576-8 (pt. III,
c. XXI, 8th para., 12th para.).

[7] Bentham, *Of Promulgation of the Laws*, in I *Works* 155; Bentham, *Principles
of the Civil Code*, in I *Works* 297, 323 (pt. I, c. XVII, 2nd para.); Bentham, *A
Fragment on Government*, in I *Works* 221, 233 n.[m] (preface, 35th para.).

[8] Bentham, *Principles of Penal Laws*, in I *Works* 365, 576 (pt. III, c. XXI,
10th para., 11th para.).

[9] Bentham, *Principles of Morals and Legislation*, in I *Works* I, 84 (c. XIII).

[10] Bentham, *Anarchical Fallacies*, in 2 *Works* 489, 511-12 (art. VIII); Bentham,
Principles of Morals and Legislation, in I *Works* I, 144 (c. XIX, 11th para.).

as slaves can reason, but simply whether they suffer.[11] Does
this not compare well with the discussion of the question in
terms of whether or not there are some men whom Nature
has fitted only to be the living instruments of others? We owe
it to Bentham more than anyone else that we have stopped
discussing this and similar questions of social policy in that
form.

So Bentham and Austin were not dry analysts fiddling with
verbal distinctions while cities burned, but were the vanguard
of a movement which laboured with passionate intensity and
much success to bring about a better society and better laws.
Why then did they insist on the separation of law as it is and
law as it ought to be? What did they mean? Let us first see
what they said. Austin formulated the doctrine:

> The existence of law is one thing; its merit or demerit is another.
> Whether it be or be not is one enquiry; whether it be or be not con-
> formable to an assumed standard, is a different enquiry. A law, which
> actually exists, is a law, though we happen to dislike it, or though it
> vary from the text, by which we regulate our approbation and disappro-
> bation. This truth, when formally announced as an abstract proposition,
> is so simple and glaring that it seems idle to insist upon it. But simple
> and glaring as it is, when enunciated in abstract expressions the enu-
> meration of the instances in which it has been forgotten would fill a
> volume.
> Sir William Blackstone, for example, says in his 'Commentaries', that
> the laws of God are superior in obligation to all other laws; that no
> human laws should be suffered to contradict them; that human laws are
> of no validity if contrary to them; and that all valid laws derive their
> force from that Divine original.
> Now, he *may* mean that all human laws ought to conform to the
> Divine laws. If this be his meaning, I assent to it without hesitation. . . .
> Perhaps, again, he means that human lawgivers are themselves obliged
> by the Divine laws to fashion the laws which they impose by that ulti-
> mate standard, because if they do not, God will punish them. To this
> also I entirely assent . . . .
> But the meaning of this passage of Blackstone, if it has a meaning,
> seems rather to be this: that no human law which conflicts with the
> Divine law is obligatory or binding; in other words, that no human
> law which conflicts with the Divine law *is a law*. . . .[12]

Austin's protest against blurring the distinction between
what law is and what it ought to be is quite general: it is a

[11] Ibid. at 142 n. § (c. XIX, 4th para. n. §).
[12] Austin, *The Province of Jurisprudence Determined* 184–5 (Library of Ideas
edn. 1954).

mistake, whatever our standard of what ought to be, whatever 'the text by which we regulate our approbation or disapprobation'. His examples, however, are always a confusion between law as it is and law as morality would require it to be. For him, it must be remembered, the fundamental principles of morality were God's commands, to which utility was an 'index': besides this there was the actual accepted morality of a social group or 'positive' morality.

Bentham insisted on this distinction without characterizing morality by reference to God but only, of course, by reference to the principles of utility. Both thinkers' prime reason for this insistence was to enable men to see steadily the precise issues posed by the existence of morally bad laws, and to understand the specific character of the authority of a legal order. Bentham's general recipe for life under the government of laws was simple: it was *'to obey punctually; to censure freely'*.[13] But Bentham was especially aware, as an anxious spectator of the French revolution, that this was not enough: the time might come in any society when the law's commands were so evil that the question of resistance had to be faced, and it was then essential that the issues at stake at this point should neither be oversimplified nor obscured.[14] Yet this was precisely what the confusion between law and morals had done, and Bentham found that the confusion had spread symmetrically in two different directions. On the one hand Bentham had in mind the anarchist who argues thus: 'This ought not to be the law, therefore it is not and I am free not merely to censure but to disregard it.' On the other hand he thought of the reactionary who argues: 'This is the law, therefore it is what it ought to be', and thus stifles criticism at its birth. Both errors, Bentham thought, were to be found in Blackstone: there was his incautious statement that human laws were invalid if contrary to the law of God,[15] and 'that

[13] Bentham, *A Fragment on Government*, in I *Works* 221, 230 (preface, 16th para.).
[14] See Bentham, 'Principles of Legislation', in *The Theory of Legislation* I, 65 n.* (Ogden edn. 1931) (c. XII, 2d para. n.*). 'Here we touch upon the most difficult of questions. If the law is not what it ought to be; if it openly combats the principle of utility; ought we to obey it? Ought we to violate it? Ought we to remain neuter between the law which commands an evil, and morality which forbids it?' See also Bentham, *A Fragment on Government*, in I *Works* 221, 287-8 (c. IV, 20th-25th paras.).
[15] I Blackstone, *Commentaries* *41. Bentham criticized 'this dangerous

spirit of obsequious *quietism* that seems constitutional in our Author' which 'will scarce ever let him recognise a difference' between what is and what ought to be.[16] This indeed was for Bentham the occupational disease of lawyers: '[I]n the eyes of lawyers — not to speak of their dupes — that is to say, as yet, the generality of non-lawyers — the *is* and the *ought to be* . . . were one and indivisible.'[17] There are therefore two dangers between which insistence on this distinction will help us to steer: the danger that law and its authority may be dissolved in man's conceptions of what law ought to be and the danger that the existing law may supplant morality as a final test of conduct and so escape criticism.

In view of later criticisms it is also important to distinguish several things that the Utilitarians did not mean by insisting on their separation of law and morals. They certainly accepted many of the things that might be called 'the intersection of law and morals'. First, they never denied that, as a matter of historical fact, the development of legal systems had been powerfully influenced by moral opinion, and, conversely, that moral standards had been profoundly influenced by law, so that the content of many legal rules mirrored moral rules or principles. It is not in fact always easy to trace this historical causal connection, but Bentham was certainly ready to admit its existence; so too Austin spoke of the 'frequent coincidence'[18] of positive law and morality and attributed the confusion of what law is with what law ought to be to this very fact.

Secondly, neither Bentham nor his followers denied that by explicit legal provisions moral principles might at different points be brought into a legal system and form part of its rules, or that courts might be legally bound to decide in

maxim', saying 'the natural tendency of such a doctrine is to impel a man, by the force of conscience, to rise up in arms against any law whatever that he happens not to like'. Bentham, *A Fragment on Government*, in I *Works* 221, 287 (c. IV, 19th para.). See also Bentham, *A Comment on the Commentaries* 49 (1928) (c. III). For an expression of a fear lest anarchy result from such a doctrine, combined with a recognition that resistance may be justified on grounds of utility, see Austin, op. cit. n. 12 *supra*, at 186.

[16] Bentham, *A Fragment on Government*, in I *Works* 221, 294 (c. V, 10th para.).

[17] Bentham, *A Commentary on Humphreys' Real Property Code*, in 5 *Works* 389.

[18] Austin, op. cit. n. 12 *supra*, at 162.

accordance with what they thought just or best. Bentham indeed recognized, as Austin did not, that even the supreme
legislative power might be subjected to legal restraints by a
constitution[19] and would not have denied that moral principles, like those of the Fifth Amendment, might form the
content of such legal constitutional restraints. Austin differed
in thinking that restraints on the supreme legislative power
could not have the force of law, but would remain merely
political or moral checks;[20] but of course he would have recognized that a statute, for example, might confer a delegated
legislative power and restrict the area of its exercise by reference to moral principles.

What both Bentham and Austin were anxious to assert
were the following two simple things: first, in the absence of
an expressed constitutional or legal provision, it could not
follow from the mere fact that a rule violated standards of
morality that it was not a rule of law; and, conversely, it could
not follow from the mere fact that a rule was morally desirable that it was a rule of law.

The history of this simple doctrine in the nineteenth century is too long and too intricate to trace here. Let me summarize it by saying that after it was propounded to the world
by Austin it dominated English jurisprudence and constitutes
part of the framework of most of those curiously English and
perhaps unsatisfactory productions — the omnibus surveys of
the whole field of jurisprudence. A succession of these were
published after a full text of Austin's lectures finally appeared
in 1863. In each of them the utilitarian separation of law and
morals is treated as something that enables lawyers to attain a
new clarity. Austin was said by one of his English successors,
Amos, 'to have delivered the law from the dead body of
morality that still clung to it';[21] and even Maine, who was

[19] Bentham, *A Fragment on Government*, in I *Works* 221, 289-90 (c. IV,
33rd-34th paras.).
[20] See Austin, op. cit. n. 12 *supra*, at 231.
[21] Amos, *The Science of Law* 4 (5th edn. 1881). See also Markby, *Elements
of Law* 4-5 (5th edn. 1896): 'Austin, by establishing the distinction between positive law and morals, not only laid the foundation for a science of law, but cleared
the conception of law ... of a number of pernicious consequences to which ... it
had been supposed to lead. Positive laws, as Austin has shown, must be legally
binding, and yet a law may be unjust. ... He has admitted that law itself may be
immoral, in which case it may be our moral duty to disobey it. ...' Cf. Holland,
Jurisprudence 1-20 (1880).

critical of Austin at many points, did not question this part
of his doctrine. In the United States men like N. St. John
Green,[22] Gray, and Holmes considered that insistence on this
distinction had enabled the understanding of law as a means
of social control to get off to a fruitful new start; they welcomed it both as self-evident and as illuminating — as a
revealing tautology. This distinction is, of course, one of the
main themes of Holmes's most famous essay 'The Path of
the Law',[23] but the place it had in the estimation of these
American writers is best seen in what Gray wrote at the turn
of the century in *The Nature and Sources of the Law*. He said:

The great gain in its fundamental conceptions which Jurisprudence
made during the last century was the recognition of the truth that the
Law of a State . . . is not an ideal, but something which actually exists.
. . . [I]t is not that which ought to be, but that which is. To fix this
definitely in the Jurisprudence of the Common Law, is the feat that
Austin accomplished.[24]

II

So much for the doctrine in the heyday of its success. Let us
turn now to some of the criticisms. Undoubtedly, when
Bentham and Austin insisted on the distinction between law
as it is and as it ought to be, they had in mind *particular* laws,
the meanings of which were clear and so not in dispute, and
they were concerned to argue that such laws, even if morally
outrageous, were still laws. It is, however, necessary, in considering the criticisms which later developed, to consider more
than those criticisms which were directed to this particular
point if we are to get at the root of the dissatisfaction felt;
we must also take account of the objection that, even if what
the Utilitarians said on this particular point were true, their
insistence on it, in a terminology suggesting a general cleavage
between what is and ought to be law, obscured the fact that
at other points there is an essential point of contact between
the two. So in what follows I consider not only criticisms of
the particular point which the Utilitarians had in mind, but
also the claim that an essential connection between law and

[22] See Green, Book Review, 6 *Am. L. Rev.* 57, 61 (1871) (reprinted in Green,
Essays and Notes on the Law of Tort and Crime 31, 35 (1933)).
[23] 10 *Harv. L. Rev.* 457 (1897).
[24] Gray, *The Nature and Sources of the Law* 94 (1st edn. 1909) (§ 213).

morals emerges if we examine how laws, the meanings of which are in dispute, are interpreted and applied in concrete cases; and that this connection emerges again if we widen our point of view and ask, not whether every particular rule of law must satisfy a moral minimum in order to be a law, but whether a system of rules which altogether failed to do this could be a legal system.

There is, however, one major initial complexity by which criticism has been much confused. We must remember that the Utilitarians combined with their insistence on the separation of law and morals two other equally famous but distinct doctrines. One was the important truth that a purely analytical study of legal concepts, a study of the meaning of the distinctive vocabulary of the law, was as vital to our understanding of the nature of law as historical or sociological studies, though of course it could not supplant them. The other doctrine was the famous imperative theory of law — that law is essentially a command.

These three doctrines constitute the utilitarian tradition in jurisprudence; yet they are distinct doctrines. It is possible to endorse the separation between law and morals and to value analytical inquiries into the meaning of legal concepts and yet think it wrong to conceive of law as essentially a command. One source of great confusion in the criticism of the separation of law and morals was the belief that the falsity of any one of these three doctrines in the utilitarian tradition showed the other two to be false; what was worse was the failure to see that there were three quite separate doctrines in this tradition. The indiscriminate use of the label 'positivism' to designate ambiguously each one of these three separate doctrines (together with some others which the Utilitarians never professed) has perhaps confused the issue more than any other single factor.[25] Some of the early American critics of the

---

[25] It may help to identify five (there may be more) meanings of 'positivism' bandied about in contemporary jurisprudence:

(1) the contention that laws are commands of human beings; see 58-62 *infra*;

(2) the contention that there is no necessary connection between law and morals or law as it is and ought to be; see 50-6 *supra*;

(3) the contention that the analysis (or study of the meaning) of legal concepts is (a) worth pursuing and (b) to be distinguished from historical inquiries into the causes or origins of laws, from sociological inquiries into the relation of law and other social phenomena, and from the criticism or appraisal of law whether in terms of morals, social aims, 'functions', or otherwise; see 64-6 *infra*;

Austinian doctrine were, however, admirably clear on just this matter. Gray, for example, added at the end of the tribute to Austin, which I have already quoted, the words: 'He may have been wrong in treating the Law of the State as being the command of the sovereign',[26] and he touched shrewdly on many points where the command theory is defective. But other critics have been less clearheaded, and have thought that the inadequacies of the command theory which gradually came to light were sufficient to demonstrate the falsity of the separation of law and morals.

This was a mistake, but a natural one. To see how natural it was we must look a little more closely at the command idea. The famous theory that law is a command was a part of a wider and more ambitious claim. Austin said that the notion of a command was 'the *key* to the sciences of jurisprudence and morals',[27] and contemporary attempts to elucidate moral judgments in terms of 'imperative' or 'prescriptive' utterances echo this ambitious claim. But the command theory, viewed as an effort to identify even the quintessence of law, let alone the quintessence of morals, seems breathtaking in its simplicity and quite inadequate. There is much, even in the simplest legal system, that is distorted if presented as a command. Yet the Utilitarians thought that the essence of a legal system could be conveyed if the notion of a command were supplemented by that of a habit of obedience. The simple scheme was this: What is a command? It is simply an expression by one person of the desire that another person should do or abstain from some action, accompanied by a threat of punishment which is likely to follow disobedience. Commands are laws if two conditions are satisfied: first, they must be general; second they must be commanded by what (as both

(4) the contention that a legal system is a 'closed logical system' in which correct legal decisions can be deduced by logical means from predetermined legal rules without reference to social aims, policies, moral standards; see 64–6 *infra*, and

(5) the contention that moral judgments cannot be established or defended, as statements of facts can, by rational argument, evidence, or proof ('noncognitivism' in ethics); see 82–3 *infra*.

Bentham and Austin held the views described in (1), (2), and (3), but not those in (4) and (5). Opinion (4) is often ascribed to analytical jurists; see 64–6 *infra*, but I know of no 'analyst' who held this view.

[26] Gray, *The Nature and Sources of the Law* 94–5 (2nd edn. 1921).

[27] Austin, op. cit. n. 12 *supra*, at 13.

Bentham and Austin claimed) exists in every political society whatever its constitutional form, namely, a person or a group of persons who are in receipt of habitual obedience from most of the society but pay no such obedience to others. These persons are its sovereign. Thus law is the command of the un-commanded commanders of society — the creation of the legally untrammelled will of the sovereign who is by definition outside the law.

It is easy to see that this account of a legal system is thread-bare. One can also see why it might seem that its inadequacy is due to the omission of some essential connection with mor-ality. The situation which the simple trilogy of command, sanction, and sovereign avails to describe, if you take these notions at all precisely, is like that of a gunman saying to his victim, 'Give me your money or your life.' The only difference is that in the case of a legal system the gunman says it to a large number of people who are accustomed to the racket and habitually surrender to it. Law surely is not the gunman situation writ large, and legal order is surely not to be thus simply identified with compulsion.

This scheme, despite the points of obvious analogy between a statute and a command, omits some of the most character-istic elements of law. Let me cite a few. It is wrong to think of a legislature (and *a fortiori* an electorate) with a changing membership as a group of persons habitually obeyed: this simple idea is suited only to a monarch sufficiently long-lived for a 'habit' to grow up. Even if we waive this point, nothing which legislators do makes law unless they comply with fun-damental accepted rules specifying the essential law-making procedures. This is true even in a system having a simple uni-tary constitution like the British. These fundamental accepted rules specifying what the legislature must do to legislate are not commands habitually obeyed, nor can they be expressed as habits of obedience to persons. They lie at the root of a legal system, and what is most missing in the utilitarian scheme is an analysis of what it is for a social group and its officials to accept such rules. This notion, not that of a com-mand as Austin claimed, is the 'key to the science of juris-prudence', or at least one of the keys.

Again, Austin, in the case of a democracy, looked past the legislators to the electorate as 'the sovereign' (or in England as part of it). He thought that in the United States the mass of the electors to the state and federal legislatures were the sovereign whose commands, given by their 'agents' in the legislatures, were law. But on this footing the whole notion of the sovereign outside the law being 'habitually obeyed' by the 'bulk' of the population must go: for in this case the 'bulk' obeys the bulk, that is, it obeys itself. Plainly the general acceptance of the authority of a law-making procedure, irrespective of the changing individuals who operate it from time to time, can be only distorted by an analysis in terms of mass habitual obedience to certain persons who are by definition outside the law, just as the cognate but much simpler phenomenon of the general social acceptance of a rule, say of taking off the hat when entering a church, would be distorted if represented as habitual obedience by the mass to specific persons.

Other critics dimly sensed a further and more important defect in the command theory, yet blurred the edge of an important criticism by assuming that the defect was due to the failure to insist upon some important connection between law and morals. This more radical defect is as follows. The picture that the command theory draws of life under law is essentially a simple relationship of the commander to the commanded, of superior to inferior, of top to bottom; the relationship is vertical between the commanders or authors of the law conceived of as essentially outside the law and those who are commanded and subject to the law. In this picture no place, or only an accidental or subordinate place, is afforded for a distinction between types of legal rules which are in fact radically different. Some laws require men to act in certain ways or to abstain from acting whether they wish to or not. The criminal law consists largely of rules of this sort: like commands they are simply 'obeyed' or 'disobeyed'. But other legal rules are presented to society in quite different ways and have quite different functions. They provide facilities more or less elaborate for individuals to create structures of rights and duties for the conduct of life within the coercive framework of the law. Such are the rules enabling individuals to make contracts, wills, and trusts, and generally to mould their legal relations with others. Such rules, unlike the criminal law, are not factors designed to obstruct wishes and choices of an antisocial sort. On the contrary, these rules provide facilities for the realization of wishes and choices. They do not say (like commands) 'do this whether you wish it or not', but rather 'if you wish to do this, here is the way to do it'. Under these rules we exercise powers, make claims, and assert rights. These phrases mark off characteristic features of laws that confer rights and powers; they are laws which are, so to speak, put at the disposition of individuals in a way in which the criminal law is not. Much ingenuity has gone into the task of 'reducing' laws of this second sort to some complex variant of laws of the first sort. The effort to show that laws conferring rights are 'really' only conditional stipulations of sanctions to be exacted from the person ultimately under a legal duty characterizes much of Kelsen's work.[28] Yet to urge this is really just to exhibit dogmatic determination to suppress one aspect of the legal system in order to maintain the theory that the stipulation of a sanction, like Austin's command, represents the quintessence of law. One might as well urge that the rules of baseball were 'really' only complex conditional directions to the scorer and that this showed their real or 'essential' nature.

One of the first jurists in England to break with the Austinian tradition, Salmond, complained that the analysis in terms of commands left the notion of a right unprovided with a place.[29] But he confused the point. He argued first, and correctly, that if laws are merely commands it is inexplicable that we should have come to speak of legal rights and powers as conferred or arising under them, but then wrongly concluded that the rules of a legal system must necessarily be connected with moral rules or principles of justice and that only on this footing could the phenomenon of legal rights be explained. Otherwise, Salmond thought, we would have to say that a mere 'verbal coincidence' connects the concepts of legal and moral right. Similarly, continental critics of the Utilitarians, always alive to the complexity of the notion of a subjective

[28] See, e.g., Kelsen, *General Theory of Law and State* 58–61, 143–4 (1945). According to Kelsen, all laws, not only those conferring rights and powers, are reducible to such 'primary norms' conditionally stipulating sanctions.
[29] Salmond, *The First Principles of Jurisprudence* 97–8 (1893). He protested against 'the creed of what is termed the English school of jurisprudence', because it 'attempted to deprive the idea of law of that ethical significance which is one of its most essential elements'. Ibid. at 9, 10.

right, insisted that the command theory gave it no place. Hägerström insisted that if laws were merely commands the notion of an individual's right was really inexplicable, for commands are, as he said, something which we either obey or we do not obey; they do not confer rights.[30] But he, too, concluded that moral, or, as he put it, common-sense, notions of justice must therefore be necessarily involved in the analysis of any legal structure elaborate enough to confer rights.[31]

Yet, surely these arguments are confused. Rules that confer rights, though distinct from commands, need not be moral rules or coincide with them. Rights, after all, exist under the rules of ceremonies, games, and in many other spheres regulated by rules which are irrelevant to the question of justice or what the law ought to be. Nor need rules which confer rights be just or morally good rules. The rights of a master over his slaves show us that. 'Their merit or demerit', as Austin termed it, depends on how rights are distributed in society and over whom or what they are exercised. These critics indeed revealed the inadequacy of the simple notions of command and habit for the analysis of law; at many points it is apparent that the social acceptance of a rule or standard of authority (even if it is motivated only by fear or superstition or rests on inertia) must be brought into the analysis and cannot itself be reduced to the two simple terms. Yet nothing in this showed the utilitarian insistence on the distinction between the existence of law and its 'merits' to be wrong.

III

I now turn to a distinctively American criticism of the separation of the law that is from the the law that ought to be. It emerged from the critical study of the judicial process with which American jurisprudence has been on the whole so beneficially occupied. The most sceptical of these critics — the loosely named 'Realists' of the 1930s — perhaps too naïvely

---

[30] Hägerström, *Inquiries Into the Nature of Law and Morals* 217 (Olivecrona edn. 1953): '[T]he whole theory of the subjective rights of private individuals . . . is incompatible with the imperative theory'. See also ibid. at 221: 'The description of them [claims to legal protection] as rights is wholly derived from the idea that the law which is concerned with them is a true expression of rights and duties in the sense in which the popular notion of justice understands these terms.'

[31] Ibid. at 218.

accepted the conceptual framework of the natural sciences as adequate for the characterization of law and for the analysis of rule-guided action of which a living system of law at least partly consists. But they opened men's eyes to what actually goes on when courts decide cases, and the contrast they drew between the actual facts of judicial decision and the traditional terminology for describing it as if it were a wholly logical operation was usually illuminating; for in spite of some exaggeration the Realists made us acutely conscious of one cardinal feature of human language and human thought, emphasis on which is vital not only for the understanding of law but in areas of philosophy far beyond the confines of jurisprudence. The insight of this school may be presented in the following example. A legal rule forbids you to take a vehicle into the public park. Plainly this forbids an automobile, but what about bicycles, roller skates, toy automobiles? What about aeroplanes? Are these, as we say, to be called 'vehicles' for the purpose of the rule or not? If we are to communicate with each other at all, and if, as in the most elementary form of law, we are to express our intentions that a certain type of behaviour be regulated by rules, then the general words we use — like 'vehicle' in the case I consider — must have some standard instance in which no doubts are felt about its application. There must be a core of settled meaning, but there will be, as well, a penumbra of debatable cases in which words are neither obviously applicable nor obviously ruled out. These cases will each have some features in common with the standard case; they will lack others or be accompanied by features not present in the standard case. Human invention and natural processes continually throw up such variants on the familiar, and if we are to say that these ranges of facts do or do not fall under existing rules, then the classifier must make a decision which is not dictated to him, for the facts and phenomena to which we fit our words and apply our rules are as it were *dumb*. The toy automobile cannot speak up and say, 'I am a vehicle for the purpose of this legal rule', nor can the roller skates chorus, 'We are not a vehicle.' Fact situations do not await us neatly labelled, creased, and folded; nor is their legal classification written on them to be simply read off by the judge. Instead, in applying legal rules, someone must take the responsibility of deciding that words do or do

not cover some case in hand, with all the practical consequences involved in this decision.

We may call the problems which arise outside the hard core
of standard instances or settled meaning 'problems of the
penumbra'; they are always with us whether in relation to
such trivial things as the regulation of the use of the public
park or in relation to the multidimensional generalities of a
constitution. If a penumbra of uncertainty must surround all
legal rules, then their application to specific cases in the penumbral area cannot be a matter of logical deduction, and so
deductive reasoning, which for generations has been cherished
as the very perfection of human reasoning, cannot serve as a
model for what judges, or indeed anyone, should do in bringing particular cases under general rules. In this area men cannot live by deduction alone. And it follows that if legal
arguments and legal decisions of penumbral questions are to
be rational, their rationality must lie in something other than
a logical relation to premises. So if it is rational or 'sound' to
argue and to decide that for the purposes of this rule an aeroplane is not a vehicle, this argument must be sound or rational
without being logically conclusive. What is it then that makes
such decisions correct or at least better than alternative
decisions? Again, it seems true to say that the criterion which
makes a decision sound in such cases is some concept of what
the law ought to be; it is easy to slide from that into saying
that it must be a moral judgment about what law ought to be.
So here we touch upon a point of necessary 'intersection between law and morals' which demonstrates the falsity or, at
any rate, the misleading character of the Utilitarians' emphatic insistence on the separation of law as it is and ought to
be. Surely, Bentham and Austin could only have written as
they did because they misunderstood or neglected this aspect
of the judicial process, because they ignored the problems of
the penumbra.

The misconception of the judicial process which ignores
the problems of the penumbra and which views the process as
consisting pre-eminently in deductive reasoning is often stigmatized as the error of 'formalism' or 'literalism'. My question
now is, how and to what extent does the demonstration of
this error show the utilitarian distinction to be wrong or
misleading? Here there are many issues which have been

confused, but I can only disentangle some. The charge of formalism has been levelled both at the 'positivist' legal theorist and at the courts, but of course it must be a very different charge in each case. Levelled at the legal theorist, the charge means that he has made a theoretical mistake about the character of legal decision; he has thought of the reasoning involved as consisting in deduction from premises in which the judges' practical choices or decisions play no part. It would be easy to show that Austin was guiltless of this error; only an entire misconception of what analytical jurisprudence is and why he thought it important has led to the view that he, or any other analyst, believed that the law was a closed logical system in which judges deduced their decisions from premises.[32] On the contrary, he was very much alive to the character of language, to its vagueness or open character;[33] he thought that in the penumbral situation judges must necessarily legislate,[34] and, in accents that sometimes recall those

[32] This misunderstanding of analytical jurisprudence is to be found in, among others, Stone, *The Province and Function of Law* 141 (1950): 'In short, rejecting the implied assumption that all propositions of all parts of the law must be logically consistent with each other and proceed on a single set of definitions ... he [Cardozo, J.] denied that the law is actually what the analytical jurist, *for his limited purposes*, assumes it to be.' See also ibid. at 49, 52, 138, 140; Friedmann, *Legal Theory* 209 (3rd edn. 1953). This misunderstanding seems to depend on the unexamined and false belief that analytical studies of the meaning of legal terms would be impossible or absurd if, to reach sound decisions in particular cases, more than a capacity for formal logical reasoning from unambiguous and clear predetermined premises is required.

[33] See the discussion of vagueness and uncertainty in law, in Austin, op. cit. n. 12 *supra*, at 202-5, 207, in which Austin recognized that, in consequence of this vagueness, often only 'fallible tests' can be provided for determining whether particular cases fall under general expressions.

[34] See Austin, op. cit. n. 12 *supra*, at 191: 'I cannot understand how any person who has considered the subject can suppose that society could possibly have gone on if judges had not legislated. . . .' As a corrective to the belief that the analytical jurist must take a 'slot machine' or 'mechanical' view of the judicial process it is worth noting the following observations made by Austin:

(1) Whenever law has to be applied, the '"competition of opposite analogies"' may arise, for the case 'may resemble in some of its points' cases to which the rule has been applied in the past and in other points 'cases from which the application of the law has been withheld'. 2 Austin, *Lectures on Jurisprudence* 633 (5th edn. 1885).

(2) Judges have commonly decided cases and so derived new rules by 'building' on a variety of grounds including sometimes (in Austin's opinion too rarely) their views of what law ought to be. Most commonly they have derived law from pre-existing law by 'consequence founded on analogy', i.e., they have made a new rule 'in *consequence* of the existence of a similar rule applying to subjects which are *analogous*. . . .' 2 ibid. at 638-9.

of the late Judge Jerome Frank, he berated the common-law
judges for legislating feebly and timidly and for blindly relying on real or fancied analogies with past cases instead of
adapting their decisions to the growing needs of society as
revealed by the moral standard of utility.[35] The villains of
this piece, responsible for the conception of the judge as an
automaton, are not the utilitarian thinkers. The responsibility,
if it is to be laid at the door of any theorist, is with thinkers
like Blackstone and, at an earlier stage, Montesquieu. The root
of this evil is preoccupation with the separation of powers
and Blackstone's 'childish fiction' (as Austin termed it) that
judges only 'find', never 'make', law.

But we are concerned with 'formalism' as a vice not of
jurists but of judges. What precisely is it for a judge to commit
this error, to be a 'formalist', 'automatic', a 'slot machine'?
Curiously enough the literature, which is full of the denunci-
ation of these vices, never makes this clear in concrete terms;
instead we have only descriptions which cannot mean what
they appear to say; it is said that in the formalist error courts
make an excessive use of logic, take a thing to 'a dryly logical
extreme',[36] or make an excessive use of analytical methods.
But just how in being a formalist does a judge make an excessive use of logic? It is clear that the essence of his error is
to give some general term an interpretation which is blind to
social values and consequences (or which is in some other way

(3) '[I]f every rule in a system of law were perfectly definite or precise', these
difficulties incident to the application of law would not arise. 'But the ideal com-
pleteness and correctness I now have imagined is not attainable in fact. . . . though
the system had been built and ordered with matchless solicitude and skill.' 2 ibid.
at 997–8. Of course he thought that much could and should be done by codifi-
cation to eliminate uncertainty. See 2 ibid. at 662–81.

[35] 2 ibid. at 641: 'Nothing, indeed, can be more natural, than that legislators,
direct or judicial (especially if they be narrow-minded, timid and unskilful), should
lean as much as they can on the examples set by their predecessors.' See also 2
ibid. at 647: 'But it is much to be regretted that Judges of capacity, experience
and weight, have not seized every opportunity of introducing a new rule (a rule
beneficial for the future). . . . This is the reproach I should be inclined to make
against Lord Eldon. . . . [T]he Judges of the Common Law Courts would not do
what they ought to have done, namely to model their rules of law and of procedure to the growing exigencies of society, instead of stupidly and sulkily adhering to the old and barbarous usages.'

[36] *Hynes* v. *New York Cent. R.R.*, 231 N.Y. 229, 235; 131 N.E. 898, 900
(1921); see Pound, *Interpretations of Legal History* 123 (2nd edn. 1930); Stone,
op. cit. n. 32 *supra*, at 140–1.

stupid or perhaps merely disliked by critics). But logic does not prescribe interpretation of terms; it dictates neither the stupid nor intelligent interpretation of any expression. Logic only tells you hypothetically that *if* you give a certain term a certain interpretation then a certain conclusion follows. Logic is silent on how to classify particulars — and this is the heart of a judicial decision. So this reference to logic and to logical extremes is a misnomer for something else, which must be this. A judge has to apply a rule to a concrete case — perhaps the rule that one may not take a stolen 'vehicle' across State lines, and in this case an aeroplane has been taken.[37] He either does not see or pretends not to see that the general terms of this rule are susceptible of different interpretations and that he has a choice left open uncontrolled by linguistic conventions. He ignores, or is blind to, the fact that he is in the area of the penumbra and is not dealing with a standard case. Instead of choosing in the light of social aims the judge fixes the meaning in a different way. He either takes the meaning that the word most obviously suggests in its ordinary non-legal context to ordinary men, or one which the word has been given in some other legal context, or, still worse, he thinks of a standard case and then arbitrarily identifies certain features in it — for example, in the case of a vehicle, (1) normally used on land, (2) capable of carrying a human person, (3) capable of being self-propelled — and treats these three as always necessary and always sufficient conditions for the use in all contexts of the word 'vehicle', irrespective of the social consequences of giving it this interpretation. This choice, not 'logic', would force the judge to include a toy motor car (if electrically propelled) and to exclude bicycles and the aeroplane. In all this there is possibly great stupidity, but no more 'logic', and no less, than in cases in which the interpretation given to a general term and the consequent application of some general rule to a particular case is consciously controlled by some identified social aim.

Decisions made in a fashion as blind as this would scarcely deserve the name of decisions; we might as well toss a penny in applying a rule of law. But it is at least doubtful whether any judicial decisions (even in England) have been quite as

---

[37] See *McBoyle* v. *United States*, 283 U.S. 25 (1931).

automatic as this. Rather, either the interpretations stigmatized as automatic have resulted from the conviction that it is
fairer in a criminal statute to take a meaning which would
jump to the mind of the ordinary man at the cost even of
defeating other values, and this itself is a social policy (though
possibly a bad one); or much more frequently, what is stigmatized as 'mechanical' and 'automatic' is a determined choice
made indeed in the light of a social aim but of a conservative
social aim. Certainly many of the Supreme Court decisions at
the turn of the century which have been so stigmatized[38] represent clear choices in the penumbral area to give effect to a
policy of a conservative type. This is peculiarly true of Mr
Justice Peckham's opinions defining the spheres of police
power and due process.[39]

But how does the wrongness of deciding cases in an automatic and mechanical way and the rightness of deciding cases
by reference to social purposes show that the utilitarian insistence on the distinction between what the law is and what
it ought to be is wrong? I take it that no one who wished to
use these vices of formalism as proof that the distinction between what is and what ought to be is mistaken would deny
that the decisions stigmatized as automatic are law; nor would
he deny that the system in which such automatic decisions
are made is a legal system. Surely he would say that they are
law, but they are bad law; they ought not to be law. But this
would be to use the distinction, not to refute it; and of course
both Bentham and Austin used it to attack judges for failing
to decide penumbral cases in accordance with the growing
needs of society.

Clearly, if the demonstration of the errors of formalism is
to show the utilitarian distinction to be wrong, the point must
be drastically restated. The point must be not merely that a
judicial decision to be rational must be made in the light of
some conception of what ought to be, but that the aims, the
social policies and purposes to which judges should appeal if

[38] See, e.g., Pound, 'Mechanical Jurisprudence', 8 *Colum. L. Rev.* 605, 615-16
(1908).
[39] See, e.g., *Lochner* v. *New York*, 198 U.S. 45 (1905). Justice Peckham's
opinion that there were no reasonable grounds for interfering with the right of free
contract by determining the hours of labour in the occupation of a baker may indeed be a wrongheaded piece of conservatism but there is nothing automatic or
mechanical about it.

their decisions are to be rational, are themselves to be considered as part of the law in some suitably wide sense of 'law'
which is held to be more illuminating than that used by the
Utilitarians. This restatement of the point would have the
following consequence: instead of saying that the recurrence
of penumbral questions shows us that legal rules are essentially incomplete, and that, when they fail to determine decisions, judges must legislate and so exercise a creative choice
between alternatives, we shall say that the social policies
which guide the judges' choice are in a sense there for them
to discover; the judges are only 'drawing out' of the rule what,
if it is properly understood, is 'latent' within it. To call this
judicial legislation is to obscure some essential continuity between the clear cases of the rule's application and the penumbral decisions. I shall question later whether this way of
talking is salutary, but I wish at this time to point out something obvious, but likely, if not stated, to tangle the issues.
It does not follow that, because the opposite of a decision
reached blindly in the formalist or literalist manner is a
decision intelligently reached by reference to some conception
of what ought to be, we have a junction of law and morals.
We must, I think, beware of thinking in a too simple-minded
fashion about the word 'ought'. This is not because there is
no distinction to be made between law as it is and ought to
be. Far from it. It is because the distinction should be between
what is and what from many different points of view ought
to be. The word 'ought' merely reflects the presence of some
standard of criticism; one of these standards is a moral standard, but not all standards are moral. We say to our neighbour, 'You ought not to lie', and that may certainly be a
moral judgment, but we should remember that the baffled
poisoner may say, 'I ought to have given her a second dose'.
The point here is that intelligent decisions which we oppose
to mechanical or formal decisions are not necessarily identical
with decisions defensible on moral grounds. We may say of
many a decision: 'Yes, that is right; that is as it ought to be',
and we may mean only that some accepted purpose or policy
has been thereby advanced; we may not mean to endorse the
moral propriety of the policy or the decision. So the contrast
between the mechanical decision and the intelligent one can
be reproduced inside a system dedicated to the pursuit of the

most evil aims. It does not exist as a contrast to be found only in legal systems which, like our own, widely recognize principles of justice and moral claims of individuals.

An example may make this point plainer. With us the task of sentencing in criminal cases is the one that seems most obviously to demand from the judge the exercise of moral judgment. Here the factors to be weighed seem clearly to be moral factors: society must not be exposed to wanton attack; too much misery must not be inflicted on either the victim or his dependants; efforts must be made to enable him to lead a better life and regain a position in the society whose laws he has violated. To a judge striking the balance among these claims, with all the discretion and perplexities involved, his task seems as plain an example of the exercise of moral judgment as could be; and it seems to be the polar opposite of some mechanical application of a tariff of penalties fixing a sentence careless of the moral claims which in our system have to be weighed. So here intelligent and rational decision is guided however uncertainly by moral aims. But we have only to vary the example to see that this need not necessarily be so and surely, if it need not necessarily be so, the utilitarian point remains unshaken. Under the Nazi regime men were sentenced by courts for criticism of the regime. Here the choice of sentence might be guided exclusively by consideration of what was needed to maintain the state's tyranny effectively. What sentence would both terrorize the public at large and keep the friends and family of the prisoner in suspense so that both hope and fear would cooperate as factors making for subservience? The prisoner of such a system would be regarded simply as an object to be used in pursuit of these aims. Yet, in contrast with a mechanical decision, decision on these grounds would be intelligent and purposive, and from one point of view the decision would be as it ought to be. Of course, I am not unaware that a whole philosophical tradition has sought to demonstrate the fact that we cannot correctly call decisions or behaviour truly rational unless they are in conformity with moral aims and principles. But the example I have used seems to me to serve at least as a warning that we cannot use the errors of formalism as something which *per se* demonstrates the falsity of the utilitarian insistence on the distinction between law as it is and law as *morally* it ought to be.

We can now return to the main point. If it is true that the intelligent decision of penumbral questions is one made not mechanically but in the light of aims, purposes, and policies, though not necessarily in the light of anything we would call moral principles, is it wise to express this important fact by saying that the firm utilitarian distinction between what the law is and what it ought to be should be dropped? Perhaps the claim that it is wise cannot be theoretically refuted, for it is, in effect, an *invitation* to revise our conception of what a legal rule is. We are invited to include in the 'rule' the various aims and policies in the light of which its penumbral cases are decided on the ground that these aims have, because of their importance, as much right to be called law as the core of legal rules whose meaning is settled. But though an invitation cannot be refuted, it may be refused, and I would proffer two reasons for refusing this invitation. First, everything we have learned about the judicial process can be expressed in other less mysterious ways. We can say laws are incurably incomplete and we must decide the penumbral cases rationally by reference to social aims. I think Holmes, who had such a vivid appreciation of the fact that 'general propositions do not decide concrete cases', would have put it that way. Secondly, to insist on the utilitarian distinction is to emphasize that the hard core of settled meaning is law in some centrally important sense and that even if there are borderlines, there must first be lines. If this were not so the notion of rules controlling courts' decisions would be senseless, as some of the 'Realists' — in their most extreme moods, and, I think, on bad grounds — claimed.[40]

By contrast, to soften the distinction, to assert mysteriously that there is some fused identity between law as it is and as it

---

[40] One recantation of this extreme position is worth mention in the present context. In the first edition of *The Bramble Bush*, Professor Llewellyn committed himself wholeheartedly to the view that 'what these officials do about disputes is, to my mind, the law itself', and that '*rules* . . . are important so far as they help you . . . predict what judges will do. . . . That is all their importance, except as pretty playthings.' Llewellyn, *The Bramble Bush* 3, 5 (1st edn. 1930). In the second edition he said that these were 'unhappy words when not more fully developed, and they are plainly at best a very partial statement of the whole truth. . . . [O]ne office of law is to control officials in some part, and to guide them even . . . where no thoroughgoing control is possible, or is desired. . . . [T]he words fail to take proper account . . . of the office of the institution of law as an instrument of conscious shaping. . . .' Llewellyn, *The Bramble Bush* 9 (2nd edn. 1951).

ought to be, is to suggest that all legal questions are fundamentally like those of the penumbra. It is to assert that there is no central element of actual law to be seen in the core of central meaning which rules have, that there is nothing in the nature of a legal rule inconsistent with *all* questions being open to reconsideration in the light of social policy. Of course, it is good to be occupied with the penumbra. Its problems are rightly the daily diet of the law schools. But to be occupied with the penumbra is one thing, to be preoccupied with it another. And preoccupation with the penumbra is, if I may say so, as rich a source of confusion in the American legal tradition as formalism in the English. Of course we might abandon the notion that rules have authority; we might cease to attach force or even meaning to an argument that a case falls clearly within a rule and the scope of a precedent. We might call all such reasoning 'automatic' or 'mechanical', which is already the routine invective of the courts. But until we decide that this *is* what we want, we should not encourage it by obliterating the utilitarian distinction.

IV

The third criticism of the separation of law and morals is of a very different character; it certainly is less an intellectual argument against the utilitarian distinction than a passionate appeal supported not by detailed reasoning but by reminders of a terrible experience. For it consists of the testimony of those who have descended into Hell, and, like Ulysses or Dante, brought back a message for human beings. Only in this case the Hell was not beneath or beyond earth, but on it; it was a Hell created on earth by men for other men.

This appeal comes from those German thinkers who lived through the Nazi regime and reflected upon its evil manifestations in the legal system. One of these thinkers, Gustav Radbruch, had himself shared the 'positivist' doctrine until the Nazi tyranny, but he was converted by this experience and so his appeal to other men to discard the doctrine of the separation of law and morals has the special poignancy of a recantation. What is important about this criticism is that it really does confront the particular point which Bentham and Austin had in mind in urging the separation of law as it is and as it ought to be. These German thinkers put their insistence on the need to join together what the Utilitarians separated just where this separation was of most importance in the eyes of the Utilitarians; for they were concerned with the problem posed by the existence of morally evil laws.

Before his conversion Radbruch held that resistance to law was a matter for the personal conscience, to be thought out by the individual as a moral problem, and the validity of a law could not be disproved by showing that its requirements were morally evil or even by showing that the effect of compliance with the law would be more evil than the effect of disobedience. Austin, it may be recalled, was emphatic in condemning those who said that if human laws conflicted with the fundamental principles of morality then they cease to be laws, as talking 'stark nonsense'.

The most pernicious laws, and therefore those which are most opposed to the will of God, have been and are continually enforced as laws by judicial tribunals. Suppose an act innocuous, or positively beneficial, be prohibited by the sovereign under the penalty of death; if I commit this act, I shall be tried and condemned, and if I object to the sentence, that it is contrary to the law of God . . . the court of justice will demonstrate the inconclusiveness of my reasoning by hanging me up, in pursuance of the law of which I have impugned the validity. An exception, demurrer, or plea, founded on the law of God was never heard in a Court of Justice, from the creation of the world down to the present moment.[41]

These are strong, indeed brutal words, but we must remember that they went along — in the case of Austin and, of course, Bentham — with the conviction that if laws reached a certain degree of iniquity then there would be a plain moral obligation to resist them and to withhold obedience. We shall see, when we consider the alternatives, that this simple presentation of the human dilemma which may arise has much to be said for it.

Radbruch, however, had concluded from the ease with which the Nazi regime had exploited subservience to mere law — expressed, as he thought, in the 'positivist' slogan 'law as law' (*Gesetz als Gesetz*) — and from the failure of the German legal profession to protest against the enormities which they were required to perpetrate in the name of law,

---

[41] Austin, *The Province of Jurisprudence Determined* 185 (Library of Ideas edn. 1954).

that 'positivism' (meaning here the insistence on the separation of law as it is from law as it ought to be) had powerfully contributed to the horrors. His considered reflections led him to the doctrine that the fundamental principles of humanitarian morality were part of the very concept of *Recht* or Legality and that no positive enactment or statute, however clearly it was expressed and however clearly it conformed with the formal criteria of validity of a given legal system, could be valid if it contravened basic principles of morality. This doctrine can be appreciated fully only if the nuances imported by the German word *Recht* are grasped. But it is clear that the doctrine meant that every lawyer and judge should denounce statutes that transgressed the fundamental principles not as merely immoral or wrong but has having no legal character, and enactments which on this ground lack the quality of law should not be taken into account in working out the legal position of any given individual in particular circumstances. The striking recantation of his previous doctrine is unfortunately omitted from the translation of his works, but it should be read by all who wish to think afresh on the question of the interconnection of law and morals.[42]

It is impossible to read without sympathy Radbruch's passionate demand that the German legal conscience should be open to the demands of morality and his complaint that this has been too little the case in the German tradition. On the other hand there is an extraordinary naïvety in the view that insensitiveness to the demands of morality and subservience to state power in a people like the Germans should have arisen from the belief that law might be law though it failed to conform with the minimum requirements of morality. Rather this terrible history prompts inquiry into why emphasis on the slogan 'law is law', and the distinction between law and morals, acquired a sinister character in Germany, but elsewhere, as with the Utilitarians themselves, went along with the most enlightened liberal attitudes. But something more disturbing than naïvety is latent in Radbruch's whole

[42] See Radbruch, 'Gesetzliches Unrecht und Übergesetzliches Recht', I *Süddeutsch Juristen-Zeitung* 105 (Germany 1946) (reprinted in Radbruch, *Rechtsphilosophie* 347 (4th edn. 1950)). I have used the translation of part of this essay and of Radbruch, 'Die Erneuerung des Rechts', 2 *Die Wandlung* 8 (Germany 1947), prepared by Professor Lon Fuller of the Harvard Law School as a mimeographed supplement to the readings in jurisprudence used in his course at Harvard.

presentation of the issues to which the existence of morally
iniquitous laws give rise. It is not, I think, uncharitable to say
that we can see in his argument that he has only half digested
the spiritual message of liberalism which he is seeking to convey to the legal profession. For everything that he says is
really dependent upon an enormous overvaluation of the importance of the bare fact that a rule may be said to be a valid
rule of law, as if this, once declared, was conclusive of the
final moral question: 'Ought this rule of law to be obeyed?'
Surely the truly liberal answer to any sinister use of the slogan
'law is law' or of the distinction between law and morals is,
'Very well, but that does not conclude the question. Law is
not morality; do not let it supplant morality.'

However, we are not left to a mere academic discussion in
order to evaluate the plea which Radbruch made for the revision of the distinction between law and morals. After the
war Radbruch's conception of law as containing in itself the
essential moral principle of humanitarianism was applied in
practice by German courts in certain cases in which local war
criminals, spies, and informers under the Nazi regime were
punished. The special importance of these cases is that the
persons accused of these crimes claimed that what they had
done was not illegal under the laws of the regime in force at
the time these actions were performed. This plea was met with
the reply that the laws upon which they relied were invalid
as contravening the fundamental principles of morality. Let
me cite briefly one of these cases.[43]

In 1944 a woman, wishing to be rid of her husband,

---

[43] Judgment of 27 July 1949, Oberlandesgericht, Bamberg, 5 *Süddeutsche
Juristen-Zeitung* 207 (Germany 1950), 64 *Harv. L. Rev.* 1005 (1951); see Friedmann, *Legal Theory* 457 (3rd edn. 1953). The text has been left as originally
written, but it has been shown by Dr H. O. Pappe of the Australian National University in his article 'On the Validity of Judicial Decisions in the Nazi Era' in 23
Mod. L. Rev. (1960), 260, that the report of the case in 64 *Harv. L. Rev.* which
was followed by the author is misleading. As Dr Pappe shows, in the actual case
the German court after accepting the theoretical possibility that statutes might
be invalid if in conflict with natural law held that the Nazi statutes in question
could not be held to violate it; the accused was held guilty of unlawfully depriving
her husband of liberty, since she had no duty to inform against him but did so for
purely personal reasons and must have realized that to do so was in the circumstances 'contrary to the sound conscience and sense of justice of all decent human
beings'. Accordingly, the case as discussed in the text must now be regarded as a
hypothetical one. Dr Pappe's careful analysis of a decision in a similar case in the
German Supreme Court should be studied. (Op. cit., 268 ff.).

denounced him to the authorities for insulting remarks he had made about Hitler while home on leave from the German army. The wife was under no legal duty to report his acts, though what he had said was apparently in violation of statutes making it illegal to make statements detrimental to the government of the Third Reich or to impair by any means the military defence of the German people. The husband was arrested and sentenced to death, apparently pursuant to these statutes, though he was not executed but was sent to the front. In 1949 the wife was prosecuted in a West German court for an offence which we would describe as illegally depriving a person of his freedom (*rechtswidrige Freiheitsberaubung*). This was punishable as a crime under the German Criminal Code of 1871 which had remained in force continuously since its enactment. The wife pleaded that her husband's imprisonment was pursuant to the Nazi statutes and hence that she had committed no crime. The court of appeal to which the case ultimately came held that the wife was guilty of procuring the deprivation of her husband's liberty by denouncing him to the German courts, even though he had been sentenced by a court for having violated a statute, since, to quote the words of the court, the statute 'was contrary to the sound conscience and sense of justice of all decent human beings'. This reasoning was followed in many cases which have been hailed as a triumph of the doctrines of natural law and as signalling the overthrow of positivism. The unqualified satisfaction with this result seems to me to be hysteria. Many of us might applaud the objective — that of punishing a woman for an outrageously immoral act — but this was secured only by declaring a statute established since 1934 not to have the force of law, and at least the wisdom of this course must be doubted. There were, of course, two other choices. One was to let the woman go unpunished; one can sympathize with and endorse the view that this might have been a bad thing to do. The other was to face the fact that if the woman were to be punished it must be pursuant to the introduction of a frankly retrospective law and with a full consciousness of what was sacrificed in securing her punishment in this way. Odious as retrospective criminal legislation and punishment may be, to have pursued it openly in this case would at least have had the merits of candour. It would have made plain that in punishing the woman a choice had to be made between two evils, that of leaving her unpunished and that of sacrificing a very precious principle of morality endorsed by most legal systems. Surely if we have learned anything from the history of morals it is that the thing to do with a moral quandary is not to hide it. Like nettles, the occasions when life forces us to choose the lesser of two evils must be grasped with the consciousness that they are what they are. The vice of this use of the principle that, at certain limiting points, what is utterly immoral cannot be law or lawful is that it will serve to cloak the true nature of the problems with which we are faced and will encourage the romantic optimism that all the values we cherish ultimately will fit into a single system, that no one of them has to be sacrificed or compromised to accommodate another.

> All Discord Harmony not understood
> All Partial Evil Universal Good

This is surely untrue, and there is an insincerity in any formulation of our problem which allows us to describe the treatment of the dilemma as if it were the disposition of the ordinary case.

It may seem perhaps to make too much of forms, even perhaps of words, to emphasize one way of disposing of this difficult case as compared with another which might have led, so far as the woman was concerned, to exactly the same result. Why should we dramatize the difference between them? We might punish the woman under a new retrospective law and declare overtly that we were doing something inconsistent with our principles as the lesser of two evils; or we might allow the case to pass as one in which we do not point out precisely where we sacrifice such a principle. But candour is not just one among many minor virtues of the administration of law, just as it is not merely a minor virtue of morality. For if we adopt Radbruch's view, and with him and the German courts make our protest against evil law in the form of an assertion that certain rules cannot be law because of their moral iniquity, we confuse one of the most powerful, because it is the simplest, forms of moral criticism. If with the Utilitarians we speak plainly, we say that laws may be law but too evil to be obeyed. This is a moral condemnation which everyone can understand and it makes an immediate and obvious claim to moral attention. If, on the other hand, we formulate our objection as an assertion that these evil things are not law, here is an assertion which many people do not believe, and if they are disposed to consider it at all, it would seem to raise a whole host of philosophical issues before it can be accepted. So perhaps the most important single lesson to be learned from this form of the denial of the utilitarian distinction is the one that the Utilitarians were most concerned to teach; when we have the ample resources of plain speech we must not present the moral criticism of institutions as propositions of a disputable philosophy.

V

I have endeavoured to show that, in spite of all that has been learned and experienced since the Utilitarians wrote, and in spite of the defects of other parts of their doctrine, their protest against the confusion of what is and what ought to be law has a moral as well as an intellectual value. Yet it may well be said that, though this distinction is valid and important if applied to any particular law of a system, it is at least misleading if we attempt to apply it to 'law', that is, to the notion of a legal system, and that if we insist, as I have, on the narrower truth (or truism), we obscure a wider (or deeper) truth. After all, it may be urged, we have learned that there are many things which are untrue of laws taken separately, but which are true and important in a legal system considered as a whole. For example, the connection between law and sanctions and between the existence of law and its 'efficacy' must be understood in this more general way. It is surely not arguable (without some desperate extension of the word 'sanction' or artificial narrowing of the word 'law') that every law in a municipal legal system must have a sanction, yet it is at least plausible to argue that a legal system must, to be a legal system, provide sanctions for certain of its rules. So too, a rule of law may be said to exist though enforced or obeyed in only a minority of cases, but this could not be said of a legal system as a whole. Perhaps the differences with respect to laws taken separately and a legal system as a whole are also true of the connection between moral (or some other) conceptions of what law ought to be and law in this wider sense.

This line of argument, found (at least in embryo form) in Austin, where he draws attention to the fact that every developed legal system contains certain fundamental notions which are 'necessary' and 'bottomed in the common nature of man',[44] is worth pursuing — up to a point — and I shall say briefly why and how far this is so.

We must avoid, if we can, the arid wastes of inappropriate definition, for, in relation to a concept as many-sided and vague as that of a legal system, disputes about the 'essential' character, or necessity to the whole, of any single element soon begin to look like disputes about whether chess could be 'chess' if played without pawns. There is a wish, which may be understandable, to cut straight through the question whether a legal system, to be a legal system, must measure up to some moral or other standard with simple statements of fact: for example, that no system which utterly failed in this respect has ever existed or could endure; that the normally fulfilled assumption that a legal system aims at some form of justice colours the whole way in which we interpret specific rules in particular cases, and if this normally fulfilled assumption were not fulfilled no one would have any reason to obey except fear (and probably not that), and still less, of course, any moral obligation to obey. The connection between law and moral standards and principles of justice is therefore as little arbitrary and as 'necessary' as the connection between law and sanctions, and the pursuit of the question whether this necessity is logical (part of the 'meaning' of law) or merely factual or causal can safely be left as an innocent pastime for philosophers.

Yet in two respects I should wish to go further (even though this involves the use of a philosophical fantasy) and show what could intelligibly be meant by the claim that certain provisions in a legal system are 'necessary'. The world in which we live, and we who live in it, may one day change in many different ways; and if this change were radical enough not only would certain statements of fact now true be false and vice versa, but whole ways of thinking and talking which

[44] Austin, 'Uses of the Study of Jurisprudence', in *The Province of Jurisprudence Determined* 365, 373, 367-9 (Library of Ideas edn. 1954).

constitute our present conceptual apparatus, through which we see the world and each other, would lapse. We have only to consider how the whole of our social, moral, and legal life, as we understand it now, depends on the contingent fact that though our bodies do change in shape, size, and other physical properties they do not do this so drastically nor with such quicksilver rapidity and irregularity that we cannot identify each other as the same persistent individual over considerable spans of time. Though this is but a contingent fact which may one day be different, on it at present rest huge structures of our thought and principles of action and social life. Similarly, consider the following possibility (not because it is more than a possibility but because it reveals why we think certain things necessary in a legal system and what we mean by this): suppose that men were to become invulnerable to attack by each other, were clad perhaps like giant land crabs with an impenetrable carapace, and could extract the food they needed from the air by some internal chemical process. In such circumstances (the details of which can be left to science fiction) rules forbidding the free use of violence and rules constituting the minimum form of property — with its rights and duties sufficient to enable food to grow and be retained until eaten — would not have the necessary non-arbitrary status which they have for us, constituted as we are in a world like ours. At present, and until such radical changes supervene, such rules are so fundamental that if a legal system did not have them there would be no point in having any other rules at all. Such rules overlap with basic moral principles vetoing murder, violence, and theft; and so we can add to the factual statement that all legal systems in fact coincide with morality at such vital points, the statement that this is, in this sense, necessarily so. And why not call it a 'natural' necessity?

Of course even this much depends on the fact that in asking what content a legal system must have we take this question to be worth asking only if we who consider it cherish the humble aim of survival in close proximity to our fellows. Natural-law theory, however, in all its protean guises, attempts to push the argument much further and to assert that human beings are equally devoted to and united in their conception of aims (the pursuit of knowledge, justice to their fellow men) other than that of survival and these dictate a further necessary content to a legal system (over and above my humble minimum) without which it would be pointless. Of course we must be careful not to exaggerate the differences among human beings, but it seems to me that above this minimum the purposes men have for living in society are too conflicting and varying to make possible much extension of the argument that some fuller overlap of legal rules and moral standards is 'necessary' in this sense.

Another aspect of the matter deserves attention. If we attach to a legal system the minimum meaning that it must consist of general rules — general both in the sense that they refer to courses of action, not single actions and to multiplicities of men, not single individuals — this meaning connotes the principle of treating like cases alike, though the criteria of when cases are alike will be, so far, only the general elements specified in the rules. It is, however, true that *one* essential element of the concept of justice is the principle of treating like cases alike. This is justice in the administration of the law, not justice of the law. So there is, in the very notion of law consisting of general rules, something which prevents us from treating it as if morally it is utterly neutral, without any necessary contact with moral principles. Natural procedural justice consists therefore of those principles of objectivity and impartiality in the administration of the law which implement just this aspect of law and which are designed to ensure that rules are applied only to what are genuinely cases of the rule or at least to minimize the risks of inequalities in this sense.

These two reasons (or excuses) for talking of a certain overlap between legal and moral standards as necessary and natural, of course, should not satisfy anyone who is really disturbed by the utilitarian or 'positivist' insistence that law and morality are distinct. This is so because a legal system that satisfied these minimum requirements might apply, with the most pedantic impartiality as between the persons affected, laws which were hideously oppressive, and might deny to a vast rightless slave population the minimum benefits of protection from violence and theft. The stink of such society is, after all, still in our nostrils, and to argue that they have (or had) no legal system would only involve the repetition of the argument. Only if the rules failed to provide these essential benefits and protection for anyone — even for a slave-owning group — would the minimum be unsatisfied and the system sink to the status of a set of meaningless taboos. Of course no one denied those benefits would have any reason to obey except fear and would have every moral reason to revolt.

VI

I should be less than candid if I did not, in conclusion, consider something which, I suspect, most troubles those who react strongly against 'legal positivism'. Emphasis on the distinction between law as it is and law as it ought to be may be taken to depend upon and to entail what are called 'subjectivist' and 'relativist' or 'noncognitive' theories concerning the very nature of moral judgments, moral distinctions, or 'values'. Of course the Utilitarians themselves (as distinct from later positivists like Kelsen) did not countenance any such theories, however unsatisfactory their moral philosophy may appear to us now. Austin thought ultimate moral principles were the commands of God, known to us by revelation or through the 'index' of utility, and Bentham thought they were verifiable propositions about utility. None the less I think (though I cannot prove) that insistence upon the distinction between law as it is and ought to be has been, under the general head of 'positivism', confused with a moral theory according to which statements of what is the case ('statements of fact') belong to a category or type radically different from statements of what ought to be ('value statements'). It may therefore be well to dispel this source of confusion.

There are many contemporary variants of this type of moral theory: according to some, judgments of what ought to be, or ought to be done, either are or include as essential elements expressions of 'feeling', 'emotion', or 'attitudes', or 'subjective preferences'; in others such judgments both express feelings or emotions or attitudes and enjoin others to share them. In other variants such judgments indicate that a particular case falls under a general principle or policy of action which the speaker has 'chosen' or to which he is 'committed' and which is itself not a recognition of what is the case but analogous to a general 'imperative' or command addressed to all including the speaker himself. Common to all these variants is the insistence that judgments of what ought to be done, because they contain such 'noncognitive' elements, cannot be argued for or established by rational methods as statements of fact can be, and cannot be shown to follow from any statement of fact but only from other judgments of what ought to be done in conjunction with some statement of fact. We cannot, on such a theory, demonstrate, e.g., that an action was wrong, ought not to have been done, merely by showing that it consisted of the deliberate infliction of pain solely for the gratification of the agent. We only show it to be wrong if we add to those verifiable 'cognitive' statements of fact a general principle not itself verifiable or 'cognitive' that the infliction of pain in such circumstances is wrong, ought not to be done. Together with this general distinction between statements of what is and what ought to be go sharp parallel distinctions between statements about means and statements of moral ends. We can rationally discover and debate what are appropriate means to given ends, but ends are not rationally discoverable or debatable; they are 'fiats of the will', expressions of 'emotions', 'preferences', or 'attitudes'.

Against all such views (which are of course far subtler than this crude survey can convey) others urge that all these sharp distinctions between is and ought, fact and value, means and ends, cognitive and noncognitive, are wrong. In acknowledging ultimate ends or moral values we are recognizing something as much imposed upon us by the character of the world in which we live, as little a matter of choice, attitude, feeling, emotion as the truth of factual judgments about what is the case. The characteristic moral argument is not one in which the parties are reduced to expressing or kindling feelings or emotions or issuing exhortations or commands to each other, but one by which parties come to acknowledge after closer examination and reflection that an initially disputed case falls within the ambit of a vaguely apprehended principle (itself no more 'subjective', no more a 'fiat of our will' than any other principle of classification), and this has as much title to be called 'cognitive' or 'rational' as any other initially disputed classification of particulars.

Let us now suppose that we accept this rejection of 'noncognitive' theories of morality and this denial of the drastic distinction in type between statements of what is and what

ought to be, and that moral judgments are as rationally defensible as any other kind of judgments. What would follow
from this as to the nature of the connection between law as it
is and law as it ought to be? Surely, from this alone, nothing.
Laws, however morally iniquitous, would still (so far as this
point is concerned) be laws. The only difference which the
acceptance of this view of the nature of moral judgments
would make would be that the moral iniquity of such laws
would be something that could be demonstrated; it would
surely follow merely from a statement of what the rule required to be done that the rule was morally wrong and so
ought not to be law or conversely that it was morally desirable and ought to be law. But the demonstration of this would
not show the rule not to be (or to be) law. Proof that the
principles by which we evaluate or condemn laws are rationally discoverable, and not mere 'fiats of the will', leaves untouched the fact that there are laws which may have any
degree of iniquity or stupidity and still be laws. And conversely there are rules that have every moral qualification to
be laws and yet are not laws.

Surely something further or more specific must be said if
disproof of 'noncognitivism' or kindred theories in ethics is
to be relevant to the distinction between law as it is and law
as it ought to be, and to lead to the abandonment at some
point or some softening of this distinction. No one has done
more than Professor Lon Fuller of the Harvard Law School in
his various writings to make clear such a line of argument, and
I will end by criticizing what I take to be its central point. It
is a point which again emerges when we consider not those
legal rules or parts of legal rules the meanings of which are
clear and excite no debate, but the interpretation of rules in
concrete cases where doubts are initially felt and argument
develops about their meaning. In no legal system is the scope
of legal rules restricted to the range of concrete instances
which were present or are believed to have been present in
the minds of legislators; this indeed is one of the important
differences between a legal rule and a command. Yet, when
rules are recognized as applying to instances beyond any that
legislators did or could have considered, their extension to
such new cases often presents itself not as a deliberate choice
or fiat on the part of those who so interpret the rule. It

appears neither as a decision to give the rule a new or extended meaning nor as a guess as to what legislators, dead perhaps in the eighteenth century, would have said had they been alive in the twentieth century. Rather, the inclusion of the new case under the rule takes its place as a natural elaboration of the rule, as something implementing a 'purpose' which it seems natural to attribute (in some sense) to the rule itself rather than to any particular person dead or alive. The utilitarian description of such interpretative extension of old rules to new cases as judicial legislation fails to do justice to this phenomenon; it gives no hint of the differences between a deliberate fiat or decision to treat the new case in the same way as past cases and a recognition (in which there is little that is deliberate or even voluntary) that inclusion of the new case under the rule will implement or articulate a continuing and identical purpose, hitherto less specifically apprehended.

Perhaps many lawyers and judges will see in this language something that precisely fits their experience; others may think it a romantic gloss on facts better stated in the utilitarian language of judicial 'legislation' or in the modern American terminology of 'creative choice'.

To make the point clear Professor Fuller uses a non-legal example from the philosopher Wittgenstein which is, I think, illuminating.

Someone says to me: 'Show the children a game.' I teach them gaming with dice and the other says 'I did not mean that sort of game.' Must the exclusion of the game with dice have come before his mind when he gave me the order?[45]

Something important does seem to me to be touched on in this example. Perhaps there are the following (distinguishable) points. First, we normally do interpret not only what people are trying to do but what they say in the light of assumed common human objectives, so that unless the contrary were expressly indicated we would not interpret an instruction to show a young child a game as a mandate to introduce him to gambling even though in other contexts the word 'game' would be naturally so interpreted. Secondly, very often, the speaker whose words are thus interpreted might say: 'Yes, that's what I mean [or 'that's what I meant all along'] though

[45] Fuller, 'Human Purpose and Natural Law', 53 *J. Philos.* 697, 700 (1956).

I never thought of it until you put this particular case to me.' Third, when we thus recognize, perhaps after argument or consultation with others, a particular case not specifically envisaged beforehand as falling within the ambit of some vaguely expressed instruction, we may find this experience falsified by description of it as a mere decision on our part so to treat the particular case, and that we can only describe this faithfully as coming to realize and to articulate what we 'really' want or our 'true purpose' — phrases which Professor Fuller uses later in the same article.[46]

I am sure that many philosophical discussions of the character of moral argument would benefit from attention to cases of the sort instanced by Professor Fuller. Such attention would help to provide a corrective to the view that there is a sharp separation between 'ends' and 'means' and that in debating 'ends' we can only work on each other non-rationally, and that rational argument is reserved for discussion of 'means'. But I think the relevance of his point to the issue whether it is correct or wise to insist on the distinction between law as it is and law as it ought to be is very small indeed. Its net effect is that in interpreting legal rules there are some cases which we find after reflection to be so natural an elaboration or articulation of the rule that to think of and refer to this as 'legislation', 'making law', or a 'fiat' on our part would be misleading. So, the argument must be, it would be misleading to distinguish in such cases between what the rule is and what it ought to be — at least in some sense of ought. We think it ought to include the new case and come to see after reflection that it really does. But even if this way of presenting a recognizable experience as an example of a fusion between is and ought to be is admitted, two caveats must be borne in mind. The first is that 'ought' in this case need have nothing to do with morals for the reasons explained already in section III: there may be just the same sense that a new case will implement and articulate the purpose of a rule in interpreting the rules of a game or some hideously immoral code of oppression whose immorality is appreciated by those called in to interpret it. They too can see what the 'spirit' of the game they are playing requires in previously unenvisaged cases.

[46] Ibid. at 701, 702.

More important is this: after all is said and done we must remember how rare in the law is the phenomenon held to justify this way of talking, how exceptional is this feeling that one way of deciding a case is imposed upon us as the only natural or rational elaboration of some rule. Surely it cannot be doubted that, for most cases of interpretation, the language of choice between alternatives, 'judicial legislation' or even 'fiat' (though not arbitrary fiat), better conveys the realities of the situation.

Within the framework of relatively well-settled law there jostle too many alternatives too nearly equal in attraction between which judge and lawyer must uncertainly pick their way to make appropriate here language which may well describe those experiences which we have in interpreting our own or others' principles of conduct, intention, or wishes, when we are not conscious of exercising a deliberate choice, but rather of recognizing something awaiting recognition. To use in the description of the interpretation of laws the suggested terminology of a fusion or inability to separate what is law and ought to be will serve (like earlier stories that judges only find, never make, law) only to conceal the facts, that here if anywhere we live among uncertainties between which we have to choose, and that the existing law imposes only limits on our choice and not the choice itself.

POSTSCRIPT

See for criticisms and comments:
1. L. Fuller, 'Positivism and Fidelity to Law: a Reply to Professor Hart', 71 *Harv. L. Rev.* 630 (1958).
2. R. A. Duff, 'Legal Obligation and the Moral Nature of Law', *Juridical Rev.* 61 (1980).
3. R. M. Dworkin, *Taking Rights Seriously* (2nd impression, 1978), ch. IV, and pp. xii, xiii, 105–8, 124–6, 326–7, 332–9, 341–3, 348–9.
4. J. Raz, *The Authority of Law* (Oxford 1979), 37–52, 146–9; 'The Purity of the Pure Theory', *Revue Internationale de Philosophie* 441 (1981).
5. J. Finnis, *Natural Law and Natural Rights* (Oxford 1980), 26, 29, 50, 363 ff., 367.
6. N. MacCormick, *H.L.A. Hart* (London 1981), 92–102.
7. D. Lyons, 'On Formal Justice', 58 *Cornell L. Rev.* 873 ff. (1973).
8. D. Lyons, 'Moral Aspects of Legal Theory', 7 *Midwest Studies in Philosophy* 223 (1982).

Essay 3

Problems of the Philosophy of Law

The existence of legal systems, even the most rudimentary, has afforded the opportunity for a variety of academic disciplines. Of these some are, or purport to be, empirical: they include the historical study of particular legal systems or specific legal doctrines and rules, and sociological studies of the ways in which the content and the efficacy of law and the forms and procedures of law-making and law-applying both influence and are influenced by their economic and social setting, and serve social needs or specific social functions. But since law in most societies soon reaches a very high degree of complexity, its administration requires the special training of judges and professional lawyers. This in turn has created the need for a specific form of legal science concerned with the systematic or dogmatic exposition of the law and its specific methods and procedures. For this purpose the law is divided into distinct branches (such as crime, tort, and contract), and general classifications and organizing concepts are introduced to collect common elements in the situations and relationships created by the law (such as rights, duties, obligations, legal personality, ownership, and possession) or elements common to many separate legal rules (such as act and intention).

No very firm boundaries divide the problems confronting these various disciplines from the problems of the philosophy of law. This is especially true of the conceptual schemes of classification, definition, and division introduced by the academic study of the law for the purpose of exposition and teaching; but even some historical and sociological statements about law are sufficiently general and abstract to need the attention of the philosophical critic. Little, however, is to be gained from elaborating the traditional distinctions between the philosophy of law, jurisprudence (general and particular), and legal theory, although importance has often been attributed to them. Instead, as with other branches of philosophy, it is more important to distinguish as belonging to the philosophy of law certain groups of questions which remain to be answered even when a high degree of competence or mastery of particular legal systems of the empirical and dogmatic studies mentioned above has been gained. Three such groups may be distinguished: problems of definition and analysis, problems of legal reasoning, and problems of the criticism of law. This division is, however, not uncontroversial; and objections to it are considered in the last section of the article.

PROBLEMS OF DEFINITION AND ANALYSIS

The definition of law. All the obscurities and prejudices which in other areas of philosophy surround the notions of definition and of meaning have contributed to the endlessly debated problems of the definition of law. In early arguments the search for the definition of law was assumed to be the task of identifying and describing the 'essence' or 'nature' of law, and thus the uniquely correct definition of law by reference to which the propriety of the use, however well established, of the expressions 'law' and 'legal system' could be tested. It is frequently difficult to distinguish from this search for the essence of law a more modest conception of definition which, while treating the task as one of identifying and describing the standards actually accepted for the use of these expressions, assumes that there is only one 'true', 'strict', or 'proper' use of them and that this use can be described in terms of a single set of necessary and sufficient conditions. A wide range of different considerations has shown how unrealistic or how sterile this assumption is in the case of law, and has compelled its surrender. Among these considerations is the realization that although there are central clear instances to which the expressions 'law' and 'legal system' have undisputed application, there are also cases, such as international law and primitive law, which have certain features of the central case but lack others. Also, there is the realization that the justification for applying general expressions to a range of different cases often lies not in their conformity to a set of necessary and sufficient conditions but in the analogies that link them or their varying relationships to some single element.

The foregoing are difficulties of definition commonly met in many areas of philosophy, but the definition of law has peculiar difficulties of its own. Thus, the assumption that the definition of law either has been or should be lexical, that is, concerned with the characterization or elucidation of *any* actual usage, has been challenged on several grounds. Thus it is often asserted that in the case of law, the area of indeterminacy of actual usage is too great and relates to too many important and disputed issues, and that what is needed is not a characterization or elucidation of usage but a reasoned case for the inclusion in or exclusion from the scope of the expressions 'law' and 'legal system' of various deviations from routine and undisputed examples. These deviant cases include not only international law and primitive law but also certain elements found in developed municipal legal systems, such as rules to which the usual sanctions are not attached and rules which run counter to fundamental principles of morality and justice.

In the above circumstances some theorists disclaim as necessarily deceptive any aim to provide an analysis or definition of law which is a neutral description or elucidation of usage; instead, they speak of the task of definition as 'stipulative', 'pragmatic', or 'constructive', that is, as designed to provide a scheme or model for the demarcation and classification of an area of study. The criterion of adequacy of such pragmatic definitions is not conformity to or the capacity to explain any actual usage but the capacity to advance the theorists' special aims, which may differ widely. Thus, a definition of law to be used for the instruction or assistance of lawyers concerned primarily with the outcome of litigation or court proceedings will differ from the definition used to demarcate and unify the fruitful area of historical study and will also differ from the definition to be used by the social critic concerned with identifying the extent to which human interests are advanced or frustrated by modes of social organization and control.

Neither the legitimacy of pragmatic definitions nor their utility for deliberately chosen objectives need be disputed. But it is clear that they avoid rather than resolve many of the long-standing perplexities which have motivated requests for the definition of law and have made it a philosophical problem. The factors which have generated these perplexities may be summarized as follows: Notwithstanding the considerable area of indeterminacy in their use, the expressions 'law', 'a law', 'legal system', and a wide range of derivative and inter-related expressions ('legislation', 'courts of law', 'the application of law', 'legal adjudication') are sufficiently determinate to make possible general agreement in judgments about their application to particular instances. But reflection on what is thus identified by the common usage of such terms shows that the area they cover is one of great internal complexity; laws differ radically both in content and in the ways in which they are created, yet despite this heterogeneity they are interrelated in various complex ways so as to constitute a characteristic structure or system. Many requests for the definition of law have been stimulated by the desire to obtain a coherent view of this structure and an understanding of the ways in which elements apparently so diverse are unified. These are problems, therefore, of the structure of law.

Reflection on the operations of a legal system disclosed problems of another sort, for it is clear that law as a mode of influence on human behaviour is intimately related to and in many ways dependent upon the use or threat of force on the one hand and on morality and justice on the other. Yet law is also, at points, distinct from both, so no obvious account of these connections appears acceptable: they appear to be not merely contingent, and since they sometimes fail, the statement of these connections does not appear to be any easily comprehensible species of necessary truth. Such tensions create demands for some stable and coherent definition of the relationships between law, coercion, and morality; but definitions of law have only in part been designed to make these important areas of human experience more intelligible. Practical and indeed political issues have long been inter-twined with theoretical ones; and as is evident from the long history of the doctrines of natural law and legal positivism, the advocacy of a submissive or a critical attitude to law, or even of obedience or disobedience, has often been presented in the form of persuasive definition of the relationship between law and morality on the one hand and between law and mere force on the other.

The analysis of legal concepts. Although legal rules are of many different types and may be classified from many different points of view, they have many common constituents; and although the law creates for both individuals and groups a great variety of different situations and relationships, some of these are constantly recurrent and of obvious importance for the conduct of social life. Both lawyers and laymen have frequent occasion to refer to these common elements and situations, and for this purpose they use classifications and organizing concepts expressed in a vocabulary which has bred many problems of analysis. These problems arise in part because this vocabulary has a more or less established use apart from law, and the points of convergence and divergence between legal and non-legal usage are not always immediately obvious or easily explicable. It is also the case that the ways in which common elements in law or legal situations are classified by different theorists in part reflect and derive from divergent conceptions of law in general. Therefore, although different writers use such expressions as 'rights' and 'duty' in referring to the same legal situations, they select different elements or aspects from these situations. A third factor calling for clarification is the fact that many of the commonest notions used in referring to legal phenomena can be explicated only when certain distinctive ways in which language functions in conjunction with practical rules have been understood. These problems of analysis are illustrated in the case of the concepts of (1) legal obligation or duty, (2) a legal transaction, and (3) intention. (Certain distinctions once made between the notions of a legal obligation and a legal duty are no longer of importance and will be disregarded.)

The situation in which an individual has a legal duty to do or to abstain from some action is the commonest and most fundamental of all legal phenomena; the reference to duty or its absence is involved in the definition of such other legal concepts as those of a right, power, a legal transaction, or a legal personality. Whenever the law of an effective legal system provides for the punishment of those who act or fail to act in certain ways, the word 'duty' applies. Thus, to take a simple example, if the law requires under penalty that persons of a certain age shall report for military service, then such persons have, or are 'under', a legal duty to do so. Thus much is undisputed, however much theorists may dispute over the analysis of 'duty' or its application to situations created not by the criminal law but by the law relating to torts or to contract.

However, even the above simple situation can be viewed

from two very different standpoints that give rise to apparently conflicting analyses of duty. From one of these (the predictive standpoint), reporting for military service is classified as a duty simply because failure to report renders likely certain forms of suffering at the hands of officials. From the other standpoint (the normative standpoint), reporting for military service is classified as a duty because, owing to the existence of the law, it is an action which may be rightly or justifiably demanded of those concerned; and failure to report is significant not merely because it renders future suffering likely but also because punishment is legally justified even if it does not always follow disobedience.

From Jeremy Bentham onward the predictive analysis of duty as a chance or likelihood of suffering in the event of disobedience to the law has been advocated by important writers for a variety of theoretical and practical reasons. On the one hand it has seemed to free the idea of legal duty from metaphysical obscurities and irrelevant associations with morals, and on the other to provide a realistic guide to life under law. It isolates what for some men is the only important fact about the operation of a legal system and what for all men is at least one important fact: the occasions and ways in which the law works adversely to their interests. This is of paramount importance not only to the malefactor but also to the critic and reformer of the law concerned to balance against the benefits which law brings its costs in terms of human suffering.

By contrast, the normative point of view, without identifying moral and legal duty or insisting on any common content, stresses certain common formal features that both moral and legal duty possess in virtue of their both being aspects of rule-guided conduct. This is the point of view of those who, although they may not regard the law as the final arbiter of conduct, nevertheless generally accept the existence of legal rules as guides to conduct and as legally justifying demands for conformity, punishment, enforced compensation, or other forms of coercion. Attention to these features of the idea of duty is essential for understanding the ways in which law is conceived of and operative in social life.

Although theorists have often attributed exclusive correctness to these different standpoints, there are various ways in which they may be illuminatingly combined. Thus, the

normative account might be said to give correctly the meaning of such statements as that a person has a legal duty to do
a certain action, while the predictive account emphasizes that
very frequently the point or purpose of making such statements is to warn that suffering is likely to follow disobedience.
Such a distinction between the meaning of a statement and
what is implied or intended by its assertion in different contexts is of considerable importance in many areas of legal
philosophy.

The enactment of a law, the making of a contract, and the
transfer by words, written or spoken, of ownership or other
rights are examples of legal transactions which are made possible by the existence of certain types of legal rules and are
definable in terms of such rules. To some thinkers, such transactions (acts in the law, or juristic acts) have appeared mysterious — some have even called them magical — because their
effect is to change the legal position of individuals or to make
or eliminate laws. Since, in most modern systems of law, such
changes are usually effected by the use of words, written or
spoken, there seems to be a species of legal alchemy. It is not
obvious how the mere use of expressions like 'it is hereby enacted . . .', 'I hereby bequeath . . .', or 'the parties hereby
agree . . .' can produce changes. In fact, the general form of
this phenomenon is not exclusively legal, although it has only
comparatively recently been clearly isolated and analysed. The
words of an ordinary promise or those used in a christening
ceremony in giving a name to a child are obvious analogues to
the legal cases. Lawyers have sometimes marked off this distinctive function of language as the use of 'operative words',
and under this category have distinguished, for example, the
words used in a lease to create a tenancy from the merely descriptive language of the preliminary recital of the facts concerning the parties and their agreement.

For words (or in certain cases gestures, as in voting or other
forms of behaviour) to have such operative effect, there must
exist legal rules providing that if the words (or gestures) are
used in appropriate circumstances by appropriately qualified
persons, the general law or the legal position of individuals is
to be taken as changed. Such rules may be conceived from
one point of view as giving to the language used a certain kind
of force or effect which is in a broad sense their meaning;

from another point of view they may be conceived as conferring on individuals the legal power to make such legal changes.
In continental jurisprudence such rules are usually referred to
as 'norms of competence' to distinguish them from simpler
legal rules that merely impose duties with or without correlative rights.

As the expressions 'acts-in-the-law' and 'operative words'
suggest, there are important resemblances between the execution of legal transactions and more obvious cases of human
actions. These points of resemblance are of especial importance to understanding what has often seemed problematic —
the relevance of the mental or psychological states of the
parties concerned to the constitution or validity of such transactions. In many cases the relevant rules provide that a transaction shall be invalid or at least liable to be set aside at the
option of various persons if the person purporting to effect it
was insane, mistaken in regard to certain matters, or subjected
to duress or undue influence. There is here an important analogy with the ways in which similar psychological facts (*mens
rea*) may, in accordance with the principles of the criminal
law, excuse a person from criminal responsibility for his
action. In both spheres there are exceptions: in the criminal
law there are certain cases of 'strict' liability where no element
of knowledge or intention need be proved; and in certain
types of legal transaction, proof that a person attached a
special meaning to the words he used or was mistaken in some
respect in using them would not invalidate the transaction,
at least as against those who have relied upon it in good faith.

Attention to these analogies between valid legal transactions and responsible action and the mental conditions that
in the one case invalidate and in the other excuse from responsibility illuminates many obscure theoretical disputes
concerning the nature of legal transactions such as contract.
Thus, according to one principal theory (the 'will' theory) a
contract is essentially a complex psychological fact — something which comes into being when there is a meeting of
minds (*consensus ad idem*) that jointly 'will' or 'intend' a certain set of mutual rights and duties to come into existence.
The words used are, according to this theory, merely evidence
of this consensus. The rival theory (the 'objective' theory)
insists that what makes a contract is not a psychological

phenomenon but the actual use of words of offer and acceptance, and that except in special cases the law simply gives
effect to the ordinary meaning of the language used by the
parties and is not concerned with their actual states of mind.
Plainly, each side to this dispute fastens on something important but exaggerates it. It is indeed true that, like an ordinary
promise, a legal contract is not made by psychological facts.
A contract, like a promise, is 'made' not by the existence of
mental states but by words (or in some cases deeds). If it is
verbally made, it is made by the operative use of language,
and there are many legal rules inconsistent with the idea that
a *consensus ad idem* is required. On the other hand, just because the operative use of language is a kind of action, the
law may — and in most civilized legal systems does — extend
to it a doctrine of responsibility or validity under which certain mental elements are made relevant. Thus a contract,
although made by words, may be vitiated or made void or
'voidable' if a party is insane, mistaken in certain ways, or
under duress. The truths latent among the errors of the 'will'
theory and the 'objective' theory can therefore be brought
together in an analysis which makes explicit the analogy
between valid transactions made by the operative use of
language and responsible actions.

The fact that the law often treats certain mental states or
psychological conditions as essential elements both in the
validity of legal transactions and in criminal responsibility has
thrust upon lawyers the task of distinguishing between and
analysing such notions as 'will', 'intention', and 'motive'.
These are concepts which have long puzzled philosophers not
primarily concerned with the law, and their application in the
law creates further specific problems. These arise in various
ways: there are divergencies between the legal and non-legal
use of these notions which are not always obvious or easily
understood; the law, because of difficulties of proof or as a
matter of social policy, may often adopt what are called external or objective standards, which treat certain forms of
outward behaviour as conclusive evidence of the existence of
mental states or impute to an individual the mental state that
the average man behaving in a given way would have had.
Although statutes occasionally use expressions like 'mali-
ciously', 'knowingly', or 'with intent', for the most part the

expressions 'intentionally' and 'voluntarily' are not the language of legal rules but are used in the exposition of such rules in summarizing the various ways in which either criminal charges or civil claims may fail if something is done — for instance, accidentally, by mistake, or under duress.

The problems that arise in these ways may be illustrated in the case of intention. Legal theorists have recognized intention as the mental element of central importance to the law. Thus, an intention to do the act forbidden by law is in Anglo-American law normally the sufficient mental element for criminal responsibility and also is normally, although not always, necessary for responsibility. So if a man intends to do the act forbidden by law, other factors having to do with his powers of self-control are usually irrelevant, although sometimes duress and sometimes provocation or deficient ability to control conduct, caused by mental disorder, may become relevant. In fact, three distinct applications of the notion of intention are important in the law, and it is necessary to distinguish in any analysis of this concept (1) the idea of intentionally doing something forbidden by law; (2) doing something with a further intention; and (3) the intention to do a future act. The first of these is in issue when, if a man is found to have wounded or killed another, the question is asked whether he did it intentionally or unintentionally. The second is raised when the law, as in the case of burglary defined as 'breaking into premises at night with the intention of committing a felony', attaches special importance or more severe penalties to an action if it is done for some further purpose, even though the latter is not executed. The third application of intention can be seen in those cases where an act is criminal if it is accompanied by a certain intention — for instance, incurring a debt with the intention never to pay.

Of these three applications the first is of chief importance in the law, but even here the law only approximates to the non-legal concept and disregards certain elements in its ordinary usage. For in the law the question whether a man did something intentionally or not is almost wholly a question concerning his knowledge or belief at the time of his action. Hence, in most cases when an action falling under a certain description (such as wounding a policeman) is made a crime, the law is satisfied, in so far as any matter of intention is concerned,

if the accused knew or believed that his action would cause
injury to his victim and that his victim was in fact a policeman.
This almost exclusively cognitive approach is one distinctive
way in which the law diverges from the ordinary idea of intentionally doing something, for in ordinary thought not all the
foreseen consequences of conduct are regarded as intended.

A rationale of this divergence can be provided, however.
Although apart from the law a man will be held to have done
something intentionally only if the outcome is something
aimed at or for the sake of which he acted, this element which
the law generally disregards is not relevant to the main question with which the law is concerned in determining a man's
legal responsibility for bringing about a certain state of affairs.
The crucial question at this stage in a criminal proceeding is
whether a man whose outward conduct and its consequences
fall within the definition of a crime had at the time he acted
a choice whether these consequences were or were not to
occur. If he did, and if he chose that in so far as he had influence over events they would occur, then for the law it is
irrelevant that he merely foresaw that they would occur and
that it was not his purpose to bring them about. The law at
the stage of assessing a man's responsibility is interested only
in his conscious control over the outcome, and discards those
elements in the ordinary concept of intention which are irrelevant to the conception of control. But when the stage of
conviction in a criminal proceeding is past, and the question
becomes how severely the criminal is to be punished, the
matter previously neglected often becomes relevant. Distinctions may be drawn at this stage between the man who acted
for a certain purpose and one who acted merely foreseeing
that certain consequences would come about.

The second and third applications of the notion of intention (doing something with a further intent and the intention
to do a future action) are closer to non-legal usage, and in the
law, as elsewhere, certain problems of distinguishing motive
and intention arise in such cases.

PROBLEMS OF LEGAL REASONING

Since the early twentieth century, the critical study of the
forms of reasoning by which courts decide cases has been a

principal concern of writers on jurisprudence, especially in America. From this study there has emerged a great variety of theories regarding the actual or proper place in the process of adjudication of what has been termed, often ambiguously, 'logic'. Most of these theories are sceptical and are designed to show that despite appearances, deductive and inductive reasoning play only a subordinate role. Contrasts are drawn between 'logic' and 'experience' (as in Holmes's famous dictum that 'the life of the law has not been logic; it has been experience') or between 'deductivism' or 'formalism' on the one hand and 'creative choice' or 'intuitions of fitness' on the other. In general, such theories tend to insist that the latter members of these contrasted sets of expression more adequately characterize the process of legal adjudication, despite its appearance of logical method and form. According to some variants of these theories, although logic in the sense of deductive and inductive reasoning plays little part, there are other processes of legal reasoning or rational criteria, which courts do and should follow in deciding cases. According to more extreme variants, the decisions of courts are essentially arbitrary.

Legislation and precedent. In Anglo-American jurisprudence the character of legal reasoning has been discussed chiefly with reference to the use by the courts of two 'sources' of law: (1) the general rules made by legislative bodies (or by other rule-making agencies to which legislative powers have been delegated) and (2) particular precedents or past decisions of courts which are treated as material from which legal rules may be extracted although, unlike legislative rules, there is no authoritative or uniquely correct formulation of the rules so extracted. Conventional accounts of the reasoning involved in the application of legislative rules to particular cases have often pictured it as exclusively a matter of deductive inference. The court's decision is represented as the conclusion of a syllogism in which the major premise consists of the rule and the minor premise consists of the statement of the facts which are agreed or established in the case. Similarly, conventional accounts of the use of precedents by courts speak of the courts' extraction of a rule from past cases as inductive reasoning and the application of that rule to the case in hand as deductive reasoning.

In their attack on these conventional accounts of judicial reasoning, sceptical writers have revealed much that is of great importance both to the understanding and to the criticism of methods of legal adjudication. There are undoubtedly crucially important phases in the use of legal rules and precedents to decide cases which do not consist merely of logical operations and which have long been obscured by the traditional terminology adopted both by the courts themselves in deciding cases and by jurists in describing the activities of courts. Unfortunately, the general claim that logic has little or no part to play in the judicial process is, in spite of its simple and monolithic appearance, both obscure and ambiguous; it embraces a number of different and sometimes conflicting contentions which must be separately investigated. The most important of these issues are identified and discussed below. There are, however, two preliminary issues of peculiar concern to philosophers and logicians which demand attention in any serious attempt to characterize the forms of legal reasonings.

It has been contended that the application of legal rules to particular cases cannot be regarded as a syllogism or any other kind of deductive inference, on the grounds that neither general legal rules nor particular statements of law (such as those ascribing rights or duties to individuals) can be characterized as either true or false and thus cannot be logically related either among themselves or to statements of fact; hence, they cannot figure as premises or conclusions of a deductive argument. This view depends on a restrictive definition, in terms of truth and falsehood, of the notion of a valid deductive inference and of logical relations such as consistency and contradiction. This would exclude from the scope of deductive inference not only legal rules or statements of law but also commands and many other sentential forms which are commonly regarded as susceptible of logical relations and as constituents of valid deductive arguments. Although considerable technical complexities are involved, several more general definitions of the idea of valid deductive inference that render the notion applicable to inferences the constituents of which are not characterized as either true or false have now been worked out by logicians. In what follows, as in most of contemporary jurisprudential literature, the general acceptability of this more generalized definition of valid inference is assumed.

Considerable obscurity surrounds the claim made by more conventional jurisprudential writers that inductive reasoning is involved in the judicial use of precedents. Reference to induction is usually made in this connection to point a contrast with the allegedly deductive reasoning involved in the application of legislative rules to particular cases. 'Instead of starting with a general rule the judge must turn to the relevant cases, discover the general rule implicit in them. . . . The outstanding difference between the two methods is the source of the major premise — the deductive method assumes it whereas the inductive sets out to discover it from particular instances'.[1]

It is of course true that courts constantly refer to past cases both to discover rules and to justify their acceptance of them as valid. The past cases are said to be 'authority' for the rules 'extracted' from them. Plainly, one necessary condition must be satisfied if past cases are in this way to justify logically the acceptance of a rule: the past case must be an instance of the rule in the sense that the decision in the case could be deduced from a statement of the rule together with a statement of the facts of the case. The reasoning in so far as the satisfaction of this necessary condition is concerned is in fact an inverse application of deductive reasoning. But this condition is, of course, only one necessary condition and not a sufficient condition of the court's acceptance of a rule on the basis of past cases, since for any given precedent there are logically an indefinite number of alternative general rules which can satisfy the condition. The selection, therefore, of one rule from among these alternatives as the rule for which the precedent is taken to be authority must depend on the use of other criteria limiting the choice, and these other criteria are not matters of logic but substantive matters which may vary from system to system or from time to time in the same system. Thus, some theories of the judicial use of precedent insist that the rule for which a precedent is authority must be indicated either explicitly or implicitly by the court through its choice of facts to be treated as 'material' to a case. Other theories insist that the rule for which a precedent is authority is the rule which a later court considering the precedent would

---

[1] G. W. Paton, *A Textbook of Jurisprudence*, 2nd edn. (Oxford 1951), 171-2.

select from the logically possible alternatives after weighing the usual moral and social factors.

Although many legal writers still speak of the extraction of general rules from precedents, some would claim that the reasoning involved in their use of precedents is essentially reasoning from case to case 'by example': a court decides the present case in the same way as a past case if the latter 'sufficiently' resembles the former in 'relevant' respects, and thus makes use of the past case as a precedent without first extracting from it and formulating any general rule. Nevertheless, the more conventional accounts, according to which courts use past cases to discover and justify their acceptance of general rules, are sufficiently widespread and plausible to make the use of the term 'induction' in this connection worth discussing.

The use of 'induction' to refer to the inverse application of deduction involved in finding that a past case is the instance of a general rule may be misleading: it suggests stronger analogies than exist with the modes of probabilistic inference used in the sciences when general propositions of fact or statements about unobserved particulars are inferred from or regarded as confirmed by observed particulars. 'Induction' may also invite confusion with the form of deductive inference known as perfect induction, or with real or alleged methods of discovering generalizations sometimes referred to as intuitive induction.

It is, however, true that the inverse application of deduction involved in the use of precedents is also an important part of scientific procedure, where it is known as hypothetic inference or hypothetico-deductive reasoning. Hence, there are certain interesting analogies between the interplay of observation and theory involved in the progressive refining of a scientific hypothesis to avoid its falsification by contrary instances and the way in which a court may refine a general rule both to make it consistent with a wide range of different cases and to avoid a formulation which would have unjust or undesirable consequences.

Notwithstanding these analogies, the crucial difference remains between the search for general propositions of fact rendered probable by confirming instances but still falsifiable by future experience, and rules to be used in the decision of cases. An empirical science of the judicial process is of course possible: it would consist of factual generalization about the decisions of courts and might be an important predictive tool. However, it is important to distinguish the general propositions of such an empirical science from the rules formulated and used by courts.

Descriptive and prescriptive theories. The claim that logic plays only a subordinate part in the decision of cases is sometimes intended as a corrective to misleading descriptions of the judicial process, but sometimes it is intended as a criticism of the methods used by courts, which are stigmatized as 'excessively logical', 'formal', 'mechanical', or 'automatic'. Descriptions of the methods actually used by courts may be distinguished from prescriptions of alternative methods and must be separately assessed. It is, however, notable that in many discussions of legal reasoning these two are often confused, perhaps because the effort to correct conventional misdescriptions of the judicial process and the effort to correct the process itself have been inspired by the realization of the same important but often neglected fact: the relative indeterminacy of legal rules and precedents. This indeterminacy springs from the fact that it is impossible in framing general rules to anticipate and provide for every possible combination of circumstances which the future may bring. For any rule, however precisely formulated, there will always be some factual situations in which the question whether the situations fall within the scope of the general classificatory terms of the rule cannot be settled by appeal to linguistic rules or conventions or to canons of statutory interpretation, or even by reference to the manifest or assumed purposes of the legislature. In such cases the rules may be found either vague or ambiguous. A similar indeterminacy may arise when two rules apply to a given factual situation and also where rules are expressly framed in such unspecific terms as 'reasonable' or 'material'. Such cases can be resolved only by methods whose rationality cannot lie in the logical relations of conclusions to premises. Similarly, because precedents can logically be subsumed under an indefinite number of general rules, the identification of *the* rule for which a precedent is an authority cannot be settled by an appeal to logic.

These criticisms of traditional descriptions of the judicial process are in general well taken. It is true that both jurists and judges, particularly in jurisdictions in which the separation of powers is respected, have frequently suppressed or minimized the indeterminacy of legal rules or precedents when giving an account of the use of them in the process of decision. On the other hand, another complaint often made by the same writers, that there is an excess of logic or formalism in the judicial process, is less easy to understand and to substantiate. What the critics intend to stigmatize by these terms is the failure of courts, when applying legal rules or precedents, to take advantage of the relative indeterminacy of the rules or precedents to give effect to social aims, policies, and values. Courts, according to these critics, instead of exploiting the fact that the meaning of a statutory rule is indeterminate at certain points, have taken the meaning to be determinate simply because in some different legal context similar wording has been interpreted in a certain way or because a given interpretation is the 'ordinary' meaning of the words used.

This failure to recognize the indeterminacy of legal rule (often wrongly ascribed to analytical jurisprudence and stigmatized as conceptualism) has sometimes been defended on the ground that it maximizes certainty and the predictability of decisions. It has also sometimes been welcomed as furthering an ideal of a legal system in which there are a minimum number of independent rules and categories of classification.

The vice of such methods of applying rules is that their adoption prejudges what is to be done in ranges of different cases whose composition cannot be exhaustively known beforehand: rigid classification and divisions are set up which ignore differences and similarities of social and moral importance. This is the burden of the complaint that there is an excessive use of logic in the judicial process. But the expression 'an excessive use of logic' is unhappy, for when social values and distinctions of importance are ignored in the interpretation of legal rules and the classification of particulars, the decision reached is not more logical than decisions which give due recognition to these factors: logic does not determine the interpretation of words or the scope of classifications. What is true is that in a system in which such rigid modes of interpretation are common, there will be more occasions when a judge can treat himself as confronted with a rule whose meaning has been predetermined.

Methods of discovery and standards of appraisal. In considering both descriptive and prescriptive theories of judicial reasoning, it is important to distinguish (1) assertions made concerning the usual processes or habits of thought by which judges actually reach their decisions, (2) recommendations concerning the processes to be followed, and (3) the standards by which judicial decisions are to be appraised. The first of these concerns matters of descriptive psychology, and to the extent that assertions in this field go beyond the descriptions of examined instances, they are empirical generalizations or laws of psychology; the second concerns the art or craft of legal judgment, and generalizations in this field are principles of judicial technology; the third relates to the assessment or justification of decisions.

These distinctions are important because it has sometimes been argued that since judges frequently arrive at decisions without going through any process of calculation or inference in which legal rules or precedents figure, the claim that deduction from legal rules plays any part in decision is mistaken. This argument is confused, for in general the issue is not one regarding the manner in which judges do, or should, come to their decisions; rather, it concerns the standards they respect in justifying decisions, however reached. The presence or absence of logic in the appraisal of decisions may be a reality whether the decisions are reached by calculation or by an intuitive leap.

Clear cases and indeterminate rules. When the various issues identified above are distinguished, two sets of questions emerge. The first of these concerns the decisions of courts in 'clear' cases where no doubts are felt about the meaning and applicability of a single legal rule, and the second concerns decisions where the indeterminacy of the relevant legal rules and precedents is acknowledged.

Even where courts acknowledge that an antecedent legal rule uniquely determines a particular result, some theorists have claimed that this cannot be the case, that courts always 'have a choice', and that assertions to the contrary can only be *ex post facto* rationalizations. Often this scepticism springs from the confusion of questions of methods of discovery with standards of appraisal noted above. Sometimes, however, it is supported by references to the facts that even if courts fail to apply a clearly applicable rule yielding a determinate result, this is not a punishable offence, and that the decision given is still authoritative and, if made by a supreme tribunal, final. Hence, it is argued that although courts may show a certain degree of regularity in decision, they are never bound to do so; they always are free to decide otherwise than they do. These last arguments rest on a confusion of finality with infallibility in decisions and on a disputable interpretation of the notion of 'being bound' to respect legal rules.

Yet scepticism of this character, however unacceptable, does serve to emphasize that it is a matter of some difficulty to give any exhaustive account of what makes a 'clear case' clear or makes a general rule obviously and uniquely applicable to a particular case. Rules cannot claim their own instances, and fact situations do not await the judge neatly labelled with the rule applicable to them. Rules cannot provide for their own application, and even in the clearest case a human being must apply them. The clear cases are those in which there is general agreement that they fall within the scope of a rule, and it is tempting to ascribe such agreements simply to the fact that there are necessarily such agreements in the use of the shared conventions of language. But this would be an oversimplification because it does not allow for the special conventions of the legal use of words, which may diverge from their common use, or for the way in which the meanings of words may be clearly controlled by reference to the purpose of a statutory enactment which itself may be either explicitly stated or generally agreed. A full exploration of these questions is the subject-matter of the study of the interpretation of statute.

The decisions of cases which cannot be exhibited as deductions from determinate legal rules have often been described as arbitrary. Although much empirical study of the judicial process remains to be done, it is obvious that this description and the dichotomy of logical deduction and arbitrary decision, if taken as exhaustive, is misleading. Judges do not generally, when legal rules fail to determine a unique result, intrude their personal preferences or blindly choose among alternatives; and when words like 'choice' and 'discretion',

or phrases such as 'creative activity' and 'interstitial legislation' are used to describe decisions, these do not mean that
courts do decide arbitrarily without elaborating reasons for
their decisions — and still less that any legal system authorizes
decisions of this kind.

It is of crucial importance that cases for decision do not
arise in a vacuum but in the course of the operation of a
working body of rules, an operation in which a multiplicity
of diverse considerations are continuously recognized as
good reasons for a decision. These include a wide variety of
individual and social interests, social and political aims, and
standards of morality and justice; and they may be formulated in general terms as principles, policies and standards.
In some cases only one such consideration may be relevant,
and it may determine decision as unambiguously as a determinate legal rule. But in many cases this is not so, and judges
marshal in support of their decisions a plurality of such considerations which they regard as jointly sufficient to support
their decision, although each separately would not be. Frequently these considerations conflict, and courts are forced
to balance or weigh them and to determine priorities among
them. The same considerations (and the same need for weighing them when they conflict) enter into the use of precedents
when courts must choose between alternative rules which can
be extracted from them, or when courts consider whether a
present case sufficiently resembles a past case in relevant
respects.

Perhaps most modern writers would agree up to this point
with this account of judicial decision where legal rules are
indeterminate, but beyond this point there is a divergence.
Some theorists claim that notwithstanding the heterogeneous
and often conflicting character of the factors which are relevant to decision, it is still meaningful to speak of a decision
as *the* uniquely correct decision in any case and of the duty
of the judge to discover it. They would claim that a judicial
choice or preference does not become rational because it is
deferred until after the judge has considered the factors that
weigh for and against it.

Other theorists would repudiate the idea that in such cases
there is always a decision which is uniquely correct, although
they of course agree that many decisions can be clearly ruled

out as incorrect. They would claim that all that courts do and can do at the end of the process of coolly and impartially considering the relevant considerations is to choose one alternative which they find the most strongly supported, and that it is perfectly proper for them to concede that another equally skilled and impartial judge might choose the other alternative. The theoretical issues are not different from those which arise at many points in the philosophical discussions of moral argument. It may well be that terms like 'choice', 'discretion', and 'judicial legislation' fail to do justice to the phenomenology of considered decision: its felt involuntary or even inevitable character which often marks the termination of deliberation on conflicting considerations. Very often the decision to include a new case in the scope of a rule or to exclude it is guided by the sense that this is the 'natural' continuation of a line of decisions or carries out the 'spirit' of a rule. It is also true that if there were not also considerable agreement in judgment among lawyers who approach decisions in these ways, we should not attach significance and value to them or think of such decisions as reached through a rational process. Yet however it may be in moral argument, in the law it seems difficult to substantiate the claim that a judge confronted with a set of conflicting considerations must always assume that there is a single uniquely correct resolution of the conflict and attempt to demonstrate that he has discovered it.

Rules of evidence. Courts receive and evaluate testimony of witnesses, infer statements of fact from other statements, and accept some statements as probable or more probable than others or as 'beyond reasonable doubt'. When it is said that in these activities special modes of legal reasoning are exhibited and that legal proof is different from ordinary proof, reference is usually intended to the exclusionary rules of the law of evidence (which frequently require courts, in determining questions of fact, to disregard matters which are logically relevant), or to various presumptions which assign greater or lesser weight to logically relevant considerations than ordinary standards of reasoning do.

The most famous examples of exclusionary rules are those against 'hearsay', which (subject to certain exceptions) make inadmissible, as evidence of the facts stated, reports tendered by a witness, however credible, of statements made by another person. Another example is the rule that when a person is charged with a crime, evidence of his past convictions and disposition to commit similar crimes is not admissible as evidence to show that he committed the crime charged. An example of a rule which may give certain facts greater or less probative weight than ordinary standards do is the presumption that unless the contrary is proved beyond reasonable doubt, a child born to a woman during wedlock is the child of both parties to the marriage.

The application of such rules and their exceptions gives rise to results which may seem paradoxical, even though they are justifiable in terms of the many different social needs which the courts must satisfy in adjudicating cases. Thus, one consequence of the well-known exception to the hearsay rule that a report of a statement is admissible as evidence of a fact stated if it is made against the interest of the person who stated it, is that a court may find that a man committed adultery with a particular woman but be unable to draw a conclusion that she committed adultery with him. A logician might express the resolution of the paradox by saying that from the fact that p entails q it does not follow that 'it is legally proved that p' entails 'it is legally proved that q'.

Apart from such paradoxes, the application of the rules of evidence involves the drawing of distinctions of considerable philosophical importance. Thus, although in general the law excludes reports of statements as evidence of the facts stated, it may admit such reports for other purposes, and in fact draws a distinction between statements of fact and what J. L. Austin called performatory utterances. Hence, if the issue is whether a given person made a promise or placed a bet, reports that he uttered words which in the context amounted to a promise or a bet are admissible. So, too, reports of a person's statement of his contemporary mental states or sensations are admissible, and some theorists justify this on the ground that such first-person statements are to be assimilated to behaviour manifesting the mental state or sensation in question.

PROBLEMS OF THE CRITICISM OF LAW

Analysis and evaluation. A division between inquiries concerned with the analysis of law and legal concepts and those concerned with the criticism or evaluation of law prima facie seems not only possible but necessary, yet the conception of an evaluatively neutral or autonomous analytical study of the law has not only been contested but also has been taken by some modern critics to be the hallmark of a shallow and useless legal positivism allegedly unconcerned with the values or ends which men pursue through law.

Many different objections to a purely analytical jurisprudence have been made. By some it has been identified with, or thought to entail commitment to, the view that a legal system is a closed logical structure in which decisions in particular cases are 'mechanically' deduced from clear antecedent rules whose identification or interpretation presents no problem of choice and involves no judgment of value. Other critics have contended that any serious demand for the definition of a legal concept must at least include a request for guidance as to the manner in which, when the relevant legal rules are unclear or indeterminate, particular cases involving the concept in question should best be determined. It is assumed by these critics that any question concerning the meaning of expressions such as 'a right' or 'a duty', as distinct from the question of what rights or duties should be legally recognized, are trivial questions to be settled by reference to a dictionary. Still others have urged that since the maintenance of a legal system and the typical operations of the law (legislation, adjudication, and the making of legal transactions) are purposive activities, any study which isolates law or legal phenomena for study without considering their adequacy or inadequacy for human purposes makes a vicious abstraction which is bound to lead to misunderstanding.

None of the above seem to constitute serious objections. The difficulties of decision in particular cases arising from the relative indeterminacy of legal rules are of great importance, but they are distinct from analytical questions such as those illustrated earlier, which remain to be answered even when legal rules are clear. Thus the isolation and characterization of the normative and predictive standpoints from which law may be viewed and the precise manner of interplay between subjective and objective factors in legal transactions are not things that can be discovered from dictionaries. But attention to them is indispensable in the analysis of the notion of a legal obligation, a legal right, or a contract. There is of course much justice in the claim that in order to understand certain features of legal institutions or legal rules, the aims and purposes they are designed to fulfil must be understood. Thus, a tax cannot be distinguished from a fine except by reference to the purpose for which it is imposed; but to recognize this is not to abandon an analytical study of the law for an evaluative one. The identification of something as an instrument for certain purposes leaves open the question whether it is good or bad, although such identification may indicate the standards by reference to which this question is to be answered. In any case, there are many features of legal rules which may profitably be studied in abstraction from the purposes which such rules may be designed to achieve.

Criteria of evaluation. None the less, protests against the severance of analytical from critical or evaluative inquiries, even if misdirected in their ostensible aim, often serve to emphasize something important. These protests are usually accompanied by and sometimes confused with a general thesis concerning the standards and principles of criticism specifically appropriate to law. This is the thesis (which has appeared in many different forms in the history of the philosophy of law) that, whatever may be the case with value judgments in other fields or with moral judgments concerning the activities of individuals, the criteria which distinguish good law from bad do not merely reflect human preferences, tastes, or conventions, which may vary from society to society or from time to time; rather, they are determined by certain constant features of human nature and the natural environment with which men must contend.

The doctrine of natural law in its various traditional forms embodies this thesis. There are, however, obscurities and metaphysical assumptions involved in the use by natural-law theorists of the notions of nature and reason which makes their formulations unacceptable to most modern secular thought; and they often confuse their important arguments concerning the principles by which law and social institutions should be judged with arguments designed to show that a reference to morality or justice must be introduced into the definition of law or legal validity. None the less, it is possible to segregate these tangled issues, and some important modern philosophical arguments concern the possibility of restating in an acceptable form the claim that there are certain objective and rationally determined criteria for the evaluation and criticism of law. These arguments will be sketched here in relation to substantive law, procedural law, and the ideas of justice and utility.

Substantive law. The purposes which human beings pursue in society and for the realization of which they employ law as an instrument are infinitely various, and men may differ in the importance they attach to them and in their moral judgments about them. But the simplest form of the argument that there are certain constant criteria for the evaluation of a legal system consists in the elaboration of the truth that if law is to be of any value as an instrument for the realization of human purposes, it must contain certain rules concerning the basic conditions of social life. Thus it is not only true that the legal system of any modern state and any legal system which has succeeded in enduring have contained rules restricting the use of violence, protecting certain forms of property, and enforcing certain forms of contract; it is also clear that without the protections and advantages that such rules supply, men would be grossly hampered in the pursuit of any aims. Legal rules providing for these things are therefore basic in the sense that without them other legal rules would be pointless or at least would operate only fitfully or inefficiently. Criticism of a legal system on the grounds that it omitted such rules could be rebutted only by the demonstration that in the particular case they were unnecessary because the human beings to which the system applied or their natural surroundings were in some way quite extraordinary, that is, that they lacked certain of the salient characteristics which men and things normally have. This is so because the need for such rules derives from such familiar natural facts as that men are both vulnerable to violence and tempted to use it against each other; that the food, clothes, and shelter necessary to existence do not exist naturally in limitless abundance but must be grown or manufactured by human effort and need legal protection from interference during growth and manufacture and safe custody pending consumption; and that to secure the mutual co-operation required for the profitable development of natural resources, men need legal rules enabling them to bind themselves to future courses of conduct.

Argument along these lines may be viewed as a modest empirical counterpart to the more ambitious teleological doctrine of natural law, according to which there are certain rules for the government of human conduct that can be seen by men endowed with reason as necessary to enable men to attain the specifically human optimum state or end (*finis, telos*) appointed for men by Nature or (in Christian doctrine) by God. The empirical version of this theory assumes only that, whatever other purposes laws may serve, they must, to be acceptable to any rational person, enable men to live and organize their lives for the more efficient pursuit of their aims. It is, of course, possible to challenge this assumption and to deny that the fact that there are certain rules necessary if fundamental human needs are to be satisfied has any relevance to the criticism of law. But this denial·seems intelligible only as a specifically religious doctrine which regards law as the expression of a divine will. It may then be argued that men's lives should be regulated by the law not in order to further any secular human purposes but because conformity to God's will is in itself meritorious or obligatory.

A more serious objection to the empirical argument conducted in terms of human needs for protection from violence to the person and property and for co-operation is the contention that although these are fundamental human needs, the coercive rules of a legal system need not provide for them. It may be said that the accepted morality of all societies provides a system of restraint which provides adequately for these needs, and that the vast majority of men abstain from murder, theft, and dishonesty not from fear of legal sanctions but for other, usually moral, reasons. In these circumstances it may be no defect in a legal system that it confines itself to other matters in relation to which the accepted morality is silent.

It seems clear, however, that social morality left to itself could not provide adequately for the fundamental needs of social life, save in the simplest forms of society. It may well be that most men, when they believe themselves to be protected from malefactors by the punishments, threats of punishment, and physical restraints of the law, will themselves voluntarily submit to the restraints necessary for peaceful and profitable coexistence. But it does not follow that without the law's protections, voluntary submission to these restraints would be either reasonable or likely. In any case, the rules and principles of social morality leave open to dispute too many questions concerning the precise scope and form of its restraints. Legal rules are needed to supply the detail required to distinguish murder and assault from excusable homicide and injury, to define the forms of property to be protected, and to specify the forms of contract to be enforced. Hence, the omission of such things from the legal system could not be excused on the ground that the existence of a social morality made them unnecessary.

Procedural law. Laws, however impeccable their content, may be of little service to human beings and may cause both injustice and misery unless they generally conform to certain requirements which may be broadly termed procedural (in contrast with the substantive requirements discussed above). These procedural requirements relate to such matters as the generality of rules of law, the clarity with which they are phrased, the publicity given to them, the time of their enactment, and the manner in which they are judicially applied to particular cases. The requirements that the law, except in special circumstances, should be general (should refer to classes of persons, things, and circumstances, not to individuals or to particular actions); should be free from contradictions, ambiguities, and obscurities; should be publicly promulgated and easily accessible; and should not be retrospective in operation are usually referred to as the principles of legality. The principles which require courts, in applying general rules to particular cases, to be without personal interest in the outcome or other bias and to hear arguments on matters of law and proofs of matters of fact from both sides of a dispute are often referred to as rules of natural justice. These two sets of principles together define the concept of the rule of law to which most modern states pay at least lip service.

These requirements and the specific value which conformity with them imparts to laws may be regarded from two different points of view. On the one hand, they maximize the probability that the conduct required by the law will be forthcoming, and on the other hand, they provide individuals whose freedom is limited by the law with certain information and assurances which assist them in planning their lives within the coercive framework of the law. This combination of values may be easily seen in the case of the requirements of generality, clarity, publicity, and prospective operation. For the alternative to control by general rules of law is orders addressed by officials to particular individuals to do or to abstain from particular actions; and although in all legal systems there are occasions for such particular official orders, no society could efficiently provide the number of officials required to make them a main form of social control.

Thus, general rules clearly framed and publicly promulgated are the most efficient form of social control. But from the point of view of the individual citizen, they are more than that: they are required if he is to have the advantage of knowing in advance the ways in which his liberty will be restricted in the various situations in which he may find himself, and he needs this knowledge if he is to plan his life. This is an argument for laws which are general in the sense of requiring courses of action and not particular actions. The argument for generality in the sense of applicability to classes of persons is different: it is that such rules confer upon the individual the advantage of knowing the restrictions to which the conduct of others besides himself will be subject. Such knowledge in the case of legal restrictions which protect or benefit the individual increases the confidence with which he can predict and plan his future.

The value of the principles of natural justice which concern the process of adjudication are closely linked to the principles of legality. The requirement that a court should be impartial and hear arguments and proofs from both sides of a dispute are guarantees of objectivity which increase the probability that the enacted law will be applied according to its tenor. It is necessary to ensure by such means that there will be this congruence between judicial decisions and the enacted law if the commitment to general rules as a method of government is taken seriously.

Care must be taken not to ascribe to these arguments more than they actually prove. Together they amount to the demonstration that all men who have aims to pursue need the various protections and benefits which only laws conforming to the above requirements of substance and procedure can effectively confer. For any rational man, laws conferring these protections and benefits must be valuable, and the price to be paid for them in the form of limitations imposed by the law on his own freedom will usually be worth paying. But these arguments do not show, and are not intended to show, that it will always be reasonable or morally obligatory for a man to obey the law when the legal system provides him with these benefits, for in other ways the system may be iniquitous: it may deny even the essential protections of the law to a minority or slave class or in other ways cause misery or injustice.

Justice and utility. The equal extension to all of the fundamental legal protections of person and property is now generally regarded as an elementary requirement of the morality of political institutions, and the denial of these protections to innocent persons, as a flagrant injustice. Even when these protections are denied, lip service is often paid to the principle of equal distribution by the pretence that the persons discriminated against are either criminal in intention, if not in deed, or are like children who are incapable of benefiting from the freedom which laws confer and are in need of some more paternalistic regime.

Different moral philosophies offer different vindications of the principle of equality. The matter is considered here in order to illustrate the philosophical problems which arise in the criticism of law concerning the relative place of the notions of utility and justice. The central principle of utilitarianism, in so far as it supplies a moral critique of law, may be stated as the doctrine that there is only one vice in legal arrangements, namely, that they fail to produce the greatest possible total of happiness in the population within their scope. The concept of a total of happiness or pleasure or satisfaction is of course open to well-known objections. But on any interpretation, utilitarian principles, if unrestricted, must endorse legal or social arrangements if the advantages they give to some persons outweigh the disadvantages imposed on others. For a consistent utilitarian there can be no necessary commitment to any principles requiring an equal distribution.

However, in some cases, if allowance is made for principles of diminishing marginal utility, it may be shown that an equal distribution is the most efficient, in the sense of producing the greatest total of happiness. But for the utilitarian this is a

contingent matter to be established in each case, not a matter
of moral principle or justice; and where the question concerns
the distribution of the fundamental legal protections of person and property, there seems no compelling utilitarian argument in favour of an equal distribution. Thus, a slave-owning
class might derive from the system of slavery benefits outweighing the misery of the slaves. Bentham urged that this was
not the case, owing to the inefficiency of slave labour, and
therefore he rejected slavery; but he rejected it as inefficient
rather than as unjust. Plainly, this form of argument is a very
insecure foundation for the principle that all men are morally
entitled to the equal protection of the laws, and it seems clear
that utilitarian principles alone cannot give any account of
the moral importance attached to equality and in general to
the notion of the just, as distinguished from an efficient, distribution as a means of happiness.

The simplest moral argument in support of the equal distribution of the law's fundamental protections is one that
combines the idea that no rational person could wish himself
to be denied these fundamental legal protections with the
principle of the universalizability of moral judgment: moral
judgments concerning social and legal arrangements must conform to the requirement that no man could regard as morally
acceptable the withholding from others, with needs and in
circumstances similar to his own, of those benefits which he
would not wish to be withheld from himself. If this principle
is admitted, it follows that it cannot be a sufficient moral
ground for accepting legal arrangements that the advantages
they give to some outweigh the disadvantages for others. The
equal extension to all of the law's protections satisfies both
the principle of utility, which requires that the law should advance human happiness, and the independent principle of justice, that the gain in happiness should be distributed fairly.
According to this qualified form of utilitarianism, the best
legal and social arrangements realize the most efficient of just
distributions.

More ambitious arguments have been advanced to show
that in spheres other than the distribution of the fundamental
protections of the law, utilitarianism is acceptable only if
qualified by independent principles of just distribution, and
also to demonstrate that the distribution required by justice

is in all spheres prima facie that of equality, unless inequalities can be shown to work ultimately for the equal benefit of all. Whatever the strength of these more general arguments may be, it is true that in relation to many legal institutions, utilitarianism unrestricted by other principles of justice yields results which would not be regarded as morally tolerable. This is particularly true of punishment. In all civilized legal systems it is recognized that no man should be punished except for his own conduct, and (with certain exceptions in the case of minor offences) only then for such of his actions as were voluntary or within his power to control. Such limitations on the scope of punishment seem obvious requirements of justice to the individuals punished, but it is at least doubtful whether they can be adequately supported on purely utilitarian grounds.

The obligation to obey the law. The philosophical investigation of the obligation to obey the law requires a distinction between the utilitarian and other moral aspects of this subject similar to that outlined in the case of justice. It seems clear that the mere existence of a legal system, irrespective of the character of its laws, is not sufficient in any intelligible theory of morality to establish that a person ought morally to do what its laws require him to do. Yet there are also powerful arguments against a purely utilitarian theory of the obligation to obey law which would regard this obligation as simply a special case of the obligation to promote happiness, with the corollary that disobedience to bad laws is justified if the consequences of disobedience (including any harm done to others through the weakening of the authority of the legal system) are better in utilitarian terms than the consequences of obedience. Among features of the moral situation for which this utilitarian theory fails to account there are two of peculiar importance. The first is that the obligation to obey law is one which is considered as owed by the citizen specifically to the members of his own society in virtue of their relationship as fellow members, and is not conceived merely as an instance of an obligation to men in general not to cause harm, injury, or suffering. Second, men are often held to be subject to an obligation to obey the law even though it is clear that little or no harm will be done to the authority of the legal system by their disobedience, as in cases (like that of the conscientious objector) where those who disobey the law willingly submit to punishment.

The theory of a social contract focused on these two aspects of the obligation of obedience to law, and it is possible to detach from what is mythical or otherwise objectionable in contract theory certain considerations which show that the obligation to obey the law may be regarded as the obligation of fairness to others, which is independent of and may conflict with utility. The principle involved, stated in its simplest form, is that when a number of persons restrict their liberty by certain rules in order to obtain benefits which could not otherwise be obtained, those who have gained by the submission of others to the rules are under an obligation to submit in their turn. Conflicts between this principle and the principle of utility are possible because often the benefits secured by such restrictions would arise even if considerable numbers failed to co-operate and submit to the rules in their turn. For the utilitarian, there could be no reason for anyone to submit to rules if his co-operation was not necessary to secure the benefits of the system. Indeed, if a person did co-operate, he would be guilty of failing to maximize the total happiness, for this would be greatest if he took the benefits of the system without submitting to its restraints. The consideration that the system would fail to produce the desired benefits or would collapse if all were to refuse their co-operation is irrelevant in a utilitarian calculation if, as is often the case, it is known that there will be no such general refusal.

POSTSCRIPT ·

See for criticisms and comments:
1. R. Nozick, *Anarchy, State, and Utopia* (Oxford, 1974), 90-5.
2. A. J. Simmons, *Moral Principles and Political Obligations* (Princeton, 1979), 101-42.
3. D. Lyons, *Forms and Limits of Utilitarianism* (Oxford, 1965), 190, 195.
4. R. J. Arneson, 'The Principle of Fairness and Free-Rider Problems' *Ethics*, xcii (1982), 616-33.

PART II

AMERICAN JURISPRUDENCE

American Jurisprudence through English Eyes: The Nightmare and the Noble Dream

It is with some sense of audacity that I venture to address an American audience on the theme of American jurisprudence. You may well think that justice could not possibly be done to so huge a subject in the confines of a single lecture, and that if it is to be done at all, it is for an American and not for a visiting Englishman to do it. I confess I have no very convincing answer to this objection except to say that there are important aspects of even very large mountains which cannot be seen by those who live on them but can be caught easily by a single glance from afar.

Of course I recognize that there is need for caution. In *The American Scene*, the greatest of your country's novelists, Henry James, remarks that 'the seer of great cities is liable to easy error, I know, when he finds this, that or the other caught glimpse the supremely significant one. . . .'[1] This is a warning against hasty generalization and oversimplification, and surely the warning is salutary, for, vast and various as it is, America has often tempted European observers to characterize some area of American life or thought in terms of a single salient feature presenting a strong contrast with Europe. And I confess I find myself strongly inclined to surrender to just this temptation and to characterize American jurisprudence, that is, American speculative thought about the general nature of law, by telling you in unqualified terms that it is marked by a concentration, almost to the point of obsession, on the judicial process, that is, with what courts do and should do, how judges reason and should reason in deciding particular cases. And I could quote in support of this the most prominent American jurists over the last eighty years. Thus Justice Oliver Wendell Holmes in 1894 said, 'The prophecies of what the courts will do in fact, and nothing more pretentious,

---

[1] Henry James, *The American Scene* 99-100 (1907).

is what I mean by the law.'[2] The great Harvard lawyer John Chipman Gray wrote at the turn of the century, 'The Law of the State or of any organized body of men is composed of the rules which the courts, that is, the judicial organs of that body, lay down for the determination of legal rights and duties.'[3] A later jurist, Karl Llewellyn, in 1930 said, 'What these officials [that is, mainly judges] do about disputes, is, to my mind, the law itself.'[4] And only a few years ago Professor Jaffe of Harvard said, while lecturing to us in Oxford, that the question, what is the function of the judiciary in a democratic state, was tearing at the vitals of American law faculties.[5] But great areas of thought are not to be assessed by aphorisms torn from their context, and remembering Henry James's warning, I shall, in devoting most of this lecture to the concentration of American thought on the judicial process, claim only that this *is* one salient feature of American jurisprudence contrasting strongly with our own.

The simple explanation of that concentration is, no doubt, the quite extraordinary role which the courts, above all the United States Supreme Court, play in American government. In de Tocqueville's famous words, 'scarcely any political question arises in the United States that is not resolved, sooner or later, into a judicial question'.[6] An English lawyer notes that two things have secured for the Supreme Court a role and a status unlike that of any English court and indeed unlike any courts elsewhere. The first was of course the Supreme Court's own decision that it had power to review and declare unconstitutional and so invalid enactments of Congress as well as of the state legislatures.[7] The second was its doctrine that the clause of the Fifth Amendment, and the later Fourteenth Amendment, providing that no person should be deprived of life, liberty, or property without due process of law, referred not merely to matters of form or procedure but also to the

[2] Holmes, 'The Path of the Law', in O. W. Holmes, *Collected Legal Papers* 173 (1920).

[3] J. C. Gray, *The Nature and Sources of the Law* 84 (2nd edn. 1921).

[4] K. Llewellyn, *The Bramble Bush* 3 (1930). But see the retraction in the second edition of these words as 'unhappy' and 'at best a very partial statement of the whole truth'. Ibid. at 9 (2nd edn. 1951).

[5] L. Jaffe, *English and American Judges as Law Makers* 9 (1969).

[6] A. De Tocqueville, *Democracy in America* 280 (P. Bradley edn. 1945).

[7] See *McCulloch* v. *Maryland*, 17 U.S. (4 Wheat.) 316 (1819); *Marbury* v. *Madison*, 5 U.S. (1 Cranch) 137 (1803).

content of legislation, so that, to an English lawyer's astonishment, even a statute of Congress of impeccable clarity, passed by an overwhelming majority and conforming to all procedural requirements specified in the Constitution, might still be held invalid because its interference with individual liberty or with property did not satisfy the requirement of a vague undefined standard of reasonableness or desirability, a doctrine which came to be called 'substantive due process'.[8]

This doctrine, once adopted, secured for the power of review a vast scope and set the American courts afloat on a sea of controversial value judgments, and it became plain that in exercising these wide powers to monitor not only the form and formalities of legislation but also its content, the courts were doing something very different from what conventional legal thought in all countries conceives as the standard judicial function: the impartial application of determinate existing rules of law in the settlement of disputes. And what the courts were doing seems to the English lawyer, at first sight at any rate, particularly hard to justify in a democracy.

In fact the most famous decisions of the Supreme Court have at once been so important and so controversial in character and so unlike what ordinary courts ordinarily do in deciding cases that no serious jurisprudence or philosophy of law could avoid asking with what general conception of the nature of law were such judicial powers compatible. Certainly American jurisprudence has not evaded this question, but in developing theories to explain — or explain away — this extraordinary judicial phenomenon, it has oscillated between two extremes with many intermediate stopping-places. For reasons which I hope will become plain, I shall call these two extremes, respectively, the Nightmare and the Noble Dream.

---

[8] For the development of this doctrine see *Allgeyer* v. *Louisiana*, 165 U.S. 578 (1897) (Fourteenth Amendment 'liberty of contract' prohibits state from regulating property owners contracting for marine insurance with foreign insurance company); *Lochner* v. *New York*, 198 U.S. 45 (1905) (Fourteenth Amendment 'liberty of contract' prohibits state from regulating the maximum hours per day or week a bakery employee may work); *Adair* v. *United States*, 208 U.S. 161 (1908) (Fifth Amendment 'liberty of contract' bars federal prohibition of 'yellow dog' employment contracts for employees of interstate railroads); *Coppage* v. *Kansas*, 236 U.S. 1 (1915) (Fourteenth Amendment 'liberty of contract' bars state prohibition of 'yellow dog' employment contracts); *Adkins* v. *Children's Hosp.*, 261 U.S. 525 (1923) (Fifth Amendment 'liberty of contract' prohibits District of Columbia from prescribing minimum wages for women).

I

The Nightmare is this. Litigants in law cases consider themselves entitled to have from judges an application of the existing law to their disputes, not to have new law made for them.
Of course it is accepted that what the existing law *is* need not
be and very often is not obvious, and the trained expertise of
the lawyer may be needed to extract it from the appropriate
sources. But for conventional thought, the image of the judge,
to use the phrase of an eminent English judge, Lord Radcliffe,
is that of the 'objective, impartial, erudite, and experienced
declarer of the law',[9] not to be confused with the very different image of the legislator. The Nightmare is that this image
of the judge, distinguishing him from the legislator, is an illusion, and the expectations which it excites are doomed to
disappointment — on an extreme view, always, and on a moderate view, very frequently. Certainly a clear-eyed scrutiny of
the course of American constitutional decision seems to support the Nightmare view of things and suggests to an Englishman a cynical interpretation of de Tocqueville's observation
that political questions in the United States sooner or later
become judicial questions. 'Perhaps they do so,' the Englishman may say, 'but the fact that they are decided in American
law courts by judges does not mean that they are not there
decided politically. So, if your Constitution has made law of
what elsewhere would be politics, it has done so at the risk of
politicizing your courts.'

So an Englishman habituated to the less spectacular activities of the English courts is tempted to agree with the many
contemporary and later American jurists who accused the
Justices of acting as a third legislative chamber when, in the
first period of the Supreme Court's activism between the Civil
War and the New Deal, they ruled unconstitutional, under the
due process clause, social and economic welfare legislation of
every sort, statutes fixing maximum hours, minimum wages,
price controls, and much else.[10] The Justices of that period,
according to their many critics, were availing themselves of
conventional myths about the judicial process to pass off their
personal political and economic doctrine of *laissez-faire* and

[9] Radcliffe, *The Path of the Law from 1967*, at 14 (1968).
[10] See n. 8 *supra*.

to erect a Magna Carta for American big business as if this was the impartial application of determinate legal provisions, somehow already latent in the phrase 'due process' and supposedly above the level of politics or merely political judgment. But economic liberties are not the only form of liberty, and in its second modern period of activism in our own day, the courts' use of their powers of judicial review to effect major law reforms, which in other countries have been brought about, if at all, only after bitterly fought parliamentary battles, has provided a different series of examples to support the Nightmare view of the judicial process as mere crypto-legislation. To an Englishman the most striking modern instance is the Court's decision in 1973 sweeping away century-old legislation against abortion in many states of the union on an issue where much moral opinion was against reform.[11] It achieved at a single judicial blow more than the last of eight English parliamentary struggles over a period of fifty years secured in my country. And this was done in the name of a right of the mother to privacy which is nowhere mentioned in the Constitution but was read into the due process clause as a fundamental liberty. Justice Oliver Wendell Holmes, in a famous dissenting opinion, protested against the *laissez-faire* decisions of his day that the Fourteenth Amendment had not enacted Herbert Spencer's *Social Statics* and its *laissez-faire* philosophy.[12] Had he survived into the modern period he might have protested that the Fourteenth Amendment had not enacted John Stuart Mill's *On Liberty*.

Given this history, it is not surprising that one great branch of American jurisprudential thought should be concerned to present the Nightmare view that, in spite of pretensions to the contrary, judges make the law which they apply to litigants and are not impartial, objective declarers of existing law, All this is comprehensible to the English lawyer after he has acquainted himself with the relevant constitutional history. What remains surprising is that in some variations of this jurisprudence the Nightmare view should be presented by serious American jurists not merely as a feature of certain types of difficult adjudication — as in the case of constitutional adjudication in which hugely general phrases like 'due process'

---

[11] *Roe* v. *Wade*, 410 U.S. 113 (1973); *Doe* v. *Bolton*, 410 U.S. 179 (1973).
[12] *Lochner* v. *New York*, 198 U.S. 45, 75 (1905) (Holmes, J., dissenting).

or 'equal protection of the laws' have somehow to be fitted
to particular cases — but as if adjudication were *essentially* a
form of law-making, never a matter of declaring the existing
law, and with the suggestion that until this truth was grasped
and the conventional myths that obscured it dissipated, the
nature of law could not be understood. I have said that serious
jurists wrote *as if* this were the case, not that they believed
it; for I agree with a recent historian of what is called the
American Realist movement of the 1920s and 1930s, with
which the Nightmare view is most identified, that many who
seemed to preach this message and send it forth in bold pro-
vocative slogans almost always meant something far less ex-
travagant than what the slogans seemed to say.[13] This is
certainly true of Holmes's famous remark that '[t]he prophecies of what the courts will do in fact and nothing more
pretentious, are what I mean by the law'.[14] It is also doubtless
true of Karl Llewellyn's '[w]hat [judges] do about disputes is
. . . the law itself', though it is scarcely possible to take the
same view of Jerome Franks's *Law and the Modern Mind*,[15]
hailed as a classic in the 1930s, in which the belief that there
could be legal rules binding on judges and applied by them,
not made by them, in concrete cases is stigmatized as an im-
mature form of fetishism or father fixation calling for psycho-
analytical therapy.

Holmes certainly never went to these extremes. Though he
proclaimed that judges do and must legislate at certain points,
he conceded that a vast area of statutory law and many firmly
established doctrines of the common law, such as the requirement of consideration for contracts, and the demands of even
the comparatively loose American theory of binding precedent, were sufficiently determinate to make it absurd to
represent the judge as primarily a law-maker. So for Holmes
the judge's law-making function was 'interstitial'.[16] Holmes's
theory was not a philosophy of 'full steam ahead and damn
the syllogisms'.

None the less, in a way which an English jurist finds

[13] See W. Twining, *Karl Llewellyn and the Realist Movement* 380 (1973).
[14] Holmes, 'The Path of the Law', *supra* n. 2, at 173.
[15] See J. Frank, *Law and the Modern Mind* 175, 178, 193, 203, 244, 264
1930).
[16] *Southern Pacific Co.* v. *Jensen*, 244 U.S. 205, 221 (1917) (Holmes, J., dissenting).

puzzling and without parallel in his own literature, the drive towards the Nightmare vision of the judicial process as a legally uncontrolled act of law-making has at times figured largely in American legal theory even though the writers caught up in it have often modified it in the face of recalcitrant facts. A most striking example of the hold of this theory on American juristic thought is John Chipman Gray's *The Nature and Sources of the Law*, which first appeared in 1909. This is much more like an English textbook on jurisprudence covering many different topics than any other American book, and the author, a distinguished Harvard lawyer, had been exposed to and acknowledged the influence of Bentham and Austin. Like an English book it surveys a wide range of topics — legal rights and duties, statutes, precedents, equity, law and morals — but it pursues throughout these topics a most un-English theme: that the law consists of the rules laid down by the courts used to decide cases and that all else, statutes and past precedents included, are merely sources of law. For this theory the words of the eighteenth-century Bishop Hoadly are three times invoked in support: 'Whoever hath an *absolute authority* to *interpret* any written or spoken laws, it is *he* who is truely the *Law-giver* to all intents and purposes, and not the person who first wrote or spoke them'.[17] It is true that even in Gray's book this radical theme is blurred by inconsistencies and concessions to ordinary ways of thought and expression, as if common sense will out even in a work of jurisprudence. But the fact that an extremely able lawyer of great practical as well as academic experience should have committed himself so far to such a method of expressing general views about the nature of law manifests the strong hold on the American legal imagination of the Nightmare view of things.

Intertwined with the Nightmare there is another persistent theme. Perhaps the most misused quotation from any American jurist is Holmes's observation of 1884 that '[t]he life of the law has not been logic: it has been experience'.[18] This in its context was a protest against the rationalist superstition (as Holmes thought it) that the historical development of the law by courts could be explained as the unfolding of the consequences logically contained in the law in its earlier

---

[17] J. C. Gray, *supra* n. 3, at 102, 125, 172.
[18] O. W. Holmes, *The Common Law* 1 (1881).

phases.[19] Judicial change and development of the law were, Holmes insisted, the expression of judges' 'instinctive preferences and inarticulate convictions' in response, as he said, to the 'felt necessities'[20] of his time. And his protest was made to secure a conscious recognition by lawyers of the legislative powers of the courts so that judicial change and readjustment of the law should be made after an explicit weighing of what he termed 'considerations of social advantage'.[21] But by one American philosopher-historian, Professor Morton White, Holmes's remarks about logic have been taken as an example of a great movement of American thought which he terms the 'Revolt against Formalism' and Holmes, together with John Dewey in philosophy, Thorsten Veblen in economics, and others, is taken as an example of a great reaction against excessive reliance on thought that is deductive, formal, abstract, or split into firmly separated distinct disciplines.[22] The revolt was born of a wish to cross sterile, arbitrary, academic divisions and to substitute for formalism a vivid, realistic attention to experience, life, growth, process, context, and function. Whatever the truth of this interesting piece of American cultural history, attacks on 'logic' or the 'excessive use' of logic made by some American jurists discussing judicial reasoning became, at any rate for the English jurist trying to understand the American scene, a most confusing and confused theme. Thus the *laissez-faire* interpretation of the due process clause of the Constitution, erecting freedom of contract into an almost absolute principle and striking down in its name much progressive social welfare legislation, was stigmatized as an example of the vices of formalism, black letter law, and excessive use of logic or of 'slot machine' or mechanical jurisprudence.[23] But logic does not of course dictate the interpretation of laws or of anything else, and no reliance upon it, excessive or otherwise, could account for the Supreme Court at the period in question reading into the Constitution the doctrines of *laissez-faire*. But what the critics

---

[19] Ibid. at 36.

[20] Ibid. at 1.

[21] Holmes, 'The Path of the Law', *supra* n. 2, at 184.

[22] Morton White, *Social Thought in America: The Revolt Against Formalism* (2nd edn. 1957).

[23] See, e.g. Pound, 'Mechanical Jurisprudence', 8 *Colum. L. Rev.* 605, 609-10, 616 (1908).

were attacking in this confused way was really not the method by which the courts had arrived at their interpretations of the Constitution but the freezing of any single interpretation of any rule of law into a fixed premise, immune from revision and to be used in all further cases of its application. So they denounced, waving the banner of pragmatism, a purely backward-looking style of adjudication according to which particular decisions in particular cases owed their legal justification exclusively to their relation to the predetermined meaning of existing legal rules; and they urged upon judges a forward-looking form of adjudication according to which legal rules are treated as displaceable presumptions or working hypotheses, to be modified or rejected if the predictable consequences of their application in a shifting social context proved unsatisfactory.[24]

The themes I have described, though originating earlier, all figured in the 1920s and 1930s in the movement called Legal Realism.[25] But in what did the realism of the Realists consist? I find it very difficult to say because this active group of jurists differed from as much as they resembled each other. All, certainly, were concerned to stress the legislative opportunities of the courts and to dissipate the myths of conventional thought which they believed obscured this. Some accompanied this with a tough-minded insistence that to understand law all that mattered was what courts did and the possibility of predicting this, not what paper rules said and not the reasons given by judges for their decisions. Some claimed that knowledge of the judge's character, habits of life, political, social or economic views, even the state of his health, was at least as important a basis for successful prediction of a decision as legal doctrine. Others cherished a vision of a down-to-earth, truly scientific jurisprudence, inspired by the belief that the only profitable, or even the only rational, study of the law was investigations, using the methods of the

---

[24] See J. Dewey, 'Logical Method and Law', 10 *Cornell L. Rev.* 17 (1924).

[25] For general accounts of the legal realist movement see W. Rumble, *American Legal Realism* (1968); G. Tarello, *Il Realismo Giuridico Americano* (1962); W. Twining, *Karl Llewellyn and the Realist Movement, supra* n. 13, at 70 (endorsing Llewellyn's protest — see Llewellyn, 'Some Realism About Realism — Responding to Dean Pound', 44 *Harv. L. Rev.* 1222 (1930), reprinted in K. Llewellyn, *Jurisprudence, Realism in Theory and Practice* 42 (1962) — against alleged misrepresentation by Pound and others).

natural sciences, into the course of judicial decision and its effects on men's behaviour.

What did all this amount to? Seen from afar it appears to many English jurists not to have advanced legal theory far or to have added much to the stock of valuable jurisprudential ideas. But the virtues and beneficent influence of the Realist movement lay elsewhere. For the English lawyer the best work of the less extreme Realists was not found in explicit general theorizing about the nature of law and adjudication, but was often implicit in their writings on many different branches of the substantive law. This had a large and still visible influence on the style of adjudication in American courts and upon legal education which at any rate some English lawyers now much envy. For its main effect was to convince many judges and lawyers, practical and academic, of two things: first, that they should always suspect, although *not* always in the end reject, any claim that existing legal rules or precedents were constraints strong and complete enough to determine what a court's decision should be without other extra-legal considerations; secondly, that judges should not seek to bootleg silently into the law their own conceptions of the law's aims or justice or social policy or other extra-legal elements required for decision, but should openly identify and discuss them.

II

I turn now to the opposite pole, which I have called the Noble Dream. Like its antithesis the Nightmare, it has many variants, but in all forms it represents the belief, perhaps the faith, that, in spite of superficial appearances to the contrary and in spite even of whole periods of judicial aberrations and mistakes, still an explanation and a justification can be provided for the common expectation of litigants that judges should apply to their cases existing law and not make new law for them even when the text of particular constitutional provisions, statutes, or available precedents appears to offer no determinate guide. And with this goes the belief in the possibility of justifying many other things, such as the form of lawyers' arguments which, entertaining the same expectations, are addressed in courts to the judges as if he were looking for, not creating, the law; the fact that when courts overrule some past decision, the later new decision is normally treated as stating what the law has always been, and as correcting a mistake, and is given a retrospective operation; and finally, the fact that the language of a judge's decision is not treated, as is the language of a statute, as the authoritative canonical text of a law-making verbal act.

Of course the Declaration of Independence spoke the language of universal natural rights and of a universal natural law. And the conception that behind or above positive law there is a universal natural law discoverable by human reason and applicable to all men at all times and places has indeed had its place in American jurisprudence, especially in the early years of the republic. Though I might add that its importance is not to be judged by the fact that the journal which began life as the *Natural Law Forum* now calls itself the *American Journal of Jurisprudence*. But, perhaps surprisingly, the Noble Dream, that even when a particular provision of the positive law is indeterminate there is none the less an existing law somewhere which judges can and should apply to dispose of the case, does *not*, in the work of the most renowned American jurists, take the form of an invocation of a universal natural law. The American Noble Dream has generally been that of something not universal, but specifically related to the concerns and shape of an individual legal system and the specific ends and values pursued through law in a particular society.

This particularist idea, that guidance for a particular society must, as Llewellyn said, 'plant its feet'[26] in that society and its actual practices, is one feature common to all forms of the American Noble Dream. Another common feature is a rejection of a belief which has sustained the Nightmare view of adjudication. This is the belief that, if a particular legal rule proves indeterminate in a given case so that the court is unable to justify its decision as the strict deductive conclusion of a syllogism in which it appears as a major premise, then the decision which the court gives *can* only be the judge's legally uncontrolled choice. Llewellyn attacked this belief when, in pleading for a 'grand style' of judicial decision, he denounced as a blinding error the assumption that if the outcome of a

[26] K. Llewellyn, *Jurisprudence, Realism in Theory and Practice, supra* n. 25, at 114.

law case is not, as he termed it, 'foredoomed in logic',[27] it can only be the product of the judge's uncontrolled will. So a judge faced with the indeterminacy of a particular legal rule does not have as his only recourse what Holmes called the 'sovereign prerogative of choice'.[28] He is not at once forced into the position of a law-maker, even an interstitial law-maker. The illusion that he is so forced is due to a failure to give proper weight to the fact that legal decision-making does not proceed *in vacuo* but always against a background of a system of relatively well-established rules, principles, standards and values. By itself, a given legal provision in its paper formulation may give no determinate guidance, but in the whole system of which the given provision is a member there may be, either expressed or latent, principles which, if consistently applied, would yield a determinate result.

Both the features which I have mentioned — which we might call particularism and holism — are to be found, with much else, in the work of Roscoe Pound, whose gigantic production, extending across seventy years of research, culminated in the publication in 1959, when the author was eighty-nine, of a 3,000-page work on jurisprudence.[29] In the 1920s Pound introduced the notion, much stressed and further developed by other jurists, that a legal system was too narrowly conceived if it was represented as containing only rules attaching closely defined legal consequences to closely defined, detailed factual situations and enabling decisions to be reached and justified by simple subsumption of particular cases under such rules.[30] Besides rules of this kind, legal systems contain large-scale general principles; some of these are explicitly acknowledged or even enacted, whereas others have to be inferred as the most plausible hypotheses explaining the existence of the clearly established rules. Such principles do not serve merely to explain rules in which they are manifested, but constitute general guidelines for decision when particular rules appear indeterminate or ambiguous or where no relevant authoritative, explicitly formulated rule seems available. Courts should not consider themselves free to legislate for such

---

[27] K. Llewellyn, *The Common Law Tradition, Deciding Appeals* 4 (1960).

[28] Holmes, 'Law in Science and Science in Law', in O. W. Holmes, *Collected Legal Papers* 239 (1920).

[29] R. Pound, *Jurisprudence* (1959).

[30] See Pound, 'The Theory of Judicial Decision', 36 *Harv. L. Rev.* 641 (1923).

cases, not even in accordance with their conceptions of justice or social good, but should instead search in the existing system for a principle or principles which singly or collectively will both serve to explain the clear existing rules and yield a determinate result for the instant case.

To an English lawyer this suggested recipe for the elimination of judicial choice may seem to make too much of, or to hope for too much from, a much admired style of adjudication followed by some great English common law judges. In the most famous modern instance, Lord Atkin, in our House of Lords, faced the question whether a manufacturer was liable to a consumer with whom he stood in no contractual relationship for injuries caused by a negligently manufactured product. In this famous English case, *Donoghue v. Stevenson*,[31] the product was a bottle of ginger beer containing the toxic remnants of a dead snail. Before this decision the situations in which one person was liable to another for injuries caused by his carelessness were the subject of a number of separate rules specifying relationships where what the English lawyer calls 'a legal duty of care' was said to exist. Such rules specified, for example, the liability of owners or occupiers of premises to persons coming upon them, of parties standing in contractual relationships, and of persons using the highways, but did not include nor plainly exclude the liability of a manufacturer to a consumer with whom he had no contract. Nor was there any clear explicit principle stating in general terms what was common to all these cases showing the general considerations that established whether or not a relationship gave rise to a duty. Lord Atkin in this leading case ruled that the manufacturer was liable under the broad principle that whoever undertakes any activity which may foreseeably be harmful to those who are likely to be affected by it must take reasonable care to avoid inflicting foreseeable harm on those who are their neighbours, so understood. Though pinched and narrowed in subsequent cases, this broad principle, when first enunciated by Lord Atkin, served both to define the relationships and so explain the already established clear rules and to provide an answer in the instant unsettled case.

This style of decision is characteristic of the general holistic approach urged by Pound and later jurists whose theories of

[31] [1932] A.C. 562.

adjudication at least approximate the Noble Dream, and is enough to refute superficial theories that when a particular legal rule proves indeterminate the judge can only then push aside his law books and proceed to legislate. But plainly, merely to adopt this style of decision is not in itself sufficient to banish the Nightmare. Many questions arise. May not the legal system contain conflicting principles? May not a given rule or set of specific rules be equally well explained by a number of different alternative hypotheses? If so, will there not be need at these higher levels for judicial choice, and if so, will not adjudication still fall short of the Noble Dream since such a choice will be an act of law-making, not a further discovery of existing law? Pound in his long life addressed himself intermittently to such questions, and one of his answers seems to have been that, at still higher levels of the legal system above that of principles, there are the received values or ideals of the system, again either explicitly acknowledged or inferable from its established rules and principles, and that recourse to these would suffice to determine which of a number of conflicting or alternative principles should prevail. But of course the same questions could be pushed further. Will not the same conflicts or alternatives present themselves at this highest level of received values or ideals? What are the grounds for thinking that there must be some unique resolution of such conflicts awaiting the judge's discovery and not calling for his choice? To be fair to Pound, it must be said that he probably conceived of the idea that a whole system with its principles and received values would provide a determinate, unique answer when particular legal rules ran out, not as a literal truth about legal systems but rather as a regulative ideal for judges to pursue; this process would dictate a salutary style of judicial decision and operate as a powerful constraint upon judicial choice rather than eliminate altogether the need for such a choice. This relatively modest version of the Noble Dream as a constraint upon rather than as an always-available substitute for judicial choice is, I think, in the end also the message preached by Karl Llewellyn in his rich and turbulent advocacy of what he termed the grand style of judicial decision. This message is presented not in general theoretical terms, for which he had a great distaste, but in the terminology of the craftsman. The judge, in cases where particular rules — paper rules as they are sometimes deprecatingly called — prove indeterminate, is to 'carve' his decision with the 'grain' of the system as a whole,[32] that is, in accordance with its broad principles and established values. Faced with the indeterminacies of the positive law the judge is not simply to decide, without further attention to the system, as he thinks best. This is the most important constraint upon judicial choice and what accounts for the high measure of predictability of judicial decision in appellate cases. I confess there is much in Llewellyn's writing on this subject which I do not fully understand in spite of the patient, lucid, and exhaustive examination of it by his sympathetic English interpreter, Professor Twining.[33] I think, however, that in Llewellyn's version of the Noble Dream it is enough that when the judges choose, as they may have to, at the higher level of principles or received values, the alternatives presented to them at this level will all have the backing of great areas of the legal system comprehended under them, and so whichever alternative is chosen, it will have its feet firmly planted in the existing system and may be ranked as a decision warranted because controlled by law.

Professor Ronald Dworkin's contemporary version of the Noble Dream[34] does not make any such compromise on these points, and he is, if he and Shakespeare will allow me to say so, the noblest dreamer of them all, with a wider and more expert philosophical base than his predecessors, and he concentrates formidable powers of argument on the defence of his theory. His theory of adjudication is marked by stress on many new distinctions, such as that between arguments of principle about existing entitlements or rights, which he thinks it is the proper business of judges to use in support of decisions, as contrasted with arguments of policy about aggregate welfare or collective goals, which are not the judge's business but the legislator's. None the less his theory, in the

---

[32] See K. Llewellyn, *The Common Law Tradition, supra* n. 27, at 222, where, in writing on 'Appellate Judging as a Craft of Law', Llewellyn states that 'I have tried to reach the idea in terms of working with rather than across or against the grain. . . . to carve with the grain . . . to reveal the latent rather than to impose new form, much less to obtrude an outside will.'

[33] See W. Twining, *supra* n. 13.

[34] See Dworkin, 'Hard Cases', 88 *Harv. L. Rev.* 1057 (1975), reprinted in R. Dworkin, *Taking Rights Seriously* 81 (1977).

senses I have already explained, is a holistic and particularistic one. Like Pound he rejects the idea that a legal system consists only of its explicit authoritative rules and emphasizes the importance of implicit unformulated principles; and like Llewellyn he rejects the idea, which he attributes to positivist jurisprudence, that the judge must, when the explicit rules prove indeterminate, push aside his law books and start to legislate in accordance with his personal morality or conceptions of social good or justice.

So for Dworkin, even in the hardest of hard cases where each of two alternative interpretations of a statute or two conflicting rules seems to fit equally well the already clearly established law, the judge is never to make law. So Oliver Wendell Holmes was, in Dworkin's view, wrong in claiming that at such points the judge must exercise what he called 'the sovereign prerogative of choice'[35] and must legislate even if only 'interstitially'. According to the new theory, the judge, however hard the case, is never to determine what the law *shall* be; he is confined to saying what he believes *is* the law before his decision, though of course he may be mistaken. This means that he must always suppose that for every conceivable case there is some solution which is already law before he decides the case and which awaits his discovery. He must not suppose that the law is ever incomplete, inconsistent, or indeterminate; if it appears so, the fault is not in *it*, but in the judge's limited human powers of discernment, so there is no space for a judge to make law by choosing between alternatives as to what shall be the law.

Of course on this view the judge has to present arguments for what he believes to be the law. Very often his reasoning will take just the form I have illustrated from the great English case on products liability. That is, he must construct a general principle which will both justify and explain the previous course of decision in relation to this subject-matter and will also yield a definite answer for the new case. But of course that is only the start of his inquiry, for there may be a plurality of such general principles fitting equally well the existing law but yielding different solutions for the instant case. This position was reached in the English courts when the general

---

[35] Holmes, 'Law in Science and Science in Law', *supra* n. 28, at 239.

principle announced by Lord Atkin in relation to negligence
came to be applied to cases of negligent misstatements on
which persons had acted to their detriment.[36] Professor
Dworkin recognizes that at any level of inquiry into the system and the general principles which may be said to be immanent in the existing law there may be unresolved questions of
this sort. To deal with them the judge must, ideally at any
rate, open up much wider-ranging questions of justice and
political morality. In Professor Dworkin's words, he:

> must develop a theory of the constitution, in the shape of a complex set
> of principles and policies that justify that scheme of government. . . .
> He must develop that theory by referring alternately to political philos-
> ophy and institutional detail. He must generate possible theories justi-
> fying different aspects of the scheme and test the theories against the
> broader institution.[37]

When the discriminating power of this test is exhausted, he
must 'elaborate the contested concepts that the successful
theory employs'.[38] The judge thus must decide what conception of the fundamental values protected by the system, such
as liberty or personal dignity or equality, is superior. Plainly
this is a Herculean task and Professor Dworkin rightly calls
the judge, whom he imagines embarked on the construction
of such a theory, Hercules. He admits that different judges
coming from different backgrounds may construct different
and conflicting Herculean theories, and, when this is so, it
cannot be demonstrated that one of these is uniquely correct
and the others wrong. Indeed, *all* may be wrong. None the
less, to make sense of what they do, judges must believe that
there is some single theory, however complex, and some single
solution for the instant case derivable from it, which is
uniquely correct.

Professor Dworkin's theory will, I am sure, much excite
and stimulate both jurists and philosophers for a long time on
both sides of the Atlantic. It has indeed already added much
to the stock of valuable jurisprudential ideas. But if I may
venture a prophecy, I think the chief criticism that it will attract will be of his insistence that, even if there is no way

---

[36] *Mutual Life & Citizens Assurance Co. v. Evatt*, [1971] A.C. 793.

[37] Dworkin, 'Hard Cases', *supra* n. 34, at 1085; *Taking Rights Seriously*
at 107.

[38] Ibid.

of demonstrating which of two conflicting solutions, both equally well warranted by the existing law, is correct, still there must always be a single correct answer awaiting discovery. Lawyers might think that if a judge has conformed before he decides to all those constraints which distinguish judicial law-making from law-making by a legislator, above all if he has considered conscientiously and impartially what Professor Dworkin well calls the 'gravitational force'[39] of the clearly established law and has arrived at a conclusion as to which of the alternatives open to him is most fair or just, no purpose is served by insisting that if a brother judge arrives after the same conscientious process at a different conclusion there is a unique right answer which would show which of the two judges, if either, is right, though this answer is laid up in a jurist's heaven and no one can demonstrate what it is.

Similarly, philosophers may dispute the claim that as a matter of logical coherence anyone who attempts to answer a question of value, whether it be the question which of two legal answers to a litigant's claims is more just or fair, or which of two competitors in a beauty competition is more beautiful, or which of Shakespeare's comedies is the funniest, must, in order to give sense to such questions, assume that there is a single objective right answer in all such cases. The corollary in the case of law is that what litigants are always entitled to have from the judge is the right answer (though there is no means of demonstrating what it is), just as they would be entitled to have a right answer to the question which of two buildings is the taller, where of course the correctness of the answer can be demonstrated by a public objective test. Perhaps both philosophers and lawyers might agree with Professor Kent Greenawalt of Columbia Law School who, after a patient examination of Professor Dworkin's attack on the idea that judges have a discretion in hard cases, concludes that '[d]iscretion exists so long as no practical procedure exists for determining if a result is correct, informed lawyers disagree about the proper result, and a judge's decision either way will not widely be considered a failure to perform his judicial responsibilities'.[40]

[39] Ibid. at 1089, *Taking Rights Seriously* at 111.
[40] Greenawalt, 'Discretion and Judicial Decision: The Elusive Quest for the Fetters that Bind Judges', 75 *Colum. L. Rev.* 359, 386 (1975).

Professor Dworkin's version of the Noble Dream challenges at two crucial points two themes which have dominated English jurisprudence ever since Jeremy Bentham, in the year of American Independence, laid its foundations when he published his first book.[41] The first theme relates to the question just discussed. It is the insistence that, though the law may be at points incomplete or indeterminate, so far as it is determinate there are means of demonstrating what it is by reference to a legal system's criteria of validity or its basic provisions concerning the sources of law. All variants of English positivist jurisprudence subscribe to this view. The second theme dominating so much English jurisprudence is the utilitarian conception that both judges and legislators, in considering what the law ought to be, may and indeed must at many points take account of general utility and of what will most advance the general welfare. Even a judge, though subject to many constraints from which the legislature is free, may properly allow his decision between competing answers, each supported by the existing law, to be tipped by such utilitarian considerations. That is, he is not confined to asking what is the most fair or most just in accordance with distributive principles of justice. But for Professor Dworkin, a judge who thus steps into the area of what he calls policy, as distinct from principles determining individual rights, is treading forbidden ground reserved for the elected legislature. This is so because for him not only is the law a gapless system, but it is a gapless system of rights or entitlements, determining what people are entitled to have as a matter of distributive justice, not what they should have because it is to the public advantage that they should have it. This exclusion of 'policy considerations' will, I think, again run counter to the convictions of many lawyers that it is perfectly proper and indeed at times necessary for judges to take account of the impact of their decisions on the general community welfare.[42]

Professor Dworkin's exclusion of such considerations from the judge's purview is part of the general hostility to utilitarianism that charcterizes his work, and this point takes me

---

[41] J. Bentham, *A Fragment on Government* (1776).

[42] Others have reached the same conclusion. See Greenawalt, *supra* n. 40, at 391; John Umana, 'Dworkin's "Rights Thesis"', 74 *Mich. L. Rev.* 1167, 1179-83 (1976).

back to my general theme. It seems to the English observer that, in the United States, utilitarianism is currently on the defensive in the face not only of Professor Dworkin's work but also of the two very important contributions to political philosophy made by Professor Rawls's *Theory of Justice*[43] and Professor Nozick's *Anarchy, State, and Utopia.*[44] These works have much affinity with the eighteenth-century doctrines of the unalienable rights of man. In any case utilitarianism as a critique of law and society has generally been overshadowed in America by doctrines of individual rights. None the less, it has penetrated, though not very far, into American theories of the judicial process. It has done this mainly in a form which leads easily into welfare economics, where the aggregate utility to be maximized is defined not in terms of pleasure, as in classical utilitarianism, but in terms of the satisfaction of expressed wants or revealed preferences. In this form it is to be found in scattered hints thrown out by Oliver Wendell Holmes that judges might soon have at their disposal to guide them in their necessary law-making tasks a science of law which would 'determine, so far as it can, the relative worth of our different social ends',[45] or, as he also puts it, would establish the postulates of the law upon 'accurately measured social desires',[46] and that this would replace the present inarticulate and intuitive methods of judicial law-making. In this context Holmes spoke of the man of the future as the man of statistics and as the master of economics.[47]

A similar conception of science applied to law seems to underlie Pound's sociological jurisprudence and its attempt to analyse the conflicts which the law is called upon to resolve in terms of underlying interests, that is, in terms of wants or desires expressed as claims to legal recognition and enforcement. Many of the pages of this immensely prolific writer are dedicated to the classification of such interests as individual, social, and public.[48] But coupled with this analysis is the conception of a science of social engineering which would show how conflicting interests might be ordered with what Pound

---

[43] J. Rawls, *A Theory of Justice* (1971).
[44] R. Nozick, *Anarchy, State, and Utopia* (1974).
[45] Holmes, 'Law in Science and Science in Law', *supra* n. 28, at 242.
[46] Ibid. at 226.
[47] Holmes, 'The Path of the Law', *supra* n. 2, at 187.
[48] 3 R. Pound, *Jurisprudence* 16–324 (1959).

calls the least friction or waste or with the least sacrifice of the total scheme of interests as a whole.[49] To do this Pound acknowledges that there must be some method of weighing or valuing the conflicting items, and so some form of quantification, but his discussion does not provide it.

If these two flirtations with the idea of a science of lawmaking, whether by legislator or judge, rest on any coherent philosophy, it is that of utilitarianism. But utilitarianism is quite explicitly acknowledged as the inspiration of the contemporary Chicago-bred school of the economic analysis of law,[50] which now has a great hold upon American teaching of the law of torts. This school of thought claims to have laid bare a profound relationship between law and economic order. As an explanatory theory it is the claim that great areas of the common law may be illuminatingly seen as mimicking an economic market, for many established legal rules are consistent with the conception of law as a system of incentives, used to ensure that economic resources are allocated to uses which are economically most efficient, where efficiency is defined as maximizing aggregate want-satisfaction. This is said to be the implicit economic logic of the law. But on its critical or normative side, the theory claims to provide a rational, impartial, and objective standard for the determination of legal disputes where the question is who should bear a loss. Thus, to take one of its simplest examples, for this theory the point of the imposition of legal liability for negligence causing harm to others is to provide an incentive to take economically justified, utility-maximizing precautions against causing such harm, that is, precautions the cost of which is less than the loss caused by their neglect discounted by the probability of its occurrence. This theory of incentives runs strongly counter not only to Professor Dworkin's theory that the judge must not concern himself with considerations of general utility but also with the conventional idea that liability in negligence is

[49] 1 R. Pound, *Jurisprudence* 545 (1959); 3 R. Pound, *Jurisprudence* 330-1; R. Pound, *Justice According to Law* 3 (1951); R. Pound, *Social Control Through Law* 64-5 (1942).
[50] See R. Posner, *Economic Analysis of Law* (1972). Professor Posner has since distinguished his theory from utilitarianism on the ground that it does not require the maximization of aggregate utility or want-satisfaction but the maximization of wealth. See his 'Utilitarianism, Economics and Legal Theory' in 8 *J. Legal Stud.* 104 (1979).

at least sometimes imposed as a matter of justice between the parties, on the footing that the victim of another's negligence has a moral *right* to have his loss made good by the negligent party, so far as monetary compensation can do this. To the question why, if the law is only concerned with the provision of incentives, should not this be done by fines payable to the state, instead of by damages paid in private litigation to the victims, the theory returns the answer, which is perhaps more ingenious than convincing, that the latter (damages paid to the victim), in its turn, is an incentive for victims to bring cases of negligence to official notice, and that the result will be a far more effective deterrent than could be provided by any central criminal-law-type agency policing negligent conduct and imposing fines.[51]

No one who has read Professor Posner's elaborate and refined work and the large literature which has grown out of it, designed to establish these utilitarian underpinnings of the law, could fail to profit. This is not, I think, because it succeeds in its ostensible purpose, but because its detailed ingenuity admirably forces one to think what else is needed besides a theory of utility for a satisfactory, explanatory, and critical theory of legal decisions. It becomes clear that in general what is needed is a theory of individual moral rights and their relationship to other values pursued through law, a theory of far greater comprehensiveness and detailed articulation than any so far provided.

In conclusion let me say this: I have portrayed American jurisprudence as beset by two extremes, the Nightmare and the Noble Dream: the view that judges always make and never find the law they impose on litigants, and the opposed view that they never make it. Like any other nightmare and any other dream, these two are, in my view, illusions, though they have much of value to teach the jurist in his waking hours. The truth, perhaps unexciting, is that sometimes judges do one and sometimes the other. It is not of course a matter of indifference but of very great importance which they do and when and how they do it. That is a topic for another occasion.

[51]   See Posner, 'A Theory of Negligence', 1 *J. Legal Stud.* 29, 48 (1972).

Essay 5

1776–1976: Law in the Perspective
of Philosophy

I

As an Englishman I am delighted to add my contribution to
this celebration of the great events of 1776. You did well, if
I may say so, for yourselves, for us, and for the world to make
that break, of which not the least important product has been
the development here of fresh and, as we see them, characteristically American interpretations of the nature and significance of law.

The perspective in which I shall invite you to see the law is
to relate certain ideas now astir, particularly in this country, in
political philosophy and jurisprudence to those which sprang
into vigorous life just two hundred years ago. No English lawyer, certainly no English philosopher of law, could forget
that year of wonders 1776, which saw the publication of the
Declaration of Independence, the first volume of Gibbon's
Decline and Fall of the Roman Empire, and Adam Smith's
Wealth of Nations, was also the year of the anonymous publication of Jeremy Bentham's first book, *The Fragment on
Government*, which contained his first formulation of the
principle of utility and the germ of nearly all his later thinking
about law and the science of law. It is, I think, less well
known that in the same year, 1776, Bentham contributed,
again anonymously, to *An Answer to the Declaration of the
American Congress*,[1] a brief, brusque, and satirical attack on
the philosophical preamble of the Declaration and on the

---

[1] *An Answer to the Declaration of the American Congress* (London 1776).
The author of the main part of this work was John Lind (1737-81), Bentham's
close friend and collaborator who began with him the project of a strict examination of Blackstone's *Commentaries* from which grew Bentham's *Comment on
the Commentaries* and of which *A Fragment on Government* was an offshoot.
Bentham's contribution is included in the 'Short Review of the Declaration' at
pp. 120-2 of Lind's book and is identified as Bentham's work by his letter to
Lind written in September 1776 now published in *The Correspondence of
Jeremy Bentham*, i. 341-4 in *The Collected Works of Jeremy Bentham* (London
1970).

doctrines of the natural equality of men and of their unalienable rights.

In *The Fragment on Government*, published four months
before the Declaration of Independence, Bentham described
the principle of utility as 'the fundamental axiom according
to which the greatest happiness of the greatest number is the
measure of right and wrong'. In Bentham's hands this maxim
was to provide among other things the justification for the
exercise of government of men by coercive laws and the justification both for obedience to laws and, when occasion required it, for withholding obedience. So utilitarianism became
a justificatory theory of government and of the limits of
government. In his contribution to the *Answer to the Declaration of the American Congress*, Bentham attacked the alternative justification for these things which was offered by the
doctrine of unalienable rights of man. In so doing he fired the
first, light shots of destructive analysis, which developed into
a lengthy and heavy bombardment when seventeen years later
the doctrine reappeared in the French Declaration of the
Rights of Man.[2]

Jeremy Bentham thus opened in 1776 with these two
works a whole epoch in that area of philosophy which is of
peculiar relevance and concern to the lawyer. Moreover even
if, in the narrow English style, we conceive of jurisprudence
as lying outside the scope of political philosophy or theory,
it is true that in jurisprudence also Bentham's thoughts, published just two hundred years ago, have been enormously
influential and persistent. During the years since his death in
1832 much argument and counter-argument about the nature
of law, about the relation between law and morality, and
about the forms of legal reasoning appropriate to legal adjudication have circled round ideas to be found in Bentham's
works. The most fundamental of these ideas is that law,
good or bad, is a man-made artifact which men create and
add to the world by the exercise of their will: not something
which they discover through the exercise of their reason to
be already in the world. There are indeed good reasons for
having laws, but a reason for a law, even a good reason, is

[2] *Anarchical Fallacies*, being an examination of the Declaration of Rights issued
during the French Revolution, in Bentham's *Works* (Bowring edn., 1838-43), ii.
491-534.

not a law any more, so Bentham thought, than 'hunger is bread'.[3] On this foundation rested the famous definition of laws as the commands, prohibitions, or permissions of a sovereign legislature, either issued explicitly and directly by the sovereign, or indirectly through subordinates whose mandates the sovereign explicitly authorizes or tacitly adopts.[4]

With these fundamental ideas went the sharp severance which Bentham made in *The Fragment on Government* between law as it is and law as it ought to be (and between an analytical or, as he termed it, expository jurisprudence and a critical or censorial jurisprudence), and his insistence in the same work that the foundations of a legal system are not to be found in any moral or justificatory theory, but are properly described in the morally and evaluatively neutral terms of a general habit of obedience to a sovereign legislature. This cluster of ideas opened the long positivist tradition in English jurisprudence. Transmitted through the medium of John Austin's work, in a style more easily assimilable than Bentham's by lawyers who were not also philosophers, this tradition has of course profoundly and, as some think, disastrously, influenced English legal education and the English conception of the judicial function, and left its profound imprint on English legal thought in general.

Even in the United States the leading themes of Benthamite jurisprudence have reverberated, though, to continue the musical metaphor, they have been transposed into another key, the American law-making court replacing the British sovereign legislature as the chief focus of attention. John Chipman Gray in *The Nature and Sources of Law* explicitly endorsed and indeed applauded the Benthamite and Austinian distinction between law as it is and law as an ideal of what ought to be,[5] and Holmes, who had read with care and responded to much of Austin's work, finding its apparent toughness congenial to his temperament, was advocating what was in essence the same distinction when he argued that the clear-minded jurist should wash the notion of legal obligation and

[3] Op. cit. n. 2 *supra*, p. 501, and *Pannomial Fragments* in Bentham's *Works*, iii. 221.
[4] See *Of Laws in General*, chs. 1 and 2, at 1–33 in *Collected Works of Jeremy Bentham* (London, 1970).
[5] *The Nature and Sources of Law* (first published New York 1909), ch. 4, sections 213–14.

duty in 'cynical acid'[6] so as to free law from a perennial and obscuring confusion with morality.

Such then were the leading ideas with which an epoch opened in both political and legal theory in 1776. But there are signs that this epoch may now be closing. Utilitarianism, which for long was regarded as the sober, workmanlike English manifestation of the European Enlightenment, and was certainly the fountain of great reforms of the archaic English legal system and the inspiration of progressive thought in England and elsewhere, is now seen by many thinkers to have a darker, more sinister side licensing anything to be done to individuals, any sacrifice, in the pursuit of the ultimate goal of maximizing the aggregate or average welfare of a community. Moreover, much of the most interesting current work among American political philosophers — and I am thinking here of John Rawls's *Theory of Justice* and Robert Nozick's *Anarchy, State, and Utopia* — is not only frankly hostile to utilitarianism but identifies as utilitarianism's cardinal sin its failure to recognize that the division of humanity into separate individuals is a fact of great moral importance which confers on certain interests of individuals a title to inviolability, to be maintained even where to maintain it may reduce the level of aggregate or average welfare below that which could otherwise be achieved. Plainly a social philosophy in this temper has much affinity with the eighteenth-century doctrines of the unalienable rights of man which were for long thought to have succumbed to their great utilitarian critic. In jurisprudence, in suggesting that we may be at the end of an epoch and the beginning of a new one, I am thinking of the work of my American successor in the Chair of Jurisprudence at Oxford, Professor Ronald Dworkin. This is marked by the same antipathy to utilitarianism[7] and the same insistence on the independent importance of individual rights, but is also marked by a new form[8] of the ancient theory that there are vital conceptual connections between law and principles of justice which justify the law, to which, it is said, positivism has been blind and blinded its victims.

---

[6] Oliver Wendell Holmes, 'The Path of the Law' (an address of 1897), in *Collected Legal Papers* (London 1920), 174.

[7] 'On Taking Rights Seriously', in *Oxford Essays in Jurisprudence*, 2nd series, ed. A. W. B. Simpson.   [3] 'Hard Cases' 88 *Harv. L. Rev.* 1057 (1975).

Of course criticism of Bentham's form of utilitarianism is no new thing. For a century at least in England and America there has been a stream of intermittent, unsystematic, and piecemeal criticism of Bentham's legacy to political philosophy and jurisprudence. Till recently the criticisms had been absorbed as matters calling for refinement, qualification, or reinterpretation of the doctrines and not outright rejection, even if in the case of some of the reinterpretations, notably John Stuart Mill's distinctively libertarian and individualistic version of the notion of utility, it might seem that the spirit of Bentham's doctrine was quite transformed and only the terminology in which it is formulated remains the same. But the three contemporary writers whom I have mentioned are different and it is a phenomenon of importance that in spite of many differences of doctrine and political implications, the liveliest and most interesting modern writings in political and legal theory contain frank and fundamental challenges to Bentham's thought about law and politics. So in the remainder of this short paper I shall take two examples of the new ideas and I shall raise the question — no more — whether we should do well to regard them as disposing finally of Bentham's thought in these fields.

II

First, then, the doctrine of natural unalienable rights. In his attack in 1776 on the Declaration of Independence Bentham allows that the concept of a non-positive right, that is one not created by the law or social custom, is coherent and not self-contradictory, though his own view was that it was indeed self-contradictory and a species of nonsense. Within the framework of this provisional concession, Bentham focused his criticism of the Declaration of Independence on the absurdity of combining the assertion that there are unalienable rights with the assertion that government is necessary to protect them and legitimate when it does so. This was absurd in Bentham's view because the exercise of the necessary powers of any government must constantly restrict the exercise by the individual of his alleged unalienable rights.

They see not or will not seem to see that nothing that was ever called government ever was or could be in any instance exercised save at the

expense of one or other of those rights: that, in as many instances as
government is ever exercised some one or other of these pretended unalienable rights is alienated. . . . If the right of pursuit of happiness is a
right unalienable, why are thieves restrained from pursuing it by theft,
murderers by murder and rebels by rebellion?[9]

Taken strictly as offering unqualified guarantees of certain
liberties, the doctrine is essentially anarchical, and anarchists
have not been slow to invoke it in support of their claim that
the State is, morally speaking, illegitimate. Bentham insisted
that no political principles with the rigidity of the doctrine of
unalienable specific rights could have any application in the
real world where men live their lives. Such principles belong
to Utopia; that is Nowhere or an imaginary world, and accordingly he stigmatized the doctrine as the product not of reason
but of mere imagination,[10] and complained that such principles were 'deaf, unyielding and inflexible, principles which will
hear of no modification, which will look at no calculation',[11]
which, if instead of imagination reason were consulted, would
be seen to be unnecessary.

This form of criticism was amplified by Bentham when he
came to deal with the French Declaration of the Rights of
Man by the demonstration that unalienable rights construed
as guarantees of specific liberties of action were not only incompatible with government but were doomed to constant
conflict with each other. Simple and crude as this form of
criticism may seem, it became and remained for decades the
standard objection to the doctrine of fixed natural rights. Indeed its vitality is paradoxically confirmed by one of the
works which I have already mentioned, Nozick's *Anarchy,
State, and Utopia*. For at the outset Nozick raises precisely
Bentham's question and asks 'How much room do individual
rights leave for government?'[12] What is astonishing is that
Nozick in effect gives Bentham's answer: 'No room except in

[9] The passages quoted here are from Bentham's draft of his letter to Lind of
September 1776 (see n. 1 *supra*). The text published by Lind in his *Answer to the
Declaration of the American Congress* differs in certain points of detail but re-
produces the substance of these passages. The published text adds however (122)
the words 'Here they have put the axe to the root of all Government.'
[10] 'Imagination with its favourite instrument the word "right"'. *Plan of Parliamentary Reform* in Bentham's *Works*, iii. 515, cf. *Anarchical Fallacies*, ibid.
523.
[11] *Plan of Parliamentary Reform*, Bentham's *Works*, iii. 467 n.
[12] Nozick, *Anarchy, State, and Utopia* 1 (1974).

an imaginary world'. For that is the message of his ingenious and brilliant work. Thus Nozick argues that, granted a set of natural rights, such as not to be killed, assaulted, coerced, and not to have property taken or destroyed, and not to be limited in the use of property, only a minimal form of State, the so-called nightwatchman State, whose functions are limited to the punishment of violations of such rights, can be legitimate. Moreover given these natural rights even this minimal form of State could be justified only under conditions of which Bentham never thought and must be forgiven for failing to do so, for they are conditions produced out of Nozick's lively imagination which are highly unlikely to be satisfied in the real as contrasted with the imaginary world. The conditions in question are that the State should have arisen through individuals voluntarily joining a private association which might eventually achieve, without infringing any natural rights, dominance in a limited territory even if not everyone joined it. But all this seems indeed imaginary and to have little relevance to a world where States do not arise in this way.

So Nozick's theory seems just tailor-made for Bentham's accusation that talk of unalienable rights taken strictly belongs only to the world of the imagination. Bentham of course realized that defenders of the doctrine would disclaim such rigid unqualified interpretations of it and while speaking of rights as 'unalienable' would admit limitations of scope, qualifications and exceptions and balancing, both of right against right, and right against general welfare, or would even be content to view them merely as ideal directions to governments to do the best they can for certain individual interests. But he claimed that the doctrine would then be nugatory. To support this point he could have cited some famous — or infamous — examples from America, where express declarations of natural rights to liberty incorporated into State constitutions were held not to affect the slave-owner's rights to property in his slaves.[13] So he depicted the French advocates of natural rights

---

[14] E.g. the interpretation of the 'free and equal' clause of the Virginia Bill of Rights (1776) in *Hudgins* v. *Wright* 11 Va. (1 Hen & M.) 133 at 141 discussed by Professor R. M. Cover in *Justice Accused: Anti-slavery and the Judicial Process* (Yale 1976), 52-4. See Bentham's observations on such declarations of rights in *An Introduction to the Principles of Morals and Legislation*, 309-10 in *Collected Works of Jeremy Bentham*, op. cit. n. 1 *supra*.

as on the horns of a dilemma between the impossible and the nugatory.[14] In this I think he was wrong: there is certainly more to be said about the relationship between basic human rights and other values than he allows. But in spite of recent work I do not think we yet have a satisfactory theory showing how respect for such rights is to be combined with the pursuit of other values. Some theories seem to me to throw out the baby (that is basic rights compatible with each other and with government) with the bath-water of excessive rigidity. Other theories — perhaps Professor Nozick's among them — do worse: they throw out the baby and keep the bath-water.

III

I turn now to my second topic, the modern challenge to the legal positivism inherited from Bentham. Here I can only consider, although very briefly, one aspect of this modern challenge: namely the new form of the old indictment that the positivist has misrepresented the nature of the judicial process. Here there has been an astonishing volte-face among the critics. Indeed, if I may use the language of 1776, it is 'the world turned upside down'. I say this because twenty years ago when I came to Harvard to lecture on my own brand of legal theory, the sin imputed to positivist conceptions of the judicial function was 'formalism', 'conceptualism', 'mechanical' or 'slot machine' jurisprudence or an excessive belief in the use of 'logic' in reaching decisions. The positivist was said to believe (though in fact neither Bentham nor Austin ever did believe this) that correct judicial decisions were always the conclusions of syllogisms reached by pure deductive reasoning from clear predetermined legal rules serving as major premises. It was said that the positivist jurists, and judges misled by them, ignored the indeterminacy at the borderline of many constitutional provisions, the open-ended character of many statutes and the unsettled or conflicting scope of many precedents which left leeways open to the judge and made a choice on his part inescapable. So that ultimately, the critics urged, to reach a decision, the judge has to choose between competing alternatives, and such a

---

[14] *Anarchical Fallacies*, op. cit. n. 10 *supra*, 493, 502 ('nonsensical or nugatory and in both cases mischievous: such is the alternative'), 502, 507, 510 and 534.

choice, if rational, would have to be made in the light of social policies and values that took him outside what the positivist called law. So on this view, intended to correct the then errors of positivism, the judge sometimes made law, though unlike a legislator he was no doubt constrained in various ways, hemmed in by the existing law which ruled out many alternatives and imposed on him a duty to weigh, as best he could, before reaching a decision various, sometimes competing, presumptions representing the received values of the legal system.

But the new critique of positivism expounded with great power and subtlety and also complexity by Professor Dworkin reverses these accusations against positivism and holds the positivists' cardinal sin no longer to be 'formalism' or belief in a 'mechanical' theory of judicial decision but to consist in a mistaken assimilation of the judge's task in deciding hard cases to a legislative or law-making choice.[15] Litigants, it is said, are always entitled to have from judges an application of existing law to them, not the making of new law for them. For a judge to make such law would not only be unjust where decisions have retroactive force, but, where judges are not elected, they would be undemocratic.

But the old and new errors of positivism do not, according to this new critique, exhaust the alternatives. There is a third alternative which is also a *via media* between classical natural law theory and positivism. For over every legal system — or rather over the mass of constitutional law, statutes, and precedents which a community at a given time accepts as clear and settled law — there is exactly what Oliver Wendell Holmes denied, 'a brooding omnipresence' of general principles of fairness and justice. These are not to be identified with positive constitutional provisions, enactments or authoritative decisions, but are presupposed by these taken together as their implicit justification and are to be inferred from them. From this body of principles, which, in our system, includes conceptions of individual dignity and freedom, rules can be deduced to solve correctly those hard cases where separate positive constitutional provisions, enactments, and precedents give incomplete, ambiguous, or conflicting guidance. It is to

[15] See his 'Hard Cases', op. cit. n. 8 *supra*.

these implicit principles manifested in the body of existing clear positive law that judges must turn to find the law which will serve to decide hard cases, and they exist as law before he turns to them. So the belief that judges can in deciding such cases properly make law even 'interstitially' can be discarded as a misleading positivist error. On this view Holmes was wrong in stating that when the law is in doubt 'even if it is disguised and unconscious the judges are called upon to exercise the sovereign prerogative of choice'.[16] On the contrary, according to the new theory with its expanded version of what law is, there always awaits the judge's discovery some pre-existing law adequate to dispose of the case with superior claims over competing alternatives, which might also be regarded as implicit in the body of existing positive law, to be best fitted to it.

Of course only a superhuman being (Dworkin calls him 'Hercules') commanding a god's-eye view of the whole legal system could be certain that he had identified correctly the one consistent set of principles which will both explain and justify the whole mass of clear and settled positive law, and also yield *the* correct rule of decision for the instant controversial case. Ordinary mortals, including judges, can only infer from the body of already decided or settled law these general abstract principles. They can only attempt to determine them by framing explanatory and justificatory hypotheses. The hypotheses of different judges may conflict, but when a judge adopts one rather than another he is not on this theory choosing what is to be the law and so 'making' it, but acting on what he thinks is the best evidence as to what the law already is; for the law itself on this view is not, as the positivist claims it sometimes is, ever incomplete or indeterminate. The fault is not in *it*; but in *our* limited powers of discernment. Even when the positive law has proved to be unsettled something always already was the law for every case, however 'hard'.

Professor Dworkin has recently provided a most striking example of the working of this theory in his recent reflections on Professor Cover's admirable study of anti-slavery and the

---

[16] 'Law in Science; Science in Law' (address of 1899) in *Collected Legal Papers*, 239.

judicial process.[17] Before the Civil War famous judges like
Joseph Story and Lemuel Shaw in Massachusetts, who were
passionately opposed to slavery, none the less after much
agony enforced the Fugitive Slave Acts passed by Congress,
and ordered slaves who had escaped to free States to be taken
back by their masters. The judges did this, distasteful as it
was to them, because according to Professor Dworkin they
thought it was their judicial duty to follow the clear intentions of the legislators in Congress who had enacted the Fugitive Slave Acts and the clearly manifested intention of the
Constitutional Convention embodied as part of the grand compromise between the slave States and free States in Article 4
of the Constitution. This provided that the escaped slave 'shall
not in consequence of any law or regulation of a State to
which he had escaped be discharged from that service but
shall be delivered up on claim of the party to whom his service or labour may be due'. The judges who with such agony
suppressed their own moral qualms in this way in order to do
what they saw as their duty to enforce the law were guilty
according to Professor Dworkin's theory of a 'failure in jurisprudence'. If only they had been willing to think along the
lines proposed by this new theory, they could have found implicit principles better fitting the existing law than any rivals
and strong enough to yield a clear decision in favour of the
slaves. For according to this theory:

The general structure of the American Constitution presupposed a conception of individual freedom antagonistic to slavery, a conception of
procedural justice that condemned the procedures established by the
Fugitive Slave Acts, and a conception of federalism inconsistent with the
idea that the State of Massachusetts had no power to supervise the capture of men and women within its territory. These principles were not
simply the personal morality of a few judges, which they set aside in the
interests of objectivity. They were rather, on this theory of what law is,
more central to the law than were the particular and transitory policies
of the slavery compromise.

So judges like Story and Shaw could and should have given
effect to them in discharge of their duty to apply the law.

    Much that Professor Dworkin says in the course of devel-
oping this conception of the unity of law with its justificatory

---

[17] Review of Cover, *Justice Accused: Anti-slavery and the Judicial Process*, in
Times Literary Supplement, 5 December 1975, p. 1437.

theory seems to me exceedingly well taken against some in-cautious descriptions of what judges do, and against some hasty claims as to what they should do in those cases where particular parts of the law offer no clear guidance. As he rightly says, judges on reaching that juncture do not and should not put their law books aside and choose without fuller reference to the existing law, according to their own social policy or moral intuition. They do seek and often find fuller guidance in the body of existing positive law which im-poses constraints upon their decision and exercises what, in a striking phrase, Professor Dworkin well calls 'a gravitational pull' (even if it is only one of analogy) over it. So that the decision, when it comes, may seem to the judge to have been latent or immanent in the law. None the less anyone consider-ing this theory and especially its application to the Fugitive Slave cases must I think be visited by doubts on two main scores. The first is the latitude which Professor Dworkin per-mits himself and so would allow to the courts in drawing the line of distinction between what is to be taken as settled law from which the guiding justificatory principles are to be de-rived, and what as unsettled law providing the hard cases to be decided by reference to the principles so derived. Thus for the theory to have any application to the Fugitive Slave Act cases the relevant law must at the time of the decision be taken not to have been settled. But the judges themselves, as Professor Dworkin says, said that it was settled. 'The law was not already settled though the judges said it was.' He implies that the judges could not have believed what they said for according to him in spite of what they said they believed they were making new law. 'The decisions were surprising not be-cause the judges refused to bend the law to their own con-victions but because though they believed they were making new law, they made law they themselves thought immoral.'

More important is the doubt whether Professor Dworkin has established something which is central to his case, namely that a judge will not frequently be faced with alternative equally correct ways of applying this theory, when, in seeking to avoid 'the failure in jurisprudence' of which Story and Shaw were guilty, he tries to extract from the existing law

[18] Cf. *Times Literary Supplement*, 5 December 1975, p. 1437, with Professor Dworkin's letter in ibid., 9 January 1976, p. 35.

the principle that will yield the correct decision in a hard case. It is right and illuminating to speak of the existing law as exerting a gravitational pull over the judge, but that there will not quite often be equal gravitational pulls in different directions seems to me something still to be shown. It is plain from Professor Dworkin's exposition that the underlying justificatory theory of the existing law from which the judges are to extract rules of decision includes principles that are hugely general and abstract and I find it difficult to believe that among these just one principle or set of principles can be shown to fit the existing settled law better than any other. Principles *supporting* the decisions against the slaves seem to fit the then existing law at least as well as those proffered by Professor Dworkin.[19]

How would Bentham have viewed this intriguing and suggestive new theory and the claim that in failing to take this wider view of the law judges like Joseph Story were guilty of a failure in jurisprudence, exposing themselves to needless agonies? He would undoubtedly have thought it was an extension to the law as a whole of Blackstone's theory of the common law according to which the judge's decisions do not make the law but are merely evidence of what the law is. The crucial question is whether the new theory can escape the criticism which Bentham made of Blackstone's theory, namely that it was a fiction which would enable the judge, in the misleading guise of finding what the law behind the positive law really is, to invest his own personal, moral or political views with a spurious objectivity as already law. All depends on the claim which Professor Dworkin makes with great

[19] Thus Joseph Story and Lemuel Shaw, had they followed Professor Dworkin's theory, might have extracted from the then existing law the following principles instead of those formulated by Professor Dworkin (155 *supra*):

(1) The general structure of the American Constitution presupposes that a compromise between different states with different institutions is to be maintained even at the cost of individual liberty involved in the effective enforcement of a slave-owner's rights, where slavery is recognized by an individual state.

(2) The conception of federalism and procedural justice presupposed by the existing law consequently requires that a slave-owner's claims to the return of an alleged escaped slave be adjudicated in the owner's state which recognizes the institution of slavery and where the best evidence of the status of the alleged slave is likely to be found.

(I am indebted to J. L. Mackie's article 'The Third Theory of Law', *Philosophy and Public Affairs* (1971), 37, for the suggestion that principles of this kind might be extracted by Professor Dworkin's method from the then-existing 'settled' law.)

power and subtlety, to which I have been unable to do justice here, that when hard cases arise equally plausible and well-based explanatory hypotheses as to what the latent law is will not be available. This is a claim I think has still to be evaluated.

So to sum up: in my perspective for the future of law and philosophy, there is much unfinished business. At a time when, both in my country and in yours, substantive issues of social policy are much discussed in terms of individuals' rights, we still need a satisfactory theory of basic human rights and their relationship to other values pursued through law. So too, if positivism in jurisprudence is to be finally laid to rest, we still need a demonstration that an expanded concept of law which includes for every legal system a unique set of justificatory principles as a reserve for the solution of hard cases, will illumine and not obscure the description and the performance of the judge's task. But judging from the work in progress the prospects that we shall have at least some of these things are good. Certainly American philosophers are more likely than any others to provide them; but let us hope it will not take them another two hundred years.

POSTSCRIPT

See for criticisms: R. Dworkin, *Taking Rights Seriously* (2nd impression 1978), 360-3.

PART III

SCANDINAVIAN JURISPRUDENCE

Essay 6

Scandinavian Realism

English and Scandinavian legal theory have long shared many
points of view. Among these are the belief that law is something man-made and made for men; hostility or indifference
to doctrines of natural law at least in the scholastic form; and
a general disbelief in the capacity of philosophical systems to
throw light either on what law is or what it ought to be. Yet
notwithstanding these similarities the principal Scandinavian
tradition in legal theory has a different *tone* from its English
counterpart. Though professedly sceptical in aim and empirical in method, it is much more like a kind of philosophy. The
work of the founder of this tradition, Axel Hägerström, had
for its motto *Censeo metaphysicam esse delendam*, and is a
sustained effort to show that notions commonly accepted as
essential parts of the structure of law such as rights, duties,
transfers of rights, and validity, are in part composed of
superstitious beliefs, 'myths', 'fictions', 'magic' or rank confusion. This tradition, continued in the work of his disciples
Lundstedt, Olivecrona and Alf Ross, has made contact with
both American 'rule-scepticism' and contemporary linguistic
philosophy. Its latest most sophisticated product is Ross's
book *On Law and Justice*.[1]

This is in many ways an interesting book, and at points a
brilliant one, though by no means free from the fiery dog-
matism of Scandinavian 'realist' jurisprudence. Ross is less
tortuous and obscure than Hägerström, less naïve and pro-
fessorial than Lundstedt; and richer in illuminating examples
and concrete detail, if less urbane, than Olivecrona. He writes
in a clear, interesting, and at times racy style; though these
felicities may be in part due to the great skill of the translator.
Moreover, whatever may be thought of the author's general
theory, his eye for legal detail is always shrewd and discerning.
Many a lawyer and judge would be better off for reading his
powerful pages dealing with interpretation of statute.

[1] *On Law and Justice* (London 1958).

The inspiration of the book generally is a *saeva indignatio* against metaphysical confusions and pseudo-rational concepts which still lurk, according to Ross, in conventional accounts of the structure of law, and in theories concerning the standards of morals and justice used in the criticism or evaluation of law. So the author is hostile both to the tradition of natural law and to formalism, even when it is the formalism of 'positivists' like Kelsen. Both these sin against the author's guiding principle that law and the criticism of law must be interpreted in terms of 'social facts'. The methods of 'modern empirical science' must be used, and legal thinking must be explained in terms of 'the same logic as that on which other empirical sciences are based'.

Though there is much that is questionable, indeed blinding, in the attempt to force the analysis of legal concepts or of any rules into the framework adapted for the empirical sciences, Ross's sceptical attack on conventional doctrines is far more sophisticated than many previous attempts to uncover behind legal forms and theories the 'facts of social reality'. The book falls into two parts. The first nine chapters are concerned with the structure of law and the analysis of its leading notions; the last eight with the standards used in its criticism. In both cases the author's aim is to dispel misconceptions often ingrained in the vocabulary of law and morals, and to replace these either by rational empirical conceptions or by frank acknowledgment of the points at which 'irrational' elements must intrude into the management of social life.

I shall deal first with the second part of the book. Though interesting, this is less original than the first, owing much to Popper's *The Open Society and its Enemies* and Stevenson's *Ethics and Language*. It contains a critique of classical and Thomist Natural Law, of the idea of justice, and of utilitarianism, and also three chapters concerned with what the author terms 'legal politics'. This is a discipline, still undeveloped, which the author favours, and thinks lawyers should pursue. Its central task is to discover *not* the aims or ends of law but the best methods of adjustment of law to changing technical or 'ideological' conditions, and to equip the lawyer to referee between experts when they disagree concerning social changes. It is an art where the value of the result is measured 'by being in fact accepted by others, particularly those in power'. With this modest, relativistic conception, we should contrast the arch-error of thinking that moral standards or values are part of the fabric of the universe awaiting our discovery by rational methods. Moral values are attitudes which human beings adopt, not facts about the world to be established. Though they may be changed either by non-rational methods (propaganda) or by rational change in beliefs about facts, they cannot be proved or disproved by rational argument.

In his elaboration of these not unfamiliar themes, the author says much still worth saying, especially concerning the concept of social welfare, and the relationship between private and public 'interests' left in so cloudy a state by Pound. He can also strike a ringing phrase: 'Like a harlot, natural law is at the disposal of everyone. The ideology does not exist that cannot be defended by an appeal to the law of nature.'[2]

Yet the author's misplaced affection for the battle-cry of 'meaningless', and his readiness to smell the rat of 'Natural Law' in every moral position not prostrate before the methods of the sciences, leads him into some absurdities. Surely it is wrong to say that the words 'just' and 'unjust' applied to a legal rule as distinct from a particular decision are 'devoid of meaning'.[3] When we assert that a rule forbidding black men to sit in the public park is unjust we no doubt use, as our criterion of just treatment, the unstated principle that, in the distribution of rights and privileges among men, differences in colour should be neglected. In any full defence of this assertion the implicit criterion would have to be made explicit. But the dependence of concepts like justice on implicit, varying and challengeable criteria does not render them meaningless when applied to law. What is true of justice is true of all concepts into which variable standards are built. Words like 'long', 'short', 'genuine', 'false', and 'useful' exhibit the same feature.

It would take too long to defend Hegel here against the charge of 'fantastic nonsense'.[4] But why should Kant's statement that 'a course of action is lawful if the liberty to pursue it is compatible with the liberty of every other person [to do likewise] under a general rule' be called *meaningless*? Clearly, further consideration of the meaning of 'meaningless' is

---

[2] Ibid., 261.   [3] Ibid., 274.   [4] Ibid., 251.

needed. And was Mill really guilty of incorporating 'pure natural law ideas' when he said that the only justification for legal coercion was to prevent one man from harming another? Even if it is true, as Ross asserts, that harm means infringing the moral right of others (an assertion which may well be disputed), the implication that men have moral rights need not entail belief in 'Natural Law', unless the latter is used simply as a misleading expression for morality. Has the author never acknowledged that someone has a moral right, though no legal right, to some promised service, or never denied that another has a moral right to interfere in his affairs?

For many, the main interest of the book will lie in the treatment of the concept of legal validity in the early chapters. Yet interesting as this is, it displays very clearly the peculiar dogmatic insistence of the Scandinavian school that if a statement cannot be analysed as a statement of fact or expression of feeling it *must* be 'metaphysical'. The statement that, e.g., the provision in section 9 of the Wills Act, 1837 (concerning the number of witnesses required in a will), is a valid rule of English law might seem innocent enough and not difficult to establish as 'true' or at least 'correct'. But for Ross legal validity is a dangerously septic notion; unless we handle it carefully, wearing the protective rubber gloves of an 'empirical methodology' determined to admit into our stock of notions only hard empirically verifiable facts, we shall catch the infection of 'metaphysics'. For in Ross's view the analysis of this and many other legal notions must take one of two forms: either it refers to the actual future behaviour and feelings of people (mainly judges), or it must refer to some mysterious unobservable quality which some rules have and others lack. So our choice is between taking 'X is a valid rule of English law' as a prediction of judicial behaviour and feeling – or metaphysics. Kelsen's insistence that legal thinking must be interpreted in terms not of facts or 'is-propositions' but of 'ought-propositions' is therefore to be rejected as a metaphysical construction 'raising the law above the world of facts'.

Ross starts his analysis of legal validity by considering the simpler case of the rules of chess, though it is of some importance to note that we do not usually speak of rules as 'valid' except where, as in the legal case, the system contains some general criteria for the *identification* of the rules. Ross claims that a chess rule, e.g., that the bishop must be moved diagonally (my example), is a 'valid rule of chess' if (1) players regularly move the bishop in this way and (2) they do so because they experience a feeling of compulsion to follow this pattern of behaviour. Accordingly the rule is, in these circumstances, something which enables us (a) to understand or interpret the players' actions as coherent motivated conduct and (b) to predict their future behaviour. The rule-formula therefore serves both as a 'scheme of interpretation' and a basis of prediction. The parallel analysis in the case of legal validity is as follows. Legal rules are essentially directives to courts to apply sanctions under certain conditions. (This Kelsenian dogma is adopted without much argument.) To say that a legal rule is valid is to say (1) that courts will under specifiable conditions apply it or at least regard it as especially important in reaching their decisions and (2) they will do so because they have an emotional experience of 'being bound' by the rules. A valid law is a verifiable hypothesis about future judicial behaviour and its special motivating feeling.

Apart from the reference to feeling and the treatment of a legal rule as a 'scheme of interpretation' as well as a basis of prediction, Ross's analysis is not very different from the cruder American Realist theories which treat statements of legal rights and duties as predictions of official action. Like these simpler theories, Ross's predictive analysis of legal validity is open to two objections which he never squarely faces. First, even if in the mouth of the ordinary citizen or lawyer 'this is a valid rule of English law' is a prediction of what a judge will do, say or feel, this cannot be its meaning in the mouth of a judge who is not engaged in predicting his own or others' behaviour or feelings. 'This is a valid rule of law' said by a judge is an act of recognition; in saying it he recognizes the rule in question as one satisfying certain accepted general criteria for admission as a rule of the system and so as a legal standard of behaviour. Secondly, even if (though this may well be doubted) non-judicial statements of the form 'X is a valid rule' are always predictions of future judicial behaviour and feelings, the basis for such predictions is the knowledge that the judges use and understand the statement 'this is a valid rule' in a non-predictive sense.

Ross is right in thinking that we must distinguish an *internal* as well as an external aspect of the phenomenon presented by the existence of social rules. This is true and very important for the understanding of any kind of rule. But unfortunately he draws the line between these aspects in the wrong places and misrepresents the internal aspect of rules as a matter of 'emotion' or 'feeling' — as a special psychological 'experience'. Only by doing this is he able to create the impression that what Kelsen terms 'ought-propositions' may be dispensed with in the analysis of legal thinking. In fact the elucidation of the internal aspect of any normative discourse requires such propositions, and if we carefully study them we shall see that there is nothing 'metaphysical' about them, though their 'logic' or structure is different from statements of fact or expressions of feeling.

The required distinction between external and internal is not one dividing physical behaviour from feeling, though of course that can be drawn; it is one dividing two radically different types of statement for which an opportunity is afforded whenever a social group conducts its affairs by rules. Thus an external observer of the group who does not accept or endorse the rules may report the fact that the group behaves in certain uniform ways and regularly reacts to deviations in adverse or hostile ways either through officials or private persons. He may predict both the future behaviour of the group and the future reaction of officials. Such statements are external statements of fact *about* the group and the efficacy of its rules. But if the group really has rules and not merely a set of convergent habits, members of the group display this by use of expressions of a different kind. These expressions do not state the fact that they follow or will follow regular patterns of behaviour; but members of the group use these expressions in the *criticism* of their own and each other's conduct by reference to the regular patterns of behaviour which they accept as a *standard*. They do not merely react to deviations from the regular pattern in a predictable adverse manner, but treat deviations as a *reason* for such reaction and demands for conformity as *justified*.

When a pattern of behaviour is thus taken as a standard the criticism of conduct in terms of it and the claims and justifications based on it are expressed by the distinctive normative vocabulary of 'ought', 'must', 'should', 'may', 'right', 'wrong', and special variants like 'duty' and 'obligation'. The forms 'I (you, he, they) ought to do that' and 'I (you, etc.) ought not to have done that' are the most general ones used to discharge these critical normative functions which indeed constitute their meaning. They are not external statements of fact predicting likely behaviour in accordance with the standards; they are internal statements in the sense that they manifest acceptance of the standards and use and appeal to them in various ways. But the internal character of these statements is not a mere matter of the speaker having certain 'feelings of compulsion'; for though these may indeed often accompany the making of such statements they are neither necessary nor sufficient conditions of their normative use in criticizing conduct, making claims and justifying hostile reactions by reference to the accepted standard.

Ross treats statements of legal validity (e.g., 'this is a valid rule of Danish law') as an external statement of fact predicting judicial behaviour and feeling. Yet the normal central use of 'legally valid' is in an internal normative statement of a special kind, and Ross's failure to give a plausible account of the use of this expression in the mouth of a judge, where its internal character is clear, is due to his more general failure to allow for the internal non-factual, non-predictive uses of language inseparable from the use of rules. The internal statement 'This is a valid rule', as distinct from the external predictive statement 'In England they will follow this rule', is appropriate when a system of rules contains, as legal systems do, not only primary rules forming legal standards of behaviour, but also rules for recognizing, or general criteria identifying, the primary rules of the system by certain marks. So when a judge recognizes a statutory provision as 'valid' he identifies this as a primary rule, using for this purpose an unstated rule of recognition or criteria of identification which might be formulated as 'What the Queen in Parliament enacts is a legal standard of behaviour.'

The concept of legal validity is in some respects different from that of a chess rule to which Ross compares it and much more like that of a score in a game. When the scorer records a run or goal he is using an accepted, unstated rule in the recognition of critical phases of the game which count towards winning. He is not predicting his own or others' behaviour or feelings, nor making any other form of factual statement about the operation of the system. The temptation to misrepresent such internal statements in which use is made of an unstated, accepted rule or criterion of recognition as an external statement of fact predicting the regular operation of the system is due to the fact that the general acceptance of the rules and efficacy of the system is indeed the *normal context* in which such internal normative statements are made. It will *usually* be pointless to assess the validity of a rule (or the progress of a game) by reference to rules of recognition (scoring) which are not accepted by others in fact, or are not likely to be observed in future. We do, however, sometimes do this, in a semi-fictional mood, as a vivid way of teaching the law of a dead legal system like classical Roman law. But this normal *context* of efficacy presupposed in the making of internal statements must be distinguished from their normative meaning or content.

It is therefore vital if we are to understand social rules and the normative uses of language which are an inseparable part of this complex phenomenon of social life not to accept Ross's dilemma: 'Either construe these as predictions of judicial behaviour and feelings or as metaphysical assertions about unobservable entities above the world of facts.' The dimensions of legal language are far richer than this allows. It is, however, equally important to stress that though 'ought-propositions' and other forms of normative internal statements are both necessary and harmless in the analysis of legal thinking, it does not in the least follow that a legal system is 'a closed logical system' alleged to be dear to the formalist's heart, or that legal statements of rights and duties or validity are all deducible from clear determinate legal rules. Of course, it is here, as everywhere in law, a matter of a central core of certain meaning and a wide penumbra of uncertainty leaving room for judicial choice. Sometimes, where the rules are vague, all we can do is to predict what judges will say, and to do this we may use, in a guarded way, the word 'valid' or the cautious form 'I think this is valid.' Among the many good things in the first part of this book, none are better than Ross's discussion of judicial reasoning. But even here, even where the system's criteria for identifying particular rules of the system are vague or indeterminate, Ross's predictive analysis cannot hold good for 'This is a valid rule' said by a judge. And surely, until the central function of assertions of legal validity as a species of internal statements is recognized for what it is in the *clear* cases, we shall not understand their use in the more debatable area of the penumbra.

POSTSCRIPT

See for criticism and comments:
1. A. Ross, 'Validity and the Conflict between Legal Positivism and Natural Law', *Revista Juridica de Buenos Aires* (1961), 46; Review of Hart, *The Concept of Law*, *Yale L. J.* (1962), 118. (Note: Ross claims that his theory does not differ in any important respects from mine and that the appearance of conflict is due to misunderstanding arising from the erroneous translation in his *On Law and Justice* of the Danish word *gaeltende* (meaning 'in force' or 'effective') as 'valid'. For an assessment of this claim see Hierro, *El Realismo Juridico Escandinavo* (Valencia 1981), esp. 172, 216, 283-5, 219-21, 295 n. 802.)
2. F. A. Siegler, 'Hart on Rules of Obligation', *Australian Journal of Philosophy* (1967), 341-55.
3. N. MacCormick, in *H.L.A. Hart* (London 1981), 30, 32, 34-6, 43-44, 166.

Self-referring Laws

In Kelsen's *General Theory of Law and State* there is a section entitled 'The Never-ending Series of Sanctions'[1] about which I have long entertained certain doubts, and I shall air these doubts in the first section of this essay. It will be seen that in this section I assume that a law may perfectly well refer to itself so long as it also refers to other laws. I do not myself think that in this idea of a partly self-referring law there is any incoherence or 'meaninglessness' or any other logical or linguistic vice. Indeed, there are many examples of such self-referring laws to be found in the field of constitutional law, especially in the constitutional law of the British Commonwealth. I find, however, that Professor Alf Ross, in his book on law and justice,[2] expresses the view that in spite of the existence of such examples as Article V of the United States Constitution self-referring laws are logically objectionable. In the second section of this contribution, I therefore say why I think such a wholesale rejection of self-referring laws is wrong.

I

Kelsen, in his section entitled 'The Never-ending Series of Sanctions', considers one argument against the doctrine that coercion is an essential element of law. In this argument the doctrine in question is interpreted to mean that a rule, to qualify as a legal rule, must be 'guaranteed' or 'secured' by another legal rule prescribing a sanction for the breach of the former rule, and the argument simply is that this is a stipulation which cannot logically be fulfilled by a legal system which consists of a finite set of legal rules. For, on this interpretation of the doctrine that coercion is a necessary element of law, a rule forbidding e.g. theft could not be a legal rule unless there was a legal rule prescribing a sanction for it, i.e. a

[1] *General Theory of Law and State* (Harvard 1949), 28-9.
[2] *On Law and Justice* (London 1958) 80-4.

rule requiring what Kelsen terms 'an organ of the community' (a judge) to punish theft; and this could not be a legal rule unless there was yet a further rule requiring another judge to punish any judge who failed to punish theft and so on. So such a stipulation requiring each rule of a legal system to be sanctioned by another rule leads to an infinite regress. 'In order to secure the efficacy of a rule of the nth degree, a rule of the $n + 1$ degree is necessary.'[3]

Kelsen accepts this argument as correct but he does not think that it constitutes any objection to his own interpretation of the doctrine that coercion is an essential element of law; for, unlike Austin, Kelsen does not think that it is necessary that a sanction be provided for every legal rule or, to use his words, that a legal rule must be a rule the efficacy of which is 'guaranteed' by a sanction. Instead Kelsen's view is that 'a rule is a legal rule because it provides for a sanction'. All the rules of a legal system are coercive in the sense that they provide for sanctions, but among these rules there are some which are not themselves secured or guaranteed by any coercive rule. To show this he sketches a simplified legal order. 'Norm n runs as follows. If an individual steals, another individual, an organ of the community, shall punish him. The efficacy of this norm n is secured by the norm $n + 1$: if the organ does not punish the thief, another organ shall punish the organ who violated his duty of punishing the thief. There is no norm $n + 2$ securing the efficacy of the norm $n + 1$ . . . But all the norms of this legal order are coercive norms.'[4]

Kelsen is right in accepting as correct the argument about the infinite regress. He is also right in thinking that his own interpretation of the doctrine that coercion is an essential element of law is not vulnerable to that argument. But it seems to me that this is not the end of the matter. Austin or any other theorist who might wish to insist that no rule is a rule of law unless a sanction or punishment is provided for its breach could state this requirement in a form which does not involve an infinite regress. For it is not essential to this requirement that the sanction provided for a breach of a rule must be provided by another rule. There is no reason why a

---

[3] Kelsen (op. cit. n. 1 *supra* 28) quotes this observation from Timasheff, *An Introduction to the Sociology of Law* (1939), 264.

[4] Op. cit. n. 1 *supra*, 29.

rule should not provide a sanction for the breach both of other rules and of itself.

This suggestion may sound strange at first. But it is certainly a theoretical possibility that should be considered before a theory like Austin's is rejected as logically absurd. To show the logical possibility of such a theory I shall adapt Kelsen's sketch of a legal system as follows.

Rule I — No individual shall steal.

Rule II — An organ of the community (a judge) shall punish anyone who breaks any law including this one.

What, it may be asked, is the content of Rule II? This question may best be answered by setting out the initial members of the series of possible duties which may arise under it.

Case I — A judge must punish any individual who steals.

Case II — A judge must punish any judge who fails to punish an individual who steals.

Case III — A judge must punish any judge who fails to punish any judge who fails to punish any individual who steals.

And so on.

This series is certainly a 'never-ending' one; but it is a series of duties and breaches of duty not of rules. Rule II when spelt out, does indeed refer to an infinite series of duties the breach of each of which (except the first) presupposes a breach of its predecessors in the series. But this, unlike the requirement that every legal rule must be sanctioned by another legal rule, generates no vicious infinite regress of rules. There is nothing logically objectionable in a rule referring to an infinite series of cases of its application related to each other in this way. Why, as far as logic goes, should there not be a rule forbidding any one to write down the successor in the series of natural numbers to the largest number previously written down by anyone. Each time this rule is broken another new way of breaking it becomes possible, and, as is the case with Rule II, every breach of this rule except the first presupposes all the earlier breaches of the rule.

One important feature of Rule II must be noted. Though it does refer to itself it does not *only* refer to itself but to a class of laws including itself. A self-referring rule about sanctions which stood alone in the sense of only referring to itself

would be logically objectionable; for it would be essentially
incomplete. This can be shown if we substitute for rule II the
purely self-referring formula:

Rule II A — A judge shall punish any individual who breaks
this rule.

If in the case of this purely self-referring formula we try to
set out as we did for Rule II the series of possible duties or
breaches of duty which arise under it we shall find that we
can never start. All we shall get is the asymptotic stutter,
namely 'A judge shall punish any judge who fails to punish
any judge who fails to punish any judge who etc. etc. . . .' *ad
infinitum*.

The reason for this difference between Rule II and Rule
IIA does not lie in any recondite logical doctrine about self-
reference. It is a simple consequence of the obvious fact that
the idea of punishing for a breach of a rule is essentially incomplete. It is incomplete without the idea of a rule which
requires behaviour other than punishment. This means that,
though it is perfectly good sense to provide a series of punishments for a series of failures to punish, there must be some
ultimate reference to punishment for something else. In this
respect we might compare the notion of a copy which is
similarly incomplete without the idea of something which is
not a copy. We may indeed order the making of copies of
copies of copies etc., but the series, if it is to start at all, must
start with the copy of an original.

II

Examples of explicitly self-referring laws are to be found in
the constitutional law of the British Commonwealth among
those clauses which English lawyers now speak of as being
'entrenched'. These are clauses which are designed to protect
certain provisions of a constitution from repeal by the ordinary legislative processes, and they do this by prescribing a
special procedure for their repeal. Plainly the prescription of
such a special procedure 'entrenching' these clauses would
be nugatory if this prescription could itself be repealed in
the ordinary way. So a skilful draftsman will entrench also
the clause prescribing the special procedure by making the

provisions of his clause apply both to the other clauses and to itself.

One of the most famous of such self-entrenched clauses is section 152 of the South Africa Act, 1909. This statute of the British Parliament enacted a constitution for the Union of South Africa and two clauses of it (sections 35 and 137), which were designed to exclude discriminations based on race and colour and to secure the equal status of the Dutch and English languages, were protected against repeal or alteration by the ordinary bicameral processes of legislation. This 'entrenchment' was secured by section 152, which was itself entrenched, and ran as follows:

> Parliament may by law repeal or alter any of the provisions of this Act ... provided ... that no repeal or alteration of the *provisions contained in this section*[5] or in sections 35 or 137 shall be valid unless the Bill embodying such repeal or alteration shall be passed by both Houses of Parliament sitting together and at the third reading be agreed to by not less than two-thirds of the total number of members of both Houses ...

In 1952 the South African government, which was anxious to disfranchise coloured voters, claimed that it was competent for the Union Parliament to repeal these entrenched clauses by the ordinary processes of legislation. This claim was not based on any theory that self-referring laws were as such inoperative or invalid but on the nature of certain subsequent legislation, particularly the Statute of Westminster which, according to the government's case, had converted the Union Parliament into a 'sovereign' or 'absolute' legislature. This claim was rejected by the South African courts,[6] and the South African government, in order to effect its policies, was forced to use an expedient which actually recognized the validity of the self-entrenched section 152. It increased the membership of the legislature and 'packed' it so as to obtain the special majority required by that section for its own repeal.

It is to be noted that this self-entrenched clause, like the self-sanctioning rule discussed earlier, refers both to itself and to other clauses. A *purely* self-referring clause of this kind, providing only for its own repeal, like a purely self-referring law prescribing sanctions only for itself, would be logically

---

[5] Emphasis added.
[6] See *Harris* v. *Dönges* (1952) 1 T.L.R. 1245. Cf. G. Marshall, *Parliamentary Sovereignty and the Commonwealth* (Oxford 1957), ch. XI.

incomplete and for similar reasons. For the idea of a law relating to the repeal of a law is parasitic upon the idea of a law which does not only refer to repeals. Given an ultimate reference to such other laws there is, it seems to me, no reason why a law should not also refer to its own repeal.

Professor Alf Ross in his fascinating chapter on legislation takes the view that neither a statute nor a constitution can state the conditions for its own amendment. He says that 'reflexivity' of this sort is logically impossible and concludes that Article V of the American constitution which provides for the amendment of the constitution including itself cannot have any legal effect. 'Any amendment of article V which is in fact carried out is an alegal act and not the creation of law by way of a procedure that has been instituted.'[7] Professor Ross does not go so far as to say that such self-referring laws are meaningless; and indeed he says several things which imply that they are not only meaningful but understood. He admits that 'all politicians in positions of authority do in fact act on the assumption that Article V legally can be amended and only be amended by a certain procedure, namely that indicated in Article V itself'.[8] But this he says is merely a 'social psychological fact'. He even concedes that 'it is difficult to imagine Article V of the constitution being changed except by a process which looks like a legal procedure determined by Article V itself',[9] but he attributes this to the domination of ideas which can be expressed only in 'magical' terms. 'The procedure laid down by Article V is the magical act which alone can loose the bond forged by the article itself.'[10]

I find this position very puzzling. If, as Professor Ross says, it is difficult to imagine a change in Article V except by the process it prescribes, it must be clear not only to Professor Ross or to 'politicians' but also to courts of law what that process is. If the courts distinguish changes made by that process from changes or purported changes not so made and treat the former as valid and the latter as invalid surely the former cannot be an 'alegal' act or 'a merely factual social-psychological change'. Even if it were the case that the judges who apply Article V according to its terms would not do this

---

[7] Op. cit. n. 2 *supra*, 81.   [8] Ibid.
[9] Ibid. 83.   [10] Ibid.

if they believed with Professor Ross that it is logically impossible for a law to refer to itself, the distinction still remains
between a constitutional change which is valid according to
the law as interpreted by the courts and one which is invalid.
And must not such a change be a legal act? Does it matter
that the courts themselves only decide as they do because
they are under the sway of 'magical' ideas in the sense (if it
is one) that they, unlike Professor Ross, believe a law may
refer to itself?

Professor Ross in support of his view that no statute or
constitution can provide for its own amendment invokes the
doctrine which he says is generally recognized by logicians
that no proposition can refer to itself.[11] But he uses one argument which seems independent of this general doctrine. He
says 'if Article V of the Constitution is in fact amended in
conformity with its own rules, it is not possible to regard the
new Article V as derived from the old one or as valid because
derived from it. Any such derivation presupposes the validity
of the superior norm and thereby the continued existence of
the same, and by derivation cannot be established a new norm
which conflicts with the source of the derivation'.[12]

Two points in this argument seem to me questionable. The
first is the statement that a derivation of a new norm presupposes not only the validity of the superior norm but its
continued existence after the creation of the new norm. The
second is the suggestion that if Article V were amended in
conformity with its own rules the new norm so created would
'conflict with the source of derivations'. Perhaps both these
points neglect the following consideration. If Article V is
interpreted as providing for its own amendment its effect is
to prescribe the use of a certain procedure until that procedure is replaced by a new procedure introduced by the old
procedure. Surely we would distinguish this as a legally valid
change and a 'derivation' as compared with an attempt to introduce the new procedure in some totally different way. It
may be true, at least in some cases, that a new norm cannot
be derived from 'a source of derivation' with which it conflicts. But there is no conflict if Article V is amended in accordance with its own provisions. For the original Article V

---

[11] Ibid. 81.   [12] Ibid. 82.

and the amended article relate to different periods of time: the original procedure is to be used *until* it is replaced by the new, and the new procedure is to be used thereafter.

Professor Ross illustrates these arguments about Article V by appealing to what he considers a less complicated case. This is the case of an 'absolute' monarch who purports to grant by the exercise of his powers a new constitution limiting his powers and intended to be irrevocable. This Professor Ross says 'cannot be regarded as deriving from his absolute power'.[13] His reason for saying this is 'that it is not possible that anything can appear in the conclusion of a valid deductive inference which is in conflict with the premises'. To this it might be objected that the exercise of legislative powers to introduce new norms is not a deductive inference and it is not clear how this logical principle applies to a legislative act. But even if we waive this point and treat it simply as reassertion of the previous point that no norm can be derived from a norm with which it conflicts, there is surely no conflict in this case. The statement that a monarch has unlimited powers until he limits them is quite compatible with the statement that after he limits them they are limited.

Of course all depends on what is meant in this context by an 'absolute monarchy'. If it means that at each moment of the monarch's existence he has a *continuing* power to legislate as he pleases on any topic except the limitation of his powers, then of course he cannot irrevocably limit his powers. But it is quite possible to give a *'self-embracing'* interpretation to 'absolute power' so that the monarch has power to legislate on all topics including the irrevocable limitation of his powers. These two alternative forms of absolute power, continuing and self-embracing, are both intelligible as constitutional arrangements, and they have both been considered by lawyers with reference to the sovereignty of the British Parliament and by philosophers with reference to the omnipotence of God.[14]

Finally, a word about the logical doctrine that no proposition can refer to itself, which Professor Ross says is generally recognized by logicians. It might be objected that laws are

---

[13] Ibid.
[14] See my *Concept of Law* (Oxford 1961), 145-9; and J. L. Mackie, 'Evil and Omnipotence', *Mind*, 64 (1955), 212.

not propositions and the application of this principle to laws cannot be assumed. Nor can it be assumed that, even if it applies to purely self-referring laws, it also applies to laws which like Article V refer also to other laws. In any case I am sure a wholesale rejection of self-reference is not generally accepted by logicians.[15] There are many different forms of self-reference requiring separate consideration. Some forms of self-reference such as 'This statement is written in English' or 'I am whispering this statement' are patently innocent of any logical vice. Professor Popper has collected some of these and also reminded us that Gödel, in the proof of one of the greatest logical discoveries of modern times, actually demonstrates and uses the self-referring sentence 'This expression is a well-formed formula'. No doubt 'This is false' can be shown to lead to well-known contradictions, and 'This is true' is no doubt empty and incomplete. But neither section 152 of the South Africa Act nor Article V of the American Constitution lead to contradictions, nor are they incomplete. This excites the suspicion that there is no general principle of logic which leads to the strange conclusion that, even though law courts hold these self-referring provisions valid, yet when changes are made in them by the procedure which they prescribe these changes are 'alegal' or merely 'magical' acts.[16]

POSTSCRIPT

See for criticisms: A. Ross, 'On Self Reference as a Puzzle in Constitutional Law', *Mind*, 78 (1969), 1–24.

---

[15] See, for example, L. R. Popper, 'Self-Reference and Meaning in Ordinary Lanugage', *Mind*, 63 (1954).

[16] Perhaps 'This is true', like a purely self-referring law, is objectionable, though it leads to no contradictions, because the idea of a statement being true is incomplete unless it refers ultimately to statements which do not only refer to truth or falsity. So, like a partly self-referring law, a partly self-referring statement which referred to its own truth as well as that of other statements may be unobjectionable. Compare (in this aspect only in spite of many important differences) with the two-rule legal system on 172 *supra* a list of two statements, namely (1) Grass is green (2) Every statement on this list is true including this one. But statements ascribing *falsity* to themselves require separate consideration. See, on partly self-referring statements, J. L. Mackie, *Truth, Probability, and Paradox* (Oxford 1973), 285–90.

PART IV

LIBERTY, UTILITY, AND RIGHTS

Essay 8

Utilitarianism and Natural Rights

I

Just over 200 years ago when Britain's American colonies finally broke away and declared their independence, two major political philosophies confronted each other across the Atlantic. The American Declaration of Independence of 1776 invoked, in some famous brief sentences, the doctrine that all men are created equal and possessed of the natural unalienable rights of man: rights to life, liberty, and the pursuit of happiness, and that it was to secure these rights that governments, deriving their just powers from the consent of the governed, were instituted among men. But only three months before the Declaration of Independence was signed, Jeremy Bentham had announced to the world in his first book *A Fragment on Government* his famous formulation of the principles of utilitarianism, according to which both government and the limits of government were to be justified by appeal to very different principles: *not* by reference to the rights of individuals, and certainly not by reference to an allegedly natural species of right, but by reference to 'the greatest happiness of the greatest number'.[1] Later the same year Bentham inserted into an *Answer to the Declaration*, published by a close friend and collaborator,[2] a brief critical attack on the whole conception of natural and unalienable rights. In this work the doctrine of natural rights is rudely dismissed, partly as self-contradictory nonsense and partly as an intelligible but dangerous doctrine quite incompatible, if taken seriously, with the exercise of any powers of government whatsoever: as Bentham in this *Answer to the Declaration* asked, 'If the right of pursuit of happiness is a right *unalienable*, why are thieves restrained

---

[1] Bentham, *A Fragment on Government*, in 1 *Works* 221, 227 (Bowring edn. 1838-43).

[2] J. Lind, *An Answer to the Declaration of the American Congress* 120-2 (London 1776). For the identification of Bentham's contribution see Hart, 'Bentham and the United States', 19 *J.L. & Econ.* 547, 555 n. 37 (1976), reprinted in my *Essays on Bentham* (Oxford 1982), ch. III.

from pursuing it by theft, murderers by murder, and rebels by rebellion . . .?'[3]. These charges Bentham later repeated in a much expanded form in his essay on *Anarchical Fallacies*[4] which he wrote in response to the French Declaration of the Rights of Man of 1791. Though in this later attack the criticism is much more detailed and sophisticated, the main charges are the same: the doctrine of natural rights is in part nonsense and in part dangerously anarchical, undermining good and bad government alike: it was, said Bentham, so much '*bawling* upon paper',[5] not only 'nonsense' but 'nonsense upon stilts'.[6] Government among men exists not because men have rights prior to government which government is to preserve, but because without government and law men have no rights and can have none. The test of good government is not natural right, but the general happiness of the governed.

The crucial difference between these two doctrines thus opposed in 1776 is that utilitarianism is a *maximizing* and collective principle requiring governments to maximize the total net sum or balance of the happiness of all its subjects, whereas natural right is a *distributive* and individualizing principle according priority to specific basic interests of each individual subject.

Bentham knew that he had special talents for setting ideas to work in changing the world as well as understanding it. So he dedicated his energies throughout his long life to the detailed elaboration and application of the 'greatest happiness' principle (as he preferred to call the principle of utilitarianism), secure in the conviction that he was endowed with a unique capacity for this task and able to perform it more powerfully, more fully, more clearly, and with more patience and convincing detail than any previous thinker who had based criticism of government and society on utilitarian principles.

It was, I think, in part due to Bentham's extraordinary powers of exposition and his passion for working out in many detailed schemes of reform the practical consequences

---

[3] Letter from Jeremy Bentham to John Lind (2 Sept. 1776), in 1 *Correspondence of Jeremy Bentham* 343 (T. Sprigge edn. 1968) (vol. 1 of *Collected Works of Jeremy Bentham* (London 1968); see Lind, *supra* n. 2, at 121.

[4] Bentham, *Anarchical Fallacies*, in 2 *Works* 491 (Bowring edn. 1838–43).

[5] Ibid. at 494.

[6] Ibid. at 501.

of utilitarianism that, although his doctrines were at first ignored and later much criticized, eventually they came to dominate English social thought for a long time. For much of the nineteenth century 'utilitarianism' became in England almost synonymous with progressive political and social thought. As Elie Halévy said, it seemed as if all reforms during the nineteenth century were forced to speak the language of utilitarianism.[7] By contrast, the doctrine of natural rights (which had at the time of the American Revolution many English supporters) seemed to disappear from practical policies and controversy, as if vanquished by Bentham's onslaughts. Few advocates of constitutional or legal reforms in nineteenth-century England or even America invoked this conception. Of course utilitarianism — or as it was often called Benthamism — had many critics in nineteenth-century England, and during Bentham's lifetime much of his work, famous abroad, was ignored at home. But the critics' own positive political or social philosophies, so far as they had any, were not framed in terms of the doctrine of the rights of man. Even in America, when after Independence the thirteen revolting colonies began to fashion constitutions first for themselves and then for the Union finally formed in 1789, their efforts were inspired by principles which fell far short of those announced in the Declaration of Independence of 1776. Slavery was accepted both by the constitutions of most individual states and of the Union, without any serious attempt to show how this could be reconciled with a theory that all men were created equal and equally endowed with a natural unalienable right to liberty. Even among the free, white, male population in America the advance after independence to a full democratic franchise was very slow.

Read in the light of these facts the famous opening words of the American Constitution of 1789, which state that it is 'to establish justice, ensure domestic tranquility, provide for the common defence, promote the general welfare and secure the blessings of liberty', seem to express a theory that the main aim of government was not the maintenance of universal individual rights, but the maximization of general welfare and the interests of the new nation as a whole, even if that

[7] E. Halévy, *The Growth of Philosophic Radicalism* 153–4 (M. Morris trans. 1952).

involved, as it did in the case of slaves, the sacrifice for some of individual liberty and happiness.

So Bentham's successive attacks on the doctrine of natural rights had a long-enduring success throughout the nineteenth century. I shall consider here a little more closely the detail of that attack as it appears in the essay on *Anarchical Fallacies* which is the most elaborate expression of his view. This work, written in 1795 but not published till after Bentham's death, is curious. It is prolix and pedantic but also written with great vehemence and passion. Bentham condemned 'the rights of anarchy' (as he called natural rights) as compatible only with 'the order of chaos';[8] their advocates were, he said, 'subverters of government'[9] and 'assassins of security'[10] who discussed serious political issues in a foolish terminology out of which Bentham said 'may start a thousand daggers'.[11] Indeed he thought the doctrine so apt to inflame unthinking passions that its repression by the criminal law might be justified.

To understand Bentham's extravagances it must be remembered that this work was written when the Jacobin Terror was at its height and this had turned Bentham, as many others, from initial support of the French revolution into scared opposition. Indeed in Bentham's case it had done something more important. Bentham in 1776 was no democrat, and for at least ten years afterwards he held that there was no need for reform in constitutional England where vast numbers had no vote. In 1790 however[12] he sketched out a utilitarian case for democracy and full manhood suffrage. But fear of anarchy and horror of the excesses of the Terror caused Bentham to put aside consideration of democratic reforms and to devote his time to writing strongly conservative pamphlets, arguing that in England there was no need for constitutional reform or any move towards democracy. It was not till 1809 that Bentham recovered his nerve from the shock of the Terror. Then, convinced that there was a case for democracy based not on the illusory rights of man but on the sure foundation

---

[8] Bentham, *supra* n. 4, at 522.
[9] Ibid. at 523.
[10] Ibid.
[11] Ibid. at 497.
[12] For an account of this unpublished work entitled 'On the Efficient Cause and Measure of Constitutional Liberty', see Hart, *supra* n. 2, at 558-9.

of utilitarianism, he became a fervent advocate of radical democratic reforms of the British Constitution.[13]

Bentham was converted to democracy because he had learnt to take a deeply pessimistic view of all governments, the 'ruling few' as he called them. He viewed governments as gangs of potential criminals, tempted like robbers to pursue their own interests at the expense of those over whom they had power, 'the subject many'.[14] But democracy, by placing the power of appointment and dismissal of governments in the hands of the majority was, he thought, the best device for securing that governments worked for the general interest by making it in their interests to do so, just as the threat of punishment for ordinary crime effected an artificial harmony of interests of the individual and society by securing that potential criminals conformed, however reluctantly, to the requirements of the general welfare. These plain, indeed blunt, considerations were what Bentham offered as a sane and sober man's guide to democracy, instead of the half intelligible and wild assertions of natural right.

Bentham attacked the notion of natural rights in two main ways. First he claimed that the idea of a right not created by positive law was a contradiction in terms like 'cold heat' or 'resplendent darkness':[15] rights, he claimed, are all fruits of positive law, and the assertion that there were rights antecedent to and independent of human law was only saved from immediate exposure as manifest absurdity because men had been misled into talking of a natural *law* as a source of a natural right. But both these were nonentities, as is shown by the fact that if there is a dispute as to whether a man has some legal right and what its scope is, this is an issue about an objective ascertainable fact which can be rationally resolved by reference to the terms of the relevant positive law, or failing that, by reference to a court of law. No such rational resolution or objective decision-making procedure is available to settle the question whether a man has a natural non-legal right, say to freedom of speech or assembly. There is no similar agreed

[13] See Bentham, *Plan of Parliamentary Reform*, in 3 *Works* 433, 451-8 (Bowring edn. 1838-43) (with an introduction stressing the need for radical and not moderate reform).

[14] Ibid. at 441.

[15] Bentham, *Supply Without Burthen*, in 1 *Jeremy Bentham's Economic Writings* 279, 335 (W. Stark edn. 1952).

test to establish the existence or non-existence of a natural right, no settled law by which it can be known. So Bentham said, 'Lay out of the question the idea of *law* and all that you get by the use of the word *right*, is a sound to dispute about.'[16] There are no rights anterior to law and no rights contrary to law, so though it may express a speaker's feelings, wishes, or prejudices, the doctrine of natural rights cannot serve, as utilitarianism can, as an objective limit rationally discernible and discussable on what laws may properly do or require. Men speak of their natural rights, said Bentham, when they wish to get their way without having to argue for it.[17]

Bentham's second criticism is that the use of the notion of natural non-legal rights in political controversy and in criticism of established laws and social institutions must either be impossible to reconcile with the exercise of any powers of government, and so dangerously anarchical, or it will be totally empty or nugatory.[18] It will be the former if the natural rights which men claim are absolute in form allowing no exceptions or compromise with other values. Men who have strong feelings against some established law will, by using the objective-sounding language of unalienable rights, be able to present such feelings as something more: as claims of something superior to established law, rendering established law 'void' and setting limits to what laws can do or require. Alternatively, if natural rights are not represented as absolute in form but allow for general exceptions (as the French Declaration did) — if, for example, the alleged natural right of freedom is put forward as something never to be abridged except when the law allows this — they are 'nugatory', empty guides both to legislators and their subjects. It had been thus nugatory in some of the new American states where express declarations in their constitutions of a natural right to liberty was held not to affect the slave-owner's rights to property in his slaves. So, concludes Bentham, natural rights are either impossible to reconcile with ordered government, since the exercise of governmental powers always involves some limitation of freedom or property, or they are nugatory, empty, and useless.

[16] Bentham, *Securities Against Misrule*, in 8 *Works* 555, 557 (Bowring edn. 1838–43).
[17] Bentham, *supra* n. 15, at 335.
[18] Bentham, *supra* n. 4, at 493, 502.

Bentham's lengthy critique of natural rights, scattered over his various works, comprised many other objections besides the two I have mentioned, but these two took a firm root in English political theory. In particular the thesis that there are only legal rights, that the idea of rights anterior to or contrary to law is absurd, became for a time part of conventional wisdom and was accepted almost as a truism by many English social thinkers. So much so that even the poet and critic Matthew Arnold, who was only marginally concerned with political philosophy or constitutional theory, and was certainly in general unsympathetic to utilitarianism, when arguing in 1878 that many unsatisfactory features in the social life of mid-Victorian England were due to its great economic and social inequality, felt it incumbent upon him to disclaim any belief in any moral or non-legal right to equality or to anything else. Using language exactly conforming to Bentham's ideas he said, 'So far as I can sound human consciousness, I cannot, as I have often said, perceive that man is really conscious of any abstract natural rights at all. . . . It cannot be too often repeated: peasants and workmen have no natural rights, not one. Only we ought instantly to add, that kings and nobles have none either. If it is [a] sound English doctrine that all rights are created by law . . . certainly that orthodox doctrine is mine.'[19]

II

The first serious challenge to the 'sound English doctrine', as Matthew Arnold called it, that there are no rights except those created by law and hence no moral and above all no natural rights, came paradoxically from Bentham's most famous disciple John Stuart Mill, who always proclaimed himself a utilitarian though in many ways it seems to us now that he preserved only the letter while changing the spirit of the original utilitarian doctrine in many important ways.

Mill claimed, as a good utilitarian, to abjure the use of what he termed 'abstract right',[20] but he reached the conclusion that, unless the idea of a moral non-legal right is admitted, no

[19] Arnold, 'Equality', in *Mixed Essays, Irish Essays and Others* 36, 46 (1883).
[20] J. S. Mill, *On Liberty*, in 18 *Collected Works of John Stuart Mill* 213, 224 (J. Robson edn. 1977).

account of justice as a distinct segment of morality could be given. This is so, he thought, because justice consists principally in respect for fundamental moral rights which all men have, whether or not any particular society recognizes such rights in its law or social practice. Mill claimed that there could be no conflict between justice so defined as respect for fundamental rights and utilitarian political morality.[21] In this, I think, he was mistaken, for in the last resort there is an unbridgeable gap between pure utilitarianism, for which the maximization of the total aggregate general welfare or happiness is the ultimate criterion of value, and a philosophy of basic human rights, which insists on the priority of principles protecting, in the case of each man, certain aspects of individual welfare and recognizing these as constraints on the maximizing aggregative principle of utilitarianism.

None the less, Mill's arguments deserve serious consideration. They are a most illuminating precursor of present twentieth-century thought on these matters. He hoped to show that in spite of common opinion to the contrary, justice and the respect for individual rights which justice requires do not conflict with utility but are part of it. This indeed follows from his definition of what it is to have a moral right. 'To have a right', Mill says, is 'to have something which society ought to defend me in the possession of. . . . If the objector goes on to ask why it ought [to do so], I can give him no other reason than general utility'.[22] Mill, in his attempted reconciliation of justice with utility, argued that justice and respect for fundamental rights represent a particular 'kind or branch of general utility'[23] which men recognized as having a superior binding force to ordinary claims of utility. He says that in the case of individual rights the interests of the individual which are at stake constitute '[an] extraordinarily important and impressive kind of utility' which he describes in a number of striking phrases: '[something] no human being can possibly do without'; 'the very groundwork of our existence'; 'the essentials of human wellbeing'.[24] He explains that

[21] J. S. Mill, *Utilitarianism*, in 10 *Collected Works of John Stuart Mill* 203, 240-1 (J. Robson edn. 1969).
[22] Ibid. at 250.
[23] Ibid. at 241.
[24] Ibid. at 250-1.

among the interests included in this special kind of utility of fundamental rights are the individual's security from harm inflicted by others, and from wrongful interference with his freedom to pursue his own good. These he says are 'utilities which are vastly more important, and therefore more absolute and imperative',[25] than any others and are to be sharply distinguished from the mere idea of promoting human pleasure, happiness, or convenience. The sentiment which guards these essential individual utilities is 'not only different in degree, but also in kind', says Mill, from the milder feeling attaching to the promotion of human pleasure or convenience.[26] Mill's conception of this special kind of utility consisting in certain specific protections of individual freedom and basic interests, and his consequent characterization of the particular moral rights in the recognition of which justice consists, corresponds very closely to some elements stressed in formulations of natural or human rights from the French Declaration of the Rights of Man of the eighteenth century to the United Nations Declaration of Human Rights of our own day. For claims to such rights are centrally claims to what is necessary, not merely to secure increases in totals of pleasure or happiness, but to what men, endowed with distinctively human capacities of thought, rational choice and action, need if they are to be able to pursue their own individual ends as progressive beings; that is they need first, a wide area of freedom from interference and second, protection from the most palpable forms of physical harm. Jefferson, it will be remembered, distinguished between happiness and the right to pursue happiness, and freedom of thought and choice has always been the organizing centre of assertions of human rights.

It is most important that Mill conceived that these fundamental rights described by him as a special kind of utility should be respected by society in the case of each individual. The principles at stake, he says, 'protect every individual from being harmed by others',[27] and he adds that '[i]t is by a person's observance of these [moralities] that his fitness to exist as one of the fellowship of human beings, is tested and decided'.[28] Mill therefore recognizes an equal distribution as vital where these fundamental rights are concerned: *all* are to

---

[25] Ibid. at 259.   [26] Ibid.
[27] Ibid. at 256.   [28] Ibid.

have them respected. Yet he nowhere demonstrates or even attempts to demonstrate the doctrine that general utility, as Bentham conceived it, is the basis of such individual rights, since he does not show that general utility treated as an aggregate would be maximized by an equal distribution to all individuals in society of these fundamental rights. There is therefore nothing to counter the sceptic who would argue that if general utility had any meaning it must be logically possible that the total net balance of ease, pleasure and happiness of a society over pain or unhappiness might be greater, *not* where those fundamental rights were equally distributed to all members alike, but where a minority, say a small slave population, or even a few individuals, were denied these essentials of human well-being in order that the vast majority should receive increments in the means of pleasure or happiness, each small in themselves but large in the aggregate. The difficulty for Mill arises from the possibility that a society might protect the vast majority of its members by rules which made exceptions for a small oppressed minority. Utilitarian principles as ordinarily understood might be satisfied by this, but a doctrine of natural rights could not be.

Perhaps Mill's invocation of 'general utility' as the foundation of basic rights to which *all* men are entitled is to be understood (though not, I think, successfully defended) in the following way. The freedom and interests protected by such rights constitute a distinct segment of utility; they are, as Mill says, the 'primary moralities', the maximization of which is to have priority over any advance, however great, in other forms of utility, which Mill variously calls 'the mere idea of promoting human pleasure or convenience' or 'ordinary expediency'. Since the basic rights impose mainly negative constraints on others, requiring their abstention from certain kinds of harmful conduct, the 'maximization' of this distinct segment of utility can only mean the total utility of respecting such rights in the case of every individual. This distinct form of utility could not be increased by denying such rights to some individuals; if, on the other hand, it were not kept distinct from and given priority over other forms of utility, but simply added to them, then total utility might be increased by denial to some individuals of benefits, even by denial of the basic rights.

But though the priority thus accorded to the utility of the basic rights is perfectly intelligible, Mill leaves obscure the sense in which 'general utility' can be said to be their foundation. For if the 'maximization' of this distinct segment of utility consists only in respecting the basic rights in the case of every individual, then respecting the rights of any one individual necessarily increases general utility because it *is* such an increase and the only thing that could count as an increase. It is difficult therefore to see how 'general utility' could be the *reason*, as Mill says it is, for respecting an individual's rights. Surely only if an increase in general utility was a value distinct from respecting an individual's rights could it be the reason for respecting them.

III

Bentham's utilitarianism met, as I have said, with much criticism even during the nineteenth century at the time of its greatest influence on the thought of political and social reformers. But very few of any of those criticisms were accompanied by any revival of the doctrine of natural right. The most serious philosophical criticisms concerned the theoretical and practical difficulties facing a utilitarian 'calculus' or reckoning of totals of net happiness, pleasure, or welfare. This required the pains and pleasures of different persons to be compared, added, and subtracted in order to determine what course of conduct would produce the greatest net balance of happiness over all. The most widespread criticisms of Bentham's utilitarianism were made by some of the great literary figures of the time. These were often based on a gross misunderstanding of Bentham's thought. Whereas Bentham explicitly identified the utility which was to be maximized with pleasure and happiness arising from any source — from the intellect, from friendship, from honours, as well as the senses — some of his critics identified it with mere sensuous pleasure. Other critics like Hazlitt,[29] Carlyle,[30] and Dickens[31]

---

[29] W. Hazlitt, *The Spirit of the Age*, in 11 *Complete Works of William Hazlitt* 1 (P. Howe edn. 1932).
[30] T. Carlyle, *Sartor Resartus*, in 1 *Collected Works of Thomas Carlyle* 116, 213–14, 226–8 (1887).
[31] C. Dickens, *Hard Times* (New York 1868).

even contrasted utility with enjoyment of life or happiness as if it meant solely the production of material goods at the cost of grinding labour. The utilitarian spirit, said Dickens, was an iron-binding of the mind to grim realities.[32]

Many refinements, some very sophisticated, designed to meet these and other criticisms, were made of Bentham's original doctrine by later utilitarians in the nineteenth century. The most important amendment made to avoid the difficulties of the utilitarian calculus was to restate the doctrine not in terms of pleasure or of happiness but in terms of the satisfaction of desires or what the welfare economists would call 'revealed preferences'. The ultimate criterion for governments to follow would then become maximum satisfaction and minimum frustration of such wants or preferences, and in this reformulation some of the difficulties of measurement and interpersonal comparison were avoided, with the aid of ideas drawn from economists, notably Pareto.

But all these were matters of comparative detail, leaving untouched the central idea of utilitarianism both as a standard of personal morality and as a critique of government, that all that matters morally is the maximization of a single collective or aggregate or total value whether it is called pleasure, happiness, or want satisfaction.

The first fundamental criticism of this central maximizing principle is again to be found implicit in John Stuart Mill's work. It is implicit in his account of justice already mentioned, but even more importantly in his influential reflections on liberty, in the essay of that name. Bentham, it will be recalled, in making his own slow transition from Tory supporter of the unreformed British Constitution to radical democrat, thought that utilitarianism provided entirely adequate reasons for preferring democracy with manhood suffrage to any other form of government, because only a government dependent on popular election could have sufficient incentive to work for the general interest rather than the sinister interest of a governing few. So his critique of constitutional or political structures was rather like that of a business efficiency expert on a grand scale examining the structure of a firm, and political theorists of our own day have produced some highly

---

[32] C. Dickens, *Household Words* (issue of 30 March 1850).

sophisticated versions of this type of quasi-economic approach to political theory. But Mill valued democracy for quite other reasons: not merely as the protection of the majority against exploitation by the few and against the inefficiency of governments, but as affording the opportunity to all to develop their distinctive human capacities for thought, choice and self-direction by partaking in political decisions, even in the minimal form of voting at intermittent elections. But Mill also thought that the tyranny of the majority over a minority was as great a danger as the tyranny of a minority government or despotism against which Bentham thought democracy the best protection. So a political morality which like utilitarianism places political power in the hands of the majority is not enough to secure a good, liberal society. It matters very much what the majority do with the power which is put in their hands; so there is need for constraints in the form of distinct principles of political morality whether or not they are translated into law in the form of a bill of rights. 'The limitations of the power of government over individuals,' said Mill, 'loses none of its importance when the holders of power are regularly accountable to the community — that is to the strongest party therein.'[33]

Hence, when Mill came to discuss the liberty of the individual he argued that it was only to be interfered with or restricted (whether by law or social pressure) when the conduct of the individual is harmful to others, whereas a strict maximizing utilitarian would have to allow that the freedom of an individual might always be restricted if this would increase the total aggregate welfare of society. Mill's doctrine of liberty is on this point a striking departure from the maximizing principle of utilitarianism and the effect of it is to secure for each individual an area of freedom for the whole range of his activities which are not harmful to others. Since it offers this protection to the freedom of the individual *as such*, it secures the same area of liberty for all individuals and thus a measure of equality, whereas pure utilitarianism is in no way committed to equality of treatment as an independent value. Of course Mill's doctrine is not without its famous ambiguities or difficulties, mainly flowing from the open-textured or

<hr>

[33] Mill, *supra* n. 20, at 219.

vague character of the concept of 'harm to others', but it is a striking departure from the maximizing principle of utilitarianism.

However, only in our own time has a direct frontal attack been made on the central maximizing principle of utilitarianism. This modern critique has been developed largely in the United States in the last twenty years, most notably in John Rawls's *A Theory of Justice*,[34] which is the most important work of political philosophy written in English since John Stuart Mill. Rawls's work is already profoundly influential, though both its critique of utilitarianism and its positive theory of basic rights is controversial and incomplete. A similar critique of utilitarianism is now to be found in many other modern writers, American and English.[35]

The thrust of this modern critique consists of a claim that utilitarianism 'does not take seriously the distinction between persons',[36] since it licenses the imposition of sacrifices in individual cases whenever this can be shown to advance aggregate welfare. Persons on this view are of no intrinsic value, but are merely the receptacles for the experiences which will increase or diminish the sole intrinsic value, namely aggregate welfare.

These considerations show why utilitarianism, once regarded as the great inspiration of progressive social thought, also possesses a darker sinister side permitting the sacrifice of one individual to secure the greater happiness of others.

Accordingly, the contemporary modern philosophers of whom I have spoken, and pre-eminently Rawls in his *Theory of Justice*, have argued that any morally adequate political philosophy must recognize that there must be, in any morally tolerable form of social life, certain protections for the freedom and basic interests of individuals which constitute an essential framework of individual rights. Though the pursuit of the general welfare is indeed a legitimate and indeed necessary concern of governments, it is something to be pursued

[34] J. Rawls, *A Theory of Justice* 22–4, 27, 181, 183, 187 (1971).
[35] E.g., R. Dworkin, *Taking Rights Seriously* (1977); J. Mackie, *Ethics: Inventing Right and Wrong* (1977); R. Nozick, *Anarchy, State, and Utopia* (1974); B. Williams, *Morality: An Introduction to Ethics* (1972).
[36] See Rawls, op. cit. n. 34 *supra* at 187. I examine this claim in detail in my 'Between Utility and Rights', Essay 9 *infra*.

only within certain constraints imposed by recognition of such rights.

The modern philosophical defence put forward for the recognition of basic human rights does not wear the same metaphysical or conceptual dress as the earlier doctrines of the seventeenth- and eighteenth-century rights of man, which men were said to have in a state of nature or to be endowed with by their creator. None the less, the most complete and articulate version of this modern critique of utilitarianism has many affinities with the theories of social contract which in the seventeenth and eighteenth centuries accompanied the doctrine of natural rights. Thus Rawls has argued in *A Theory of Justice* that though any rational person must know that in order to live even a minimally tolerable life he must live within a political society with an ordered government, no rational person bargaining with others on a footing of equality could agree to regard himself as bound to obey the laws of any government if his freedom and basic interests, what Mill called 'the groundwork of human existence', were not given protection and treated as having priority over mere increases in aggregate welfare, even if the protection cannot be absolute.

Both the philosophical foundations of this new critique of utilitarianism and the detailed application of its doctrine of basic rights to contemporary constitutional, social and economic problems of society are still highly controversial. It cannot be said that we have had, either from the European or from American political theorists who have now become acutely conscious of the defects of an undiluted maximizing utilitarianism, a sufficiently detailed or adequately articulate theory showing the foundation for such rights and how they are related to other values which are pursued through government. Nothing is yet available of this kind comparable in clarity and detailed articulation to Bentham's elaborate exposition and application of utilitarianism. Indeed the revived doctrines of basic rights, as currently presented, are in spite of much brilliance still unconvincing. In fact, I think, this is due to their authors seeking to define their point of view too exclusively in terms of the ways in which utilitarianism has ignored certain values taken to be uncontroversial, whereas what is first needed is some more radical and detailed consideration of the ways in which rights relate to other values pursued in society. Among such writers examples could now be found in both the Conservative Right and the Liberal Left of the political spectrum. The work of these writers certainly demands careful assessment, but that is a task for another time.[37]

Yet it is plain that a theory of rights is urgently called for. During the last half century man's inhumanity to man has been such that the most basic and elementary freedoms and protections have been denied to innumerable men and women guilty, if of anything, only of claiming such freedoms and protections for themselves and others, and sometimes these have been denied to them on the specious pretence that this denial is demanded by the general welfare of a society. So the protection of a doctrine of basic human rights limiting what a state may do to its citizens seems to be precisely what the political problems of our own age most urgently require, or at any rate they require this more urgently than a call to maximise general utility. And in fact the philosophical developments which I have sketched have been accompanied by a growth, recently accelerated, of an international human rights movement. Since 1946 when the signatories of the United Nations Charter affirmed their faith in fundamental human rights and the dignity and worth of the human person, no state can claim that the denial of such rights to its own citizens is solely its own business. I cannot here assess how much or how little the world has gained from the fact that in the thirty years which separate the signing of the United Nations Charter from the recent Helsinki Agreement, pressure for the implementation of basic human rights has become increasingly a feature of international relations, coventions, and diplomacy. Nor can I assess here how often cynical lip service to the doctrine has been, and still is, accompanied by cynical disregard of its principles. There is however no doubt that the conception of basic human rights has deeply affected the style of diplomacy, the morality, and the political ideology of our time, even though thousands of innocent persons still imprisoned or oppressed have not yet felt its benefits. The doctrine of human rights has at least temporarily replaced the doctrine of maximizing utilitarianism as the prime

---

[37] I attempt such an assessment in 'Between Utility and Rights', Essay 9 *infra*.

philosophical inspiration of political and social reform. It remains to be seen whether it will have as much success as utilitarianism once had in changing the practices of governments for human good.

POSTSCRIPT

See for an opposed view: D. Lyons, 'Human Rights and the General Welfare', 6 *Philosophy and Public Affairs* (1977); criticized in 'Natural Rights: Bentham and John Stuart Mill' in my *Essays on Bentham* (Oxford 1982), ch. IV.

Essay 9

Between Utility and Rights

I

I do not think that anyone familiar with what has been published in the last ten years, in England and the United States,
on the philosophy of government can doubt that this subject,
which is the meeting point of moral, political, and legal philosophy, is undergoing a major change. We are currently wit-
nessing, I think, the progress of a transition from a once
widely accepted old faith that some form of utilitarianism, if
only we could discover the right form, *must* capture the essence of political morality. The new faith is that the truth
must lie not with a doctrine that takes the maximization of
aggregate or average general welfare for its goal, but with a
doctrine of basic human rights, protecting specific basic liberties and interests of individuals, if only we could find some
sufficiently firm foundation for such rights to meet some
long-familiar objections. Whereas not so long ago great energy
and much ingenuity of many philosophers were devoted to
making some form of utilitarianism work, latterly such energies and ingenuity have been devoted to the articulation of
theories of basic rights.

As often with such changes of faith or redirection of philosophical energies and attention, the new insights which are
currently offered us seem to dazzle at least as much at they
illuminate. Certainly, as I shall try to show by reference to the
work of two now influential contemporary writers, the new
faith has been presented in forms which are, in spite of much
brilliance, in the end unconvincing. My two examples, both
American, are taken respectively from the Conservative Right
and the Liberal Left of the political spectrum; and while the
former builds a theory of rights on the moral importance of
the *separateness* or *distinctness* of human persons which utilitarianism is said to ignore, the latter seeks to erect such a
theory on their moral title to *equal concern and respect*
which, it is said, unreconstructed utilitarianism implicitly

denies. So while the first theory is dominated by the duty of governments to respect the separateness of persons, the second is dominated by the duty of governments to treat their subjects as equals, with equal concern and respect.

II

For a just appraisal of the first of these two theories it is necessary to gain a clear conception of what precisely is meant by the criticism, found in different forms in very many different modern writers, that unqualified utilitarianism fails to recognize or abstracts from the separateness of persons when, as a political philosophy, it calls on governments to maximize the total or the average net happiness or welfare of their subjects. Though this accusation of ignoring the separateness of persons can be seen as a version of the Kantian principle that human beings are ends in themselves, it is none the less the distinctively modern criticism of utilitarianism. In England Bernard Williams[1] and in America John Rawls[2] have been the most eloquent expositors of this form of criticism; and John Rawls's claim that 'Utilitarianism does not take seriously the distinction between persons'[3] plays a very important role in his *A Theory of Justice*. Only faint hints of this particular criticism flickered through the many different attacks made in the past on utilitarian doctrine, ever since Jeremy Bentham in 1776 announced to the world that both government and the limits of government were to be justified by reference to the greatest happiness of the greatest number, and not by reference to any doctrine of natural rights: such doctrines he thought so much 'bawling upon paper',[4] and he first announced them in 1776 in a brief rude reply[5] to the American Declaration of Independence.

---

[1] 'A Critique of Utilitarianism', in J. Smart and B. Williams, *Utilitarianism, For and Against* 108–18 (1973); and 'Persons, Character and Morality' in *The Identity of Persons* (Rorty edn., 1977).

[2] See J. Rawls, *A Theory of Justice* 22–4, 27, 181, 183, 187 (1971).

[3] Ibid. at 187.

[4] Bentham, *Anarchical Fallacies*, in 2 *Works* 494 (Bowring edn., 1838–43).

[5] For an account of this reply included in *An Answer to the Declaration of the American Congress* (1776) by Bentham's friend John Lind, see my 'Bentham and the United States of America', 19 *J.L. & Econ.* 547, 555–6 (1976), reprinted in my *Essays on Bentham* (Oxford, 1982), ch. III.

What then does this distinctively modern criticism of utilitarianism, that it ignores the moral importance of the separateness of individuals, mean? I think its meaning is to be summed up in four main points, though not all the writers who make this criticism would endorse all of them.

The first point is this: In the perspective of classical maximizing utilitarianism separate individuals are of no intrinsic importance but only important as the points at which fragments of what *is* important, i.e. the total aggregate of pleasure or happiness, are located. Individual persons for it are therefore merely the channels or locations where what is of value is to be found. It is for this reason that as long as the totals are thereby increased there is nothing, if no independent principles of distribution are introduced, to limit permissible trade-offs between the satisfactions of different persons. Hence one individual's happiness or pleasure, however innocent he may be, may be sacrificed to procure a greater happiness or pleasure located in other persons, and such replacements of one person by another are not only allowed but required by unqualified utilitarianism when unrestrained by distinct distributive principles.

Secondly, utilitarianism is not, as sometimes it is said to be, an individualistic and egalitarian doctrine, although in a sense it treats persons as equals, or of equal worth. For it does this only by in effect treating individual persons as of *no* worth; since not persons for the utilitarian but the experiences of pleasure or satisfaction or happiness which persons have are the sole items of worth or elements of value. It is of course true and very important that, according to the utilitarian maxim, 'everybody [is] to count for one, nobody for more than one',[6] in the sense that in any application of the greatest happiness calculus the equal pains or pleasures, satisfactions or dissatisfactions or preferences of different persons are given the same weight whether they be Brahmins or Untouchables, Jews or Christians, black or white. But since utilitarianism has no direct or intrinsic concern but only an instrumental concern with the relative *levels* of total well-being enjoyed by different persons, its form of equal concern

---

[6] See J. S. Mill, *Utilitarianism* (ch. 5), in 10 *Collected Works of John Stuart Mill* 157 (1969); Bentham, *Plan of Parliamentary Reform*, in 3 *Works* 459 (Bowring edn. 1838–43).

and respect for persons embodied in the maxim 'everybody to count for one, nobody for more than one' may license the grossest form of inequality in the actual treatment of individuals, if that is required in order to maximize aggregate or average welfare. So long as that condition is satisfied, the situation in which a few enjoy great happiness while many suffer is as good as one in which happiness is more equally distributed.

Of course in comparing the aggregate economic welfare produced by equal and unequal distribution of resources account must be taken of factors such as diminishing marginal utility and also envy. These factors favour an equal distribution of resources, but by no means always favour it conclusively. For there are also factors pointing the other way, such as administrative and transaction costs, loss of incentives and failure of the standard assumption that all individuals are equally good pleasure or satisfaction machines, and derive the same utility from the same amount of wealth.

Thirdly, the modern critique of utilitarianism asserts that there is nothing self-evidently valuable or authoritative as a moral goal in the mere increase in totals of pleasure or happiness abstracted from all questions of distribution. The collective sum of different persons' pleasures, or the net balance of total happiness of different persons (supposing it makes sense to talk of adding them), is not in itself a pleasure or happiness which anybody experiences. Society is not an individual experiencing the aggregate collected pleasures or pains of its members; no person experiences such an aggregate.

Fourthly, according to this critique, maximizing utilitarianism, if it is not restrained by distinct distributive principles, proceeds on a false analogy between the way in which it is rational for a single prudent individual to order his life and the way in which it is rational for a whole community to order its life through government. The analogy is this: it is rational for one man as a single individual to sacrifice a present satisfaction or pleasure for a greater satisfaction later, even if we discount somewhat the value of the later satisfaction because of its uncertainty. Such sacrifices are amongst the most elementary requirements of prudence and are commonly accepted as a virtue, and indeed a paradigm of practical rationality, and, of course, any form of saving is an example of this form of rationality. In its misleading analogy with an individual's prudence, maximizing utilitarianism not merely treats one person's pleasure as replaceable by some greater pleasure of that same person, as prudence requires, but it also treats the pleasure or happiness of one individual as similarly replaceable without limit by the greater pleasure of other individuals. So in these ways it treats the division between persons as of no more moral significance than the division between times which separates one individual's earlier pleasure from his later pleasure, as if individuals were mere parts of a single persisting entity.

III

The modern insight that it is the arch-sin of unqualified utilitarianism to ignore in the ways I have mentioned the moral importance of the separateness of persons is, I think, in the main, a profound and penetrating criticism. It holds good when utilitarianism is restated in terms of maximum want or preference satisfaction and minimum want or preference frustration rather than in the Benthamite form of the balances of pleasure and pain as psychological states, and it holds good when the maximand is taken to be average rather than total general welfare. But it is capable of being abused to discredit all attempts to diminish inequalities and all arguments that one man's loss may be compensated by another's gain such as have inspired policies of social welfare; all these are discredited as if all necessarily committed the cardinal sin committed by maximizing utilitarianism of ignoring the separateness of individuals. This is I think the basis of the libertarian, strongly anti-utilitarian political theory developed by Robert Nozick in his influential book, *Anarchy, State, and Utopia*.[7] For Nozick a strictly limited set of near-absolute individual rights constitute the foundations of morality. Such rights for him 'express the inviolability of persons'[8] and 'reflect the fact of our separate existences'.[9] The rights are these: each individual, so long as he does not violate the same rights of others, has the right not to be killed or assaulted, to be free from all forms

---

[7] R. Nozick, *Anarchy, State, and Utopia* (1974).
[8] Ibid at 32.
[9] Ibid at 33.

of coercion or limitation of freedom, and the right not to have property, legitimately acquired, taken, or the use of it limited. He has also the secondary right to punish and exact compensation for violation of his rights, to defend himself and others against such violation. He has the positive right to acquire property by making or finding things and by transfer or inheritance from others, and he has the right to make such transfers and binding contracts. The moral landscape which Nozick explicitly presents contains only rights and is empty of everything else except possibly the moral permissibility of avoiding what he terms catastrophe. Hence moral wrongdoing has only one form: the violation of rights, perpetrating a wrong to the holder of a right. So long as rights are not violated it matters not for morality, short of catastrophe, how a social system actually works, how individuals fare under it, what needs it fails to meet or what misery or inequalities it produces. In this scheme of things the basic rights which fill the moral landscape and express the inviolability of persons are few in number but are all equally stringent. The only legitimate State on this view is one to which individuals have transferred their right to punish or exact compensation from others, and the State may not go beyond the night-watchman functions of using the transferred rights to protect persons against force, fraud, and theft or breaches of contract. In particular the State may not impose burdens on the wealth or income or restraints on the liberty of some citizens to relieve the needs or suffering, however great, of others. So a State may only tax its citizens to provide the police, the law courts, and the armed forces necessary for defence and the performance of the night-watchman functions. Taxing earnings or profits for the relief of poverty or destitution, however dire the need, or for the general welfare such as public education, is on this view morally indefensible; it is said to be 'on a par with' forced labour[10] or making the government imposing such taxes into a 'part owner' of the persons taxed.[11]

Nozick's development of this extreme libertarian position is wide-ranging. It is full of original and ingenious argument splendidly designed to shake up any complacent interventionist into painful self-scrutiny. But it rests on the slenderest

---

[10] Ibid. at 169.   [11] Ibid. at 172.

foundation. Indeed many critics have complained of the lack
of any argument to show that human beings have the few and
only the few but very stringent rights which Nozick assigns to
them to support his conclusion that a morally legitimate government cannot have any more extensive functions than the
night-watchman's. But the critics are wrong: there is argument
of a sort, though it is woefully deficient. Careful scrutiny
of his book shows that the argument consists of the assertion
that if the functions of government are not limited to the
protection of the basic stringent rights, then the arch-sin of
ignoring the separateness of persons which modern critics impute to utilitarianism will have been committed. To sustain
this argument Nozick at the start of his book envelops in
metaphors all policies imposing burdens or restraints going
beyond the functions of the night-watchman State, and the
metaphors are in fact all drawn from a description of the arch-
sin imputed to utilitarianism. Thus, not only is taxation said
to be the equivalent of forced labour, but every limitation of
property rights, every restriction of liberty for the benefit of
others going beyond the constraints imposed by the basic
rights, are described as *violating* a person,[12] as a *sacrifice* of
that person,[13] or as an outweighing of *one life* by others,[14] or
a treatment of a distinct individual as a *resource*[15] for others.
So conceptions of justice permitting a graduated income tax
to provide for basic needs or to diminish social or economic
inequalities are all said to neglect the basic truth 'that each
individual is a separate person, that his is the only life he
has'.[16] To hold that a person should bear costs that benefit
others more is represented as a *'sacrifice'* of that person and
as implying what is false: namely that there is a single social
entity with a life of which individual lives are merely part just
as one individual's desires sacrificed for the sake of his other
desires are only part of his life.[17] This imputation of the arch-
sin committed by utilitarianism to any political philosophy
which assigns functions to the state more extensive than the
night-watchman's constitutes, I think, the foundation which
Nozick offers for his system.

It is a paradoxical feature of Nozick's argument, hostile

---

[12] Ibid. at 32.   [13] Ibid. at 33.
[14] Ibid.   [15] Ibid.
[16] Ibid.   [17] Ibid. at 32-3.

though it is to any form of utilitarianism, that it yields a result identical with one of the least acceptable conclusions of an unqualified maximizing utilitarianism, namely that given certain conditions there is nothing to choose between a society where few enjoy great happiness and very many very little, and a society where happiness is more equally spread. For the utilitarian the condition is that in both societies either aggregate or average welfare is the same. For Nozick the condition is a historical one: that the patterns of distribution of wealth which exist at any time in a society should have come about through exercise of the rights and powers of acquisition and voluntary transfer included in ownership and without any violation of the few basic rights. Given the satisfaction of this historical condition, how people fare under the resulting patterns of distribution, whether grossly inegalitarian or egalitarian, is of no moral significance. The only virtue of social institutions on this view is that they protect the few basic rights, and their only vice is failure to do this. Any consequence of the exercise of such rights is unobjectionable. It is as if the model for Nozick's basic moral rights were a legal one. Just as there can be no legal objection to the exercise of a legal right, so in a morality as empty as Nozick's is of everything except rights, there can be no moral objection to the exercise of a moral right.

Why should a critic of society thus assume that there is only one form of moral wrong, namely, violation of individual rights? Why should he turn his gaze away from the consequences in terms of human happiness or misery produced by the working of a system of such rights? The only answer apparent in Nozick's work is that to treat this misery as a matter of moral concern and to require some persons to contribute to the assistance of others only makes sense if one is prepared, like the maximizing utilitarian, to disregard the separateness of individuals and share the superstition that those required to make such contributions are merely part of the life of a single persisting social entity which both makes the contributions and experiences the balance of good that comes from such contributions. This of course simply assumes that utilitarianism is only intelligible if the satisfactions it seeks to maximize are regarded as those of a single social entity. It also assumes that the only alternative to the Nozickian philosophy of right is an unrestricted maximizing utilitarianism which respects not persons but only experiences of pleasure or satisfaction; and this is of course a false dilemma. The impression that we are faced with these two unpalatable alternatives dissolves if we undertake the no doubt unexciting but indispensable chore of confronting Nozick's misleading descriptive terms, such as 'sacrifice of one individual for others', 'treating one individual as a resource for others', 'making others a part owner of a man', 'forced labour', with the realities which these expressions are misused to describe. We must also substitute for the blindingly general use of concepts like 'interference with liberty' a discriminating catalogue which will enable us to distinguish those restrictions on liberty which can be imposed only at that intolerable cost of sacrificing an individual's life or depriving it of meaning, which according to Nozick is the cost of any restriction of liberty except the restriction on the violation of basic rights. How can it be right to lump together, and ban as equally illegitimate, things so different in their impact on individual life as taking some of a man's income to save others from some great suffering, and killing him or taking one of his vital organs for the same purpose? If we are to construct a tenable theory of rights for use in the criticism of law and society we must, I fear, ask such boring questions as: Is taxing a man's earnings or income, which leaves him free to choose whether to work and to choose what work to do, not altogether different in terms of the burden it imposes from forcing him to labour? Does it really sacrifice him or make him or his body just a resource for others? Does the admitted moral impermissibility of wounding or maiming others or the existence of an absolute moral right not to have one's vital organs taken for the benefit of others in any way support a conclusion that there exists an absolute moral right to retain untaxed all one's earnings or all the income accrued from inherited property except for taxes to support the army and the police? Can one man's great gain or relief from great suffering not outweigh a small loss of income imposed on another to provide it? Do such outweighings only make sense if the gain and the loss are of the same person or a single 'social entity'? Once we shake off that assumption and once we distinguish between the gravity of the different restrictions on different specific liberties and their importance for the conduct of a meaningful life or the development of the personality, the idea that they all, like unqualified maximizing utilitarianism, ignore the moral importance of the division of humanity into separate individuals, and threaten the proper inviolability of persons, disappears into the mist.

There is of course much of value to be learned from Nozick's ingenious and diverting pages, but there are also many quite different criticisms to be made of its foundations apart from the one which I have urged. But since other critics have been busy with many such criticisms I will here mention only one. Even if a social philosophy can draw its morality, as Nozick assumes, only from a single source; even if that source is individual rights, so that the only moral wrongdoing consists in wrongs done to individuals that violate their rights, and even if the foundation for such rights is respect for the separateness of persons, why should rights be limited as they are by Nozick to what Bentham called the negative services of others, that is to abstention from such things as murder, assault, theft, and breach of contract? Why should there not be included a basic right to the positive service of the relief of great needs or suffering or the provision of basic education and skills when the cost of these is small compared with both the need to be met and with the financial resources of those taxed to provide them? Why should property rights, to be morally legitimate, have an absolute, permanent, exclusive, inheritable, and unmodifiable character which leaves no room for this? Nozick is I think in particular called upon to answer this question because he is clear that though rights for him constitute the only source of constraint on action, they are not ends to be maximized,[18] the obligations they impose are, as Nozick insists, 'side constraints', so the rights form a protective bastion enabling an individual to achieve his own ends in a life he shapes himself; and *that*, Nozick thinks, is the individual's way of giving meaning to life.[19]

But it is of course an ancient insight that for a meaningful life not only the protection of freedom from deliberate restriction but opportunities and resources for its exercise are needed. Except for a few privileged and lucky persons, the ability to shape life for oneself and lead a meaningful life is

[18] Ibid. at 28–9.   [19] Ibid. at 48–50.

something to be constructed by positive marshalling of social and economic resources. It is not something automatically guaranteed by a structure of negative rights. Nothing is more likely to bring freedom into contempt and so endanger it than failure to support those who lack, through no fault of their own, the material and social conditions and opportunities which are needed if a man's freedom is to contribute to his welfare.

IV

My second example of contemporary right-based social philosophy is that put forward with very different political implications as one ground for rights in the original, fascinating, but very complex web of theory spun by Professor Ronald Dworkin in his book *Taking Rights Seriously*.[20] Dworkin's theory at first sight seems to be, like Nozick's, implacably opposed to any form of utilitarianism; so much so that the concept of a right which he is concerned to vindicate is expressly described by him as 'an anti-utilitarian concept'. It is so described because for Dworkin 'if someone has a right to something then it is wrong for the government to deny it to him even though it would be in the general interest to do so'.[21]

In fact the two writers, in spite of this surface similarity, differ on almost every important issue except over the conviction that it is a morality of individual rights which both imposes moral limits on the coercive powers of governments, and in the last resort justifies the use of that power.

Before I turn to examine in detail Dworkin's main thesis I shall summarize the major differences between these two modern philosophers of right. For Nozick the supreme value is freedom — the unimpeded individual will: for Dworkin it is equality of concern and respect, which as he warns us does not always entail equality of treatment. That governments must treat all their citizens with equal concern and respect is for Dworkin 'a postulate of political morality',[22] and, he presumes, everyone accepts it. Consequently these two thinkers' lists of basic rights are very different, the chief difference

[20] R. Dworkin, *Taking Rights Seriously* (1977).
[21] Ibid. at 269.
[22] Ibid. at 272.

being that for Dworkin there is no general or residual right to liberty, as there is for Nozick. Indeed, though he recognizes that many, if not most, liberal thinkers have believed in such a right, as Jefferson did, Dworkin calls the idea 'absurd'.[23] There are only rights to specific liberties such as freedom of speech, worship, association, and personal and sexual relationships. Since there is no general right to liberty there is no general conflict between liberty and equality, though the reconciliation of these two values is generally regarded as the main problem of liberalism; nor, since there is no general right to liberty, is there any inconsistency, as conservatives often claim, in the liberal's willingness to accept restriction on economic but not on personal freedom. This is why the political thrust of these two right-based theories is in opposite directions. So far from thinking that the State must be confined to the night-watchman's functions of protecting a few basic negative rights but not otherwise restricting freedom, Dworkin is clear that the State may exercise wide interventionist functions; so if overall social welfare fairly assessed would be thereby advanced, the State may restrict the use of property or freedom of contract; it may enforce desegregation, provide through taxation for public education and culture; it may both prohibit discrimination on grounds of sex or colour where these are taken to be badges of inferiority, and allow schemes of reverse racial discrimination, if required in the general interest, even in the form which the Supreme Court has recently refused to uphold in *Bakke*'s case.[24] But there is no general right to liberty: so the freedom from legal restriction to drive both ways on Lexington Avenue and the freedom, later regretted but upheld in *Lochner*'s case[25] against State legislation, to enter into labour contracts requiring more than ten hours work a day were, as long as they were left unrestricted, legal rights of a sort; but they were not and cannot constitute moral or political rights in Dworkin's strong

[23] Ibid. at 267. Yet 'Hercules' (Dworkin's model of a judge) is said not only to believe that the Constitution guarantees an abstract right to liberty but to hold that a right to privacy is a consequence of it. Ibid. at 117.

[24] *Regents of the Univ. of Cal.* v. *Bakke*, 438 U.S. 265 (1978); and see R. Dworkin, *supra* n. 20, at 223–39, and *N.Y. Rev. Books*, 10 November 1977, at 11–15.

[25] See *Lochner* v. *New York*, 198 U.S. 45 (1905), and R. Dworkin, *supra* n. 20, at 191, 269–78.

'anti-utilitarian' sense, just because restriction or abolition of these liberties might properly be imposed if it advanced general welfare. Finally, notwithstanding the general impression of hostility to utilitarianism suggested by his stress on the 'anti-utilitarian' character of the concept of a right, Dworkin does not reject it wholly as Nozick does, but, as in the Lexington Avenue and labour contract examples, actually endorses a form of utilitarianism. Indeed he says 'the vast bulk of the laws which diminish my liberty are justified on utilitarian grounds'.[26] But the utilitarianism which Dworkin endorses is a purified or refined form of it in which a 'corrupting'[27] element which he finds in vulgar Benthamite utilitarianism is not allowed to weigh in determining decisions. Where the corrupting element does weigh it destroys, according to Dworkin, the fair egalitarian character, 'everybody to count for one, nobody for more than one', which utilitarian arguments otherwise have. This corrupting element causes their use or the use of a majority democratic vote (which he regards as the nearest practical political representation of utilitarianism) to violate, in the case of certain issues, the fundamental right of all to equal concern and respect.

Before we consider what this 'corrupting' element is and how it corrupts I wish to stress the following major point. Dworkin interestingly differs from most philosophers of the liberal tradition. He not merely seeks to draw a vital distinction between mere liberties which may be restricted in the general interest like freedom of contract to work more than ten hours a day, and those preferred liberties which are rights which may not be restricted, but he attempts to do this without entering into some familiar controversial matters. He does not make any appeal to the important role played in the conduct of individual life by such things as freedom of speech or of worship or of personal relations, to show that they are too previous to be allowed to be subordinated to general welfare. So he does not appeal to any theory of human nature designed to show that these liberties are, as John Stuart Mill claimed, among 'the essentials of human well-being',[28] 'the very ground

[26] Ibid. at 269. It is clear that this means 'adequately justified', not merely 'said to be justified'.
[27] Ibid. at 235.
[28] J. S. Mill, *supra* n. 6, at 255.

work of our existence',[29] or to any substantive ideal of the good life or individual welfare. Instead Dworkin temptingly offers something which he believes to be uncontroversial by which to distinguish liberties which are to rank as moral rights like freedom of speech or worship from other freedoms, like freedom of contract or in the use of property, which are not moral rights and may be overridden if they conflict with general welfare. What distinguishes these former liberties is not their greater substantive value but rather a relational or comparative matter, in a sense a procedural matter: the mere consideration that there is an 'antecedent likelihood'[30] that if it were left to an unrestricted utilitarian calculation of the general interest or a majority vote to determine whether or not these should be restricted, the balance would be tipped in favour of restriction by that element which, as Dworkin believes, corrupts utilitarian arguments or a majority vote as decision procedures and causes them to fail to treat all as equals with equal concern and respect. So anti-utilitarian rights essentially are a response to a defect — a species of unfairness — likely to corrupt some utilitarian arguments or a majority vote as decision procedures. Hence the preferred liberties are those such as freedom of speech or sexual relations, which are to rank as rights when we know 'from our general knowledge of society'[31] that they are in danger of being overridden by the corrupting element in such decision procedures.

What then is this element which may corrupt utilitarian argument or a democratic vote? Dworkin identifies it by a distinction between the personal and external preferences[32] or satisfactions of individuals, both of which vulgar utilitarianism counts in assessments of general welfare and both of which may be represented in a majority vote. An individual's personal preferences (or satisfactions) are for (or arise from) the assignment of goods or advantages, including liberties, to himself; his external preferences are for such assignments to others. A utilitarianism refined or purified in the sense that it counted only personal preferences in assessing the balance of

[29] Ibid.
[30] R. Dworkin, *supra* n. 20, at 278.
[31] Ibid. at 277.
[32] Ibid. at 234–8, 275–8.

social welfare would for Dworkin be 'the only defensible form of Utilitarianism',[33] and indeed it is that which justifies the 'vast bulk of our laws diminishing liberty'.[34] It would, he thinks, genuinely treat persons as equals, even if the upshot was not their equal treatment. So where the balance of personal self-interest preferences supported some restriction on freedom (as it did according to Dworkin in the labour contract cases) or reverse discrimination (as in *Bakke*'s case), the restriction or discrimination may be justified, and the freedom restricted; or the claim not to be discriminated against is not a moral or political right. But the vulgar, corrupt form of utilitarianism counts both external and personal preferences and is not an acceptable decision procedure since (so Dworkin argues) by counting in external preferences it fails to treat individuals with equal concern and respect or as equals.[35]

Dworkin's ambitious strategy in this argument is to derive rights to specific liberties from nothing more controversial than the duty of governments to treat their subjects with equal concern and respect. His argument here has a certain Byzantine complexity and it is important in assessing it not to be misled by an ambiguity in the way in which a right may be an 'anti-utilitarian right'. There is a natural interpretation of this expression which is not Dworkin's sense; it may naturally be taken merely to mean that there are some liberties so precious for individual human life that they must not be overridden even in order to secure an advance in general welfare, because they are of greater value than any such increase of general welfare to be got by their denial, however fair the *procedure* for assessing the general welfare is and however genuinely as a procedure it treats persons as equals. Dworkin's sense is *not* that; his argument is not that these liberties must be safeguarded as rights because their value has been compared with that of the increase in general welfare and found to be greater than it, but because such liberties are likely to be defeated by an unfair form of utilitarian argument which by counting in external preferences fails to treat men as equals. So on this view the very identification of the liberties which

---

[33] Ibid. at 276.
[34] Ibid. at 269.
[35] Ibid. at 237, 275.

are to rank as rights is dependent on the anticipated result of a majority vote or a utilitarian argument; whereas on the natural interpretation of an 'anti-utilitarian right' the liberties which are to rank as rights and prevail over general welfare are quite independently identified.

Dworkin's actual argument is more complicated[36] than this already complex story, but I do not think what is omitted is needed for its just assessment. I think both the general form of the argument and its detail are vulnerable to many different objections. The most general objection is the following. What moral rights we have will, on this view, depend on what external preferences or prejudices are current and likely at any given time in any given society to dominate in a utilitarian decision procedure or majority vote. So as far as this argument for rights is concerned, with the progressive liberalization of a society from which prejudices against, say, homosexual behaviour or the expression of heterodox opinions have faded away, rights to these liberties will (like the State in Karl Marx) wither away. So the more tolerant a society is, the fewer rights there will be; there will not merely be fewer occasions for asserting rights. This is surely paradoxical even if we take Dworkin only to be concerned with rights against the State.

---

[36] The main complications are: (1) Personal and external preferences may be intertwined in two different ways. A personal preference, e.g., for the segregated company of white men, may be parasitic on an external preference or prejudice against black men, and such 'parasitic' preferences are to rank as external preferences not to be counted (ibid. at 236). They are however to be distinguished from certain personal preferences which, although they too involve a reference to others, do so only in an instrumental way, regarding others as a means to their personal ends. So a white man's preference that black men be excluded from law school because that will increase his own chances of getting in (ibid. at 234–5) or a black man's preference for reverse discrimination against whites because that will increase the number of black lawyers, is to rank as a personal preference and is to be counted. (2) Though personal and external preferences are in principle distinguishable, in practical politics it will often be impossible to discriminate them and to know how many of each lie behind majority votes. Hence whenever external preferences are likely to influence a vote against some specific liberty, the liberty will need to be protected as an 'anti-Utilitarian right'. So the 'anti-utilitarian' concept of a right is 'a response to the philosophical defects of a utilitarianism that counts external preferences and the practical impossibility of a utilitarianism that does not' (ibid. at 277). Notwithstanding this 'practical impossibility', there are cases where according to Dworkin valid arguments may be made to show that external preferences are not likely to have tipped the balance. See his comments on *Lochner's* case (ibid. at 278) and *Bakke's* case (see n. 23 and accompanying text *supra*) and his view that most of the laws limiting liberties are justified on utilitarian grounds (R. Dworkin, *supra* n. 20, at 269).

But this paradox is compounded by another. Since Dworkin's theory is a response specifically to an alleged defect of utilitarian argument it only establishes rights against the outcome of utilitarian arguments concerning general welfare or a majority democratic vote in which external preferences are likely to tip the balance. This theory as it stands cannot provide support for rights against a tyranny or authoritative government which does not base its coercive legislation on considerations of general welfare or a majority vote. So this particular argument for rights helps to establish individual rights at neither extreme: neither in an extremely tolerant democracy nor in an extremely repressive tyranny. This of course narrows the scope of Dworkin's argument in ways which may surprise readers of his essay 'What Rights Do We Have?'.[37] But of course he is entitled to reply that, narrow though it is, the reach of this particular argument extends to contemporary Western democracies in which the allegedly corrupting 'external preferences' hostile to certain liberties are rife as prejudices. He may say that *that* is good enough — for the time being.[38]

However, even if we accept this reply, a close examination of the detail of the argument shows it to be defective even within its limited scope; and the ways in which it is defective show an important general failing. In constructing his antiutilitarian right-based theory Dworkin has sought to derive too much from the idea of equal concern and respect for persons, just as Nozick in constructing his theory sought to derive too much from the idea of the separateness of persons. Both of course appear to offer something comfortably firm and uncontroversial as a foundation for a theory of basic rights. But this appearance is deceptive: that it is so becomes clear if we press the question why, as Dworkin argues, does a utilitarian decision procedure or democratic vote which counts

[37] R. Dworkin, *supra* n. 20, at 266–78.

[38] This argument from the defect of unreconstructed utilitarianism in counting external preferences is said to be 'only one possible ground of rights' (ibid. at 272, and R. Dworkin, *supra* n. 20, at 356 (2nd printing 1977), and is stated to be applicable only in communities where the general collective justification of political decisions is the general welfare. Though Dworkin indicates that a different argument would be needed where collective justification is not utilitarian (ibid. at 365), he does not indicate how in such a case the liberties to be preferred as rights are to be identified.

both personal and external preferences, *for that reason*, fail
to treat persons as equals, so that when as he says it is 'antecedently likely' that external preferences may tip the balance
against some individual's specific liberty, that liberty becomes
clothed with the status of a moral right not to be overridden
by such procedures. Dworkin's argument is that counting external preferences corrupts the utilitarian argument or a majority vote as a decision procedure, and this of course must
be distinguished from any further independent moral objection there may be to the actual decision resulting from the
procedure. An obvious example of such a vice in utilitarian
argument or in a majority vote procedure would of course be
double counting, e.g. counting one individual's (a Brahmin's
or a white man's) vote or preference twice while counting
another's (an Untouchable's or a black man's) only once. This
is, of course, the very vice excluded by the maxim 'everybody
[is] to count for one, nobody for more than one' which Mill
thought made utilitarianism so splendid. Of course an Untouchable denied some liberty, say liberty to worship, or a
black student denied access to higher education as a result of
such double counting would not have been treated as an equal,
but the right needed to protect him against this is not a right
to any specific liberty but simply a right to have his vote or
preference count equally with the Brahmin's or the white
man's. And of course the decision to deprive him of the liberty in question might also be morally objectionable for
reasons quite independent of the unfairness in the procedure
by which it was reached: if freedom of religion or access to
education is something of which no one should be deprived
whatever decision procedure, fair or unfair, is used, then a
right to that freedom would be necessary for its protection.
But it is vital to distinguish the specific alleged vice of un-
refined utilitarianism or a democratic vote in failing, e.g.,
through double counting, to treat persons as equals, from
any independent objection to a particular decision reached
through that procedure. It is necessary to bear this in mind in
considering Dworkin's argument.

So, finally, why is counting external preferences thought
to be, like the double counting of the Brahmin's or white
man's preference, a vice of utilitarian argument or a majority
vote? Dworkin actually says that the inclusion of external

preference *is* a 'form of double counting'.[39] To understand this we must distinguish cases where the external preference is *favourable* to, and so supports, some personal preference or want for some good or advantage or liberty from cases where the external preference is hostile. Dworkin's simple example of the former is where one person wants the construction of a swimming-pool[40] for his use and others, non-swimmers, support this. But why is this a 'form of double counting'? No one's preference is counted twice as the Brahmin's is; it is only the case that the proposal for the allocation of some good to the swimmers is supported by the preferences both of the swimmer and (say) his disinterested non-swimmer neighbour. Each of the two preferences is counted only as one; and surely *not* to count the neighbour's disinterested preference on this issue would be to fail to treat the two as equals. It would be 'under-counting' and presumably as bad as double counting. Suppose — to widen the illustration — the issue is freedom for homosexual relationships, and suppose that (as may well have been the case at least in England when the old law was re-formed in 1967[41]) it was the disinterested external preferences of liberal heterosexuals that homosexuals should have this freedom that tipped the balance against the external preferences of other heterosexuals who would deny this freedom. How in this situation could the defeated opponents of freedom or any one else complain that the procedure, through counting external preferences (both those supporting the freedom for others and those denying it) as well as the personal preferences of homosexuals wanting it for themselves, had failed to treat persons as equals?

It is clear that where the external preferences are hostile to the assignment of some liberty wanted by others, the phenomenon of one person's preferences being supported by those of another, which, as I think, Dworkin misdescribes as a 'form of double counting', is altogether absent. Why then, since the charge of double counting is irrelevant, does counting such hostile external preferences mean that the procedure does not treat persons as equals? Dworkin's answer seems to be that if, as a result of such preferences tipping the balance,

---

[39] Ibid. at 235.
[40] Ibid.
[41] Sexual Offences Act, 1967, c. 60.

persons are denied some liberty, say to form certain sexual relations, those so deprived suffer because by this result their concept of a proper or desirable form of life is despised by others, and this is tantamount to treating them as inferior to or of less worth than others, or not deserving equal concern and respect. So every denial of freedom on the basis of external preferences implies that those denied are not entitled to equal concern and respect, are not to be considered as equals. But even if we allow this most questionable interpretation of denials of freedom, still for Dworkin to argue in this way is altogether to change the argument. The objection is no longer that the utilitarian argument or a majority vote is, like double counting, unfair as a procedure because it counts in 'external preferences', but that a particular *upshot* of the procedure where the balance is tipped by *a particular kind* of external preference, one which denies liberty and is assumed to express contempt, fails to treat persons as equals. But this is a vice not of the mere externality of the preferences that have tipped the balance but of their content: that is, their liberty-denying and respect-denying content. But this is no longer to assign certain liberties the status of ('anti-utilitarian') rights simply as a response to the specific defects of utilitarianism, as Dworkin claims to do. Yet that is not the main weakness in his ingenious argument. What is fundamentally wrong is the suggested interpretation of denials of freedom as denials of equal concern or respect. This surely is mistaken. It is indeed least credible where the denial of a liberty is the upshot of a utilitarian decision procedure or majority vote in which the defeated minority's preferences or votes for the liberty were weighed equally with others and outweighed by number. Then the message need not be, as Dworkin interprets it, 'You and your views are inferior, not entitled to equal consideration, concern or respect', but 'You and your supporters are too few. You, like everyone else, are counted as one but no more than one. Increase your numbers and then your views may win out.' Where those who are denied by a majority vote the liberty they seek are able, as they are in a fairly working democracy, to continue to press their views in public argument and to attempt to change their opponents' minds, as they in fact with success did after several defeats when the law relating to homosexuality was changed in England, it seems quite impossible to construe every denial of libery by a majority vote based on external preferences as a judgment that the minority whom it defeats are of inferior worth, not entitled to be treated as equals or with equal concern and respect. What is true is something different and quite familiar but no support for Dworkin's argument: namely that the procedural fairness of a voting system or utilitarian argument which weighs votes and preferences equally is no guarantee that all the requirements of fairness will be met in the actual working of the system in given social conditions. This is so because majority views may be, though they are not always, ill-informed and impervious to argument: a majority of theoretically independent voters may be consolidated by prejudice into a self-deafened or self-perpetuating bloc which affords no fair opportunities to a despised minority to publicize and argue its case. All that is possible and has sometimes been actual. But the moral unacceptability of the results in such cases is not traceable to the inherent vice of the decision procedure in counting external preferences, as if this was analogous to double counting. That, of course, would mean that every denial of liberty secured by the doubly counted votes or preferences would necessarily not only be a denial of liberty but also an instance of failing to treat those denied as equals.

I do not expect, however, that Professor Dworkin would concede the point that the triumph of the external preference of a majority over a minority is not as such a denial of equal concern and respect for the defeated minority, even if in the face of my criticism he were to abandon the analogy which he uses to support the argument between such a triumph and the procedural vice of double counting, which vice in the plainest and most literal sense of these not very clear phrases certainly does fail to treat all 'as equals' or with 'equal concern and respect'. He would, I think, simply fall back on the idea that any imposition of external preferences is tantamount to a judgment that those on whom they are imposed are of inferior worth, not to be treated as equals or with equal concern and respect. But is this true? Of course, that governments should as far as possible be neutral between all schemes of values and impose no external preferences may be an admirable ideal, and it may be the true centre of liberalism, as

Dworkin argues, but I cannot see that this ideal is explained or justified or strengthened by its description as a form of, or a derivative from, the duty of governments to show equal concern and respect for their citizens. It is not clear why the rejection of this ideal and allowing a majority's external preferences denying a liberty to prevail is tantamount to an affirmation of the inferior worth of the minority. The majority imposing such external preferences may regard the minority's views as mistaken or sinful; but overriding them, for those reasons (however objectionable on other grounds), seems quite compatible with recognizing the equal worth of the holders of such views and may even be inspired by concern for them. In any event both the liberal prescription for governments, 'impose no scheme of values on any one', and its opposite, 'impose this particular conception of the good life on all', though they are universal prescriptions, seem to have nothing specifically to do with equality or the value of equal concern and respect any more than have the prescriptions 'kill no one' and 'kill everyone', though of course conformity with such universal prescriptions will involve treating all alike in the relevant respect.[42]

Though the points urged in the last paragraphs destroy the

[42] My suspicions that the ideas of 'equal concern and respect' and treatment 'as equals' are either too indeterminate to play the fundamental role which they do in Dworkin's theory or that a vacuous use is being made of the notion of equality are heightened by his later observations on this subject. See 'Liberalism', in *Public and Private Morality* 127-8, 136-40 (Hampshire edn., 1978). Here he argues that in addition to the liberal conception of equal concern and respect there is another, conservative, conception which, far from requiring governments to be as neutral as possible between values or theories of the good life, requires them to treat all men as a 'good man would wish to be treated', according to some particular preferred theory of the good life. On this view, denials of certain forms of sexual liberty as well as the maintenance of social and economic inequalities, if required by the preferred moral theory, would be the conservative form of treating all as equals and with equal concern and respect. But a notion of equal concern and respect, hospitable to such violently opposed interpretations (or 'conceptions of the concept') does not seem to me to be a single concept at all, and it is far from clear why either of these two conceptions should be thought of as forms of equal concern and respect to all. Though the claim that liberal rights are derived from the duty of governments to treat all their citizens with equal concern and respect has the comforting appearance of resting them on something uncontroversial ('a postulate of political morality' which all are 'presumed to accept', R. Dworkin, *supra* n. 20, at 272), this appearance dissolves when it is revealed that there is an alternative interpretation of this fundamental duty from which most liberal rights could not be derived but negations of many liberal rights could.

the argument that denial of liberty on the basis of external preferences is a denial of equal concern and respect and the attempted derivation of rights from equality, this does not mean that such denials of freedom are unobjectionable or that there is no right to it: it means rather that the freedom must be defended on grounds other than equality. Utilitarian arguments, even purified by the exclusion of external preferences, can produce illiberal and grossly inegalitarian results. Some liberties, because of the role they play in human life are too precious to be put at the mercy of numbers even if in favourable circumstances they may win out. So to protect such precious liberties we need rights which are indeed 'anti-utilitarian rights' and 'anti-' much else, but in so far as they are 'anti-utilitarian' they are so in the common and not the Dworkinian sense of that expression, and they are needed as a shield not only against a preponderance of external preferences but against personal preferences also. Freedom of speech, for example, may need to be defended against those who would abridge and suppress it as dangerous to their prosperity, security or other personal interests.[43] We cannot escape, as Dworkin's purported derivation of such rights from equality seeks to do, the assertion of the value of such liberties as compared with advances in general welfare, however fairly assessed.

It is in any case surely fantastic to suppose that what, for example, those denied freedom of worship, or homosexuals denied freedom to form sexual relations, have chiefly to complain about is not the restriction of their liberty with all its grave impact on personal life or development and happiness, but that they are not accorded *equal* concern and respect: that others are accorded a concern and respect denied to them. When it is argued that the denial to some of a certain

[43] Dworkin certainly seems to endorse utilitarian arguments purified of external preferences, yet he states that his arguments against an unrestricted utilitarianism are not in favour of a restricted one. (R. Dworkin, *supra* n. 20, at 357 (2nd printing 1977).) The contrary impression is given by earlier statements such as that the vast bulk of laws which diminish our liberty are justified on utilitarian grounds (ibid. at 269), and the following comment on the right of liberty of contract claimed in *Lochner's* case: 'I cannot think of any argument that a political decision to limit such a right . . . is antecedently likely to give effect to external preferences and *in that way* offend the right of those whose liberty is curtailed to equal concern and respect. If as I think no such argument can be made out then the alleged right does not exist'. Ibid. at 278 (emphasis added).

freedom, say to some form of religious worship or to some form of sexual relations, is essentially a denial of equal concern and respect, the word 'equal' is playing an empty but misleading role. The vice of the denial of such freedom is not its inequality or unequal impact: if that *were* the vice the prohibition by a tyrant of all forms of religious worship or sexual activity would not increase the scale of the evil as in fact it surely would, and the evil would vanish if all were converted to the banned faith or to the prohibited form of sexual relationship. The evil is the denial of liberty or respect; not *equal* liberty or *equal* respect: and what is deplorable is the ill-treatment of the victims and not the relational matter of the unfairness of their treatment compared with others. This becomes clear if we contrast with this spurious invocation of equality a genuine case of a failure to treat men as equals in the literal sense of these words: namely literal double counting, giving the Brahmin or the white man two votes to the Untouchable's or black man's single vote. Here the single vote given to the latter is indeed bad just because the others are given two: it is, unlike the denial of a religious or sexual freedom, a genuine denial of *equality* of concern and respect, and this evil *would* vanish and *not* increase if the restriction to a single vote were made universal.

V

I conclude that neither Nozick's nor Dworkin's attempt to derive rights from the seemingly uncontroversial ideas of the separateness of persons or from their title to equal concern and respect succeeds. So in the rough seas which the philosophy of political morality is presently crossing between the old faith in utilitarianism and the new faith in rights, perhaps these writers' chief and very considerable service is to have shown, by running up against them, some of the rocks and shoals to be avoided, but not where the safe channels lie for a prosperous voyage. That still awaits discovery. Much valuable work has been done, especially by these and other American philosophers, but there is much still to be done to identify the peculiar features of the dimension of morality constituted by the conception of basic moral rights and the way in which that dimension of morality relates to other values pursued through government; but I do not think a satisfactory foundation for a theory of rights will be found as long as the search is conducted in the shadow of utilitarianism, as both Nozick's and Dworkin's in their different ways are. For it is unlikely that the truth will be in a doctrine mainly defined by its freedom from utilitarianism's chief defect — neglecting the separateness of persons — or in a doctrine resting, like Dworkin's, everything on 'equal concern and respect' as a barrier against an allegedly corrupt form of utilitarianism.

POSTSCRIPT

See for criticisms and comments: R. Dworkin, 'Is there a Right to Pornography?', *Oxford L. J.* 177 at 206–12 (1981).

Rawls on Liberty and Its Priority

I. INTRODUCTION

No book of political philosophy since I read the great classics of the subject has stirred my thoughts as deeply as John Rawls's *A Theory of Justice*. But I shall not in this article offer a general assessment of this important and most interesting work. I shall be concerned with only one of its themes, namely, Rawls's account of the relationship between justice and liberty, and in particular with his conception that justice requires that liberty may only be limited for the sake of liberty and not for the sake of other social and economic advantages. I have chosen this theme partly because of its obvious importance to lawyers, who are, as it were, professionally concerned with limitations of liberty and with the justice or injustice of such limitations. I choose this theme also because this part of Rawls's book has not, I think, so far received, in any of the vast number of articles on and reviews of the book which have been published, the detailed attention which it deserves. Yet, as Sidgwick found when he considered a somewhat similar doctrine ascribing priority to liberty over other values, such a conception of liberty, though undoubtedly striking a responsive chord in the heart of any liberal, has its baffling as well as its attractive aspect,[1] which becomes apparent when we consider, as Rawls intends that we should, what the application of this doctrine would require in practice.

Part of what follows is concerned with a major question of interpretation of Rawls's doctrine, and the rest is critical. But I am very conscious that I may have failed to keep constantly in view or in proper perspective all the arguments which Rawls, at different places in this long and complex work, concentrates on the points which I find unconvincing. I would

---

[1] H. Sidgwick, *The Methods of Ethics* (7th edn. 1907) bk. III, ch. V. § 4. 'I admit that it commends itself much to my mind. . . . But when I endeavour to bring it into closer relation to the actual circumstances of human society it soon comes to wear a different aspect.'

not therefore be surprised if my interpretation could be corrected and my criticisms answered by some further explanation which the author could supply. Indeed I do not write to confute, but mainly in the hope that in some of the innumerable future editions of this book Rawls may be induced to add some explanation of these points.

I hope that I can assume that by now the main features of Rawls's *A Theory of Justice* are familiar to most readers, but for those to whom it is not, the following is a minimum account required to make this article intelligible.

First, there is what Rawls terms the 'Main Idea'. This is the striking claim that principles of justice do not rest on mere intuition, yet are not to be derived from utilitarian principles or any other teleological theory holding that there is some form of good to be sought and maximized. Instead, the principles of justice are to be conceived as those that free and rational persons concerned to further their own interests would agree should govern their forms of social life and institutions if they had to choose such principles from behind 'a veil of ignorance' — that is, in ignorance of their own abilities, of their psychological propensities and conception of the good, and of their status and position in society and the level of development of the society of which they are to be members. The position of these choosing parties is called 'the original position'. Many discussions of the validity of this Main Idea have already appeared, and it will continue to be much debated by philosophers, but for the purposes of this article I shall assume that if it could be shown that the parties in the original position would choose the principles which Rawls identifies as principles of justice, that would be a strong argument in their favour. From the Main Idea Rawls makes a transition to a general form or 'general conception' of the principles that the parties in the original position would choose. This general conception of justice is as follows:

All social values — liberty and opportunity, income and wealth, and the bases of self-respect — are to be distributed equally unless an unequal distribution of any, or all, of these values is to everyone's advantage.[2]

This general conception of justice, it should be observed, refers to the equal distribution of liberty but not to its

[2] Rawls, *A Theory of Justice* 62 (1971).

maximization or extent. However, most of the book is concerned with a special interpretation of this general conception
which refers both to the maximization and the equality of
liberty. The principal features of this special conception of
justice are as follows:

First Principle ['the principle of greatest equal liberty'[3]]
> Each person is to have an equal right to the most extensive total sys-
> tem of equal basic liberties compatible with a similar system of lib-
> erty for all.

Second Principle
> Social and economic inequalities are to be arranged so that they are
> ... to the greatest benefit of the least advantaged. ....[4]

To these two principles are attached certain priority rules, of
which the most important is that liberty is given a priority
over all other advantages, so that it may be restricted or unequally distributed only for the sake of liberty and not for
any other form of social or economic advantage.

To this account two points specially relevant to this article
must be added. First, Rawls regards his two principles as
established or justified not simply by the fact that they would
be chosen, as he claims they would, by the parties in the original position, but also by the general harmony of these principles with ordinary 'considered judgments duly pruned and
adjusted'.[5] The test of his theory, therefore, is in part whether
the principles he identifies illuminate our ordinary judgments
and help to reveal a basic structure and coherence underlying
them.

Secondly, it is an important and interesting feature of
Rawls's theory that once the principles of justice have been
chosen we come to understand what their implementation
would require by imagining a four-stage process. Thus, we are
to suppose that after the first stage, when the parties in the
original position have chosen the principles of justice, they
move to a constitutional convention. There, in accordance

---

[3] Ibid. 124.

[4] Ibid. 302. I have here omitted the provisions for a just savings principle and
for equality of opportunity, which Rawls includes in this formulation of his second
principle, since they are not relevant to the present discussion.

[5] Ibid. 20. Rawls, in fact, speaks of a 'reflective equilibrium' between principles and ordinary judgments, since he envisages that where there are initial
discrepancies between these we have a choice of modifying the conditions of the
initial position in which principles are chosen or modifying in detail the judgements (pp. 20 ff.).

with the chosen principles, they choose a constitution and establish the basic rights or liberties of citizens. The third stage is that of legislation, where the justice of laws and policies is considered; enacted statutes, if they are to be just, must satisfy both the limits laid down in the constitution and the originally chosen principles of justice. The fourth and last stage is that of the application of rules by judges and other officials to particular cases.

II. LIBERTY AND BASIC LIBERTIES

Throughout his book Rawls emphasizes the distinction between liberty and other social goods, and his principle of greatest equal liberty is, as I have said, accompanied — in his special conception of justice as distinct from his general conception — by a priority rule which assigns to liberty, or at least to certain forms of liberty institutionally defined and protected, a priority which forbids the restriction of liberty for the sake of other benefits: liberty is only to be restricted for the sake of liberty itself. In the general conception of justice there is no such priority rule and no requirement that liberty must be as extensive as possible, though it is to be equally distributed unless an unequal distribution of it is justified as being to everyone's advantage.[6] The special conception is to govern societies which have developed to the point when, as Rawls says, 'the basic wants of individuals can be fulfilled'[7] and social conditions allow 'the effective establishment of fundamental rights'.[8] If these favourable conditions do not obtain, equal liberty may be denied, if this is required to 'raise the level of civilization so that in due course these freedoms can be enjoyed'.[9]

I find it no easy matter, on some quite crucial points, to interpret Rawls's complex doctrine, and there is one initial question of interpretation which I discuss here at some length. But it is perhaps worth saying that to do justice to Rawls's principle of greatest equal liberty it is necessary to take into account not only what he says when expressly formulating, expounding, and illustrating this principle, but also what he

---

[6] Ibid. 62.
[8] Ibid. 152, 542.
[7] Ibid. 543.
[9] Ibid. 152.

says about some other apparently separate issues — in particular, natural duties,[10] obligations arising from the principle of fairness,[11] permissions,[12] paternalism[13] and the common good or common interest,[14] for these may apparently supplement the rather exiguous provision for restrictions on liberty which are all that, at first sight, his principle of greatest equal liberty seems to allow.

The initial question of interpretation arises from the following circumstances. Rawls in his book often refers in broad terms to his first principle of justice as 'the principle of greatest equal liberty',[15] and in similarly broad terms to its associated priority rule as the rule that 'liberty can be restricted only for the sake of liberty'.[16] These references to liberty in quite general terms, and also Rawls's previous formulation in his articles of this first principle as the principle that everyone has 'an equal right to the most extensive liberty compatible with a like liberty for all',[17] suggest that his doctrine is similar to that criticized by Sidgwick.[18] It is probable that Sidgwick had chiefly in mind a formulation of a principle of greatest equal liberty urged by Herbert Spencer in his long-forgotten *Social Statics*.[19] This was effectively criticized by Sidgwick as failing to account for some of the most obvious restrictions on liberty required to protect individuals from harms other than constraint or deprivation of liberty, and indeed as forbidding the institution of private property, since to own anything privately is to have liberty to use it in ways denied to others. Spencer attempted to get out of this difficulty (or

---

[10] Ibid. 114 ff., 333 ff.

[11] Ibid. 108 ff.   [12] Ibid. 116 ff.

[13] Ibid. 248.   [14] Ibid. 97, 213, 246.

[15] E.g. ibid. 124.   [16] Ibid. 250, 302. ·

[17] Rawls, 'Justice as Fairness', 67 *Philosophical Review* 164, 165 (1958); see Rawls, 'The Sense of Justice', 72 *Philosophical Review* 283 (1963); Rawls, 'Distributive Justice', in *Politics, Philosophy, and Society* 61 (3rd Series, Oxford 1967). This formulation in these articles should not be confused with the formulation of the 'general conception' of justice in the book. See pp. 3 ff.

[18] H. Sidgwick, *supra* n. 1, bk. III, ch. V., § § 4–5, and ch. XI, § 5.

[19] See H. Spencer, *Social Statics* (1850). Criticisms of Spencer's theory in terms very similar to Sidgwick's criticisms were made by F. W. Maitland in 1 *Collected Papers* 247 (H. Fisher edn. 1911). Maitland treated Spencer's doctrine of equal liberty as virtually identical with Kant's notion of mutual freedom under universal law expounded in the latter's *Rechtslehre*. I am grateful to Professor B. J. Diggs for pointing out to me important differences between Rawls's doctrine of liberty and Kant's conception of mutual freedom under universal law.

rather outside it) by simply swallowing it, and reached the conclusion that, at least in the case of land, only property held in
common by a community would be consistent with 'equal
liberty'[20] and hence legitimate. Rawls in his book simply lists
without argument the right to hold personal property, but
not property in the means of production, as one of the basic
liberties,[21] though, as I shall argue later, he does this at some
cost to the coherence of his theory.

Rawls's previous formulation of his general principle of
greatest equal liberty — 'everyone has an equal right to the
most extensive liberty compatible with a like liberty for all'
— was then very similar to the doctrine criticized by Sidgwick.
But Rawls's explicit formulation of it in his book is no longer
in these general terms. It refers not to 'liberty' but to basic or
fundamental *liberties*, which are understood to be legally
recognized and protected from interference. This, with its
priority rule, as finally formulated, now runs as follows:

Each person is to have an equal right to the most extensive total system
of equal basic liberties compatible with a similar system of liberty for
all. . . .

[L]iberty can be restricted only for the sake of liberty. There are two
cases: (a) a less extensive liberty must strengthen the total system of
liberty shared by all; (b) a less than equal liberty must be acceptable to
those with the lesser liberty.[22]

Even to this, however, for complete accuracy a gloss on the
last sentence is needed because Rawls also insists that 'acceptable to those with the lesser liberty' means not acceptable just
on any grounds, but only acceptable because affording a
greater protection of their own liberties.[23]

The basic liberties to which Rawls's principle thus refers
are identified by the parties in the original position[24] from behind the veil of ignorance as essential for the pursuit of their
ends, whatever those ends turn out to be, and so as determining the form of their society. Not surprisingly, therefore,
the basic liberties are rather few in number, and Rawls gives

---

[20] H. Spencer, *supra* n. 19.

[21] Op. cit. n. 2 *supra*, 61.

[22] Ibid. 302.

[23] Ibid. 233.

[24] E.g., 'equal liberty of conscience is the only principle that parties in the
original position can acknowledge', ibid. 207.

a short list of them which he describes in the index as an 'enumeration',[25] though he warns us that these are what they are only 'roughly speaking'.[26] They comprise political liberty, that is, the right to vote and be eligible for public office; freedom of speech and of assembly; liberty of conscience and freedom of thought; freedom of the person, along with the right to hold personal property; and freedom from arbitrary arrest and seizure.

Now the question of interpretation is whether Rawls's change of language from a principle of greatest equal liberty couched in quite general terms ('everyone has an equal right to the most extensive *liberty*'), to one referring only to specific basic *liberties*, indicates a change in his theory. Is the principle of liberty in the book still this quite general principle, so that under the priority rule now attached to it no form of liberty may be restricted except for the sake of liberty? It is difficult to be sure, but my own view on this important point is that Rawls no longer holds the quite general theory which appeared in his articles, perhaps because he had met the difficulties pointed out by Sidgwick and others. There are, I think, several indications, besides the striking change in language, that Rawls's principle is now limited to the list of basic liberties, allowing of course for his statement that the actual list he gives is only rough. The first indication is the fact that Rawls does not find it necessary to reconcile the admission of private property as a liberty with any general principle of *maximum* equal liberty, or of 'an equal rights to the most extensive liberty', and he avoids the difficulties found in Herbert Spencer's doctrine by giving a new sense to the requirement that the right to hold property must be equal. This sense of equality turns on Rawls's distinction between liberty and the value or worth of liberty.[27] Rawls does not require, except in the case of the *political liberties* (the right to participate in government and freedom of speech), that basic liberties be equal in value, or substantially equal, so he does not require, in admitting the right to property as a basic equal liberty, either that property should be held in common so that everyone can enjoy the same property, or that separately

---

[25] Ibid. 540.
[26] Ibid. 61.
[27] Ibid. 204, 225 ff.

owned property should be equal in amount. That would be to insist that the value of the right to property should be equal. What is required is the merely formal condition that the *rules*[28] governing the acquisition, disposition and scope of property rights should be the same for all. Rawls's reply to the familiar Marxist criticism that in this case we shall have to say that the beggar and the millionaire have equal property rights would be to admit the charge, but to point out that, in his system, the unequal value of these equal property rights would be cut down to the point where inequality would be justified by the working of the difference principle, according to which economic inequalities are justified only if they are for the benefit of the least advantaged.[29]

The second indication that Rawls's principle of greatest equal liberty and its priority rule ('liberty can be restricted only for the sake of liberty')[30] is now limited to the basic liberties is his careful and repeated explanation that, though the right to hold property is for him a 'liberty', the choice between private capitalism and state ownership of the means of production is left quite open by the principles of justice.[31] Whether or not the means of production are to be privately owned is something which a society must decide in the light of the knowledge of its actual circumstances and the demands of social and economic efficiency. But, of course, a decision to limit private ownership to consumer goods made on such grounds would result in a less extensive form of liberty than would obtain if private ownership could be exercised over all forms of property. Rawls's admission of this restriction as allowable so far as justice is concerned would be a glaring inconsistency if he was still advancing the general principle that there must be 'an equal right to the most extensive liberty', for that, under the priority rule, would entail that *no form* of liberty must be narrowed or limited for the sake of economic benefits, but only for the sake of liberty itself.

These considerations support very strongly the interpretation that Rawls's principle of greatest equal liberty, as it is developed in this book, is concerned only with the enumerated basic liberties, though of course these are specified by him only in broad terms. But I confess that there are also

---

[28] Ibid. 63–4.   [29] Ibid. 204.
[30] Ibid. 302.   [31] Ibid. 66, 273–4.

difficulties in this interpretation which suggest that Rawls has not eliminated altogether the earlier general doctrine of liberty, even though that earlier doctrine is not, as I have explained above, really consistent with Rawls's treatment of the admissible limitations of the right of property. For it seems obvious that there are important forms of liberty — sexual freedom and the liberty to use alcohol or drugs among them — which apparently do not fall within any of the roughly described basic liberties;[32] yet it would be very surprising if principles of justice were silent about their restriction. Since John Stuart Mill's essay *On Liberty*, such liberties have been the storm centre of discussions of the proper scope of the criminal law and other forms of social coercion, and there is, in fact, just one passage in this book from which it is clear that Rawls thinks that his principles of justice are not silent as to the justice of restricting such liberties.[33] For in arguing against the view that certain forms of sexual relationship should be prohibited simply as degrading or shameful, and so as falling short of some 'perfectionist' ideal, Rawls says that we should rely not on such perfectionist criteria but on the principles of justice, and that according to these no reasonable case for restriction can be made out.

There is much that I do not understand in this short passage. Rawls says here that justice requires us to show, before restricting such modes of conduct, either that they interfere with the basic liberties of others or that 'they violate some natural duty or some obligation'. This seems an unexplained departure from the strict line so often emphasized in the case of basic liberties, that liberty may be restricted only for the sake of liberty. Is there then a secondary set of principles for

---

[32] It has been suggested to me that Rawls would regard these freedoms as basic liberties falling under his broad category of liberty of conscience, which is concerned not only with religious but with moral freedom. But Rawls's discussion of this, ibid. 205 ff., seems to envisage only a man's freedom to fulfil moral *obligations* as he interprets them, and sexual freedom would therefore only fall under this category for those to whom the promptings of passion presented themselves as calls of moral duty. Others have suggested that these freedoms would fall under Rawls's category of freedom of the person; but this seems most unlikley to me in view of his collocation of it with property ('freedom of the person along with the right to hold personal property'). It is to be noted also that sexual freedom is spoken of as a 'mode of conduct', ibid. 331, and the possibility of its interference with 'basic liberties' (not '*other*' basic liberties) is mentioned.

[33] Ibid. 331.

non-basic liberties? This solution would have its own difficulties. The natural duties to which Rawls refers here, and the
principle from which obligations, such as the obligation to
keep a promise, derive, are, according to Rawls, standards of
conduct for *individuals* which the parties in the original position have gone on to choose after they have chosen the principles of justice as standards for *institutions*, which I take it
include the law. If liberty may be restricted to prevent violation of any such natural duties or obligations, this may rather
severely narrow the area of liberty, for the natural duties include the duty to assist others when this can be done at small
cost and the duty to show respect and courtesy, as well as
duties to support just institutions, not to harm the innocent,
and not to cause unnecessary suffering. Further, since the
parties in the original position are said to choose the principles
of justice as standards for institutions *before* they choose the
natural duties for individuals, it is not clear how the former
can incorporate the latter, as Rawls suggests they do when he
says that principles of justice require us to show, before we
restrict conduct, that it violates either basic liberties or natural duties or obligations.

I hope that I have not made too much of what is a mere
passing reference by Rawls to liberties which do not appear
to fall within his categories of basic liberties, but have been at
the centre of some famous discussions of freedom. I cannot,
however, from this book see quite how Rawls would resolve
the difficulties I have mentioned, and I raise below the related
question whether liberties which are plainly 'basic' may also
be restricted if their exercise involves violation of natural
duties or obligations.

III. LIMITING LIBERTY FOR THE SAKE OF LIBERTY

I turn now to consider the principle that basic liberties may
be limited only for the sake of liberty. Rawls expresses this
principle in several different ways. He says that basic liberties
may be restricted or unequally distributed only for the sake
of a greater 'system of liberty as a whole',[34] that the restriction

---

[34] Ibid. 203.

must yield 'a greater equal liberty',[35] or 'the best total system of equal liberty'[36] or 'strengthen' that system,[37] or be 'a gain for . . . freedom on balance'.[38]

What, then, is it to limit liberty for the sake of liberty? Rawls gives a number of examples which his principle would permit. The simplest case is the introduction of rules of order in debate,[39] which restrict the liberty to speak when we please. Without this restriction the liberty to say and advocate what we please would be grossly hampered and made less valuable to us. As Rawls says, such rules are necessary for 'profitable'[40] discussion, and plainly when such rules are introduced a balance is struck and the liberty judged less important or less valuable is subordinated to the other. In this very simple case there seems to be a quite obvious answer to the question as to which of the two liberties here conflicting is more valuable, since, whatever ends we are pursuing in debate, the liberty to communicate our thought in speech must contribute more to their advancement than the liberty to interrupt communication. It seems to me, however, misleading to describe even the resolution of the conflicting liberties in this very simple case as yielding a 'greater' or 'stronger' total system of liberty, for these phrases suggest that no values other than liberty and dimensions of it, like extent, size, or strength, are involved. Plainly what such rules of debate help to secure is not a *greater* or more extensive liberty, but a liberty to do something which is more valuable for any rational person than the activities forbidden by the rules, or, as Rawls himself says, something more 'profitable'. So some criterion of the value of different liberties must be involved in the resolution of conflicts between them; yet Rawls speaks as if the system 'of basic liberties' were self-contained, and conflicts within it were adjusted without appeal to any other value besides liberty and its extent.

In some cases, it is true, Rawls's conception of a greater or more extensive liberty resulting from a more satisfactory resolution of conflicts between liberties may have application. One fairly clear example is provided by Rawls when he says that the principle of limiting liberty only for the sake of

---

[35] Ibid. 229.   [36] Ibid. 203.
[37] Ibid. 250.   [38] Ibid. 244.
[39] Ibid. 203.   [40] Ibid.

liberty would allow conscription for military service in a war genuinely undertaken to defend free institutions either at home or abroad.[41] In that case it might plausibly be said that only the quantum or extent of liberty was at stake; the temporary restriction of liberty involved in military conscription might be allowed to prevent or remove much greater inroads on liberty. Similarly, the restriction imposed in the name of public order and security, to which Rawls often refers,[42] may be justified simply as hindering greater or more extensive hindrances to liberty of action. But there certainly are important cases of conflict between basic liberties where, as in the simple rules of debate case, the resolution of conflict must involve consideration of the relative value of different modes of conduct, and not merely the extent or amount of freedom. One such conflict, which, according to Rawls's four-stage sequence, will have to be settled at a stage analogous to a constitutional convention, is the conflict between freedom of speech and of the person, and freedom to participate in government through a democratically elected legislature.[43] Rawls discusses this conflict on the footing that the freedom to participate in government is to be considered as restricted if there is a Bill of Rights protecting the individual's freedom of speech or of the person from regulation by an ordinary majority vote of the legislature. He says that the kind of argument to support such a restriction, which his principles of justice require, is 'a justification which appeals only to a greater equal liberty'.[44] He admits that different opinions about the value of the conflicting liberties will affect the way in which different persons view this conflict. None the less, he insists that to arrive at a just resolution of the conflict we must try to find the point at which 'the danger to liberty from the marginal loss in control over those holding political power just balances the security of liberty gained by the greater use of constitutional devices'.[45] I cannot myself understand, however, how such weighing or striking of a balance is conceivable if the only appeal is, as Rawls says, to 'a greater liberty'.

These difficulties in the notion of a greater total liberty,

[41] Ibid. 380.
[42] Ibid. 97, 212–13.
[43] Ibid. 228–30.
[44] Ibid. 229.   [45] Ibid. 230.

or system of liberty, resulting from the just resolution of conflict between liberties, are made more acute for me by Rawls's
description of the point of view from which he says all such
conflicts between liberties are to be settled — whether they
occur at the constitution-making stage of the four-stage sequence, as in the case last considered, or at the stage of legislation in relation to other matters.

Rawls says that when liberties conflict the adjustment
which is to secure 'the best total system' is to be settled from
the stand-point of 'the representative equal citizen', and we
are to ask which adjustment 'it would be rational for him to
prefer'.[46] This, he says, involves the application of the principle of the common interest or common good which selects
those conditions which are necessary for 'all to equally further their aims' or which will 'advance shared ends'.[47] It is, of
course, easy to see that very simple conflicts between liberties,
such as the debating rules case, may intelligibly be said to be
settled by reference to this point of view. For in such simple
cases it is certainly arguable that, whatever ends a man may
have, he will see as a rational being that the restrictions are
required if he is to pursue his ends successfully, and this can
be expressed in terms of 'the common good' on the footing
that such restrictions are necessary for all alike. But it would
be quite wrong to generalize from this simple case; other conflicts between basic liberties will be such that different resol-
utions of the conflict will correspond to the interests of different people who will diverge over the relative value they set
on the conflicting liberties. In such cases, there will be no
resolution which will be uniquely selected by reference to the
common good. So, in the constitutional case discussed above,
it seems difficult to understand how the conflict can be resolved by reference to the representative equal citizen, and
without appeal to utilitarian considerations or to some conception of what all individuals are morally entitled to have as
a matter of human dignity or moral right. In particular, the
general strategy which Rawls ascribes to the parties in the
original position of choosing the alternative that yields the
best worst position is no help except in obvious cases like the
debating rules case. There, of course, it can be argued that it

is better to be restricted by reasonable rules than to be exposed to unregulated interruption, so that it is rational to trade off the liberty to speak when you please for the more valuable benefit of being able to communicate more or less effectively what you please. Or, to put the same exceedingly simple point in the 'maximum' terms which Rawls often illuminatingly uses, the worst position under the rule (being restrained from interruption but given time to speak free from interruption) is better than the worst position without the rule (being constantly exposed to interruption though free to interrupt).

Such simple cases, indeed, exist where it can be said that all 'equal citizens', however divergent their individual tastes or desires, would, if rational, prefer one alternative where liberties conflict. But I do not understand how the notion of the rational preference of the representative equal citizen can assist in the resolution of conflicts where reasonable men may differ as to the value of conflicting liberties, and there is no obviously best worst position which a rational man would prefer. It is true that at the stages in the four-stage sequence where such conflicts have to be resolved there is no veil of ignorance to prevent those who have to take decisions knowing what proportions of the population favour which alternatives. But I do not think Rawls would regard such knowledge as relevant in arguments about what it would be rational for the representative equal citizen to prefer; for it would only be relevant if we conceive that this representative figure in some way reflects (perhaps in the relative strength or intensity of his conflicting desires) the distribution of different preferences in the population. This, however, would be virtually equivalent to a utilitarian criterion and one that I am sure is far from Rawls's thoughts. I would stress here that I am not complaining that Rawls's invocation of 'the rational preference of the representative equal citizen' fails to provide a decision procedure yielding a determinate answer in all cases. Rather, I do not understand, except in the very simple cases, what sort of argument is to be used to show what the representative's rational preference would be and in what sense it results in 'a greater liberty'.

Of course, it is open to Rawls to say, as he does, that arguments concerning the representative's rational preference will

often be equally balanced, and in such cases justice will be indeterminate. But I do not think that he can mean that justice
is to be indeterminate whenever different people value alternatives differently. Indeed, he is quite clear that, in spite of
such difference in valuation, justice does require that there
be some constitutional protections for individual freedom,
though these will limit the freedom to participate in government;[48] the only indeterminacy he contemplates here is as to
the particular form of constitutional protection to be selected
from a range of alternatives all of which may be permitted by
principles of justice. Yet, if opinion is divided on the main
issue (that is, whether there should be any or no restrictions
on legislative power to protect individual freedom), I do not
understand what sort of argument it is that is supposed to
show that the representative equal citizen would prefer an
affirmative answer on this main issue as securing 'the greater
liberty'.

This difficulty still plagues me even in relatively minor
cases where one might well accept a conclusion that principles of justice are indeterminate. Thus, suppose the legislator
has to determine the scope of the rights of exclusion comprised in the private ownership of land, which is for Rawls a
basic liberty,[49] when this basic liberty conflicts with others.
Some people may prefer freedom of movement not to be
limited by the rights of landowners supported by laws about
trespass; others, whether they are landowners or not, may prefer that there be some limitations. If justice is indeterminate
in this minor case of conflicting liberties, then no doubt we
would fall back on what Rawls terms procedural justice, and
accept the majority vote of legislature operating under a just

[48] 'The liberties of equal citizenship must be incorporated into and protected
by the constitution' (ibid. 197). 'If a bill of rights guaranteeing liberty of conscience and freedom of thought and assembly would be effective then it should be
adopted' (ibid. 231).
[49] It has been suggested to me by Mr Michael Lesnoff that Rawls might not
consider the private ownership of land to be a basic liberty since, as noted above,
justice according to Rawls leaves open the question whether there is to be private
ownership of the means of production. I am not, however, clear what is included
in the scope of the basic liberty which Rawls described as 'the right to hold [per-
sonal] property' (ibid. 61). Would it comprise ownership or (in a socialized economy) a tenancy from the state in land to be used as a garden? If not, the example
in the text might be changed to that of a conflict between pedestrians' freedom of
movement and the rights of drivers of automobiles.

constitution and a fair procedure, even if we cannot say of
the outcome that it is in itself a just one. But, presumably, in
considering what measures to promote and how to vote, the
legislators must, since this is a case, though a minor one, of
conflicting basic liberties, begin by asking which of the alternatives a representative equal citizen would, if rational, prefer,
even if they are doomed to discover that this question has no
determinate answer. But indeterminacy and unintelligibility
are different things, and it is the intelligibility of the question
with which I am concerned. What do the legislators mean
in such cases when they ask which alternative it would be
rational for the representative equal citizen to prefer as securing the greater liberty, when they know that some men may
value privacy of property more than freedom of movement,
and others not? If the question is rephrased, as Rawls says it
can be, as a question involving the principle of the common
good, then it will presumably appear as the question which
alternative will in the long run most advance the good of all,
or ends that all share. This might be an answerable question
in principle if it could be taken simply as the question which
alternative is likely most to advance everyone's general welfare, where this is taken to include economic and other advantages besides liberty. If, for example, it could be shown
that unrestricted freedom of movement over land would tend
to reduce everyone's food supply, whereas no bad consequences likely to affect everyone would result from the other
alternative, then the conflict should be resolved in favour of
restriction of movement. But this interpretation of the question in terms of welfare seems ruled out by the principle that
liberty may only be limited for the sake of liberty, and not
for social or economic advantages. So, I think that the conception of the rational choice of the representative equal citizen needs further clarification.

IV. LIMITING LIBERTY TO PREVENT HARM OR SUFFERING

I now turn to the question whether the principle of limiting
liberty only for the sake of liberty provides adequately for
restrictions on conduct which causes pain or unhappiness to
others otherwise than by constraining liberty of action. Such
harmful conduct in some cases would be an exercise of the

basic liberties, such as freedom of speech, for example, or the use of property, though in other cases it may be the exercise of a liberty not classed by Rawls as basic. It would be extraordinary if principles of justice which Rawls claims are in general in harmony with ordinary considered judgments were actually to exclude (because they limited liberty otherwise than for the sake of liberty) laws restraining libel or slander, or publications grossly infringing privacy, or restrictions on the use of private property (e.g. automobiles) designed to protect the environment and general social amenities. These restrictions on the basic liberties of speech and private property are commonly accepted as trade-offs not of liberty for liberty, but of liberty for protection from harm or loss of amenities or other elements of real utility.

There are two ways in which perhaps Rawls's principles can at least partly fill this gap.[50] In some cases more plausibly than others, he might argue that an unrestricted liberty to inflict what we call harm or suffering on others would in fact restrict the victim's liberty of action in either or both of two ways. The physical injury inflicted might actually impair the capacity for action, or the knowledge that such harmful actions were not prohibited might create conditions of apprehension and uncertainty among potential victims which would grossly inhibit their actions. But such arguments seem quite implausible except in cases of conduct inflicting serious physical harm on individuals, and even there, when such restrictions are accepted as a reasonable sacrifice of liberty, it seems clear that if pain and suffering and distress were not given a weight independent of the tendency of harmful conduct to inhibit the victim's actions or incapacitate him from action, the balance would often, in fact, not be struck as it is.

[50] Professor Dworkin and Mr Michael Lesnoff have suggested to me that what I describe here as a 'gap' may not in fact exist, since Rawls's basic liberties may be conceived by him as limited *ab initio* so that they do not include the liberty to act in a way damaging to the interests or liberties of others. But though it is certainly consistent with much of Rawls's discussion of basic liberties to treat his admittedly rough description of them as simply indicating areas of conduct within which the parties in the original position identify specific rights *after* resolving conflicts between the several liberties and the interests or liberties of others, this does not fit with Rawls's account of the basic liberties as liable to conflict, nor with his account of the conflicts as resolved not by the parties in the original position but by constitutional convention or by a body of legislators adopting the point of view of the representative equal citizen.

It is, however, necessary at this point again to take into account those natural duties which are standards of individual conduct, as distinct from principles of justice, which are standards for institutions. These duties include the duty not to harm others or cause 'unnecessary suffering' and also the duty to come to the assistance of others. In discussing the acceptance of such duties by the parties in the original position, Rawls represents them as calculating that the burdens of such duties will be outweighed by the benefits;[51] so natural duties represent cases where, like the simple rules of debate case, the best worst position for all rational men can be identified, and in these cases even from behind the veil of ignorance. Even there it will appear to the parties as rational self-interested persons that it is, for example, better to be restrained from practising cruelty to others while protected from them than to be exposed to others' cruelty while free to practise it, and better to have to provide modest assistance to others in need than never to be able to rely on such assistance being forthcoming. So it is plain that these natural duties might fill part of the gap left open by the principle that liberty may only be limited for the sake of liberty, if Rawls means (though he does not explicitly say it) that even the basic liberties may be restricted if their exercise would infringe any natural duty. But again, these natural duties chosen from behind the veil of ignorance would only account for very obvious cases where the benefits of the restrictions would, for all rational men, plainly outweigh the burdens. This will not help where divergent choices would reasonably be made by different individuals in the light of their different interests, and it seems to me that this will very often be the case. Some persons, given their general temperament, might reasonably prefer to be free to libel others or to invade their privacy, or to make use of their own property in whatever style they like, and might gladly take the risk of being exposed to these practices on the part of others and to the consequences of such practices for themselves and the general social and physical environment. Other persons would not pay this price for unrestricted liberty in these matters, since, given their temperament, they would value the protections afforded by the restrictions higher than

[51] Op. cit. n. 2 *supra*, 338.

the unrestricted liberty. In such cases restrictions on the basic liberties of speech or private property cannot be represented as a matter of natural duty on the footing that rational men, whatever their particular temperament, would opt for the restrictions just as they might opt for general restrictions on killing or the use of violence.

Of course, it is certainly to be remembered that justice for Rawls does not exhaust morality; there are, as he tells us, requirements, indeed duties, in relation to animals and even in relation to the rest of nature which are outside the scope of a theory of what is owed to rational individuals.[52] But even if there are such moral duties, regarding even rational beings, I do not think that Rawls would consider them as supplementing principles of justice which apply to institutions. I take it, therefore, that restrictions on the basic liberties excluded by the principles of justice because they are not restrictions of liberty for the sake of liberty could not be independently supported as just by appeal to other principles of morality. The point here is not that Rawlsian justice will be shown to be indeterminate at certain points as to the propriety of certain restrictions on liberty; it is, on the contrary, all too determinate, since it seems to exclude such restrictions as actually unjust because they do not limit liberty only for the sake of liberty. I take it Rawls would not wish to meet this point by simply adding to his principles of justice a further supplement permitting liberty to be restricted if its exercise violated not only the natural duties but any requirements of morality, for this would, it seems to me, run counter to the general liberal tenor of his theory.

V. THE CHOICE OF BASIC LIBERTIES

I think the most important general point which emerges from these separate criticisms is as follows. Any scheme providing for the general distribution in society of liberty of action necessarily does two things: first, it confers on individuals the advantage of that liberty, but secondly, it exposes them to whatever disadvantages the practices of that liberty by others may entail for them. These disadvantages include not only the

---

[52] Ibid. 512.

case on which Rawls concentrates, namely interference with another individual's basic liberties, but also the various forms of harm, pain, and suffering against which legal systems usually provide by restrictive rules. Such harm may also include the destruction of forms of social life or amenities which otherwise would have been available to the individual. So whether or not it is in any man's interest to choose that any specific liberty should be generally distributed depends on whether the advantages for him of the exercise of that liberty outweigh the various disadvantages for him of its general practice by others. I do not think Rawls recognizes this adequately in his discussion of conflicting liberties and his theory of natural duties. His recognition is inadequate, I think, because his doctrine insists that liberty can only be limited for the sake of liberty, and that when we resolve conflicts we must be concerned only with the extent or amount of liberty. This conceals the character of the advantages and disadvantages of different sorts which must be involved in the resolution of such conflicts; and his doctrine also leads him to misrepresent the character of all except those most simple conflicts between liberty and other benefits which are resolved by the parties in the original position when they choose the natural duties. Throughout, I think, Rawls fails to recognize sufficiently that a weighing of advantage and disadvantage must always be required to determine whether the general distribution of any specific liberty is in a man's interest, since the exercise of that liberty by others may outweigh the advantages to him of his own exercise of it. A rather startling sign that this is ignored appears in Rawls's remark that 'from the standpoint of the original position, it is rational' for men to want as large a share as possible of liberty, since 'they are not compelled to accept more if they do not wish to, nor does a person suffer from a greater liberty'.[53] This I find misleading because it seems to miss the vital point that, whatever advantage for any individual there may be in the exercise of some liberty taken in itself, this may be outweighed by the disadvantage for him involved in the general distribution of that liberty in the society of which he is a member.

The detailed criticisms which I have made so far concern

---

[53] Ibid. 143.

the *application* of Rawls's principle of greatest equal liberty. But the general point made in the last paragraph, if it is valid, affects not merely the application of the principles of justice once they have been chosen but also the argument which is designed to show that the parties would in the conditions of the original position, as rational self-interested persons, choose the basic liberties which Rawls enumerates. Even if we assume with Rawls that every rational person would prefer as much liberty as he can get if no price is to be paid for it, so that in that sense it is true that no one 'suffers from a greater liberty', it does not follow that a liberty which can only be obtained by an individual at the price of its general distribution through society is one that a rational person would still want. Of course, Rawls's natural duties represent some obvious cases where it can fairly be said that any rational person would prefer certain restrictions to a generalized liberty. In other, less simple cases, whether it would be rational to prefer liberty at the cost of others having it too must depend on one's temperament and desires. But these are hidden from the parties in the original position, and, this being so, I do not understand how they can make a rational decision, in terms of self-interest, to have the various liberties at the cost of their general distribution. Opting for the most extensive liberty for all cannot, I think, be presented as always being the best insurance against the worst in conditions of uncertainty about one's own temperament and desires.

VI. THE ARGUMENT FOR THE PRIORITY OF LIBERTY

I will end by explaining a difficulty which I find in the main argument which Rawls uses to show that the priority of liberty prohibiting exchanges of liberty for economic or other social advantages must be included among the requirements of justice. According to Rawls's theory, the rational, self-interested parties in the original position choose this priority rule from behind the veil of ignorance as part of the special conception of justice, but they choose it on the footing that the rule is not to come into play unless or until certain favourable social and economic conditions have actually been reached in the society of which they will be members. These favourable conditions are identified as those which allow the effective establishment and exercise of the basic liberties,[54] and when basic wants can be fulfilled.[55] Until this point is reached the general conception of justice is to govern the society, and men may give up liberties for social and economic gains if they wish.

I do not think that Rawls conceives of the conditions which bring the priority rule into play as a stage of great prosperity.[56] At any rate, it is quite clear that when this stage is reached there may still be in any society people who want more material goods and would be willing to surrender some of their basic liberties to get them. If material prosperity at this stage were so great that there could then be no such people, the priority rule then brought into operation could not function as a prohibitory rule, for there would be nothing for it to rule out. As Rawls says, we need not think of the surrender of liberties which men might still be willing to make for greater economic welfare in very extreme terms, such as the adoption of slavery.[57] It might be merely that some men, perhaps a majority, perhaps even all, in a society might wish to surrender certain political rights the exercise of which does not appear to them to bring great benefits, and would be willing to let government be carried on in some authoritarian form if there were good reasons for believing that this would bring a great advance in material prosperity. It is this kind of exchange which men might wish to make that the priority rule forbids once a society has reached the quite modest stage where the basic liberties can be effectively established and the basic wants satisfied.

[54] Ibid. 152.

[55] Ibid. 542–3.

[56] It is plain that under this identification the conditions for the application of the special conception of justice may be reached at very different levels of material prosperity in different societies. Thus, in a small agrarian society or in a society long used to hard conditions, men might be capable of establishing and exercising political liberties at a much lower standard of living than would be possible for inhabitants of a large, modern industrial society. But in view of the fact that Rawls describes the relevant stage as one where conditions merely 'allow' or 'admit' the effective establishment and realization of basic liberties, it is not clear to me whether he would consider the special conception of justice applicable to a very wealthy society where, owing to the unequal distribution of wealth, poverty prevented considerable numbers from actually exercising the basic liberties. Would it be unjust for the poor in such a society to support an authoritarian form of government to advance their material conditions?

[57] Op. cit. n. 2 *supra*, 61.

Why then should this restrictive priority rule be accepted as among the requirements of justice? Rawls's main answer seems to be that, as the conditions of civilization improve, a point will be reached when, *from the standpoint of the original position*, 'it becomes and then remains . . . irrational to acknowledge a lesser liberty for the sake of greater material means. . . .' because, 'as the general level of well-being rises, only the less urgent material wants remain'[58] to be satisfied and men come increasingly to prize liberty. 'The fundamental interest in determining our plan of life *eventually* assumes a prior place' and 'the desire for liberty is the chief regulative interest that the parties [in the original position] must suppose they all will have in common *in due course*'.[59] These considerations are taken to show the rationality, from the standpoint of the parties in the original position, of ranking liberty over material goods, represented by the priority rule.

The core of this argument seems to be that it is rational for the parties in the original position, ignorant as they are of their own temperaments and desires and the conditions of the society of which they are to be members, to impose this restriction on themselves, prohibiting exchanges of liberty for other goods because 'eventually' or 'in due course' in the development of that society the desire for liberty will actually come to have a greater attraction for them. But it is not obvious to me why it is rational for men to impose on themselves a restriction against doing something they may want to do at some stage in the development of their society because at a later stage ('eventually' or 'in due course') they would not want to do it. There seems no reason why a surrender of political liberties which men might want to make purely for a large increase in material welfare, which would be forbidden by the priority rule, should be permanent so as to prevent men, when great affluence is reached, restoring the liberties if they wished to do so; it is not as if men would run the risk, if there were no priority rule, of permanently losing liberties which later they might wish to have. I think, however, that probably Rawls's argument is really of the following form, which makes use again of the idea that under certain conditions of uncertainty rational beings would opt for the

---

[58] Ibid. 542.
[59] Ibid. 543 (emphasis added).

alternative whose worst consequences would be least damaging to one's interests than the worst consequences of other alternatives. Since the parties in the original position do not know the stage of development of their society, they must, in considering whether to institute a priority rule prohibiting exchanges of liberty for economic goods, ask themselves which of the following alternatives, A or B, is least bad:

A. If there is no priority rule and political liberties have been surrendered in order to gain an increase in wealth, the worst position is that of a man anxious to exercise the lost liberties and who cares nothing for extra wealth brought him by surrender.

B. If there is a priority rule, the worst position will be that of a person living at the bottom economic level of society, just prosperous enough to bring the priority rule into operation, and who would gladly surrender the political liberties for a greater advance in material prosperity.

It must, I think, be part of Rawls's argument that for any rational self-interested person B is the best worst position and for that reason the parties in the original position would choose it. I am not sure that this is Rawls's argument, but if it is, I do not find it convincing. For it seems to me that here again the parties in the original position, ignorant as they are of the character and strength of their desires, just cannot give any determinate answer if they ask which of the positions, A or B, it is then, in their condition of ignorance, most in their interests to choose. When the veil of ignorance is lifted some will prefer A to B and others B to A.

It may be that a better case along the line of argument just considered could be made out for some of the basic liberties, for example, religious freedom, than for others. It might be said that any rational person who understood what it is to have a religious faith and to wish to practise it would agree that for any such person to be prevented by law from practising his religion must be worse than for a relatively poor man to be prevented from gaining a great advance in material goods through the surrender of a religious liberty which meant little or nothing to him. But even if this is so, it seems to me that no *general* priority rule forbidding the exchange, even for a limited period, of any basic liberty which men might wish to make in order to gain an advance in material prosperity, can be supported by this argument which I have ascribed, possibly mistakenly, to Rawls.

I think the apparently dogmatic course of Rawls's argument for the priority of liberty may be explained by the fact that, though he is not offering it merely as an ideal, he does harbour a latent ideal of his own, on which he tacitly draws when he represents the priority of liberty as a choice which the parties in the original position must, in their own interest, make as rational agents choosing from behind the veil of ignorance. The ideal is that of a public-spirited citizen who prizes political activity and service to others as among the chief goods of life and could not contemplate as tolerable an exchange of the opportunities for such activity for mere material goods or contentment. This ideal powerfully impregnates Rawls's book at many points which I have been unable to discuss here. It is, of course, among the chief ideals of liberalism, but Rawls's argument for the priority of liberty purports to rest on interests, not on ideals, and to demonstrate that the general priority of liberty reflects a preference for liberty over other goods which every self-interested person who is rational would have. Though his argument throws much incidental light on the relationship between liberty and other values, I do not think that it succeeds in demonstrating its priority.

POSTSCRIPT

See for comments: J. Rawls, 'The Basic Liberties and their Priority', 3 *Tanner Lectures on Human Values* (1982).

Social Solidarity and the Enforcement of Morality

It is possible to extract from Plato's *Republic* and *Laws*, and perhaps from Aristotle's *Ethics* and *Politics*, the following thesis about the role of law in relation to the enforcement of morality: the law of the city state exists not merely to secure that men have the opportunity to lead a morally good life, but to see that they do. According to this thesis not only may the law be used to punish men for doing what morally it is wrong for them to do, but it should be so used; for the promotion of moral virtue by these means and by others is one of the ends or purposes of a society complex enough to have developed a legal system. This theory is strongly associated with a specific conception of morality as a uniquely true or correct set of principles — not man-made, but either awaiting man's discovery by the use of his reason or (in a theological setting) awaiting its disclosure by revelation. I shall call this theory 'the classical thesis' and not discuss it further.

From the classical thesis there is to be distinguished what I shall call 'the disintegration thesis'. This inverts the order of instrumentality between society on the one hand and morality on the other as it appears in the classical thesis; for in this thesis society is not the instrument of the moral life; rather morality is valued as the cement of society, the bond, or one of the bonds, without which men would not cohere in society. This thesis is associated strongly with a relativist conception of morality: according to it, morality may vary from society to society, and to merit enforcement by the criminal law, morality need have no rational or other specific content. It is not the quality of the morality but its cohesive power which matters. 'What is important is not the quality of the creed but the strength of the belief in it. The enemy of society is not error but indifference.'[1] The case for the enforcement

---

[1] P. Devlin, *The Enforcement of Morals* 114 (1965) [hereinafter cited as Devlin]. Cf. ibid. at 94: 'Unfortunately bad societies can live on bad morals just as well as good societies on good ones.'

of morality on this view is that its maintenance is necessary to prevent the disintegration of society.

The disintegration thesis, under pressure of the request for empirical evidence to substantiate the claim that the maintenance of morality is in fact necessary for the existence of society, often collapses into another thesis which I shall call 'the conservative thesis'. This is the claim that society has a right to enforce its morality by law because the majority have the right to follow their own moral convictions that their moral environment is a thing of value to be defended from change.[2]

The topic of this article is the disintegration thesis, but I shall discharge in relation to it only a very limited set of tasks. What I shall mainly do is attempt to discover what, when the ambiguities are stripped away, is the empirical claim which the thesis makes and in what directions is it conceivable that a search for evidence to substantiate this claim would be rewarding. But even these tasks I shall discharge only partially.

I

The disintegration thesis is a central part of the case presented by Lord Devlin[3] justifying the legal enforcement of morality at points where followers of John Stuart Mill and other latter-day liberals would consider this an unjustifiable extension of the scope of the criminal law. The morality, the enforcement of which is justified according to Lord Devlin, is variously described as 'the moral structure' of society, 'a public morality', 'a common morality', 'shared ideas on politics, morals, ethics', 'fundamental agreement about good and evil', and 'a

---

[2] This characterization of the conservative thesis is taken from Dworkin, 'Lord Devlin and the Enforcement of Morals', 75 *Yale L.J.* 986 (1966). Professor Dworkin distinguishes the parts played in Lord Devlin's work by the disintegration thesis and the conservative thesis, and his essay is mainly concerned with the critical examination of Lord Devlin's version of the latter. The present essay, by contrast, is mainly concerned to determine what sort of evidence is required if the disintegration thesis is not to collapse into or be abandoned for the conservative thesis.

[3] See principally the lecture by Lord Devlin entitled 'The Enforcement of Morals' which he delivered as the Second Maccabaean Lecture in Jurisprudence of the British Academy and which is reproduced in Devlin ch. I as 'Morals and the Criminal Law'.

recognised morality'.[4] This is said to be part of 'the invisible bonds of common thought' which hold society together; and 'if the bonds were too far relaxed the members would drift apart',[5] It is part of 'the bondage . . . of society' and is 'as necessary to society as, say, a recognised government'.[6] The justification for the enforcement of this recognized morality is simply that the law may be used to preserve anything essential to society's existence. 'There is disintegration when no common morality is observed and history shows that the loosening of moral bonds is often the first stage of disintegration'.[7] If we consider these formulations they seem to constitute a highly ambitious empirical generalization about a necessary condition for the existence or continued existence of a society, and so give us a sufficient condition for the disintegration of society. Apart from the one general statement that 'history shows that the loosening of moral bonds is often the first stage of disintegration', no evidence is given in support of the argument and no indication is given of the kind of evidence that would support it, nor is any sensitivity betrayed to the need for evidence.

In disputing with Lord Devlin,[8] I offered him the alternative of supplementing his contentions with evidence, or accepting that his statements about the necessity of a common morality for the existence of society were not empirical statements at all but were disguised tautologies or necessary truths depending entirely on the meaning given to the expression 'society', 'existence', or 'continued existence' of society. If the continued existence of a society meant living according to some specific shared moral code, then the preservation of a moral code is logically and not causally or contingently necessary to the continued existence of society, and this seems too unexciting a theme to be worth ventilating. Yet at points Lord Devlin adopts a definition of society ('a society *means* a community of ideas'[9]) which seems to suggest that he intended his statements about the necessity of a morality

[4] Devlin 9–11.
[5] Devlin 10.
[6] Devlin 10–11.
[7] Devlin 13.
[8] See H. L. A. Hart, *Law, Liberty, and Morality* (1963).
[9] Devlin 10 (emphasis added). But cf. ibid. at 9: 'What makes a society of any sort is community of ideas . . .'

to society's existence as a definitional truth. Of course, very often the expressions 'society', 'existence of society', and 'the same society' are used in this way: that is, they refer to a form or type of social life individuated by a certain morality or moral code or by distinctive legal, political, or economic institutions. A society in the sense of a form or type of social life can change, disappear, or be succeeded by different forms of society without any phenomenon describable as 'disintegration' or 'members drifting apart'. In this sense of 'society', post-feudal England was a different society from feudal England. But if we express this simple fact by saying that *the same English society* was at one time a feudal society and at another time not, we make use of another sense of 'society' with different criteria of individuation and continued identity. It is plain that if the threat of disintegration or 'members drifting apart' is to have any reality, or if the claim that a common morality is 'as necessary to society as, say, a recognised government' is taken to be part of an argument for the enforcement of morality, definitional truths dependent upon the identification of society with its shared morality are quite irrelevant. Just as it would be no reply to an anarchist who wished to preserve society to tell him that government is necessary to an organized society, if it turned out that by 'organized society' we merely meant a society with a government, so it is empty to argue against one who considers that the preservation of society's code of morality is not the law's business, that the maintenance of the moral code is necessary to the existence of society, if it turns out that by 'society' is meant a society living according to this moral code.

The short point is that if we *mean* by 'society ceasing to exist' not 'disintegration' nor 'the drifting apart' of its members, but a radical change in its common morality, then the case for using the law to preserve morality must rest not on any disintegration thesis but on some variant of the claim that when groups of men have developed a common form of life rich enough to include a common morality, this is something which ought to be preserved. One very obvious form of this claim is the conservative thesis that the majority have a right in these circumstances to defend their existing moral environment from change. But this is no longer an empirical claim.

II

Views not dissimilar from Lord Devlin's, and in some cases hovering in a similar way between the disintegration thesis and the conservative thesis, can be found in much contemporary sociological theory of the structural and functional prerequisites of society. It would, for example, be profitable, indeed necessary for a full appreciation of Talcott Parsons's work, to take formulations of what is apparently the disintegration thesis which can be found in almost every chapter of his book *The Social System*, and inquire (i) what precisely they amount to; (ii) whether they are put forward as empirical claims; and (iii) if so, by what evidence they are or could be supported. Consider, for example, such formulations as the following: 'The sharing of such common value patterns . . . creates a solidarity among those mutually oriented to the common values. . . . [W]ithout attachment to the constitutive common values the collectivity tends to dissolve.'[10] 'This integration of a set of common value patterns with the internalized need-disposition structure of the constituent personalities is the core phenomenon of the dynamics of social systems. That the stability of any social system is dependent on a degree of such integration may be said to be the fundamental dynamic theorem of sociology.'[11] The determination of the precise status and the role of these propositions in Parson's complex works would be a task of some magnitude, so I shall select from the literature of sociology Durkheim's elaboration of a form of the disintegration theory, because his variant of the theory as expounded in his book, *The Division of Labour in Society*, is relatively clear and briefly expressed, and is also specifically connected with the topic of the enforcement of morality by the criminal law.

Durkheim distinguishes two forms of what he calls 'solidarity' or factors tending to unify men or lead them to cohere in discriminable and enduring societies. The minimum meaning attached to 'society' here is that of a group of men which we can distinguish from other similar groups and can recognize as being the same group persisting through a period of time though its constituent members have been replaced

---

[10] T. Parsons, *The Social System* 41 (1951).
[11] Ibid. at 42.

during the time by others. One of the forms of solidarity, 'mechanical solidarity', springs from men's resemblances, and the other, 'organic solidarity', from their differences. Mechanical solidarity depends on, or perhaps indeed consists in, sharing of common beliefs about matters of fact and common standards of behaviour among which is a common morality. This blend of common belief and common standards constitutes the *conscience collective*, which draws upon all the ambiguities of the French word *conscience* as between consciousness or knowledge and conscience. The point of the use of this terminology of *conscience* is largely that the beliefs and subscription to the common standards become internalized as part of the personality or character of the members of society.

Organic solidarity by contrast depends on the dissimilarities of human beings and their mutual need to be complemented by association in various forms with others who are unlike themselves. The most prominent aspect of this interdependence of dissimilars is the division of labour, but Durkheim warns us that we must not think of the importance of this as a unifying element of society as residing simply in its economic payoff. '[T]he economic services that it [the division of labour] can render are picayune compared to the moral effect that it produces, and its true function is to create in two or more persons a feeling of solidarity.'[12] Generally, mechanical solidarity is the dominant form of solidarity in simple societies and diminishes in importance, though apparently it is never eliminated altogether as a unifying factor, as organic solidarity develops in more complex societies. According to Durkheim the law presents a faithful mirror of both forms of solidarity, and can be used as a gauge of the relative importance at any time of the two forms. The criminal law, with its repressive sanctions, reflects mechanical solidarity; the civil law reflects organic solidarity, since it upholds the typical instruments of interdependence, e.g. the institution of contract, and generally provides not for repressive sanctions, but for restitution and compensation.

Somewhat fantastically Durkheim thinks that the law can be used as a measuring instrument. We have merely to count

[12] E. Durkheim, *The Division of Labour in Society* 56 (3rd edn. Simpson trans. 1964).

the number of rules which at any time constitute the criminal law and the number of rules which constitute the civil law expressing the division of labour, and then we know what fraction to assign to the relative importance of the two forms of solidarity.[13] This fantasy opens formidable problems concerning the individuation and countability of legal rules which occupied Bentham a great deal[14] but perhaps need not detain us here. What is of great interest, however, is Durkheim's view of the role of the criminal law in relation to a shared morality. Durkheim is much concerned to show the hollowness of rationalistic and utilitarian accounts of the institution of criminal punishment. For him, as for his English judicial counterpart, utilitarian theory fails as an explanatory theory, for it distorts the character of crime and punishment, and considered as a normative theory would lead to disturbing results. Durkheim therefore provides fresh definitions of both crime and punishment. For him a crime is essentially (though in developed societies there are secondary senses of crime to which this definition does not apply directly) a serious offence against the collective conscience — the common morality which holds men together at points where its sentiments are both strong and precise. Such an act is not condemned by that morality because it is independently a crime or wrong, it is a crime or wrong because it is so condemned. Above all, to be wrong or a crime an act need not be, nor even be believed to be, harmful to anyone or to society in any sense other than that it runs counter to the common morality at points where its sentiments are strong and precise. These features of Durkheim's theory are striking analogues of Lord Devlin's observation that it is not the quality of the morality that matters but the strength of the belief in it and its consequent cohesive power, and his stipulation that the morality to be enforced must be up to what may be called concert pitch: it must be marked by 'intolerance, indignation, and disgust'.[15]

What, then, on this view, is punishment? Why punish? And how severely? Punishment for Durkehim is essentially the

---

[13] Ibid. at 68.

[14] Bentham devoted a whole book to the questions: What is one law? What is part of a law? What is a complete law? See Bentham, *Of Laws in General*, in *Collected Works of Jeremy Bentham* (London 1970).

[15] Devlin viii–ix, 17.

hostility excited by violations of the common morality which may be either diffused throughout society or administered by official action, when it will usually have the form of specifically graduated measures. His definition, therefore, is that punishment is 'a passionate reaction of graduated intensity' to offences against the collective conscience.[16] The hollowness of utilitarian theory as an explanation of criminal punishment is evident if we look at the way that, even in contemporary society, criminal punishments are graduated. They are adapted not to the utilitarian aim of preventing what would be ordinarily described as harmful conduct, but to the appropriate expression of the degree of feeling excited by the offence, on the footing that such appropriate expression of feeling is a means of sustaining the belief in the collective morality.[17] Many legal phenomena bear this out. We punish a robber even if he is likely to offend again, less severely than a murderer whom we have every reason to think will not offend again. We adopt the principle that ignorance of the law is no excuse in criminal matters, and, he might have added, we punish attempts less severely than completed offences, thereby reflecting a difference in the resentment generated for the completed as compared with the uncompleted crime.

Hence, to the question 'Why punish?' Durkheim's answer is that we do so primarily as a symbolic expression of the outraged common morality the maintenance of which is the condition of cohesion resulting from men's likenesses. Punishing the offender is required to maintain social cohesion because the common conscience, violated by the offence, 'would necessarily lose its energy if an emotional reaction of the community [in the form of punishment] did not come to compensate its loss, and it would result in a breakdown of social solidarity'.[18]

This thumbnail sketch of Durkheim's theory presents its essentials, but there are two complexities of importance, as there are also in Lord Devlin's case. Both have to do with the possibilities of change in the common morality. Both theorists seem to envisage a spontaneous or natural change and warn

[16] Durkheim, op. cit. n. 12 *supra*, 90.
[17] Cf. Devlin 114: 'When considering intangible injury to society it is moral belief that matters; immoral activity is relevant only insofar as it promotes disbelief.'
[18] Durkheim, op cit. n. 12 *supra*, 108.

us in different ways that the enforcement of morality must allow for this. Thus Lord Devlin issues prudential warnings to the legislator that '[t]he limits of tolerance shift'[19] and that we should not make criminal offences out of moral opinion which is likely soon to change and leave the law high, and, so to speak, morally dry. Durkheim similarly says that his theory does not mean that it is necessary to conserve a penal rule because it once corresponded to the collective sentiments, but only if the sentiment is still 'living and energetic'. If it has disappeared or been enfeebled, nothing is worse than trying to keep it alive artificially by the law.[20] This means that we must distinguish a natural or non-malignant change in the social morality or a natural 'shift in its limts of tolerance' from a malignant form of change against which society is to be protected and which is the result of individual deviation from its morality. It is, however, a further complexity in these theories that the function of punishment, or rather the mechanism by which punishment operates in preserving a social morality from malignant change, differs as between Durkheim and Lord Devlin. For Lord Devlin punishment protects the existing morality by repressing or diminishing the number of immoral actions which in themselves are considered 'to threaten' or weaken the common morality. For Durkheim, however, punishment sustains the common morality, not mainly by repressing the immoral conduct, but principally by giving satisfactory vent to a sense of outrage because if the vent were closed the common conscience would 'lose its energy' and the cohesive morality would weaken.

III

If we ask in relation to theories such as Lord Devlin's and Durkheim's precisely what empirical claim they make concerning the connection between the maintenance of a common morality and the existence of society, some further disentangling of knots has to be done.

It seems a very natural objection to such theories that if

---

[19] Devlin 18. Cf. ibid. at 114: '[T]here is nothing inherently objectionable about the change of an old morality for a new one . . . . [I]t is the interregnum of disbelief that is perilous'.
[20] Durkheim, op. cit. n. 12 *supra*, 107 n. 45.

they are to be taken seriously as variants of the disintegration thesis, the justification which they attempt to give for the enforcement of social morality is far too general. It is surely both possible and good sense to discriminate between those parts of a society's moral code (assuming it has a single moral code) which are essential for the existence of a society and those which are not. Prima facie, at least, the need for such a discrimination seems obvious even if we assume that the moral code is only to be enforced where it is supported by 'sentiments which are strong and precise' (Durkheim) or by 'intolerance, indignation and disgust' (Devlin). For the decay of all moral restraint or the free use of violence or deception would not only cause individual harm but would jeopardize the existence of a society since it would remove the main conditions which make it possible and worthwhile for men to live together in close proximity to each other. On the other hand the decay of moral restraint on, say, extramarital intercourse, or a general change of sexual morality in a permissive direction seems to be quite another matter and not obviously to entail any such consequences as 'disintegration' or 'men drifting apart'.[21]

---

[21] Lord Devlin in a footnote concedes that not every *breach* of a society's moral code threatens its existence. His words are: 'I do not assert that *any* deviation from a society's shared morality threatens its existence any more than I assert that *any* subversive activity threatens its existence. I assert that they are both activities which are capable in their nature of threatening the existence of society so that neither can be put beyond the law.' Devlin 13 n. 1 (emphasis in original). This passage does not mean or imply that there are any parts of a social morality which though supported by indignation, intolerance, and disgust can be regarded as not essential for society's existence: on this point Lord Devlin plainly inclines towards the conception of a social morality as a seamless web. Devlin115. But Professor Dworkin argues, convincingly in my opinion, that Lord Devlin uses the same criterion (in effect 'passionate public disapproval') to determine both that a deviation from public morality *may* conceivably threaten its existence and that it in fact *does* so, so as to justify actual punishment. Dworkin, op. cit. n. 2 *supra*, 986, 990-2 . This leaves his version of the disintegration thesis without empirical support. Thus, according to Lord Devlin, 'We should ask ourselves in the first instance whether, looking at homosexuality calmly and dispassionately, we regard it as a vice so abominable that its mere presence is an offence. If that is the genuine feeling of the society in which we live, I do not see how society can be denied the right to eradicate it.' Devlin 17. But he offers no evidence that in these circumstances the legal toleration of homosexuality would in fact endanger society's existence. Contrast the foregoing with the principles applied by Lord Devlin to fornication in relation to which 'feeling may not be so intense'. In *that* case: 'It becomes *then* a question of balance, the danger to society in one scale and the extent of the restriction in the other.' Devlin 17-18 (emphasis added).

It seems, therefore, worthwhile pausing to consider two possible ways of discriminating within a social morality the parts which are to be considered essential.

(i) The first possibility is that the common morality which is essential to society, and which is to be preserved by legal enforcement, is that part of its social morality which contains only those restraints and prohibitions that are essential to the existence of any society of human beings whatever. Hobbes and Hume have supplied us with general characterizations of this moral minimum essential for social life: they include rules restraining the free use of violence and minimal forms of rules regarding honesty, promise-keeping, fair dealing, and property. It is, however, quite clear that neither Devlin nor Durkheim means that only these elements, which are to be found in common morality, are to be enforced by law, since any utilitarian or supporter of the Wolfenden Report would agree to that. Quite clearly the argument of both Lord Devlin and Durkheim concerns moral rules which may differ from society to society. Durkheim actually insists that the common morality, violations of which are to be punished by the criminal law, may have no relation to utility: 'It was not at all useful for them [these prohibitions] to be born, but once they have endured, it becomes necessary that they persist in spite of their irrationality'.[22] The morality to be punished includes much that relates 'neither to vital interests of society nor to a minimum of justice'.[23]

(ii) The second possibility is this: the morality to be enforced, while not coextensive with every jot and tittle of an existent moral code, includes not only the restraints and prohibitions such as those relating to the use of violence or deception which are necessary to any society whatever, but also what is essential for a particular society. The guiding thought here is that for any society there is to be found, among the provisions of its code of morality, a central core of rules or principles which constitutes its pervasive and distinctive style of life. Lord Devlin frequently speaks in this way of what he calls monogamy adopted 'as a moral principle',[24] and of course this does deeply pervade our society in two principal ways. First, marriage is a *legal* institution and the recognition of

---

[22] Durkheim, op. cit. n. 12 *supra*, 107.
[23] Ibid. at 81.
[24] Devlin 9.

monogamy as the sole legal form of marriage carries implications for the law related to wide areas of conduct: the
custody and education of children, the rules relating to inheritance and distribution of property, etc. Second, the principle of monogamy is also morally pervasive: monogamous
marriage is at the heart of our conception of family life, and
with the aid of the law has become part of the structure of
society. Its disappearance would carry with it vast changes
throughout society so that without exaggeration we might say
that it had changed its character.

On this view the morality which is necessary to the existence of society is neither the moral minimum required in all
societies (Lord Devlin himself says that the polygamous marriage in a polygamous society may be an equally cohesive
force as monogamy is in ours),[25] nor is it every jot and tittle of
a society's moral code. What is essential and is to be preserved
is the central core. On this footing it would be an open and
empirical question whether any particular moral rule or veto,
e.g. on homosexuality, adultery, or fornication, is so organi-
cally connected with the central core that its maintenance and
preservation is required as a vital outwork or bastion. There
are perhaps traces of some of these ideas in Lord Devlin, but
not in Durkheim. But even if we take this to be the position,
we are still not really confronted with an empirical claim concerning the connection of the maintenance of a common
morality and the prevention of disintegration or 'drifting
apart'. Apart from the point about whether a particular rule
is a vital outwork or bastion of the central core, we may still
be confronted only with the unexciting tautology depending
now on the identification of society, not with the whole of its
morality but only with its central core or 'character', and this
is not the disintegration thesis.

IV

What is required to convert the last-mentioned position into
the disintegration thesis? It must be the theory that the maintenance of the core elements in a particular society's moral
life is in fact necessary to prevent disintegration, because the

---

[25] Devlin 114.

withering or malignant decay of the central morality is a disintegrating factor. But even if we have got thus far in identifying an empirical claim, there would of course be very many questions to be settled before anything empirically testable could be formulated. What are the criteria in a complex society for determining the existence of a single recognized morality or its central core? What is 'disintegration' and 'drifting apart' under modern conditions? I shall not investigate these difficulties, but I shall attempt to describe in outline the types of evidence that might conceivably be relevant to the issue if and when these difficulties are settled. They seem to be the following:

(a) Crude historical evidence in which societies — not individuals — are the units. The suggestion is that we should examine societies which have disintegrated and inquire whether their disintegration was preceded by a malignant change in their common morality. This done, we should then have to address ourselves to the possibility of a causal connection between decay of a common morality and disintegration. But of course all the familiar difficulties involved in macroscopic generalizations about society would meet us at this point, and anyone who has attempted to extract generalizations from what is called the decline and fall of the Roman Empire would know that they are formidable. To take only one such difficulty: suppose that all our evidence was drawn from simple tribal societies or closely knit agrarian societies (which would seem to be the most favourable application of Durkheim's theory of mechanical solidarity). We should not, I take it, have much confidence in applying any conclusions drawn from these to modern industrial societies. Or, if we had, it would be because we had some well-developed and well-evidenced theory to show us that the differences between simple societies and our own were irrelevant to these issues as the differences in the size of a laboratory can safely be ignored as irrelevant to the scope of the generalizations tested by laboratory experiments. Durkheim, it may be said, is peculiarly obscure on just this point, since it is not really clear from his book whether he means that in advanced societies characterized by extensive division of labour the mechanical solidarity which would still be reflected in its criminal law could be disregarded or not.

(b) The alternative type of evidence must be drawn presumably from social psychology and must break down into at least two sub-forms according to the way in which we conceive the alternatives to the maintenance of a common morality. One alternative is general uniform *permissiveness* in the area of conduct previously covered by the common morality. The lapse, for example, of the conception that the choices between two wives or one, heterosexuality or homosexuality, are more than matters of personal taste. This (the alternative of permissiveness) is what Lord Devlin seems to envisage or to fear when he says: 'The enemy of society is not error but indifference', and 'Whether the new belief is better or worse than the old, it is the interregnum of disbelief that is perilous.'[26] On the other hand the alternative may be not permissiveness but *moral pluralism* involving divergent sub-moralities in relation to the same area of conduct.

To get off the ground with the investigation of the questions that either of these two alternatives opens up, it would be reasonable to abandon any general criteria for the disintegration of society in favour of something sufficiently close to satisfy the general spirit of the disintegration thesis. It would be no doubt sufficient if our evidence were to show that malignant change in a common morality led to a general increase in such forms of antisocial behaviour as would infringe what seem the minimum essentials: the prohibitions and restraints of violence, disrespect for property and dishonesty. We should then require some account of the conceivable psychological mechanisms supposed to connect the malignant decay of a social morality with the increase in such forms of behaviour. Here there would no doubt be signal differences between the alternatives of permissiveness and moral pluralism. On the permissiveness alternative, the theory to be tested would presumably be that in the 'interregnum conditions', without the discipline involved in the submission of one area of life, e.g. the sexual, to the requirements of a common morality, there would necessarily be a weakening of the general capacity of individuals for self-control. So, with permissiveness in the area formally covered by restrictive sexual morality, there would come increases in violence and dishonesty

[26] Ibid.

and a general lapse of those restraints which are essential for any form of social life. This is the view that the morality of the individual constitutes a seamless web. There is a hint that this, in the last resort, is Lord Devlin's view of the way in which the 'interregnum' constitutes a danger to the existence of society: for he replied to my charge that he had assumed without evidence that morality was a seamless web by saying that though '[s]eamlessness presses the simile rather hard', 'most men take their morality as a whole'.[27] But surely this assumption cannot be regarded as obviously true. The contrary view seems at least equally plausible: permissiveness in certain areas of life (even if it has come about through the disregard of a previously firmly established sexual morality) might make it easier for men to submit to restraints on violence which are essential for social life.

If we conceive the successor to the 'common morality' to be not permissiveness but moral pluralism in some area of conduct once covered by a sexual morality which has decayed through the flouting of its restrictions, the thesis to be tested would presumably be that where moral pluralism develops in this way quarrels over the differences generated by divergent moralities must eventually destroy the minimal forms of restraint necessary for social cohesion. The counter-thesis would be that plural moralities in the conditions of modern large-scale societies might perfectly well be mutually tolerant. To many indeed it might seem that the counter-thesis is the more cogent of the two, and that over wide areas of modern life, sometimes hiding behind lip-service to an older common morality, there actually are divergent moralities living in peace.

I have done no more than to sketch in outline the type of evidence required to substantiate the disintegration thesis. Till psychologists and sociologists provide such evidence, supporters of the enforcement of morality would do better to rest their case candidly on the conservative rather than on the disintegration thesis.

POSTSCRIPT

See for criticism and comments: B. Mitchell, *Law, Morality, and Religion in a Secular Society* (Oxford 1967), chs. 1–3.

[27] Devlin 115.

PART V

FOUR LEGAL THEORISTS

Essay 12

Jhering's Heaven of Concepts and Modern Analytical Jurisprudence

I

I shall begin by expressing my regret that so few of Jhering's great works are translated into English. It is an intellectual tragedy; there is no English translation even of the masterly *Geist des Römischen Rechts* nor of *Scherz und Ernst in der Jurisprudenz*,[1] nor even of the essay *Im Juristischen Begriffshimmel* which I will discuss here, though some fragments of the latter appeared in 1951 in an English translation in an American collection of readings[2] in jurisprudence and legal philosophy. I hope this failure on our part to obtain translations of these works will one day be remedied.

The English lawyer interested in the philosophy of law will, when he reads this brilliant little work of Jhering's, have two contrasting experiences. On the one hand, he will be surprised; for, rightly or wrongly, he would not expect to find wit and gaiety in the work of a German jurist of the nineteenth century. Certainly there is no English writer on law, with the possible exception of the early Bentham, who combines such lightness of touch with such profundity of insight as Jhering does. On the other hand the English reader of this work of Jhering will have a sensation of *déjà vu*, even if not *déjà lu*. This I will explain later; but first I will attempt to identify in summary form the main intellectual failings against which Jhering's satire is directed. I believe five different though related aberrations of legal thought can be distinguished here. They are as follows:

1. Excessive preoccupation with concepts considered in

---

[1] *Scherz und Ernst in der Jurisprudenz*. All references are to the 8th edn. (Leipzig 1900).
[2] *Readings in Jurisprudence and Philosophy of Law*, ed. Cohen and Cohen (New York 1951).

abstraction from the conditions under which they have to be applied in real life.[3]

2. Blindness to the social and individual interests which must be considered, together with other practical problems, in the use and development of legal concepts.[4]

3. A belief that it is possible to distinguish between the essence (*das Wesen*) and the legal consequences (*die Folgen*) of a legal rule or concept, so that we may consider concepts *in abstracto* 'aller seiner realen Wirkungen entkleidet' as Puchta did in the case of possession.[5] This leads to a special kind of nonsense in the solution of problems: it licenses us to say of a concept like possession that it is 'seinem Wesen nach Faktum, in seinen Folgen einem Rechte gleich'.[6] So it is 'Faktum und Recht zugleich'.[7]

4. Ignoring the ends and the purposes of law and refusing to ask the question: why is the law thus and so? In the *Begriffshimmel* 'fragt Niemand nach dem Warum'[8] and all concepts deformed by considerations of utility are put into the 'Anatomisch-pathologisches Begriffskabinett'.[9]

5. A false assimilation of the concepts and methods of legal science to mathematics; so that all legal reasoning is a matter of pure calculation in which the contents of the legal concepts are unfolded by logical deduction.[10]

Such, I think, is a summary of the main features of the style of legal thinking which Jhering is concerned to attack. Nearly all of them were attacked, often in closely similar language, by a great master of the common law from whom many English lawyers have learned a critical approach to their own system. He was not an Englishman, but a great American judge of the Supreme Court and a jurist, Oliver Wendell Holmes, Jr. Between Holmes's thought and Jhering's there are many striking

---

[3] 'Die Frage der Anwendung und des Beweises kommt für ihn gar nicht in Betracht' *Scherz und Ernst*, 273.

[4] 'Badet sich hier in dem reinen Gedankenäther, unbekümmert über die reale Welt', ibid. 274.

[5] Ibid. 296.

[6] Ibid. 283 n. 8 (quotation from Savigny).

[7] Ibid. (quotation from Savigny).

[8] Ibid. 287.

[9] Ibid. 297. Cf. 'thörichte Frage nach seinem praktischen Warum' ibid. 314.

[10] Ibid. 287–8. Cf. 'Der Jurist rechnet mit seinen Begriffen, wie der Mathematiker mit seinen Grössen', ibid. 274.

parallels; yet it seems clear that the American jurist arrived at his own critical position independently. Indeed, the author of the most recent, authoritative, and detailed biography of Holmes expressly states that, though Holmes certainly read four volumes of the *Geist des Römischen Rechts* in 1879, there is no indication that he ever recognized that Jhering had uttered protests against 'the beatitudes of logic' in German legal thought which were similar to his own protests.[11]

Here are some famous phrases from Holmes: 'The common law is not a brooding omnipresence in the sky',[12] and again 'the life of the law has not been logic; it has been experience',[13] and 'it is a fallacy to believe that a system of law can be worked out like mathematics from some general axioms of conduct',[14] and again, 'the fallacy that the only force at work in the development of the law is logic',[15] and 'general propositions do not decide concrete cases'.[16] 'Where there is doubt, the simple tool of logic does not suffice.'[17]

Holmes was inspired in such criticism of what he called 'the fallacy of logical form'[18] by the pragmatism and operationalism of the American philosopher, C. S. Peirce; but he combined with the pragmatism a deep conviction, similar to Jhering's own concern for 'Zweck im Recht', that lawyers must be sensitive in the interpretation and application of law to the claim of 'social advantage'.

Holmes was the spiritual godfather of a school of sceptical American jurists whose most extreme development was to be found in the loosely-knit group of writers known as the 'legal realists' and whose main work was done in the 1930s. But between them and Holmes came the main work of Roscoe Pound who explicitly recognized Holmes and Jhering, all of whose works he had read, as equal pioneers in the work of replacing *Begriffsjurisprudenz* by *Wirklichkeitsjurisprudenz*. The influence of Jhering's thought is plain in Pound's well-known *Interpretations of Legal History*[19] and in a famous

[11] Howe, *Justice Oliver Wendell Holmes: The Proving Years*, ii. 152.
[12] *Southern Pacific Co.* v. *Jensen* (1917) 244 U.S. 205, 222.
[13] *The Common Law* (Boston 1881), 1.
[14] 'Path of the Law', in *Collected Legal Papers* (London 1920), 180.
[15] Ibid.   [16] *Lochner* v. *New York* (1904) 198 U.S. 45, 74.
[17] 'Law in Science and Science in Law', in *Collected Legal Papers*, 239.
[18] 'Path of the Law', 184 *ubi. rep.*
[19] Cambridge 1922.

essay 'Mechanical Jurisprudence',[20] in which he preached Jhering's message in his own words, and attacked as profoundly mistaken the belief that the law developed by 'rigorous logical deduction from predetermined conceptions in the disregard and often in the teeth of actual facts'. Pound had a variety of epithets to describe this mistaken method; among them are 'automatic', 'slot machine', 'formal', and 'conceptualism'.

Yet in spite of these striking similarities, the American onslaughts on *Begriffsjurisprudenz* or 'conceptualism' and Jhering's protests diverged in the following way. The objects of Jhering's attack, it will be remembered, were not practitioners but great academic expositors of the law (*Theoretiker*). Only these were allowed into the *Begriffshimmel* and it will be remembered that nearly all of them were Germans ('fast nur alle aus Deutschland'). Savigny was nearly refused admission, but obtained entry on the strength of his work on possession because it showed a proper contempt for utility. So little do these theoreticians care for the actual practice of the law that they are prepared to ignore any actual decisions of judges which run counter to their own logical calculations in which they unfold the content of legal concepts. Practice in their view 'spoils the law' and is bad for this reason; just as someone might condemn war because it spoils the appearance of soldiers ('der Krieg verderbe den Soldaten'[21]). So the theoretician if he is worthy of entry into the *Begriffshimmel* is perfectly prepared to condemn the decisions of practical lawyers as logical impossibilities,[22] and, as in the case of Roman lawyers, to attribute their deviations from rigorous conceptual thought to their falling under the evil influence of considerations of utility.[23]

The great contrast between Jhering's attack and the attack on conceptualism made by Holmes and his followers, Pound and the legal realists, is that the latter directed their main invective not against theoretical jurists but against judges and practical lawyers. For them these vices of legal thought are exhibited by lawyers and judges who place an excessive reliance on 'logic' in deciding cases, and who think that the

---

[21] *Scherz und Ernst*, 289 n. 2.
[22] Ibid. 300.
[23] Ibid. 297.

application of general rules and concepts in legal decisions was a simple exercise in syllogistic reasoning; and it is a critique of judicial technique that American jurists have preached this doctrine to English lawyers.

No doubt this difference between Jhering and his American counterparts reflects the different status of the judge in the German and Anglo-American legal systems. Later, of course, Jhering's successors directed their attacks also against judges, who believed that by using only logical operations they could establish with absolute exactness that a given decision of a particular case was predetermined by the legislator.[24] Similarly, Holmes's message was expanded by Pound and his successors, and converted into a criticism not only of judges but of juristic writing.

Notwithstanding these differences I believe the fundamental intellectual error about the nature of law and legal concepts, which drew fire from Jhering, was exactly the same as stimulated Holmes and his followers to their attack; and I will attempt to say what the root of this intellectual error is. It can I think be most simply stated in the following way. The fundamental error consists in the belief that legal concepts are *fixed* or *closed* in the sense that it is possible to define them exhaustively in terms of a set of necessary and sufficient conditions; so that for any real or imaginary case it is possible to say with certainty whether it falls under the concept or does not; the concept either applies or it does not; it is logically closed (*begrenzt*). This would mean that the application of a concept to a given case is a simple logical operation conceived as a kind of unfolding of what is already there,[25] and, in simpler Anglo-American formulation, it leads to the belief that the meaning of all legal rules is fixed and predetermined before any concrete questions of their application arises.

If we ask why this belief about the nature of legal concepts is wrong, the answer, as I have said elsewhere,[26] is that men who make laws are men, not gods. It is a feature of the human predicament, not only of the legislator but of anyone who attempts to regulate some sphere of conduct by means of

---

[24] Gnaeus Flavius, *Der Kampf um die Rechtswissenschaft* (1907), 7.

[25] 'Die Fülle des Inhalts, der in ihnen beschlossen liegt, für die Erkenntnis zu Tage zu fördern' (*Scherz und Ernst*, 287).

[26] *The Concept of Law* (Oxford 1961), 125.

general rules, that he labours under one supreme handicap —
the impossibility of foreseeing all possible combinations of
circumstances that the future may bring. A god might foresee
all this; but no man, not even a lawyer, can do so. Of course
things *could* be different: suppose that the world we live in
were in fact characterized only by a finite number of features
and suppose that we knew all the modes in which they could
combine, then provision could be made in advance for every
possibility. We could make rules and frame concepts, the
application or non-application of which to particular cases
was fixed from the beginning and never called for a further
choice, consideration of utility or of practical matters, and so
for creative development of the initial rule. Everything could
be known in advance, and so for everything something could
be specified in advance by regulation. This would be a world
in which the work of the theoretician and the practical lawyer
could coincide and both could enter the same heaven as far
as Jhering was concerned. But plainly this is not our world.
Human law-makers can have no such knowledge of all possible combinations of circumstances which the future may
bring. This means that all legal rules and concepts are 'open';
and when an unenvisaged case arises we must make a fresh
choice, and in doing so elaborate our legal concepts, adapting
them to socially desirable ends. Now all this Jhering perfectly
understood: he ridiculed, especially in his *Zweck im Recht*,
the idea of detailed rules which would provide for every case
— juristic specifications for the decision of all possible law-
suits; and he stressed the impossibility of foreseeing the infinite variety and manifold composition of all possible cases.

Of course it is possible to attempt to give to legal rules and
concepts an artificial rigour which will eliminate to the maximum extent the need for anything more than deductive
reasoning. We can so to speak 'freeze' the meaning of a legal
rule or concept by laying down certain elements and insisting
that if these are present they are sufficient to bring anything
which has them within the scope of the rule, whatever other
features the case may have and whatever may be the social
consequences of applying the rule in this rigid way. We shall
in fact then blindly prejudge what is to be done in a range of
future cases about whose composition we are ignorant. We
shall then indeed succeed in settling in advance questions

which can only reasonably be settled when the circumstances in which they arise are known. This is the vice which English and American lawyers identify as conceptualism in the judicial process; but it is in essence the same vice as Jhering identified in the works of great theoretical writers who were happy to ignore the judicial process and the work of practical lawyers.

II

So much for the *Begriffshimmel*. Let me now turn to what is called by American and English lawyers 'analytical jurisprudence'. It is necessary I think to distinguish two phases of the legal studies which have come to be so called. The first phase is associated with the names of Jeremy Bentham[27] and John Austin,[28] the great utilitarian thinkers of the nineteenth century. Indeed, one might call them the great figures of the English *Aufklärung* so far as law is concerned.

The second phase[29] is of comparatively recent development and has been inspired by a distinctive movement in philosophy in general which is much concerned with language. Its principal exponents were the Viennese Ludwig Wittgenstein, Professor at Cambridge from 1930–50, and yet another Austin, John L. Austin, Professor of Moral Philosophy at Oxford from 1952 till his death in 1959.

Let me shortly characterize the analytical jurisprudence of the first phase. As I have said, Bentham and Austin were Utilitarians and as such were passionately interested in the criticism of law, in legal reform, and the adaptation of law to rational ends which they conceived in terms of the greatest happiness principle. That was their 'Zweck im Recht' — whether it was Jhering's I am not sure. Yet both these thinkers combined with their utilitarianism certain doctrines about the nature of law and about the importance of a certain form of legal studies. Both defined law in terms of the notion of a command and so would be ranked by German thinkers as

[27] 1748–1832. See especially his *An Introduction to the Principles of Morals and Legislation* (1789), and *Of Laws in General* (London 1970); also *A Fragment on Government* (1776).

[28] 1790–1859. See his *Province of Jurisprudence Determined* (1832; ed. Hart, London 1954).

[29] See Summers, 'The New Analytical Jurists' (1966) 41 *New York Univ. L. Rev.*, 861.

exponents of the will theory (*Willenstheorie*), though, as I shall show later, the doctrine that law is the command of the sovereign did not have for them all the consequences usually attributed to the will theory. Both these thinkers further insisted on the importance of a value-free (*wertfrei*) form of legal studies which was concerned with the analysis, not only of the concept of law, but also of other fundamental legal concepts which are used in the descriptions of all mature legal systems, and in general with the structure and logical interrelation of the elements of a legal system. Bentham called this form of legal study 'expository' jurisprudence and distinguished it from the criticism of law in terms of its ends, which he styled 'censorial' jurisprudence. Similarly, Austin distinguished his analytical study of concepts and the structure of legal systems as 'general jurisprudence' and distinguished it from the utilitarian criticism of law which he called 'the art of legislation'. Both thinkers conceived these two forms of legal study, one analytical and value-free, the other critical of law in the light of utilitarian values, not as providing rival answers to the same questions, but different answers to different questions; and they thought that both these forms of study were necessary for the education of a civilized lawyer.

Bentham, in the course of his analytical studies, insisted that the concepts of the law needed for their analysis new methods. In particular, he thought that the traditional form of definition *per genus et differentiam* could not be used with profit in the case of many legal notions such as duty or obligation, because these had a distinctive structure calling for special methods of analysis; and he expounded a method which logicians of the twentieth century have called 'definition in use', because instead of attempting to define single words (e.g. 'duty' or 'obligation') the analysis takes whole sentences in which the term to be analysed appears. Thus we clarify the notion of duty not by attacking the single word 'duty' but by attacking model sentences like 'X has a duty to pay Y £100'.[30] But Bentham's innovations went deeper than this. He sought also to clarify the structural relationships between various types of legal rules and claimed that to exhibit

---

[30] See for Bentham's views on definition: *Works* (Bowring edn., 1838– 43), iii. 18; viii. 242–53; *Fragment on Government* ch. V, para. 6 n. 1, s. 6, and my 'Definition and Theory in Jurisprudence', Essay 1 *supra*.

their logical connections the Aristotelian logic, which was a logic of assertions, was useless; he worked out what he called the 'logic of the will' which was specially adapted to exhibit the connections between such notions as 'command', 'prohibit', and 'permit'.[31] Here he anticipated a form of modern logic known as deontic logic. Finally he opened up a problem which still awaits a solution. If we think of a legal system as consisting of separate legal norms or separate laws, what is *one* norm and what is merely *part* of a norm? What, in other words, is our criterion of *individuation* for laws? Till this is settled we cannot give a coherent account of the structure of a legal system.[32]

Austin followed very much in Bentham's footsteps, though he did not command his master's powers of innovation in logic. But the point which I wish to stress about both these great writers is that the form of analytical jurisprudence which they practised and preached was not in any way to be identified with the *Begriffsjurisprudenz* which Jhering attacked. It is I think quite common for continental thinkers to assume that unless a legal system is a closed logical system there is no place for any logical analysis of it, and to claim that Bentham and Austin were infected with the conceptualism[33] attacked by Jhering, so that they too had a place in the *Begriffshimmel*. I think this is a mistake due to a false inference from the fact that both Bentham and Austin held some form of the will theory, since they defined law in terms of command. But they themselves never drew from this theory the corollary which the older German will-theorists drew, that when a judge applied the law, the law was always the completely predetermined content of the legislator's will and the judge's task was simply the logical operation of subsuming a particular case under the general proposition describing the predetermined rule of law. On the contrary, Austin[34] most clearly recognized that even if English judges often spoke as if the contrary were true, in fact they frequently 'made' the law. Indeed Austin

---

[31] *Of Laws in General* (ed. Hart, *Collected Works*, London 1970), ch. X.

[32] Ibid. ch. 16. Cf. *An Introduction to Principles of Morals and Legislation*, Preface para. 33-4, ch. XVII para. 29 n. 1; *Of Laws in General*, ch. XIV.

[33] See Friedmann, *Legal Theory* (1947 edn.), 209; Bodenheimer, 'Modern Analytical Jurisprudence and the Limits of its Usefulness' (1956) 104 *University of Pennsylvania L. R.* 1080.

[34] *Province of Jurisprudence Determined* (1954 edn.), 191.

blamed the judges, not for doing this, but for failing to make the law by reference to the precepts of utilitarianism. He therefore was well aware of one fact which makes it absurd to suppose that the law was or could be developed by logical reasoning alone. But he was also aware of a second fact: namely the 'indeterminacy'[35] or open character of many legal concepts, so that they could yield only, as he said, 'a fallible test' of whether a given fact situation fell under them or not. Yet, notwithstanding all this, Bentham and Austin thought it of great importance to pursue, with new methods of definition and clarification, the analysis of words such as 'obligation', 'duty', 'right', 'property', 'possession', and other fundamental legal concepts, and to investigate the logical relationship between laws.

Let me turn now to the modern phase of analytical jurisprudence. Here, as I have said, the main stimulus has been provided by two philosophers very much concerned with language: Wittgenstein and Professor John L. Austin. They were not specifically concerned with law, but much of what they had to say about the forms of language, the character of general concepts, and of rules determining the structure of language, has important implications for jurisprudence and the philosophy of law, and has been exploited by writers on these subjects both in England and in America. Again, as with the earlier form of analytical jurisprudence, the modern writers are free of *Begriffsjurisprudenz* in Jhering's sense. Indeed, one of their most powerful doctrines is a repudiation of the conception of human thought and language on which the old *Begriffsjurisprudenz* rested. I shall lay before you two examples of the philosophy underlying this newer form of analytical jurisprudence. The first of them will show you how far from *Begriffsjurisprudenz* it is.

Porosität der Begriffe. This is a phrase used by a close adherent[36] of Wittgenstein's, for a most important feature of most empirical concepts and not merely legal concepts, namely, that we have no way of framing rules of language which are ready for all imaginable possibilities. However

---

[35] Ibid. 204–5, 207.

[36] F. Waismann. See his 'Verifiability' ('Verifizierbarkeit'), *Proc. Aristot. Soc. Suppl.* vol. 19 (1949), translated in *Sprache und Analysis* (ed. Bubner, Göttingen 1968).

complex our definitions may be, we cannot render them so precise so that they are delimited in all possible directions and so that for any given case we can say definitely that the concept either does or does not apply to it. 'Suppose I come across a being that looks like a man, speaks like a man, behaves like a man, and is only one foot tall, shall I say it is a man?'[37] Hence there can be no final and exhaustive definitions of concepts, even in science. 'The notion of gold seems to be defined with absolute precision, say, by the spectrum of gold with its characteristic lines. But what should we say if a substance was discovered which looked like gold, satisfied all the chemical tests for gold, but emitted a new sort of radiation?'[38] As we can never eliminate such possibilities of unforeseen situations emerging, we can never be sure of covering all possibilities. We can only redefine and refine our concepts to meet the new situations when they arise. This recognition of the *Porosität* or, as the English call it, 'open texture' of concepts, is, as I say, a powerful feature of the philosophy inspired by the modern form of analytical jurisprudence. Wittgenstein expressed it in words which fit the law very closely: 'Ich sagte von der Anwendung eines Wortes: sie sei nicht überall von Regeln begrenzt'[39] and 'Wir sind nict für alle Möglichkeiten seiner Anwendung mit Regeln ausgerüstet'[40] and again, 'Der Umfang des Begriffs ist durch eine Grenze nicht abgeschlossen: er ist nicht überall von Regeln begrenzt.'[41]

A second feature of the newer analytical jurisprudence has drawn upon modern linguistic philosophy in a quite different way. Wittgenstein said somewhere that words are also deeds ('Wörter sind auch Taten') and Professor Austin's most original contribution is to be seen in his posthumous book *How to do Things with Words*.[42] In it he insists that among the many different functions which language performs there is one which has been most frequently overlooked by philosophers and yet is most important if we are to understand

---

[37] Ibid. 122.
[38] Ibid.
[39] *Philosophical Investigations* (Oxford 1953), para. 84.
[40] Ibid. para. 80.
[41] Ibid. para. 68.
[42] Oxford 1962.

certain transactions in social life and especially in the law. Take for example a christening ceremony. At the crucial moment a sentence is uttered ('I hereby name this child X') and the effect of the utterance of these words is to transform the pre-existing social situation, so that it now becomes *correct* to refer to the child by the name X. Here, against a background of social conventions, words are used not as they most frequently are to *describe* the world, but to *bring about certain changes*. The same is true of the utterance of the words of a promise. 'I promise to take you in my car to the station' is not a *description* of anything but it is an utterance which has the *effect of creating* a moral obligation for the person who utters it. It binds the speaker. It is obvious that this use of language is of great importance in the law. We find it in a will when a testator writes 'I hereby bequeath my gold watch to my friend X' and also in the language of enactments used by legislators, e.g. 'It is hereby enacted . . . that . . .'. Here in the law the utterances of sentences by duly qualified persons on appropriate occasions have legal effects.

English lawyers sometimes refer to language so used as 'operative' words, but this general function of language which extends widely outside the law is known to most philosophers in England as 'performative'. The performative use of language both in and out of the law has many interesting special features which differentiate it from our use of language when we are concerned to make true or false statements describing the world. I do not think the general character of acts in the law (*Rechtsgeschäfte*) can be understood without reference to this idea of the performative use of language. Some legal philosophers, notably Hägerström,[43] were profoundly puzzled by the fact that it is possible to create obligations, to transfer rights, and generally to change legal situations merely by using language. This seemed to him a species of magic or legal alchemy, but surely all that is needed to understand it is to recognize a special function of language: given a background of rules or conventions which provide that if a certain person says certain words then certain other rules shall be brought into operation, this determines the function or, in a broad sense, the meaning of the words in question.

---

[43] *Der Römische Obligationsbegriff* (Uppsala 1927), ii. 399 and *Inquiry into Law and Morals* (Stockholm 1953), Preface and chs. XVII and XVIII.

The two examples that I have given where modern analytical jurisprudence is indebted to modern linguistic philosophy (*Porosität der Begriffe* and performative utterances) are only two out of many possible examples. A fuller account would discuss such things as the displacement of the old idea that when a general term or concept is applied to many different instances all the instances must share a single set of common properties. This is a dogma; there are many different ways in which the several instances of a general term are linked together, besides this simple way; and an understanding of these many different ways is plainly of particular importance in the case of legal terms.[44] In general however I should claim a great affinity between Jhering's sense of the need to get nearer to the point of the actual use and application of our concepts, and the spirit and new doctrines of contemporary analytical philosophy. Wittgenstein once said that if we wish to understand our concepts we must consider them when they are 'at work', not when they are 'idling' or 'on holiday'.[45] If I am not mistaken this is entirely in accord with Jhering's rejection of the *Begriffshimmel,* and the need to return to earth: *wieder auf Erden*!

[44] See my *Concept of Law* (1961), 66–7, 234.
[45] *Philosophical Investigations* para. 132.

Diamonds and String: Holmes on the Common Law

Holmes's famous book, *The Common Law*, admirably reintroduced to the general reader by Professor Mark Howe of Harvard,[1] resembles a necklace of splendid diamonds surprisingly held together at certain points by nothing better than string. The diamonds are the marvellous insights into the genius of the common law and the detailed explorations of the dynamic of its growth; they still flash their illuminating light on the dark areas beneath the clear and apparently stable forms of legal thought. The string is the sometimes obscure and hasty argument, the contemptuous dismissal of rival views, and the exaggerations with which Holmes sought to build up the tendencies which he found actually at work in the history of the law into a tough, collective philosophy of society. Holmes's genius as displayed here is that of a historian especially of early law, and his historical work, though since corrected on many details, made, as Maitland immediately recognized, 'an epoch'. By comparison the philosophy which Holmes drew from his history was shallow, in spite of its interesting connections, noted by Professor Howe, with the Darwinism and empiricism of his day. It now seems of value mainly as a stimulant, and to have little claim to finality even as a critique of the Kantian metaphysics to which it was opposed.

The range of the book is vast; its topics include the basis of liability for crime and for civil wrongs or torts in early and later law, the nature of contract, the law's use of the elusive idea of possession and the slow emergence of modern ideas of the transferability of legal rights. But the range is matched by the scholarship. In the first thirty pages, besides the texts of Roman law and English statutes and cases from the earliest times onwards, there are references to Plato, Demosthenes, Plutarch, Pausanias, Livy, Cicero, Aulus Gellius, Pliny, and

[1] O. W. Holmes, *The Common Law* (1881; ed. M. Howe 1963).

many others. This learning is always gracefully deployed and never degenerates into pedantry, and it is amazing that so much could have been amassed by a man of forty.

In his preface of 1881 Holmes told his readers that his object in writing the book (which he had delivered as lectures to a partly lay and surely somewhat puzzled audience at the Lowell Institute in Boston) was to construct a theory. 'Nous faisons une théorie et non un spicilège.' The theory was to hold together and render intelligible the forests of detail, some of it very ancient lumber, of which the common law appeared to consist. Perhaps the boldness of this enterprise appears greater today than it did then. Sir Henry Maine, gifted with somewhat similar talents for pregnant epigram and historical generalization, though with perhaps less learning, had successfully attempted something similar for Roman law in his *Ancient Law*. The day had not yet then dawned when a 'law book' would mean, for Americans, a vast tome constructed mainly with scissors and paste in and for law schools, or would mean for Englishmen, a slightly smaller textbook uneasily designed to serve the needs of both practitioners and students. The delineation of first principles was still a respectable speculative enterprise even for a lawyer.

When Holmes first began to write in the 1870s he found that academic law was dominated by a theory which had been begotten by German philosophy on the body of Roman law. The great names were those of Kant, Hegel, and Savigny, and the theory's focal point was the respect, indeed the reverence, due to the individual and the individual will. To this, all that was problematic or in need of justification was referred. Punishment was to be justified as a return for or even a cancelling out of the blameworthy exercise of the will; contracts were to be enforced because they were made by the meeting of human wills which they expressed; possession — even the possession by a thief of his stolen goods — was to be protected by the law because it was 'the objective realisation of the will'. To Holmes, this *Willenstheorie* seemed either unintelligible or a romantic fiction incapable of explaining even the institutions of Roman law on which it purported to be a gloss. Apart from its detailed errors this whole metaphysical approach appeared simply to ignore the practical aims and exigencies which shape any living body of law. In this ruling theory of his day Holmes discerned two pathetic fallacies, and devoted much of his book to their exposure. The first fallacy was that a legal system had a simple logical structure and that its complexities could all be explained as the deductive consequences of a few leading principles. The second fallacy was that there was a close affinity, if not identity, between legal and moral duty and legal and moral wrong. These were the ideas which, as he wrote elsewhere, were to be washed — perhaps washed away — in 'cynical acid', and he turned to English legal history to find it. In so doing he professed himself convinced that in the common law there was 'a system far more civilised than the Roman, framed on a plan irreconcilable with the *a priori* doctrines of Kant and Hegel'.

In spite of the originality and generality of its main themes no part of this book is easy reading. It is essentially the work of a professional legal historian in search of a general theory, not that of a social prophet. The most difficult passages are in the last chapters describing the slow involved process by which modern notions of contract, and of legal rights as easily transferable things, emerged from cruder primitive conceptions. Here Holmes probed deep into the technicalities of the medieval common law, and the often rebarbative detail is difficult even for a lawyer to follow. But it is precisely here that Holmes's greatest gifts were manifested. He opened up fresh ground in this area of legal science because he was so greatly endowed with the ability to question what had long seemed obvious. 'The difficulty', he observes, 'in dealing with a subject is to convince the sceptic that there is anything to explain.' So he set out to understand and to expound how familiar modern legal conceptions first became 'thinkable in legal terms'. More — more even of philosophy — is to be learned from following Holmes's sympathetic reconstruction of the difficult birth of modern legal ideas than from attending to his overt philosophizing. To learn how men came with the aid of the strange fictions and analogies depicted here to acknowledge that not only concrete things but abstractions like legal rights might be transferred from person to person is to gain a new comprehension of the natural history of human thought. Indeed Holmes's touch was very much that of the naturalist and was perhaps influenced by the biological theories of his day. Though he never adulated the past he thought recourse to it indispensable for explanation of its remnants still present in modern legal rules. It is, he said, 'just as the clavicle in the cat tells of the existence of some earlier creature to which a collar bone was useful'.

From his historical studies Holmes distilled a number of maxims to be used as prophylactics against the excessive rationalization and moralization of the law which were the occupational diseases of the legal theorist. Among these maxims is the famous warning (too frequently torn from its context and misapplied) that 'the life of the law has not been logic; it has been experience', and his insistence on the importance to the understanding of law of 'instinctive preferences and inarticulate convictions'. In his famous lectures, Holmes's *idée maitresse*, which in the end became something of an obsession, was the principle that though the law often seems to make liability to punishment or to paying compensation for harm done dependent on the individual's actual intention to do harm, this is most often not to be taken at its face value. Here, he thought, lay one of the cardinal differences between early and modern law: 'acts should be judged by their tendency under the known circumstances not by the actual intent which accompanies them'; 'Though the law starts from the distinctions and uses of the language of morality it necessarily ends in external standards not dependent on the actual consciousness of the individual'. Or again, 'the law considers what would be blameworthy in the average man, the man of ordinary intelligence and prudence, and determines liability by that'. These were indeed powerful heuristic maxims dissipating much misunderstanding especially in the fields of contract and tort. But Holmes came to regard them as more than valuable pointers to neglected tendencies in the law. He sometimes treats them as statements of necessary truths ('by the very necessity of its nature the law is continually transmuting moral standards into external or objective ones'), and he erects these principles into a form of social philosophy justifying what he describes as 'the sacrifice of the individual'.

Such was Holmes's greatly debated theory of objective liability. Its central contention is that when the law speaks of an intention to do harm as a necessary constituent of a crime, all it does, and can, and should require (these three things are never adequately discriminated by Holmes) is that the person accused of the crime should have done what an average man would have foreseen would result in harm. In spite of its subjective and moralizing language the law does not require proof of the accused's actual wickedness or actual intention or actual foresight that harm would result. Of course for common sense as for the law there are important *connections* between the proposition that a man in acting in a certain way intended harm and the proposition that an average man who acted in that way would have foreseen it or intended it. For the latter is good though not conclusive evidence for the former. None the less the two propositions are distinct. Holmes, however, though well aware of the distinction, thought that in general law did not and should not attend to it. This was not because he was a philosophical behaviourist or because he thought that subjective facts were too elusive for the courts to ascertain. There is no echo in Holmes of the medieval Chief Justice Brian of the Common Pleas: 'The thought of man is not triable; the devil alone knoweth the thought of man.'[2] Though many of Holmes's followers accepted his theory of objective liability because of the difficulties of legal proof of actual knowledge or intention, Holmes does not rest his doctrine on these merely pragmatic grounds but on a social theory. 'Objective liability' for Holmes meant not an evidential test but a substantive standard of behaviour. His view was that the function of the criminal law was to protect society from harm, and in pursuit of this objective it did and should set up 'objective standards of behaviour which individuals must attain at their peril.' The law may exempt those who like the young child or lunatic are obviously grossly incapable, but apart from this, if men are too weak in understanding or in will-power they must be sacrificed to the common good.

Certainly the criminal law bears traces of such objective standards; indeed the elimination of these has been the aim of many liberal-minded reformers of the law for many years. But though Holmes at one point says that he does not need to defend the law's use of 'objective standards' but only to record it as a fact, he devotes much of this chapter to showing that the law here is reasonable and even admirable. The arguments he uses are the poorest in the book. He considers

[2] Y. B. 17 Edward IV Pasch. fol. 2.

the objection that the use of external standards of criminal responsibility taking no account of the incapacities of individuals is to treat men as things, not as persons, as means and not as ends. He admits the charge but thinks it irrelevant. He asserts that society frequently treats men as means: it does so when it sends conscripts 'with bayonets in their rear' to death. But this reply is cogent only against a stupidly inaccurate version of the Kantian position on which the objection rests. Kant never made the mistake of saying we must never treat men as means. He insisted that we should never treat them *only* as means 'but in every case as ends also'. This meant that we are justified in requiring sacrifices from some men for the good of others only in a social system which also recognizes their rights and their interests. In the case of punishment the right in question is the right of men to be left free and not punished for the good of others unless they have broken the law when they had the capacity and a fair opportunity to conform to its requirements.

Apart from this, Holmes's main argument is a fallacy and unfortunately an infectious one. He adopts the acceptable position that the general aim justifying a modern system of criminal punishment is not to secure vengeance or retribution in the sense of a return of pain for an evil done, but is the aim of preventing harmful crime. On this basis he seeks to prove that there can be no reason why the law should concern itself with the actual state of the offender's mind or inquire into his actual capacity to do what the law requires. His proof is that since the law only requires outward conformity to its prescriptions and does not care, so long as the law is obeyed, what were the intentions or motives of those who obeyed or whether they could have done otherwise, so it should equally disregard these subjective matters in dealing with the offender when the law has been broken. This is of course a *non sequitur*. Even if the general justification of punishment is the utilitarian aim of preventing harm and not vengeance or retribution it is still perfectly intelligible that we should defer to principles of justice or fairness to individuals and not punish those who lack the capacity or fair opportunity to obey. It is simply not true that such a concern with the individual only makes sense within a system of retribution or vengeance. Holmes, indeed, in discussing liability in tort stresses the

importance of such principles of justice to individuals, but
thinks that in the criminal law their requirements are adequately satisfied if the individual is punished only for what
would be blameworthy in the average man. No doubt there
are practical difficulties in ascertaining the actual knowledge
or intention or capacity of individuals in every case, but there
is no reason in principle why a maximum effort should not
be made to do it.

'The law will not enquire whether he did actually foresee
this consequence or not. The test of foresight is not what
this very criminal foresaw but what a man of reasonable prudence would have foreseen.' Twice at least when a judge in
Massachusetts, Holmes applied this principle in murder cases,
and the influence of his doctrine has been great both on the
body and the theory of the law. In 1961 the English House
of Lords endorsed it[3] and quoted Holmes's words. But little
support for it is now to be found in American legal opinion
and it is firmly rejected in the Model Penal Code of the
American Law Institute. The decision of the English House
of Lords was greeted with a storm of criticism and it is now
clear that Holmes's doctrine is unlikely to be invoked in
English cases other than murder.[4] But paradoxically some of
Holmes's opponents even in America have darkened counsel
as much as his followers. For they have accepted from Holmes
the false suggestion implicit in his argument that it is pointless to bother about the individual's mind or capacity to conform to law except where the aim of punishment is retribution
for moral wickedness. They have asserted against Holmes that
we should indeed be concerned with these subjective facts
about the individual, but agreed with him that this is so only
because it is necessary to establish the wickedness of those
who are punished. This is a blinding oversimplification of the
complex issues surrounding the institution of punishment,
and it ignores the claims of those liberal forms of utilitarianism which hold that, though it is for the protection of society
that law-breakers are to be punished, no individual is to be
punished who lacks the capacity to obey.

Though these and other weaknesses are to be found in this

---

[3] *DPP* v. *Smith* [1961] A. C. 290.
[4] The decision of the House of Lords on this point was later reversed by statute. See Criminal Justice Act 1967, S.8.

book, almost everything which Holmes said in it still rever-
berates. This is not only a tribute to the magic and sonority
of his style. In thinking about any subject on which Holmes
touched here it still pays handsome dividends to start with
what he said, even though, in some cases, it seems no longer
possible to stay with it.

Kelsen Visited

In November 1961 I had the enjoyable and instructive experience of meeting Hans Kelsen and debating with him at
the Law School of the University of California in Berkeley
some topics which I had previously selected for discussion
from his *General Theory of Law and State*.[1] The meeting was
arranged by Professor Albert Ehrenzweig who introduced us.
We warned our very large audience that they might be disappointed or bored or both disappointed and bored: for the
questions we proposed to discuss might excusably appear to
them to be dry and technical, and our differences to be mere
disputes over detail within the 'positivist' camp of jurisprudence, of no great interest to those outside it. I explained that
my view was that Kelsen's great work deserved the compliment of detailed scrutiny, and that it had too often been
used as an excuse for the debate of vast and vaguely defined
issues, such as the hoary perennial known as 'Natural Law
versus Legal Positivism'. In spite of the technical nature of
our discussion it was I think enjoyed by our audience, which
included, as well as lawyers, a sprinkling of philosophers, political theorists, and students of other disciplines. Certainly it
proved most instructive to me: it made me understand better
the point of certain Kelsenian doctrines which had long perplexed me, even if it did not finally dispel my perplexities. I
am reluctant to believe that I am alone in finding these difficulties in Kelsen's work; so some account of our discussion
may be of use to others. In what follows I shall try to explain
both why the points I raised seem to me important as well as
to delineate our respective positions.

The points which I chose for discussion were these:

I. Kelsen's expression: 'Rules of Law in a descriptive
    sense'.[2]

---

[1] Kelsen, *General Theory of Law and State* (1949). This work is referred to in
this essay as the *General Theory*.

[2] Ibid. at 45–6, 50, 163–4.

II. The definition of delict.[3]
III. The relationship between Positive Law and Morality.[4]

Besides these three issues there were others which we agreed to discuss if there was time. In fact there was no time for any of these others at our public discussion.

Before concluding this brief introduction I should like to record the fact that our discussion had its entertaining moments. The first was when Kelsen remarked that the dispute between us was of a wholly novel kind because though he agreed with me I did not agree with him. The second was towards the end of our debate, when upon Kelsen emphasizing in stentorian tones, so remarkable in an octogenarian (or in any one), that 'Norm was Norm' and not something else, I was so startled that I (literally) fell over backwards in my chair.

I. RULES OF LAW IN A DESCRIPTIVE SENSE

In the following passages taken from the *General Theory* I have italicized the particular expressions which I found difficult to understand.

It is the task of the science of law to represent the law of a community, i.e. the material produced by the legal authority in the law making procedure, in the form of statements to the effect that 'if such and such conditions are fulfilled, then such and such a sanction shall follow'. These statements, by means of which the science of law represents law, must not be confused with the norms created by the law making authorities. It is preferable not to call these statements norms, but legal rules. The legal norms enacted by the law creating authorities are prescriptive; *the rules of law formulated by the science of law are descriptive*. It is of importance that the term *'legal rule' or 'rule of law' be employed here in a descriptive sense*.[5]

The rule of law, *the term used in a descriptive sense*, is a hypothetical judgment attaching certain consequences to certain conditions. . . . The rule of law says: if *A* is, *B* ought to be. *The rule of law is a norm (in the descriptive sense of that term)*. . . .[6]

The ought-statements in which the theorist of law represents the norms have a merely descriptive import; they, as it were, descriptively reproduced the 'ought' of the norms. . . .[7]

[3] Ibid. at 54-6.
[4] Ibid. at 373-6, 407-10.
[5] Ibid. at 45. (Emphasis added.)
[6] Ibid. at 45-6. (Emphasis added.)
[7] Ibid. at 163. (Emphasis added.)

The general drift of these passages is of course tolerably clear. Kelsen has told us, in his introduction to the *General Theory* and elsewhere, that the 'general orientation' of his Pure Theory of Law and of analytical jurisprudence are the same. Neither of these disciplines is concerned with the moral or political evaluation of law, nor with the sociological description or explanation of law or legal phenomena. Instead both are concerned with the analysis or elucidation of the meaning of positive law. They differ according to Kelsen because the Pure Theory is more consistent and so avoids certain errors made, e.g., by Austin in the analysis of rights and duties and of the relationship between law and state.

This characterization of the Pure Theory of Law as a stricter, more consistent, and more systematic version of analytical jurisprudence, together with Kelsen's frequent references to the task of juristic theory as being that of 'grasp[ing] the specific meaning of the legal rules',[8] naturally leads one to expect that the main product of this form of jurisprudence will be statements giving or explaining the meaning of expressions such as 'law', 'legal system', 'legal rule', 'right', 'duty', 'ownership', and 'possession'. Austin certainly was much occupied with such analysis, and indeed conceived the elucidation of the law's fundamental notions to be the special task of the analytical science which he styled 'General Jurisprudence'.[9] Of course the ideas of 'analysis', 'elucidation', and even 'definition' are vague, and can take many forms. It is not to be expected that the analytical jurist should always, or even usually, provide definitions *per genus et differentiam* of single words in which the definition provided is a synonym for the word to be defined. If the distinctive feature of analytical jurisprudence is its concern, in Kelsen's words, to grasp the 'specific meaning of legal rules', there are many different ways in which this may be done. The analytical jurist may give not definitions of single words, but synonyms or 'translations' of whole sentences ('definitions in use'); or he may even forgo altogether the provision of synonyms and instead set out to describe the standard use of certain expressions.

Now, undoubtedly, in Kelsen's *General Theory* there are

[8] Ibid. at 164.
[9] Austin, 'The Uses of the Study of Jurisprudence', in *The Province of Jurisprudence Determined* 367 (1954).

some statements which seem to be definitions or analyses. They are statements which directly or indirectly explain the meaning of certain expressions distinctive of the law in terms of other more familiar or better understood expressions. One example of these (about which I say more later) is what Kelsen himself terms the 'juristic definition' of delict as a 'behavior of the individual against whom the sanction as the consequence of this behavior is directed'.[10] Another related example is Kelsen's statement that to be legally obligated to a certain behaviour 'means that the contrary behavior is a delict and as such is the condition of a sanction stipulated by a legal norm'.[11] But though these and numerous other instances could be found in Kelsen's book of what might be construed as definitions or analyses of expressions, it is plain that it is not the main concern of the Pure Theory of Law to provide these, but to do something rather different. More often than not Kelsen seems concerned to introduce new expressions and with them new ideas rather than to define old ones. Such definitions as there are of current legal expressions are incidental to the task which Kelsen at the outset says is the main task of the Pure Theory of Law: to enable the jurist concerned with a particular legal system to understand and to describe as exactly as possible that system of positive law. For this purpose the Pure Theory 'furnishes the fundamental concepts by which the positive law of a definite legal community can be described'.[12]

It is important to observe that such a description of a particular system of law is not the task of the Pure Theory of Law; it is the task of 'the normative science of law' or 'normative jurisprudence'. It is very easy especially for an Englishman trained in Austin's jurisprudence to think that all these three quoted expressions mean the same thing and can be simply identified with 'analytical jurisprudence'. It is indeed true that all these forms of jurisprudence have some important features in common; they are all sciences whose subject-matter is positive law; they are not concerned to evaluate or criticize that subject-matter in moral, ideological, or in any other ways; they are not concerned to provide factual descriptions

---

[10] Kelsen, *General Theory*, 55.
[11] Ibid. at 59.   [12] Ibid. at xiii.

or explanations of the actual operations of the law. They are thus all 'pure' or free of ideology and sociology. But in spite of these similarities it is vital to distinguish the Pure Theory of Law from the normative science of law or normative jurisprudence, which last two are I think synonymous for Kelsen. The Pure Theory is a general theory which in effect tells the jurist concerned with some particular legal system how to 'represent' or describe that system; what sorts of 'concepts' he should use and what he should not use; and generally what form his description or 'representation' of the legal system is to take if it is to be fit to rank as the normative science of that system. Now it is at this point that Kelsen introduces the notions that I and others have found so puzzling. Speaking in the character of the Pure Theorist, Kelsen tells the jurist engaged in the normative science of a particular legal system that his description or representation of it must take the form of 'rules' or 'ought-statements', but 'in a descriptive sense'. This is such a surprise because what we should naturally expect from a lawyer who tells us that he is engaged in the description or a representation of English or California law would not be a set of rules or 'ought-statements', but a set of statements explaining what the rules of English or California law as found in, e.g., statutes, mean. So we would expect the general form of the statements of the normative science of English or California law if its task is simply that of describing or representing the law of those systems, to be of the kind indicated by the following blank schemata:

Section 2 of the Homicide Act 1957 which provides . . . means that . . .

or

Section 18, subsection 2 of the California Penal Code means the same as . . .

Statements of the form of these two schemata are of course *about* the rules of English or California law in the sense that they tell us what these rules mean, but they are not themselves to be identified with the rules whose meaning they explain. They are a jurist's statements *about* law, not legislative pronouncements *of* law. To add to the puzzle, Kelsen himself, as can be seen from the quotations set out above, warns against identifying these two diverse things. Yet he insists on calling the statements of the normative science of law 'rules of law' or 'ought-statements' in a 'descriptive sense'. Why?

Two admirable writers on jurisprudence have been concerned with this question before me, and it is a diverting, if also, in a way, a discouraging, fact that whereas one of them condemns Kelsen's talk of rules in a descriptive sense as both confused and confusing the other does not find much difficulty with it. Thus Professor Alf Ross thinks that Kelsen in using this terminology is perpetuating a very bad continental tradition that it is possible to conduct a science of law or a science of 'norms' *in norms*.[13] This would be to use the expression 'normative science' not in the innocuous sense of a science that had norms or legal rules for its subject-matter but in a sense, laden with the theory of natural law, of a science whose *conclusions* are laws. On the other hand Professor Martin Golding, in his important article 'Kelsen and the Concept of a "Legal System"',[14] plainly thinks that no such charges are warranted. He concedes that the expression 'normative jurisprudence' is an unhappy name for the jurist's task of representing or describing the law of a particular system in the forms prescribed by the Pure Theory; and he notes that some passages in Kelsen's work may suggest that in order to carry out his task the jurist must exercise a mysterious faculty of 'norm cognition' instead of an ordinary ability to say what the laws of some legal system are and what they mean. But it is manifestly Professor Golding's view that all that is needed to dissipate confusion and to do justice to Kelsen's meaning is to bring in at this point a distinction familiar to modern logicians between the *use* and the *mention* of words.

The force of this distinction may be sufficiently conveyed (to the uninitiated and for my present limited purposes) by a single example. Consider the statement: 'The word "puppy" means in English the same as the expression "young dog"'. In this statement certain words are mentioned or referred to as words and we are told that these mentioned words are equivalent in meaning. So the statement is in a pretty obvious sense about the meaning of the words which are enclosed in internal inverted commas. Contrast with this the statements 'Fido is a

[13] Ross, *On Law and Justice* 9-10 n. 4 (1959).
[14] Golding, 'Kelsen and the Concept of "Legal System"', 47 *Archiv Für Rechts und Sozialphilosophie* 355, 364 (Germany 1961).

puppy' and 'Fido is a young dog'. These latter two statements
are not about words but about the animal Fido, and in them
the words 'puppy' and 'young dog' are *used*, not mentioned,
and not enclosed in internal inverted commas. In these latter
statements the meaning of words is not discussed but taken
as known.

   If we apply this distinction to the law we can say that the
legislature in enacting a law *uses* certain words and the jurist
who undertakes to tell us what the law means *mentions* both
the words of the law and the words which he gives by way of
paraphrase or explanation of meaning. So the schemata set
out above will be filled out with words that are mentioned,
not used. On this footing we might say that all Kelsen meant
by the puzzling assertion that the statements of the normative
science of law are themselves 'rules' and 'ought-statements'
though 'in a descriptive sense' is that his statements explaining the meaning of a legislative enactment will mention certain ought-statements or rules as the equivalent in meaning of
the enactment. They will have the form of 'Section 2 of the
Homicide Act 1957 means the same as the rule "If *B* . . . then
A . . . ought to be".'

   On this view therefore we could regard Kelsen as having
most acutely anticipated the important distinction between
the use and mention of words, but as having expressed it un-
happily as a distinction between a prescriptive and descriptive
sense of words like 'ought'. Now in our debate I pressed this
point of view on Kelsen, though as I had not then seen Professor Golding's article, I, no doubt, did not put the point
with his clarity. I thought this was the way in which Kelsen
might reply to Professor Alf Ross's strictures, which I also
quoted. To my surprise Kelsen would have none of it. He insisted that the statements of the normative science of law
representing the law of a given system were *not* paraphrases
at all: he said they were not 'second order' statements about
the law in which words were mentioned, not used. He stood
by his terminology of rules and ought-statements 'in a descriptive sense' and he urged me to read the works of the
nineteenth-century logician Sigwart who also spoke of a
descriptive sense of 'ought'. I teased Kelsen a little with the
suggestion that perhaps since Sigwart (whom I had not and
have not read) logic had made some progress. *Vixere fortes*

post Agamemnona. But here our argument on this point came to a stop.

At the time I thought Kelsen was wrong in not accepting the solution in terms of the distinction between the use and mention of words. Since our debate however I have come to think that he was perhaps right, and that that distinction is too crude to characterize precisely the relationship between the statements of the normative science of law as Kelsen conceives of them and the law of the system which they represent. To understand that relationship we should consider that between a speaker of a foreign language and his English interpreter. Suppose a German commandant in a prisoner-of-war camp barks out to his English or American prisoners the order *'Stehen Sie auf!'* The interpreter, doing his duty, shouts out 'Stand up!' No doubt, without consciously mimicking the tone or mien or gesture of the commandant, the interpreter will reproduce enough to make clear to the men that the original was an order, and not, e.g., a plea or a request. How shall we classify in relation to its German original the interpreter's speech-act in uttering the English sentence 'Stand up'? Shall we say that it was the giving of an order? But plainly the interpreter had no authority to give orders: he had a duty to interpret the commandant's orders and if the men obeyed or disobeyed it was not he but the commandant who was obeyed or disobeyed. Does the use-and-mention distinction fit the situation? Does the interpreter make a second-order statement mentioning the German words and say that they mean the same as the English words 'Stand up'? This seems very far from a literal description of the situation. It would be like saying that when one man imitates another's words, conversation or gestures he is *talking about* them. Of course between the interpreter's words in the situation I have envisaged and the explicit second-order statement that the commandant's German words meant the same as the interpreter's English words there is an important relationship. If asked why he said 'Stand up' when he did, he would have to include in any full explanation his belief that the second-order statement was true; just as the mimic of another's gestures would have to include in any full *explanation* of his activities his belief that his own gestures resembled his victim's. But (to use Kelsen's language) the interpreter and the mimic manage to 'represent'

their originals without *mentioning* them, though of course
without doing or being exactly the same kind of thing as the
originals. Theirs is a special use of language, not a mention of
it. From this we *might* go further with Kelsen and say of the
interpreter that he represented the original order by 'an order
in the descriptive sense' and his use of the grammatical imperative mood was 'descriptive' not prescriptive. At least we
can see the reasons for inventing such terms even if we can
also see the danger of using them.

All this can be transferred back to the law to justify Kelsen's
terminology in characterizing as he does the statements of
normative science which represent the law. Moreover I think
Kelsen's whole picture of the jurist's activity may be misunderstood if we do not stress the points made in the last paragraph. For, as Professor Golding points out,[15] Kelsen does not
conceive of the jurist's statements as having a simple one-to-
one correspondence with the laws of the system in question.
His finished representation of the system will have a clarity,
consistency, and order not present in the original: indeed it
will include for example a basic norm 'postulated' by the
jurist which may not ever have been explicitly formulated
within the system but will explain the validity and the systematic interrelation of the subordinate norms. Even this
aspect of the jurist's 'representation' of the system we might
reproduce, and so come to understand a little better, in a further use of the analogue of the interpreter. Suppose the commandant to be a somewhat stupid man and very much afraid
of fire. Whenever he sees anything inflammable lying around
he orders the prisoners to pick it up. Day in and day out he
stomps round the camp shouting in German 'Pick up that
box', 'Pick up that paper', 'Pick up that bundle of straw'. The
interpreter dutifully barks out the English equivalents, and
then one day, being a man of superior intelligence, adds on his
own motion 'and pick up all inflammable material'. The commandant on being told of what he has said says 'Good: that's
exactly what I would have said: only I couldn't think of
the right words. What a fine interpreter you are! In fact you
do more than interpret my orders: you do what Professor
Golding says the normative science of law does for the

law of a particular system: you *rationally reconstruct*[16] my orders.'

Now it seems to me that this feature of the jurist's activity explains further why Kelsen would be reluctant to identify his representation of the law with mere statements about the meaning of laws or paraphrases in which rules and 'oughts' are mentioned but not used. I do not think his terminology of rule and ought 'in a descriptive sense' happy, but I do think he was wise to reject the alternative I proffered; for, again like the interpreter's words, the statements of the jurist representing the law are a specific kind of use of language and not a mention of it.

II. THE DEFINITION OF DELICT

Kelsen offers in his book what he terms a 'juristic definition' of delict or, as English and American lawyers would say, of civil and criminal wrongs. In our debate I discussed this definition only so far as it related to crime, and I was mainly concerned with the following quotations from the *General Theory*. These seem to me important because they show that Kelsen's Pure Theory differs from the usual conception of analytical jurisprudence in certain further respects beyond those already discussed above. They also seem to me to suggest certain limitations on the capacity of the Pure Theory to further the aim which Kelsen attributes to it of promoting the understanding of a system of positive law.

> From a purely juristic point of view, the delict is characterized as a condition of the sanction. But the delict is not the only condition. . . . What then is the distinctive characteristic of that condition which is called the 'delict'? Could no other criterion be found than the supposed fact that the legislator desires conduct contrary to that which is characterized as 'delict', then the concept of delict would be incapable of a juristic definition. The concept of delict defined simply as socially undesired behavior is a moral or political, in short, no juristic but a metajuristic, concept. . . .[17]
> A juristic definition of delict must be based entirely upon the legal norm. And such a definition can in fact be given. Normally, the delict is the behavior of that individual against whom the sanction as a consequence of his behavior is directed. . . . The criterion of the concept of

[16] Ibid. at 357–9.
[17] Kelsen, *General Theory*, 53.

'delict' is an element which constitutes the content of the legal norm. . . .
It is an element of the norm by which the legislator expresses his intention in an objectively cognizable way; it is an element which can be
found by an analysis of the legal norm. . . .

The definition of delict as the behavior of the individual against
whom the sanction, as a consequence of his behavior, is directed presupposes—although it does not refer to the fact—that the sanction is
directed against the individual whose behavior the legislator considers
to be detrimental to society . . .[18]

. . . The legal concept of delict presupposes in principle that the individual whose behavior has from a political point of view a socially detrimental character, and the individual against whom the sanction is directly
or indirectly executed, coincide. Only on this condition is the juristic
definition of the delict, as the behavior of the individual against whom
the sanction as a consequence of this behavior is directed, correct.[19]

The general outline of this definition of delict is clear: a
delict, e.g. a crime, is simply the behaviour upon which according to law a sanction becomes applicable to the person
whose behaviour it is. What is not clear is what Kelsen means
by on the one hand insisting that this is all that a juristic definition of delict can and should say and, on the other hand,
acknowledging that this definition presupposes, though it
does not refer to, the socially detrimental character of the
delict and is only correct if the condition thus presupposed is
satisfied.

It is of course plain from many passages in Kelsen's book
(and it is an important fact) that the Pure Theory imposes
certain very severe restrictive conditions on the permissible
forms of definition. It also seems clear that a science of positive law which disregarded these would not for Kelsen be a
'normative' science. These restrictions indeed constitute one
reason why no simple identification between analytical jurisprudence and either the Pure Theory or a 'normative science'
of law can be made in spite of their similarity in spirit and
general orientation. For though Austin and his followers distinguish as sharply as Kelsen does between the analysis of
law and moral, political, or ideological evaluations of it, there
is no counterpart in their work to Kelsen's distinctive insistence that in defining or analysing only certain restricted elements may be used. In general the Pure Theory insists that the
clarificatory task of a normative science of law be performed

[18] Ibid. at 54.   [19] Ibid. at 56.

with elements drawn from the law itself, and care must be taken in defining or analysing legal concepts to avoid using moral, political, or psychological elements which are not, in Kelsen's words, 'part of the legal material'.

It is not very easy to make out precisely what elements these restrictions allow, but there are clear examples in Kelsen's book of what they exclude. Thus in criticizing Austin's analysis or definition of legal obligation Kelsen considers the definition that to be obliged is to fear the sanction, but he does not simply treat this, as a modern analytical jurist might, as an example of a mistaken definition. So he does not, for example, criticize it on the footing that a person may very well be under a legal obligation and yet not fear a sanction. What he does say is that such definition is 'incompatible with the principles of analytical jurisprudence'[20] because 'no analysis of the contents of commands can establish the psychological fact of fear'.[21] His point is that it is wrong in principle to bring into the juristic definition of a concept psychological elements such as fear, or other elements which are not part of the contents of the law. Kelsen's own juristic definition of obligation states that legal duty is 'the behavior by the observation of which the delict is avoided, thus the opposite of the behavior which forms the condition of the sanction'. No doubt Kelsen thinks that this definition is correct as complying with the restrictive condition that a juristic definition may use only elements which form part of the content of law. It is worth noting, however, in order to prevent a common misunderstanding that though Kelsen rejects Austin's 'psychological' conception of duty or obligation, he does not mean that a juristic definition can never use any psychological element. For Kelsen expressly says that in a case where the law itself makes such elements relevant, e.g. where *mens rea* is a condition of criminal responsibility, then the sanction is directed to a psychologically qualified delict. The idea of responsibility based on fault is thus defined by Kelsen, and no doubt he would claim that it is a sound juristic definition because though it uses psychological terms these are elements found in the relevant law.[22]

[20] Ibid. at 72.
[21] Ibid. at 72-3.
[22] Ibid. at 55, 66.

Though these examples throw some light on Kelsen's restricted form of juristic definition, it is not easy to understand
why, given the aims of the Pure Theory, the restrictions it imposes should be observed; nor precisely how we are to determine what elements are to count as 'found by an analysis of
the content of the legal norm'[23] or 'are expressed in the content of the norm'[24] or 'are expressed in the material produced
in the law-creating procedure'[25] or are 'manifested in the contents of the legal order'.[26] Kelsen certainly does insist that we
must not bring into the definition of delict such elements as
the supposed desire of the legislator, or the fact that the de-
lictual conduct is socially harmful or against the purpose of
the law: the juristic definition of delict must be 'based entirely upon the legal norm'[27] and he considers his own definition of it to be so based. But this leaves much unexplained.
Suppose that in fact the laws of a given system always contained (as Bentham wished) an explanatory statement that
the actions to which the law attached criminal sanctions were
regarded as social evils and that was why they were punished.
Would the juristic definition of delict then rightly include a
reference to such social facts? I am fairly sure that Kelsen's
answer would be 'No', though I much regret not having raised
this point with him. He would, I think, in consistency with
his general doctrine, have to say that the laws of an actual system, before they have passed through the clarifying filter of
the normative science of law, contain much that is irrelevant
to that science. For the representation or description of the
law which is the concern of that science is concerned only
with its strictly normative elements; that indeed is why it is,
in spite of Professor Alf Ross's protests, properly called a
'normative science' and not merely a science *of* norms. I
think this means that the permitted elements which may be
used in juristic definition are those contained in the canonical form for the representation of the law which Kelsen lays
down: statements that if such and such conditions are fulfilled then such and such a sanction shall follow. These are
the statements by which the normative science of law is said
by Kelsen to describe or represent law. They are 'hypothetical

<hr>

23 Ibid. at 54.   24 Ibid.
25 Ibid. at 51.   26 Ibid.
27 Ibid. at 54.

judgement[s] attaching certain consequences to certain conditions':[28] if A is, B ought to be. So the explanatory statement of the law's purpose which would have pleased Bentham would, even if it were contained in the text of a statute, be quite irrelevant to normative science.

At this point Kelsen's restrictive conception of juristic definition can be seen to have points of contact with some themes of American Legal Realism. We must compare the restrictions insisted on by Kelsen to Holmes's 'bad man' theory[29] that we should include in our definition, e.g., of duty, only those elements which the 'bad man' would want to know. Of course the permitted elements are quite different in the case of the two theories. The Realist permits only elements relevant to the *prediction* of the sanction; whereas Kelsen permits only elements which according to the legal rule are conditions under which the sanction 'ought' to be applied. But notwithstanding these differences the comparison does suggest a criticism of Kelsen's definition of delict and indeed of the whole programme of his severely restricted juristic definition.

Briefly, the criticism is that such definitions will not serve any useful purpose, theoretical or practical, and may introduce at points a confusion. That confusion may be generated is perhaps evident from the following simple case. Sanctions may take the form of compulsory money payments, e.g. fines; but taxes also take this form. In both cases alike, to use Kelsen's terminology, certain behaviour of the subject is a condition under which an official or organ of the system ought to demand a money payment from the subject. So if we confine our attention to the contents of the law as represented in the canonical form 'If A, then B ought to be' it is impossible to distinguish a criminal law punishing behaviour with a fine from a revenue law taxing certain activities. Both when the individual is taxed and when he is fined the law's provisions when cast into the Kelsenian canonical form are identical. Both cases are therefore cases of delict unless we distinguish between them by reference to something that escapes the net of the canonical form, i.e. that the fine is a punishment for an activity officially condemned and the tax is not. It may perhaps be objected that a tax, though it consists of a compulsory

---

[28] Ibid. at 45.
[29] Holmes, 'The Path of the Law', in *Collected Legal Papers* 171 (1920).

money payment as some sanctions also do, is not a 'sanction' and that Kelsen's juristic definition of delict refers to a 'sanction'. But this does not really avoid the difficulty; it only defers it; for we shall have to step outside the limits of juristic definition in order to determine when a compulsory money payment is a sanction and when it is not. Presumably it is a sanction when it is intended as or assumed to be a punishment to discourage 'socially undesired behavior'[30] to which it is attached; but this is precisely the element which Kelsen considers to be excluded from the juristic definition of delict.

It is plain that Kelsen himself is aware of these difficulties, because he concedes that the juristic definition only holds good on the presupposition that the behaviour, which is the condition of the sanction, is considered detrimental to society. But does not this concession show that the severely restricted juristic definition is useless as well as confusing? Here it is important to stress that many of the illuminating definitions of the Pure Theory are not and could not be *juristic* definitions in the severely restricted sense that Kelsen intends. Plainly for the reasons given above the definition of a sanction is not.[31] It is even possible to doubt whether the definition of a legal norm (quite apart from its dependence on the definition of a sanction) conforms to the strict requirements of juristic definition. For Kelsen tells us that the norm 'is the expression of the idea that something ought to occur, especially that an individual ought to behave in a certain way'.[32] But though a norm may *be* an expression of an idea it is not clear that 'an expression' or 'an idea' or 'an expression of an idea' are *contents* or *elements* of the norm or fit any other of the descriptions given by Kelsen of what may be used in a strictly juristic definition. So we should perhaps distinguish the most fundamental definitions of the Pure Theory to which the jurist conducting the normative science of law will *conform* in representing the law of a particular system as 'metajuristic' definitions, to mark the distinction between them and the juristic definitions which the jurist will actually *use* in

---

[30] Kelsen, *General Theory*, 53. The difficulty of distinguishing a penalty from a tax for the purpose of art. I, § 8, of the United States Constitution is well known. See, e.g., *Steward Mach. Co.* v. *Davis*, 301 U.S. 548 (1937).

[31] See the discussion of coercion and the distinction between civil and criminal sanctions in Kelsen, *General Theory*, 18–19, 50–1.

[32] Kelsen, *General Theory*, 36.

representing the law of some particular system. He will not use in his representation of the system, but will take for granted, definitions of 'sanction' or of 'legal rule', but he will use definitions of delict. Perhaps indeed some such distinction between definitions which are metajuristic and those which are juristic is needed for any analytical account of law.

I pressed these points on Kelsen in our debate, but I cannot say that he retreated or was moved by my claim that he had in fact given his case away by saying that his definition of delict held good on the 'presupposition in principle that the behavior against which the sanction is directed has or is considered to have a socially detrimental character'. I did however learn from our discussion two important things. The first is that Kelsen had an interesting and possibly good reason for talking not merely of a science of norms but of a 'normative' science of law, and this is not open to Professor Ross's criticism, though it may be to others. The second is that any one who, like myself, would wish to bring into the definition of crime or delict the idea that the behaviour to which sanctions are attached is unlike behaviour which is simply taxed and differs from it because it is in some way condemned, must be careful to state how in the case of any given law the presence of this factor of condemnation is ascertained.

III. THE RELATIONSHIP BETWEEN LAW AND MORALITY

Let us consider the case of a conflict between a norm of positive law and a norm of morality. Positive law can, for instance, stipulate an obligation to render military service, which implies the duty to kill in war, while morality, or a certain moral order, unconditionally forbids killing. Under such circumstances, the jurist would say that 'morally, it may be forbidden to kill, but that is irrelevant legally'. From the point of view of positive law as a system of valid norms, morality does not exist as such; or, in other words, morality does not count at all as a system of valid norms if positive law is considered as such a system. From this point of view, there exists a duty to perform military service, no contrary duty. In the same way, the moralist would say that 'legally, one may be under the obligation to render military service and kill in war, but that is morally irrelevant'. That is to say, law does not appear at all as a system of valid norms if we base our normative considerations on morality. From this point of view, there exists a duty to refuse military service, no contrary duty. Neither the jurist nor the moralist asserts that both normative systems are valid. The jurist ignores morality as a system of valid norms, just as the moralist ignores positive law as such a system.

Neither from the one nor from the other point of view do there exist two duties simultaneously which contradict one another. And there is no third point of view.[33]

Against our thesis that two contradictory norms cannot both be valid, one might argue that, after all, there are such things as collisions of duties. Our answer is that terms like 'norm' and 'duty' are equivocal. On the one hand, they have a significance that can be expressed only by means of an ought-statement (the primary sense). On the other hand, they also are used to designate a fact which can be described by an is-statement (the secondary sense), the psychological fact that an individual has the idea of a norm, that he believes himself to be bound by a duty (in the primary sense) and that this idea or this belief (norm or duty in the secondary sense) disposes him to follow a certain line of conduct. It is possible that the same individual at the same time has the idea of two norms, that he believes himself bound by two duties which contradict and hence logically exclude one another; for instance, the idea of a norm of positive law which obligates him to render military service, and the idea of a norm of morality which obligates him to refuse to render military service. The statement describing this psychological fact, however, is no more contradictory than, for instance, the statement that two opposite forces work at the same point. A logical contradiction is always a relation between the meaning of judgments or statements, never a relation between facts. The concept of a so-called conflict of norms or duties means the psychological fact of an individual's being under the influence of two ideas which push him in opposite directions; it does not mean the simultaneous validity of two norms which contradict one another.[34]

These passages from the *General Theory* concerning the relationship between law and morals are to my mind among the most difficult of that difficult book. They are also to many people very alarming, because statements like 'the jurist ignores morality as a system of valid norms just as the moralist ignores positive law as such a system' seem to exclude the possibility of a moral criticism of law, and this has of course always been among the errors or even sins imputed, if somewhat indiscriminately, to legal 'positivists' by their opponents.

Involved in these passages are some complex issues which stem from Kelsen's highly idiosyncratic views concerning the possible relations between sets of valid norms and concerning the very idea of validity. I cannot deal with all these views here, and at our debate I did little more than scratch the surface of Kelsen's approach to these problems, which I thought instructive but mistaken. I shall proceed here as I did there by

---

[33] Ibid. at 374.   [34] Ibid. at 375.

noting that we have in these passages two main tenets. There is first a destructive doctrine, namely, that contrary to common beliefs, there *cannot* be a relationship between law and morals such that a valid rule of law conflicts with or, as Kelsen puts it, is 'contradicted' by a valid moral rule; secondly, there is a constructive account of the idea of 'a collision of duties' designed to reconcile it with this destructive doctrine. For ease of exposition I shall consider the constructive account first.

Kelsen notes as a possible objection to his theory that two contradictory norms cannot be valid that there are such things as 'collisions' of duties. People indeed think and speak of these (usually calling them 'conflicts of duties') as an important feature of life. But he does not mention another case, equally important, where law and morals are thought of as conflicting: namely, the case of the moral criticism of law. This, as much as the conflict of duties, calls for explanation from any one who asserts, as Kelsen does, that 'two contradictory norms cannot both be valid'.[35] The difference between these two cases is as follows. We speak of a collision, or more usually of a conflict, of duties when a person recognizes that he is required by a valid rule of the law of his country to do something, e.g. kill another human being, and also recognizes that he is required not to do this by a moral rule or principle which he accepts. But in the case of the moral criticism of law the conflict between law and morals need not thus bear on a particular person or his actions. Thus an Englishman (whom we will call 'the critic') who is not himself liable to military service may morally condemn on the ground that no one should kill, not only the law of England in regard to military service, but contemporary American law and the law of ancient Rome. In each case he considers the law in question valid but to be in conflict with morality. There is, however, in this case no conflict of duties for the critic himself or for any Englishman, American, or ancient Roman except those who were *both* liable to military service *and* had moral objections to it. Plainly the two cases are so different that separate consideration is needed of the bearing of Kelsen's destructive doctrine upon them.

Kelsen's account of the conflict of duties is that though we

[35] Ibid.

may naïvely think that in such cases a valid legal norm is in
conflict with a valid moral norm, this is not so and cannot be
so. But there is an ambiguity in words like 'norm' or 'duty'
which suggests that it is so. Sometimes these words stand for
what can be expressed by an ought-statement such as 'I ought
to do military service'. This is their primary normative sense;
but there is a secondary sense in which they refer to psychological facts such as that a person believes himself to be bound
to do something and is therefore disposed to do it. We can
therefore (and according to Kelsen we must) interpret the
statement that a given person has a conflict of duties as simply
a reference to the psychological fact that he is 'under the influence of two ideas which push him in opposite directions'.[36]
This does not mean, according to Kelsen, that two valid norms
are simultaneously valid; this, according to his destructive
doctrine, is logically impossible. Interpreted in Kelsen's way,
the statement that a person has a conflict of duties is a mere
statement of fact like the statement that two opposite forces
work at the same point, and does not state a relation between
the meaning of norms or ought-statements. It is therefore, so
interpreted, admissible, and is indeed the kind of statement
that a psychologist or sociologist makes. But they are not concerned with the normative aspect of law. They, according to
Kelsen, do not conceive of law or morality as valid norms.
Their standpoint is that of 'factuality', not of 'normativity'.[37]

This account seems to me to be wrong, for the following
among other reasons. If a man says that he has a conflict of
legal and moral duties and we ask him to say why or how this
is so, it plainly would be no adequate answer if he replied that
he felt disposed to do and also not to do something; or, to
use Kelsen's phrase, that he felt pushed in opposite directions.
More is required if we are to count him as having a conflict of
legal and moral duties. It must be the case that a valid rule of
law actually requires him to do something and that a moral
principle or rule requires him to abstain from doing it; it must
also be the case that he believes all this to be the case and
that it is impossible for him to fulfil the requirements of both
the legal and the moral rule. It is very important to notice
that if it turned out that he was mistaken in believing that a

---

[36] Ibid.   [37] Ibid. at 376.

valid rule of law required him to do what the moral rule forbids (as he might be if he did not know that the law in question had been repealed) then he would not in fact have a
conflict of duties. We would tell him that though he *believed*
his duties conflicted, in fact they did not really do so, for he
was mistaken about the law.

It is plain, I hope, from the foregoing that it is an essential
element in what we call a conflict of duties that the requirements of a valid law should conflict with those of a moral rule
or principle. To discover therefore whether or not there is
such a conflict in a given case we must consider the meaning
of the legal rule and the moral rule, treating them for this
purpose (to use Kelsen's terminology) as ought-statements.
Only if they are inconsistent in the sense that they cannot be
simultaneously fulfilled can we truthfully say that there is a
conflict of duties. An assertion that a person has a conflict of
duties is, contrary to Kelsen's view, made 'from the point of
view of normativity'. It is not a mere statement of psychological fact, like 'He feels disposed to act in contrary ways' or
'He fancies that he has a conflict of duties.'

Kelsen's psychological analysis of the conflict of law and
morals must also, and perhaps more obviously, fail as an account of the case of the moral criticism of law. For a moral
critic who condemns the law of his own or some other system
because it requires behaviour contrary to that required by
some moral principle is not committed to any statement of
psychological fact about individuals being under the 'influence of ideas that push [them] in opposite directions'. The
critic plainly considers the meaning of what Kelsen calls
ought-statements, viewing them as norms, and finds that they
conflict.

Consider now Kelsen's destructive doctrine. Why does he
insist that valid norms *cannot* exist side by side and conflict?
He has I think two principal reasons. The first may be summarized in his own words: 'The jurist ignores morality as a
system of valid norms just as the moralist ignores positive law
as such a system. Neither from the one nor from the other
point of view do there exist two duties simultaneously which
contradict each other.'[38] Now in one sense these words seem

to me to be quite true, but irrelevant to our question, which is whether valid norms can conflict. For if by a 'jurist' Kelsen means, as he often does, a student of the law setting out to describe or 'represent' a particular system of law, it is quite true that he would disregard non-legal norms whether they were in conflict with the law or not; for they would simply be outside the scope of his task. The same is true *mutatis mutandis* of the moralist if he is a person engaged exclusively in describing a moral code. It is therefore true that neither *moralist* nor *jurist* would make statements about conflicts between law and morals. But this does not show that such statements cannot be made both meaningfully and truthfully. Kelsen denies this when he adds, 'And there is no third point of view.'[39] But this seems just a blank assertion which I see no reason to accept. No human being is *just* a lawyer or *just* a moralist. Some at least think about both legal and moral norms and consider their meaning as norms and find that they conflict. No doubt Kelsen would say that this is possible only if he abandons the point of view of 'normativity' for that of 'factuality' and look upon law not as valid norms but as facts, as a psychologist or a sociologist would. But this for the reason already stated seems untrue.

Kelsen's second destructive argument is that a statement that a valid legal rule and moral principle conflict is itself a logical impossibility. For him, it is tantamount to the assertion of both '*A* ought to be' and '*A* ought not to be' (where *A* is some human action); and this, he says, is like asserting both '*A* is' and '*A* is not', a contradiction in terms and hence logically impossible.[40] To this argument there are many objections, and I shall conclude by briefly outlining the main ones. First, the argument assumes that a statement that a legal rule is valid simply means that the actions it refers to ought to be done ('*A* ought to be'). But this, it seems to me, is to confuse a statement about a law either with the pronouncement of the law by the legislator, or with a jurist's statement of its meaning, or, as Kelsen would say, with his 'representation' of the law. For it is a tolerable (though I think not wholly acceptable) theory that the law as enunciated by the legislator or 'represented' by the jurist is an ought-statement. But the

[39] Ibid.   [40] Ibid.

statement *that* the law is valid surely does not merely repeat the law: it refers to the place of the law within the legal system. I will not elaborate on this point here, partly because I have discussed the meaning of validity at length elsewhere,[41] but also because even if we waived this objection Kelsen's conclusion would still not follow. For even on Kelsen's interpretation of validity the statement that a valid legal rule *conflicted* with a valid moral rule would not be equivalent to the joint assertion of 'A ought to be' and 'A ought not to be' which he considers a contradiction; it would be equivalent to the statement *about* 'A ought to be' and 'A ought not to be' to the effect that they conflict. This certainly is not a contradiction or logically impossible, though Kelsen would be entitled to argue that it was false.

Let us however waive, for the sake of argument, both these points, and concede that the statement that a valid rule of law conflicts with a valid moral rule does mean the same as 'A ought to be and A ought not to be'. Is this a contradiction? Technically the contradictory of (1) 'A ought to be' is not (2) 'A ought not to be', but (3) 'It is not the case that A ought to be'; and of course the joint assertion of (1) and (3) does sound pretty meaningless. But if, which has been doubted, any of the usual logical terms are applicable to ought-statements, 'A ought to be' and 'A ought not to be' are contraries, not contradictories. This however is not a serious objection because Kelsen might well say that the joint assertion of contraries is a logical impossibility. What is serious is the point that there are many interpretations which we could reasonably give to ought-statements which would explain both why 'A ought to be done and A ought not to be done' expresses a conflict between law and morals and yet does not amount to an attempt to state a logical impossibility. Here I will suggest only one possible interpretation. An intuitively acceptable meaning for 'A ought to be done' is that 'there are good reasons for doing A'. If we give 'ought' this meaning then 'A ought legally to be done and A ought morally not to be done' is equivalent to 'There are good legal reasons for doing A and good moral reasons for not doing A.' This expresses a conflict because it is logically impossible for one person at the same

[41] *The Concept of Law* 100-7, 245-7 (1961).

time to *do* both *A* and not *A*. But it does not, as far as I can see, assert anything contradictory or logically impossible.

Finally I should say that in our debate we did not get far into these rather complex matters concerning the logical relations of law and morals. Kelsen did however say that he was considering afresh the question of the possible logical relations between norms, and particularly the possibility that one norm might logically conflict with another. I do not record this to show that Kelsen was impressed by my arguments, for I think he had in mind quite different considerations. But it is very much to be hoped that on this most difficult of subjects we shall have more from the most stimulating writer on analytical jurisprudence of our day.

POSTSCRIPT

See for criticisms and comments: J. Raz, 'The Purity of the Pure Theory', 138 *Revue Internationale de la Philosophie* 441 (1981).

Essay 15

Kelsen's Doctrine of the Unity of Law

INTRODUCTION

In this essay I propose to examine one of the most striking doctrines expounded by Kelsen in his *General Theory of Law and State* and his more recent *Pure Theory of Law*.[1] Its central positive contention is that all valid laws necessarily form a single system,[2] and its central negative contention is that valid laws cannot conflict.[3] This is the strongest form of Kelsen's doctrine of the unity of law; but arguments are also to be found in Kelsen's books which support a weaker form of this doctrine, namely, that though it is not necessarily true that all valid laws form a single system and cannot conflict, it just is the case that they do form a single system and do not conflict. For Kelsen, this doctrine of the unity of law yields certain conclusions concerning the possible or actual relationships between international law and all systems of municipal law.[4] On the strong version of his theory international law and systems of municipal law necessarily form one single system,[5] and there can be no conflicts between the laws of international law and municipal law.[6] On the weaker version it just

---

[1] I refer to the *General Theory of Law and State* (Harvard 1949) as *GT* and to the *Pure Theory of Law* (University of California 1967) as *PTL*. I refer to the fuller and generally more accurate French version of the original of the latter work, *Théorie Pure de Droit* (Dalloz, 1962) as *TP*.

[2] *GT*, 363. 'It is logically not possible to assume that simultaneously valid norms belong to different mutually independent systems'; cf. *PTL*, 328.

[3] Kelsen in *GT* and *PTL* regards conflicting norms as 'contradictory' (see *infra*, section II) and so expresses his doctrine that valid laws cannot conflict by saying 'two norms which by their significance contradict and hence logically exclude one another cannot be simultaneously assumed to be valid', *GT*, 375; cf. *PTL*, 74. Note that from *PTL*, 18 (end of second paragraph) the translator has omitted the crucial words which appear in *TP*, 25, 'on peut considerer comme valable soit l'une, soit l'autre norme; il est par contre impossible de les considerer comme valable et l'une et l'autre à la fois'.

[4] The unity of international law and municipal law in one system is called by Kelsen an 'epistemological postulate', *GT*, 373, and to comprehend them as such is 'inevitable'. *PTL*, 332–3, and cf. *PTL*, 328.

[5] *PTL*, 329.

[6] *PTL*, 328.

is the case that all these laws form a single system and there are in fact no conflicts between them.[7] Kelsen develops similar, though not identical, views concerning the relationships between law and morals. He does not however contend that valid legal and moral norms either necessarily or in fact form a single system. Instead he argues that from one point of view there are only legal norms and from another point of view there are only moral norms; that these two points of view are exclusive of each other; and that they are exhaustive, so there is no third point of view from which there are both valid legal and valid moral norms.[8]

I believe, and shall attempt to show, that Kelsen's doctrine of the unity of all valid laws, and his conclusions concerning the possible and actual relationships between international law and municipal laws, are mistaken. But I think for a number of different reasons that much is to be learned from examining his doctrine. The effort of criticism of these difficult doctrines is, I think, rewarding because it brings to light at least two things. First, it shows that there is a good deal of unfinished business for analytical jurisprudence still to tackle, and this unfinished business includes a still much needed clarification of the meaning of the common assertion that laws belong to or constitute a *system* of laws, and an account of the criteria for determining the system to which given laws belong, and of what individuates one system from another. Secondly, the examination of certain features of Kelsen's doctrine takes us to the frontiers at least of the logic of norms and their interrelationships, and perhaps points beyond the frontiers to the need for something more comprehensive than the present familiar forms of deontic logic.

I shall discuss the main issues which I have mentioned in the following order. In section I, I shall consider Kelsen's theory of the unity of international law and municipal law, dealing first with the weaker version and then with the stronger version. In section II, I shall consider the 'no conflict' theory of international law and municipal law, dealing first with the strong version and then with the weaker version. In section III, I shall attempt to draw some morals from these criticisms of Kelsen's theories that may help in the

---

[7] *PTL*, 330–1. The same doctrine in a different terminology in *GT*, 371–2.
[8] *GT*, 374 ff.; *PTL*, 329.

construction of a more satisfactory analysis of the notion of a legal system, and of the nature of the criteria determining its membership, and of the principles of individuation of legal systems.

I shall not, in this paper, discuss Kelsen's doctrine concerning the possibility of simultaneously valid legal and moral norms, and of their conflict. I omit this topic not only because I have discussed some aspects of it elsewhere,[9] but also because, though Kelsen repeats this doctrine in his latest book, he neither repeats his previous arguments for it nor adduces new ones.

I. THE UNITY OF INTERNATIONAL LAW AND MUNICIPAL LAW

(A) Monistic and pluralistic theory

Kelsen calls his own theory that international law and municipal law form one system a 'monistic' theory, and contrasts it with the traditional view that they are independent systems, which he terms a 'pluralistic' theory.[10] It is however a complication of Kelsen's doctrine that there are two possible forms of monistic theory:[11] 'two different ways of comprehending all legal phenomena as parts of a single system'.[12] For according to Kelsen it is possible to structure or arrange the components of the single system which comprehends both international law and all systems of municipal law in either of two ways. One of these ways ('primacy of international law') treats international law (or, more accurately, the basic norm of international law) as the foundation of a single unified system and all the rest, including all systems of municipal law, as subordinate parts of the system ultimately deriving their validity from this foundation. The other way ('primacy of municipal law') treats one (any *one*) system of municipal law (or, more accurately, its basic norm) as the foundation of a single unified system, and all the rest, including international law and all other systems of municipal law, as subordinate parts of the single system deriving their validity from its foundation. The choice between these two alternative points of

---

[9] 'Kelsen Visited', Essay 14 *supra*.
[10] *GT*, 363-4; *PTL*, 328-9.
[11] *GT*, 376-83; *PTL*, 333-9.   [12] *GT*, 387.

view (primacy of international law or primacy of municipal law) is, according to Kelsen, a matter of political ideology, not law, and is guided by ethical and political considerations.[13] However, the contents of both international law and municipal law are totally unaffected by this choice: the legal rights and obligations of states and individuals remain the same whichever of the two alternative systems is adopted.[14] I shall not in this essay question this complication of Kelsen's theory (though in fact I think it eminently questionable), for it is in fact not relevant to the main monistic doctrine of the necessary unity of all law, and Kelsen's arguments for the monistic theory of the relations of international law and municipal law are unaffected by his view that there is a choice between according primacy to international law or to a system of municipal law.

Kelsen claims that an analysis of the actual systems of international law and municipal law shows that they form a single system. But this claim rests on a special interpretation of the legal phenomena which seems to me, for the reasons I give below, profoundly mistaken. But before I examine this interpretation it may be helpful to characterize in general terms, with the aid of a simple example, the kind of error which in my view infects Kelsen's interpretation. Suppose the question arose whether I, Hart, wrote this paper in obedience to someone's order that I should write it. Let us assume that evidence is forthcoming that just before I sat down to write this paper the Vice-Chancellor of Oxford University dispatched to me a document purporting to order me to write a paper on Kelsen's Doctrine of the Unity of Law. It is plain that whether or not I wrote this paper in obedience to that order could not be settled by comparing the contents of the order ('Hart: write a paper on Kelsen's Doctrine of the Unity of Law') with a true description of my later conduct ('Hart wrote a paper on Kelsen's Doctrine of the Unity of Law'). This comparison would indeed show correspondence between the content of the order and the description of my conduct, in that the action-description contained in the order is applicable to my subsequent conduct. But though in order to establish that I did write this paper in obedience to this order it would be *necessary* to show this correspondence between the content of the order and the description of my conduct, plainly this would not be *sufficient*. It would also be necessary to establish certain facts that have to do not with the content of the order, but with the circumstances surrounding the issue and reception of the order, involving consideration of such questions as the following. Did Hart receive the Vice-Chancellor's missive? Did he recognize it as an order? Did he write the paper in order to comply with this order? Did anyone else give such an order? If so, whose order did Hart intend to obey? A 'pure theory' of imperatives that ignored such facts and circumstances surrounding the issue and reception of orders, and restricted itself to the characterization of the relationships between the contents of orders and the description of actions, would necessarily be incompetent to settle the question whether any person had obeyed a particular order. However, since the correspondence relationship between content and action-description is a necessary condition of obedience, the theory would be competent to identify cases where orders had not been obeyed; though it is important to remember that 'not obeyed' is not the same as 'disobeyed'.

I will try to show that in somewhat the same way, though not precisely the same way, the pure theory of law suffers from the defects of my imaginary pure theory of imperatives, for it concentrates too exclusively on the contents of laws and pays too little attention to circumstances that concern the making or origin of laws (rather than what laws say) and whether they are recognized as authoritative and by whom. When we have laws that explicitly or implicitly refer to other laws, or their existence or validity, we cannot determine from these relationships alone whether they belong to the same or different systems. This depends on facts concerning the making and recognition of laws. The pure theory of law is too pure to attend to such facts; and, as I shall attempt to show, by treating what are at best necessary conditions as if they were sufficient conditions of laws belonging to the same system, the pure theory reaches false conclusions as to the unity of international and municipal law. With this general characterization of the type of error which I think is inherent in the content-obsessed pure theory of law, let me turn to the examination of Kelsen's interpretation of the legal phenomena.

(B) The completion relationship between laws

Kelsen attacks with some force a crude and misleading dichotomy between international law and municipal law. International law, it is sometimes said, imposes obligations and confers rights on states, whereas municipal law imposes obligations and confers rights on individuals. This distinction is often used to support the pluralistic theory. It is said that international law and municipal law are independent legal systems because they regulate different subject-matters: international law regulates the behaviour of states and municipal law regulates the behaviour of individuals. Kelsen criticizes this argument for pluralism in two ways.[15] He shows that there are rules of international law, no doubt exceptional, that apply directly to individuals in the same way as the rules of municipal law. Examples of these are the laws against piracy, and the rules of international law making punishable acts of illegitimate warfare, ie. hostile acts on the part of individuals not belonging to the armed forces of the country. But quite apart from these exceptional cases, Kelsen maintains that if we understand the logical structure of such expressions as 'the state' as a technique or method of referring indirectly to individuals identified by certain legal rules and lay aside the misconception of a state as an entity over and above the individuals that compose it, it is apparent that laws which purport to apply directly to states in fact apply to individuals, though the manner of their application is indirect. Hence the description of the rules of international law as 'applying to states' should not be construed as contrasting with 'applying to individuals'; it is to be contrasted with applying *directly* to individuals, i.e. without the aid of, or supplementation by, other rules identifying the individuals to whom the first rules are applicable.[16] The rules of international law, according to Kelsen, when they purport to apply to states are 'incomplete': they specify themselves only *what* is to be done or not to be done, but they leave or, as Kelsen says, 'delegate' the identification of the individuals who are or are not to do these things to the rules of municipal law,[17] and the

---

[15] *GT*, 342–8; *PTL*, 324–8.
[16] *GT*, 342; *PTL*, 325, 327.
[17] *GT*, 348–9; *PTL*, 325.

latter rules, identifying the individuals, 'complete' the rules of international law.

Kelsen illustrates this completion of international law by the rules of municipal law by the following simple example.

There is a time-honoured rule of common international law to the effect that war must not be begun without previous, formal declaration of war. The third Hague Convention of 1907 codified this rule in the stipulation (art. 1) that hostilities 'must not commence without a previous and unequivocal warning, which shall take the form either of a declaration of war giving reasons, or of an ultimatum with a conditional declaration of war'. This norm states only that a declaration of war has to be delivered, not by whom,—that is to say, by which individual as organ of the State —it has to be done. Most constitutions empower the head of the state to declare war. The constitution of the United States (art. 1 s.8) says that 'the Congress shall have the power to declare war'. By this determining the personal element, the American constitution completes the norm of international law just mentioned. The characteristic of international law that it 'obligates States only' consists merely in the fact that its norms generally determine only the material element, leaving the determination of the personal element to national law.[18]

Let us call the relationship between a set of rules one of which leaves to the other or others the identification of the individuals to whom the first applies, the 'completion relationship', and let us call the set of rules so related 'a completing set'. Kelsen's insistence that many rules of international law and municipal law are related by the completion relationship is in many ways illuminating, and I shall not quarrel with his use of this idea in attacking the crude and confused theory that international law and municipal law are independent or different systems because international law applies to states and municipal law to individuals. It is however very important to appreciate that the fact that the completion relationship holds between certain rules is not itself sufficient to show that the rules between which it holds belong to one and the same system: for unless it can be independently shown that the very idea of the existence of different systems of legal rules is illusory, and that there is only *one* system of rules, it seems quite clear that the completion relationship may hold either between the rules of the same system or between rules of different systems. It is necessary to stress this fact because it may be obscured by Kelsen's frequent (and, again, often

[18] *GT*, 343.

illuminating) insistence on the similarity between the relationships holding on the one hand between the rules of
international law, and municipal law, and on the other hand
between a statute of municipal law and the by-laws or regulations of a corporation.[19] This similarity, obscured by the
personifying or reifying terminology of 'state' and 'corporation', resides in the following facts. When a rule of international law purports to impose some duty directly on a state
it is in fact indirectly imposing those duties on the individuals
identified by the state's municipal system, and those individuals' actions and obligations are imputed to the state. Similarly, when a statute of a municipal legal system imposes
some duty on a corporation it indirectly imposes that duty
on the individuals (officers or members of the corporation)
identified by the internal by-laws or regulations of the
corporation. Both cases thus exemplify the completion
relationship.

The relation between the total legal order constituting the state, the so-
called law of the state or national legal order, and the juristic person of
a corporation is the relation between two legal orders, a total and a
partial legal order, between the law of the state and the by-laws of the
corporation. To be more specific it is a case of delegation.[20]

In considering this interesting parallel between the relationships of municipal statutes to corporation by-laws on the one
hand and international law to municipal law on the other, it
is important not to lose sight of the fact that when a rule of
municipal law, e.g. an English statute, imposes obligations on
a corporation incorporated under English law, the regulations
or by-laws of the corporation which identify the individuals
who, as officers or members of the corporation are to execute
this duty, derive their validity from other English statutes
determining the manner in which corporation regulations may
be made and limiting their content. As Kelsen says, the by-
laws constituting the corporation are created by a legal transaction determined by the national legal order. Hence, the
statute imposing the obligation on the corporation, and the
earlier statutes under which the company regulations were
made, belong to the same legal system quite independently of
the completion relationship holding between the statute imposing the obligation on the corporation and its regulations.

[19] *GT*, 349; *PTL*, 325; cf. *PTL*, 179.   [20] *GT*, 100.

These statutes and by-laws all belong to the same system because they satisfy the criteria recognized by English courts as identifying the laws which they are to enforce. Of course, an English statute might impose obligations on a foreign corporation. Here too, the completion relationship would hold between the English statute and the regulations of the Swedish corporation, for the latter would identify those individuals who as officers or members of the corporation were bound to execute the duty. But the regulations of the Swedish corporation which would thus complete the English statute derive their validity from a statute of the Swedish legislature determining the manner in which Swedish corporation regulations are to be made. This Swedish statute exists as part not of English law but of Swedish law, and so existed before the enactment of the English statute imposing obligations on the Swedish corporation, whereas in the case where the English statute imposes obligations on the English corporation the regulations of the corporation existed as part of English law.

It is perhaps worth observing that completion relationships between laws of the same or different systems are not confined to cases where we speak of abstract juristic entities such as 'state' or 'corporation'. Thus an English statute might confer certain rights, e.g. the right to vote, on individuals whom it might define only as persons liable to pay certain rates and taxes under some other English statute, or it might exempt from taxation certain foreigners if they are liable under the law of their own country to certain similar taxes. In the first case the completion relationship would hold between laws of the same system; in the second case it holds between laws of a different system.

(C) The relationship of validating purport

In spite of some ambiguity of language,[21] Kelsen does not, I think, conceive of the completion relationship between laws as in itself sufficient to show that they belong to the same system, for he writes: 'Since the international legal order not only requires the national legal orders as a necessary complementation, but also determines their spheres of validity in all respects, international and national law form one inseparable

---

[21] Notably *GT*, 349; and *PTL*, 325.

whole.'[22] The words which I have quoted introduced Kelsen's central argument for the monistic theory and, as I believe, his central mistake. The argument, reduced to its essentials, is this. International law contains among its rules one that Kelsen terms the 'principle of effectiveness' which 'determines' or 'is the reason for' the validity of the national legal orders and their territorial and temporal sphere of validity. The contents of this principle of effectiveness are spelt out by Kelsen in his latest formulation of it, as follows:

> A norm of general international law authorises an individual or a group of individuals on the basis of an effective constitution, to create and apply as a legitimate government a normative coercive order. That norm thus legitimises this coercive order for the territory of its actual effectiveness as a valid legal order and the community constituted by this coercive order as a 'state' in the sense of international law.[23]

Because the principle of effectiveness thus legitimizes or validates the separate coercive orders effective in different territories, international law, to which the principle of effectiveness belongs, forms a single system together with the various systems of municipal law, which it legitimizes or validates. It forms with them, Kelsen says, 'one separable whole'.[24] In considering this argument it is important to understand precisely what in Kelsen's view is the relationship between the principle of effectiveness and the various municipal legal systems which it is said to legitimate, or the validity of which it is said to determine. The principle of effectiveness says that the other rules of a certain description (i.e., roughly, coercive rules effective in certain territories) are valid; and it is a fact that there are certain rules (the actual systems of municipal law) that satisfy this description. Let us call this relationship the relationship of validating purport. I shall argue that what was said above about the completion relationship applies also to the relationship of validating purport: it is not sufficient in order to establish that two rules form part of a single system to show that one of them provides that rules of a certain description satisfied by the other are valid. I shall also argue that when such a relationship holds between two rules it is dangerously misleading to express this fact by

---

[22] *GT*, 351.
[23] *PTL*, 215; cf. *PTL*, 336-40; and *GT*, 121.
[24] *GT*, 351.

stating, *without stressing a very important qualification*, that one rule 'determines the validity' of the other or is 'the reason for its validity'.

Kelsen's argument depends on the use he makes of the fact that the relationship of validating purport holds between the principle of effectiveness considered as a rule of international law and the rules of municipal legal systems. The inadequacy of this argument and also the character of the important qualification I have just mentioned can be seen from the following wild hypothetical example. Suppose the British Parliament (or *mutatis mutandis*, Congress) passes an Act (the Soviet Laws Validity Act, 1970) which purports to validate the law of the Soviet Union by providing that the laws currently effective in Soviet territory, including those relating to the competence of legislative and judicial authorities, shall be valid. The enactment of this Act by Parliament or Congress would not be a reason for saying that English (or American) law together with Soviet law formed one legal system, or for using *sans phrase* any of the Kelsenian expressions such as that Soviet law 'derives its validity' from English law or that English law was 'the reason for the validity' of Soviet law. The reason for refusing to assent to these propositions is surely clear and compelling: it is that the courts and other law-enforcing agencies in Soviet territory do not, save in certain special circumstances,[25] recognize the operations of the British (or American) legislature as criteria for identifying the laws that they are to enforce, and so they do not recognize the Soviet Laws Validity Act, though a valid English (or American) statute, as in any way determining or otherwise affecting the validity of Soviet law in Soviet territory. It is true indeed that the relationship of validating purport holds between that Act and the laws made by the Soviet legislature, which the Soviet courts do recognize; but the division of laws into distinct legal systems cuts across the relationship of validating purport, for that relationship, like the completion relationship examined above, may hold either between laws of different systems or between laws of the same system.

The important qualification that should be made in drawing any conclusion from the existence of the relationship of

---

[25] Cases involving a 'foreign element': see *infra*, 340–2.

validating purport between rules is perhaps obvious. On the passing of the Soviet Laws Validity Act it would be right to say that *for the purposes* of English law, or according to English law, Soviet laws were validated by or derive their validity from an English statute, and the effect of this would be that English courts would apply Soviet law in adjudicating upon any transaction or conduct to which the Soviet authorities would apply Soviet law. The Soviet Laws Validity Act would make Soviet law part of English law for such purposes. But the two pairs of questions:

A1. Do English law and Soviet law form part of a single system of law?
A2. Does Soviet law derive its validity from English law?

and:

B1. Does English law treat Soviet law as forming part of a single system with itself?
B2. Is Soviet law valid according to English law?

are questions of different kinds. The first pair are not questions that concern merely the content of laws and so are to be settled by considering what laws say; whereas the second pair are questions concerning the content of laws and are settled in that way.

There is the same difference in kind between the pairs of questions:

C1. Do international law and municipal law form a single system?
C2. Does municipal law derive its validity from international law?

and:

D1. Does international law treat (e.g., by its principle of effectiveness) municipal law as forming part of a single system with itself?
D2. Is municipal law valid according to the international law (e.g., through its principle of effectiveness)?

The pure theory blurs the distinctions between these very different types of question; it does so because it concentrates too much on what laws of validating purport *say* about other laws, and pays too little attention to matters that do not concern the content of laws but their mode of recognition. The pure theory, therefore, has a juristic Midas touch, which transmutes all questions about laws and their relationship into questions of the content of law or questions concerning what laws say; but the touch is perverse, for not all questions are of this kind.

I conclude that the arguments in support of the weaker version of Kelsen's version of the doctrine of the unity of international law and municipal law fail. This is not to say that arguments different from Kelsen's might not succeed in establishing the weaker version of his thesis — at least up to a point. For whether or not international law and the law of a state form one system depends on the manner in which and extent to which a given state recognizes international law. If in cases where international law conflicts with the law of the state the courts of the state treat the state law as invalid or overridden by international law, this would be a good reason for saying that international law and the law of that state form parts of a single system of law — or at any rate it would resemble the reason for saying that the law of a state of the United States and federal law form part of a single system. But Kelsen's arguments fail because the fact that the relationship of validating purport exists between the principle of effectiveness treated as a rule of international law (or any other rules of international law purporting to determine the validity of municipal law), and the rules of municipal law, does not show that the latter derive their validity from the former, and does not show that 'pluralists' are wrong in denying that international law and municipal law form a single system.[26]

I now turn to the examination of the stronger form of Kelsen's thesis that international law and minicipal law necessarily form one system.

(D) The necessary unity of all valid law
Very little by way of argument is to be found in support of Kelsen's stronger thesis that all valid law *necessarily* forms a

---

[26] I consider later the possibility of *introducing* a meaning for 'legal system' such that the mere existence of the relationship of validating purport between laws is sufficient to constitute the laws of a single system. This would not of course refute the conventional pluralist for it is not in this sense of 'system' that he asserts that international law and municipal law are separate systems.

single system, with its corollary that international law and municipal law necessarily constitute such a system. Kelsen asserts that this is a 'postulate of legal theory'.[27] 'The unity of national law and international law is an epistemological postulate. A jurist who accepts both sets of valid norms must try to comprehend them as parts of one harmonious system.'[28] This postulate is frequently referred to in the terminology of logical necessity. 'It is logically not possible to assume that simultaneously valid norms belong to different mutually independent systems.'[29]

For these assertions I have identified only two arguments. Neither need occupy us long. The first argument reduces to the contention that all that is law forms a single system because there is a form of knowledge ('jurisprudence'[30] or 'connaissance juridique'[31]) or a science of law which studies both international law and municipal law as falling under the single description 'valid laws' and thus represents 'its object' as a unity. Kelsen expresses this argument in the following words:

[The] pluralistic construction is untenable if both the norms of international law and those of the national legal orders are to be considered as simultaneously valid legal norms. This view implies already the epistemological postulate: to understand all law in one system . . . as one closed whole. Jurisprudence subsumes the norms regulating the relations between states, called international law, as well as the national legal orders under one and the same category of law. In so doing it tries to present its object as a unity.[32]

Surely we might as well attempt to deduce from the existence of the history of warfare or the science of strategy that all wars are one or all armies are one.

The second argument really shows that Kelsen's argument

---

[27] *GT*, 373.
[28] Ibid.
[29] *GT*, 363.
[30] *PTL*, 328.
[31] *TP*, 430
[32] *PTL*, 328. Professor J. L. Mackie has pointed out to me that Kelsen's claim that there can only be one system of valid laws resembles Kant's claim that there is only one space. 'For . . . we can represent to ourselves only one space; and if we speak of diverse spaces, we mean only parts of one and the same unique space' (*Critique of Pure Reason* A25). I have the impression that underlying Kelsen's theory of law there is the *assumption* that there is a single 'normative space' which must be describable by a consistent set of 'rules in a descriptive sense'. (See *infra*, 327 ff.)

for the necessary unity of valid law is dependent on his thesis that there can be no conflicts between valid laws, for he says:

> If there should be two actually different systems of norms, mutually independent in their validity . . . both of which are related to the same object (in having the same sphere of validity), insoluble logical contradiction between them could not be excluded. The norm of one system may prescribe conduct A for a certain person, under a certain condition, at certain time and place. The norm of the other system may prescribe, under the same conditions and for the same person, conduct non-A. This situation is impossible for the cognition of norms.[33]

Of course this does not deal with the possibility that there might be two legal systems simultaneously effective in different territories in which the possibility of conflicts is excluded because the constitution of each system secured that what Kelsen calls 'the sphere of validity' of the laws of each system should be different. The laws of the two systems should be different. The laws of the two systems might, for example, according to their constitutions apply to conduct in different territories. Kelsen asserts[34] that such a limitation would have to be imposed by a single superior law to which both systems with limited scope would be subordinate and with which they would form a single system. But he does not support this assertion with any arguments, and it is difficult to see why it should not just be the case that two communities chose independently to adopt constitutions limiting the scope of the laws in this way. However, the argument from the alleged impossibility of conflict, though it does not cover this case, remains Kelsen's only remaining argument for the necessary unity of all valid law.[35] I examine the thesis that conflict between valid laws is impossible in the next section.

---

[33] *GT*, 408.

[34] *GT*, 407–8.

[35] Quite apart from its failure to cover the case mentioned, this argument for the necessary unity of all valid law in one system is incomplete, even if conflict between valid laws is (contrary to the argument of the next section) admitted to be logically impossible. To complete the argument it would have to be shown that what Kelsen calls 'insoluble logical contradictions', which he thinks might arise in the case of two independent systems, could not arise in the case of one system.

II. THE 'NO CONFLICTS' THEORY[36]

Kelsen claims that in spite of appearances there really are no conflicts between international law and municipal law. He admits that if there were such conflicts the monistic theory that international law and municipal law form one system could not be sustained: indeed he says the absence of conflict is the 'negative criterion'[37] of the unity of international law and municipal law in a single system. If, however, there were such conflicts the result would be, according to Kelsen, not that international law and municipal law would constitute separate systems of valid laws, as the conventional 'pluralist' holds; instead we would have a choice between treating international law as valid while ignoring any conflicting rules of municipal law, or treating a system of muncipal law as valid while ignoring any conflicting rules of international law. This is, according to Kelsen, actually the position with regard to laws and morality: when their norms conflict we have a choice between treating the legal rules as valid, ignoring conflicting moral norms, or treating moral norms as valid, ignoring any conflicting laws.[38]

Before we can evaluate these somewhat surprising doctrines it is plainly necessary to canvass some preliminary questions. What is it for laws or systems of laws to conflict? How is a conflict between laws related to logical inconsistency or contradiction? Unfortunately, Kelsen's own analysis in his books of the notion of conflicts between laws and norms consists only of a few scattered observations, though what he has to say touches upon some important and indeed controversial logical issues. This is not the place for full investigation of these issues, but in my statement and criticism of Kelsen's doctrines I will use, as undogmatically as I can, some relatively simple distinctions which have been drawn by writers on

[36] This section is concerned with Kelsen's views on conflicts as expounded in *GT* and *PTL*. In a later essay on 'Derogation' in *Essays in Honour of Roscoe Pound* (New York 1962) Kelsen admits the logical possibility of conflicting valid norms. He does not however explain why he has abandoned his previous views or refer to the exposition of them in *GT* and *PTL*. Nor does he withdraw or modify the monistic theory of international law and municipal law expounded in these books. See, for an examination of this phase of Kelsen's thought, A. G. Conte, 'In Margine All'Ultimo Kelsen' in *Studi Giuridici* (Studia Ghisleriana, Pavia, 1967), 113.

[37] *PTL*, 328.

[38] *GT*, 410; *PTL*, 329.

deontic logic and the logic of imperatives, who have concerned themselves with similar questions about conflicts.

(A) Conflict as the logical impossibility of joint conformity
Many writers favour the idea (which seems intuitively acceptable) that conflict between two rules requiring or prohibiting
actions is to be understood in terms of the logical possibility
of joint obedience to them. Two such rules conflict if and
only if obedience to them both ('joint obedience') is logically
impossible. The crudest[39] case of such a conflict are rules
which respectively require and forbid the same action on the
part of the same person at the same time or times. The logical
impossibility of joint obedience may be exhibited in the following way.[40] For any rule requiring or prohibiting action,
we can form a statement (an 'obedience statement') asserting
that the action that is required by the rule is done, or the
action prohibited by the rule is not done. Two such rules conflict if their respective obedience statements are logically inconsistent and so cannot both be true. Thus (to take one of
Kelsen's examples), suppose one rule requires certain persons
to kill certain other human beings, and another rule prohibits
the same persons from killing the same other human beings,
the obedience statements corresponding to those rules would
be of the general form, 'killing is done', and 'killing is not
done'. Of course, before we can determine whether two statements of this general form are logically inconsistent or not,
they would have to be filled out with specifications of the
agents and victims and times to which the rules, explicitly or
implicitly, related. If the same agents are required by one rule
to do, and by another rule to abstain from, the same action
at the same time this will be reflected in the corresponding
obedience statements which would be logically inconsistent.
Joint obedience to the rules would be logically impossible.

It is to be observed that this definition of conflict between
rules leaves entirely open the question whether or not it is

[39] Crude, since most cases of conflict between two rules arise because some
contingent fact makes it impossible only on particular occasion to obey them
both, and not because the rules by explicitly forbidding and requiring the same
action are such that on no occasion could they both be obeyed.

[40] See B. A. O. Williams, 'Consistency and Realism', *Proc. Aristot. Soc.
Suppl.* xxxix (1965), 103. I am much indebted to this lucid account of the
logical issues involved.

logically possible for two conflicting rules to coexist as valid rules either of the same or different systems. To most people it would certainly seem possible for a law of one legal system made by one set of legislators to conflict with the law of another legal system made by another set of legislators; and it would perhaps seem equally obvious that one such law could conflict with some moral rule or principle. Joint obedience to these rules would be logically impossible, but their coexistence as valid rules would be logically possible. Further, though it would certainly be deplorable on every practical score if laws of a single legal system conflicted and the system provided no way of resolving such conflicts, it is still far from obvious that even this is a logical impossibility. So far as the nature and logical possibilities of conflict are concerned, there seems little difference between rules requiring and prohibiting action and simple second person orders and commands addressed by one person to another. Two such orders ('kill' and 'do not kill') conflict if joint obedience to them is logically impossible, and this can be shown in the form of logically inconsistent obedience statements. But it is certainly logically possible for conflicting orders to be given by different persons to the same person, and though we might think a person who gave inconsistent orders at short intervals to the same person mad or split-minded or lacking a coherent will and perhaps in need of clinical attention, such situations do not seem logically impossible. In the end no doubt, if he insisted on producing streams of inconsistent orders and these could not be explained, e.g. by lapse of memory, we should conclude that he did not understand what he was saying, and might well refuse to classify what he said as constituting orders at all.

In one important respect, however, which is relevant to Kelsen's theory, conflict between laws and other rules is more complicated than conflict between such simple orders. Laws and rules, as Kelsen acknowledges,[41] instead of requiring or forbidding action, may either expressly permit action, or by not forbidding them, tacitly permit them; and it is clear that there may be conflicts between laws that forbid and laws or legal systems that expressly or tacitly permit. To meet such

---

[41] *PTL*, 16. Kelsen described such permissive rules (express or tacit) as 'negative regulation' of conduct, and distinguishes a positive sense of permission when rules prohibit interference with another's conduct.

cases, we should have to use not only the notion of obedience, which is appropriate to rules requiring or forbidding action, but the notion of acting on or availing oneself of a permission. We might adopt the generic term 'conformity' to comprehend both obedience to rules that require or prohibit and acting on or availing oneself of permission, and we could adopt the expression 'conformity statements' to cover both kinds of corresponding statement. In fact, the conformity statement showing that a permissive rule (e.g. permitting though not requiring killing) had been acted on will be of the same form as the obedience statement for a rule requiring the same action (killing is done). So if one rule prohibits and another rule permits the same action by the same person at the same time, joint conformity will be logically impossible and the two rules will conflict.[42]

(B) Conflict and logical inconsistency

Kelsen would I think accept such a definition of conflict between rules in terms of the logical impossibility of joint conformity. Certainly his few examples of conflicting rules and of what he sometimes terms 'opposite' or 'incompatible' behaviour are consistent with this, and he makes at least one passing though informal reference to what is in substance the joint conformity test of conflict.[43] But Kelsen's account of the connection between conflict between norms and logical inconsistencies is different and more controversial. For his doctrine as expounded in his books is that the statement that two valid norms conflict is or entails a contradiction; for Kelsen it is a logical impossibility that there should coexist valid but conflicting norms either of the same or different systems. And it is not merely the case for him that joint conformity to them is logically impossible.[44]

Kelsen's arguments for these conclusions depend on the use which he makes of a distinction (itself important and illuminating) between laws made or applied by legal authorities, e.g.

[42] *PTL*, 18, but note text of *TP* (n. 3 *supra*); *PTL*, 25, 205.

[43] The 'joint-conformity' test of conflict is applicable only to rules all or all but one of which require or prohibit action. Permissive rules cannot conflict, but joint conformity with two permissive rules may be logically impossible (e.g. 'Opening the window is permitted'; 'Shutting the window is permitted'). I am indebted to Professor J. L. Mackie for this point.

[44] *GT*, 409; *PTL*, 18, 205–8, 329.

statutes of a legislature, which cannot be either true or false, and a class of statements describing the content of laws, which Kelsen called 'legal rules in a descriptive sense' and which can be either true or false. These rules in a descriptive sense are of the following general form: 'according to a certain positive legal order a certain consequence ought to take place' or 'according to a certain legal norm something ought to be done or ought not to be done'. In such statements 'ought' according to Kelsen is used in a descriptive sense, and I shall refer to such statements as 'descriptive-ought statements'.[45]

A simple illustration of this doctrine is as follows. If there exists a legal order, e.g. the English legal system, and among its duly enacted laws there is a statute requiring under certain penalties men on attaining the age of twenty-one to report for military service, these facts constitute part of the truth grounds for the descriptive-ought statement 'according to English law the following persons . . . ought to report for military service . . .'. If there is such a law the descriptive-ought statement is true; if there is not, it is false. Three things however should be borne in mind when considering Kelsen's descriptive-ought statements.

1. 'Ought' is used by Kelsen in a special, wide sense, so that 'ought' statements include not only descriptions of laws that forbid or require action, but also those that describe laws or legal systems which expressly or tacitly permit actions. 'Ought' in Kelsen's usage is a kind of deontic variable ranging over what he terms prescriptions (or commands), permissions and authorizations.[46]

2. Descriptive-ought statements are not confined to the law. Similar statements, similarly capable of truth or falsity, may be made concerning non-legal, e.g. moral norms:

L'ethique décrit les normes d'une morale determinée, elle nous enseigne comment nous devons nous conduire selon cette morale, mais, en tant

---

[45] *PTL*, 73, 78. The corresponding term in *TP* is 'proposition de droit' as distinguished from 'norme juridique'; and in the original German is 'Rechstatz' as distinguished from 'Rechtsnorm'. In the long note to *TP*, 99 (omitted by the translator in *PTL*), Kelsen cites Sigwart in support of the notion of 'ought in a descriptive sense'. Cf. the similar views of von Wright on normative statements in *Norm and Action* (London 1963), 78 ff.; cf. Castaneda on 'deontic assertables' in 'Actions, Imperatives and Obligations', *Proc. Aristot. Soc.* lxviii (1967–8), 25.
[46] *PTL*, 5.

que science, elle ne nous préscrit pas de nous conduire de telle ou telle façon. Le moraliste n'est pas l'autorité morale qui pose les normes qu'il décrit en propositions normatives.[47]

3. The words which appear at the beginning of the formulation of descriptive-ought statements in the above quotations ('according to a certain positive legal order') and the words 'selon cette moral [déterminée]', are important for the following reasons. Kelsen has sometimes been accused of holding a metaphysical belief that there is a realm of 'ought' (including the 'ought' of legal rules) which is not man-made, but awaits man's cognition or discovery, and of believing that it is this realm of ought, over and above the world of facts, that true descriptive-ought statements describe. Against such critics, Kelsen insists that for him all norms are made and not merely discovered by human beings, and although, given the existence of positive legal orders or systems, true descriptive statements can be made about their content in the form of ought statements, the truth of such statements is not 'absolute' but relative[48] to the particular legal system or order concerned. Indeed it could be argued in support of Kelsen that so long as we bear in mind this essential relativity to a given system his account of descriptive-ought statements clarifies a certain kind of discourse frequent among lawyers. Lawyers often ask such questions as 'What is the legal position with regard to military service?', and tender in answer to such questions such statements as 'Men on attaining the age of 21 must report for military service', and regard the answers as true or false. There is frequent occasion for lawyers to describe what they might call the 'legal position' in relation to some subject without referring to the particular enactments or regulations or other sources of the relevant law, though of course it would be always understood that the 'legal position' thus described is that arising under the laws of a particular system, and a more accurate formulation would make this explicit by including such words as 'according to English law . . .'.

The immediate relevance of Kelsen's descriptive-ought

---

[47] *TP*, 99, note (omitted from *PTL*).
[48] *PTL*, 18.

statements to the question of conflicts between laws can be seen from the following quotation:

> Since legal norms, being prescriptions (that is commands, permissions, authorisations), can neither be true nor false the question arises: How can logical principles especially the Principle of the Exclusion of Contradiction and the rules of inference be applied to the relation between legal norms if, according to traditional views, these principles are applicable only to assertions that can be true or false? The answer is: Logical principles are applicable indirectly to legal norms to the extent that they are applicable to rules of law which describe the legal norms and which can be true or false. Two legal norms are contradictory and can therefore not both be valid at the same time if the two rules of law that describe them are contradictory . . .[49]

Kelsen explains several times that descriptive-ought statements describing two legal rules requiring what he terms 'opposite' behaviour would be of the form 'A ought to be' and 'A ought not to be', and statements of this form referring to actions to be done by the same agents at the same time are said by Kelsen to 'contradict each other',[50] and their joint assertion is said to be meaningless: 'to say that A ought to be and at the same time ought not to be is just as meaningless as to say that A is and at the same time that it is not'.[51] Accordingly, it is a logical impossibility for two such rules to be valid: only one of them can be regarded as valid. Kelsen thus speaks throughout his books as if conflicts between laws were a form of logical inconsistency, so that it is logically impossible that conflicting rules should coexist and not merely that joint conformity with them is logically impossible.

Kelsen's arguments raise a host of difficulties;[52] fortunately not all of them need detailed consideration here. We may waive for the moment (while noting for later use) the objections that if 'A ought to be' and 'A ought not to be' are logically inconsistent they are not, as Kelsen says, contradictory but contraries. The contradictory of 'A ought not to be done' is 'it is not the case that A ought not to be done', and two ought-statements of this form would describe not two rules that require and prohibited the same action, but two rules,

---

[49] *PTL*, 74.   [50] *PTL*, 206.   [51] Ibid.

[52] Among these difficulties, much in need of exploration, is the determination of the meaning for Kelsen of 'valid'. Sometimes he writes as if to say that a norm is 'valid', is to say that it is a final and uniquely correct standard of conduct and so excludes the validity of conflicting norms, e.g. *GT*, 410.

one of which prohibited and the other of which permitted the same action. But apart from this, it is not a self-evident truth of logic that 'A ought to be done' and 'A ought not to be done', even if they describe rules of the *same* system, are logically inconsistent at all. Certainly some argument is required to show that they are. No doubt, if we assume certain premises (namely 1. 'ought' implies can, and 2. 'A ought to be done and A ought not to be done' entails 'A ought both to be done and not to be done') it would then follow that 'A ought to be done' and 'A ought not to be done' cannot logically both be true.[53] It is also of course possible to define 'ought' in such a way that 'A ought to be done' entails 'it is not the case that A ought not to be done'; but it is worth noting that logicians of repute in constructing systems of deontic logic have allowed for the possibility of conflicting obligations ('one ought to do A' and 'one ought not to do A'). There seems no formal inconsistency in such a notion, and a logical calculus which is out to catch the logical properties of actual human codes of behaviour should not rule out such possibilities of conflict in advance by taking it as an axiom that 'one ought to do A' entails that it is not the case that one ought not to do A.[54]

It is not necessary, however, in order to assess Kelsen's thesis that international law and municipal law cannot conflict, to press the point that conflict even between laws of the same system is not a logical impossibility. For Kelsen's arguments that there can be no such conflicts between international law and municipal law are intended by him to be independent of the thesis that they form one system.[55] Kelsen's arguments for the possibility of conflicts turn entirely on his view of the logical relations between the descriptive-ought statements describing conflicting laws, and his arguments seem to be vitiated by a simple error. He disregards the important fact that, as he had previously himself observed, descriptive-ought statements when true are true only relatively to the systems that they describe, and accurately formulated, should

[53] See Williams, loc. cit. n. 40 *supra*.

[54] See for a clear discussion of this point E. J. Lemmon, 'Deontic Logic and the Logic of Imperatives', *Logique et Analyse* (1965), esp. 45–51.

[55] His position is that if there were such conflicts we could not regard international law and municipal law as one system, and absence of conflict is the negative criterion of unity of system. See 324 *supra*.

be prefixed with such words as 'according to English law'.[56] Hence if we were to concede for the sake of argument that '*A* ought to be' and '*A* ought not to be' are, as Kelsen claims, logically inconsistent, or that laws of the same system could not conflict, it would not follow, nor is it the case, that descriptive-ought statements of the form 'according to international law *A* ought to be' and 'according to English law *A* ought not to be' are logically inconsistent. Indeed there seems no reason at all, once the relativity of descriptive-ought statements is borne in mind, for thinking that two statements of this form cannot both be true. Since Kelsen therefore has given no satisfactory reason for saying that international law and municipal law form one system, there seems nothing to support the thesis that their rules cannot conflict.

(C) The weaker version of the 'no conflict' theory
With these rather top-heavy but necessary preliminaries we may turn to the evaluation of Kelsen's claim that there are in fact no conflicts between valid rules of international law and municipal law. His proof that there are no conflicts between international law and municipal law takes the following form.[57] According to a conventional 'pluralist' theory, a conflict between international law and municipal law arises if a state enacts a statute which is incompatible with a provision of a treaty to which it is a party, and which is valid according to international law. He cites as an example the case of a treaty between two states, which I shall call *A* and *B*. The treaty provides that the members of a minority group in the population of a State *B* should have the same political right as the majority. If in State *B* a law is enacted depriving the minority of all political rights notwithstanding the treaty, conventional pluralist theory would claim that here the statute, valid according to the law of State *B*, and the treaty, valid according to international law, conflicted: it would be impossible to comply both with the treaty and with the statute, for this would be both to allow and not to allow the minority to exercise certain rights.

Kelsen argues that to regard such cases in this way is to misinterpret the rules of international law according to which

---

[56] E.g. *PTL*, 73, 205.   [57] *PTL*, 330.

such treaties are binding on states. Such rules make the enactment by a state of statutes, which are incompatible with the
terms of a valid treaty to which it is a party, an offence or
delict under international law, exposing the state to the sanctions of international law. But though the *enactment* of such
a statute is forbidden by international law, once enacted it is
none the less valid even according to international law (though
illegally enacted), and does not conflict with the rules of international law relating to treaties; for their true force is exhausted in making the enactment by the state of such a statute
illegal,[58] i.e., a delict or offence against international law. In
other words, the rule of international law does not seek to
determine directly the content of state statutes, but only the
legality or illegality of their enactment. There is therefore no
conflict between the rule of international law, so interpreted,
and the statute, though the latter's enactment violates the
rule. Kelsen cites, as a parallel, one interpretation of constitutional provisions protecting fundamental rights in those systems of municipal law which contain no provision for judicial
review or for the nullification of statutes which are unconstitutional because they violate the fundamental rights which
the constitution purports to protect. Instead of judicial review
the constitution, in such cases, is interpreted as making officials or legislators liable to punishment for their part in the
enactment of such unconstitutional statutes. In such cases
the constitution does not directly determine the content of
statutes, but only the legality of their enactment; and there
is no conflict between the constitution so interpreted and the
statute which remains valid though its enactment constitutes
a punishable offence under the constitution.

This argument is ingenious, but even if we concede the suggested interpretation of the rules of international law relating
to treaties it does not, in fact, banish conflict between international and municipal law; it merely locates such conflict at
a different point and shows it to be a conflict not between
rules requiring and prohibiting the same action (the treaty and
the statute) but between rules prohibiting and *permitting* the
same action, i.e., the enactment of the statute. It is a conflict
of this latter form that arises when a state enacts a statute in

violation of its treaty obligations, if its enactment is an offence according to international law, but is not so according
to municipal law. There are certainly many systems of municipal law, among them the English, according to which it is not
an offence to enact or procure the enactment of any statute,
and so this is permitted. It is logically impossible to conform
(in the wider sense of this expression noted above) both to the
permissive rule of municipal law permitting the enactment of
any statute and the rule of international law relating to treaties which (if we accept Kelsen's interpretation of them) prohibits such an enactment and makes it an offence or delict.
This being the case, even if we accept Kelsen's interpretation
of the rules of international law, this does not establish that
they do not conflict with municipal law.[59]

III. MEMBERSHIP OF A LEGAL SYSTEM

In this concluding section I shall try to distil from the above
criticisms of Kelsen some more constructive points that may
help our understanding of the concept of a legal system and
of the criteria of the membership of different laws in a single

---

[59] It is to be observed that throughout this section I have ignored, as Kelsen
himself does, an argument in favour of the weaker form of the 'no conflict' theory
which would be available if his own controversial interpretation of all laws as
'sanction-stipulating norms' addressed to organs or officials determining the condition under which sanctions 'ought' to be applied were taken seriously. According to this interpretation 'only the coercive act functioning as a sanction ought to
be' (*PTL*, 119), i.e., the only persons who 'ought' to do anything according to law
are the 'organs' or officials, and what they 'ought' to do is to apply sanctions if
the conditions stated in the law are fulfilled. Since in different states these organs
or officials are different persons, no conflict would ever arise between the laws of
different states: joint conformity to the laws would always be possible. Thus, even
if laws of State *A* stipulated that sanctions ought to be applied by its officials to
certain persons in the event of their doing certain specified actions, and the laws
of State *B* forbade the application by its officials of sanctions under those same
conditions, no conflict would arise since the officials of the two states would be
different persons. Similarly, since the sanction-applying agencies in international
law are (according to Kelsen) the representatives of the states against whom a
delict or offence has been committed, whereas the sanction-applying agencies of
a state are its own officials, no conflict could arise. There is nothing in Kelsen's
accounts of what it is for laws to conflict which excludes this argument. I do not
myself accept Kelsen's interpretation of law as sanction-stipulating norms and so
would not regard this argument as sound. Kelsen might also have used as an argument in support of the 'no conflicts' theory his own (in my view erroneous) doctrine that the legal 'ought' must (to avoid a vicious regress) have the sense of
'permitted' or 'authorized' rather than 'commanded' (*PTL*, 25).

system. I certainly am not able to advance a comprehensive analysis of these difficult notions. Such an analysis is, as I have said, part of the still unfinished business of analytical jurisprudence and I am not yet competent to finish it. Yet the general form or direction of such an analysis may perhaps be at least glimpsed from what follows.

(A) Recognition and validating purport
Let us reconsider that relationship between laws which I called the relationship of validating purport, and recall the Soviet Laws Validity Act, which I dreamed up in order to exhibit the absurdity of the view, which Kelsen seems to share, that this relationship is sufficient to make the laws between which it holds members of the same legal system. I argued that this view is absurd because the Soviet Laws Validity Act, though it purports to validate the law-making operations of Soviet legislators, would not be recognized by the Soviet law-identifying and law-enforcing agencies as having any bearing on the validity of Soviet law. Without such recognition, we can only say the Soviet Laws Validity Act purports to validate the laws of the USSR, or that according to English law, or for the purposes of English law, Soviet law is a subordinate part of the English legal system; we cannot, unless there is such recognition, say that the validity of the laws of the USSR is derived from the Soviet Laws Validity Act, or that the law of the USSR and the UK form parts of a single system. Perhaps some qualification is needed of this last point. No doubt we could collect together all laws between which the relationship of validating purport holds, irrespective of the legal system from which they come, and call the group of laws so collected 'a single legal system'. This would be to introduce a new meaning for the expression 'legal system'; for a group of laws linked together solely by the relationship of validating purport would not correspond to the concept of a legal system that lawyers and political theorists or any serious thinkers about law and politics actually use. The new definition would have very little utility and would be retrograde if it displaced the existing sense of a legal system, and so barred us from saying that the laws of the UK and the USSR belong to different systems, notwithstanding the existence of the Soviet Laws Validity Act. 'Systems' of laws constructed solely

out of the relationship of validating purport would ignore the dividing line introduced by the idea that recognition by the law-identifying and law-enforcing agencies effective in a given territory is of crucial importance in determining the system to which laws belong. It is surely obvious that these dividing lines could not be ignored by any fruitful legal or political theory. To deny their importance would be tantamount to denying the importance to lawyers and political theorists of the division between nation states.

(B) The individuation of laws

When we turn our attention away from the relationship of validating purport to consider how the idea of recognition by courts or other identifying agencies effective in different territories is used to distinguish between legal systems, and as a criterion of membership of laws in a single system, some important points thrust themselves upon us. For example, an important contrast now emerges between two different ways of individuating or distinguishing between different laws. On the one hand, we may individuate or distinguish a law simply by referring to its content (e.g., as 'the law making the possession of LSD a criminal offence'). However, since the idea of two different laws with the same content is perfectly intelligible we may, and sometimes actually need to, individuate or distinguish laws not only by their content (i.e. by what the laws say or provide) but also by reference to their authors, mode of enactment, and date (e.g., as 'the law making possession of LSD a criminal offence enacted by the British Parliament on 30 December 1967').

The relevance of this to our present problem is as follows. The relationship of validating purport is a relationship between the content of those laws that purport to validate other laws or law-making operations and those other laws or operations. The most important examples of this relationship are laws that confer powers to legislate upon persons or bodies of persons. The simplest example of such power-conferring laws is a law conferring power upon an individual X (a monarch or a minister) to make laws or regulations. The law conferring such power in effect says 'the laws which X enacts are to be obeyed'. In Kelsen's terminology, such a law conferring legislative power 'authorizes' X to create new laws, and X's enactment is 'a law-creating act or event', while the laws created by X are said to 'derive their validity' from the law conferring the legislative power which is 'the reason for their validity'. Clearly in such cases if a law conferring legislative power is to be a reason for the validity of other laws it is necessary that the description of those other laws (in this case 'enacted by X') should correspond to the description used in the law conferring the legislative power (e.g., 'laws enacted by X are to be obeyed'). In order that the relationship of validating purport should hold between the law conferring the power and the enacted laws, this correspondence is not merely necessary but is sufficient. But, as I have argued above, though this is necessary, it is not sufficient to show that the laws made by X actually do derive their validity from the law purporting to confer upon X the power to make laws. What is needed in order that we may move from 'This law purports to validate laws enacted by X' to 'The laws enacted by X actually derive their validity from this law' is that the courts or law-identifying agencies of the territory concerned should recognize a particular law purporting to confer powers on X and treat it as a reason for recognizing also the laws it purports to validate. But in answering the question whether this law is so recognized, we must identify it not by its content alone as we did when we were concerned only with the relationship of validating purport, but by its authors or mode of creation or date or all of these. We must, in other words, shift our attention from the content to these other individuating elements. That this shift in attention is necessary is evident from the following considerations. The actual constitution of the USSR and the Soviet Laws Validity Act may have precisely the same content, and both have the relationship of validating purport to the law-making operations of the Soviet legislature. But the Soviet courts would distinguish between them; and in recognizing, not the Soviet Laws Validity Act, but only the Soviet constitution, as relevant to the validity of Soviet laws and belonging to the same system as those laws, they distinguish between them by such individuating factors as I have described above, notwithstanding the identity of content.

(C) Derivations of validity and criterion of membership

These considerations show that in considering whether two laws belong to the same system or different systems we cannot use as our criterion of belonging to the same system the fact that one of them derives its validity from the other. This is so because until the question of membership is settled by the independent test of recognition we cannot discover whether one of the laws does derive its validity from the other. We can only know that one purports to validate the other. The criterion of membership of laws in a single system is therefore independent of and indeed presupposed when we apply the notion of one law deriving validity from another. Only when we know that the Soviet constitution is recognized by the Soviet courts as a reason for recognizing laws enacted in accordance with its provisions, and so belongs to the same system as those laws, are we in a position to state that the latter derive their validity from the former. Until we know that the constitution is so recognized all we can say is that this constitution, like the Soviet Laws Validity Act, purports to validate such laws.

(D) The basic norm as a criterion of membership

Readers of Kelsen will recall that in all the versions of his theory he adheres to the view that what unites different laws in a single system is the basic norm,[60] and it does so because all the positive laws of the system, according to him, derive their validity directly or indirectly from the basic norm. The basic norm, according to Kelsen, unlike all other norms of a system, is not a positive or created norm:[61] unlike all the other laws of a system (positive laws) it does not derive its validity from any other laws. It is a 'presupposed' norm, which is 'the reason for the validity' of the constitution; it may be formulated as 'one ought to behave as the constitution prescribes',[62] and is presupposed by anyone who regards the constitution as a valid norm.[63]

Since the basic norm is the reason for the validity of the

---

[60] *GT*, 110, 367; *PTL*, 195, 201.

[61] *PTL*, 199.

[62] *PTL*, 201; its formulation will be different if municipal law is regarded as a subordinate part of international law.

[63] *PTL*, 204 n. 72.

constitution that derives its validity directly from it, all the other laws of the system that derive their validity directly or indirectly from the constitution derive it indirectly and ultimately from the basic norm. Kelsen's view is that laws form one system because their validity is thus to be traced back and derived from one basic norm. If, however, as I have argued above, we can only trace back the validity of laws to other laws (as distinct from the relationship of validating purport), if we already know by the test of recognition to what system the laws belong, it cannot be traceability back to the basic norm that tells us to what system laws belong or accounts for their unity in a single system. Again, our hypothetical example makes this clear. The basic norm of the American constitution is (roughly) that the constitution is valid; but unless we have some independent criterion of what it is for laws to belong to one system we cannot trace the validity of laws back to the constitution and thence to its basic norm; we can only trace relationships of validating purport, and these, as we have seen, will cut across different legal systems. They will link together with the American constitution not only the Soviet Laws Validity Act (supposing it to be enacted by Congress) but all the Soviet legislation that it purports to validate. If our sole criterion for membership of the system is the traceability of validating purport we cannot break off at the dividing line at which we would wish to break off. We cannot, as the Soviet courts do, stop at the Soviet constitution, and ignore the Soviet Laws Validity Act as belonging to a different system, although it purports to validate Soviet law; we have to go on from the laws enacted by the Soviet legislator to the Soviet Laws Validity Act and thence to the American constitution, and thence to its basic norm, beyond which by definition no further relationship of validating purport is to be traced. But the journey is fruitless, because it shows neither that these laws derive their validity from the basic norm nor that they belong to a single legal system.

IV. PROBLEMS OF RECOGNITION

The previous section, as I have said, constitutes no more than a tentative account of the appropriate criterion for determining the membership of a legal system and for the individuation of different legal systems. It is plain that the notion of recognition that I have stressed will need refinement in different directions, and I shall end by explaining very briefly some of the considerations that have caused me to express myself thus tentatively.

1. I have spoken of recognition by the law-identifying and law-enforcing agencies effective in different territories. This obviously envisages arrangements of modern municipal legal systems where there are courts and special agencies for the enforcement of law. But we cannot leave out of sight more primitive arrangements: there may be no courts and no specialized enforcement agencies, and the application of sanctions for breach of the rules may be left to injured parties or their relatives, or to the community at large. International law, at least according to Kelsen, is itself such a decentralized system. Presumably, in such cases we shall have to use as our test of membership the notion of recognition by the society or the community, and certain problems in defining what constitutes sufficient recognition will have to be faced.

2. Even in the case of modern municipal legal systems the notion of recognition by a court is not without ambiguities. On a narrow interpretation, recognition by a court as a criterion of membership could mean that a rule could not be said to belong to a legal system until it had been actually applied by a court disposing of a case. This interpretation would come nearer to Gray's[64] theory and to the doctrine ascribed to some later American Legal Realists; but it is surely very unrealistic, for there seems little reason to deny that a statute enacted by the legislature of a normally functioning legal system is a law of the system even before it is applied by the courts in actual cases. However, the precise formulation of a wider interpretation of the idea of recognition which would include rules that courts would apply as well as those actually applied would not be uncontroversial.

3. All civilized legal systems contain special rules for dealing with cases containing a foreign element (e.g. contracts or marriages made abroad). These special rules determine both when courts have jurisdiction to try cases with such foreign elements and which legal systems should guide the courts in the

---

[64] See his *Nature and Sources of Law* (New York 1909).

exercise of this jurisdiction. These are the rules known as private international law or conflicts of law, and if we are to take account of them the notion of recognition by courts will have to be refined in further different directions. If a man and his wife whose marriage is valid according to the laws of the country where it was celebrated travel through many different countries, they can be confident that the courts of most of these countries will treat their marriage as valid, at least as far as the formalities of its celebration are concerned. This is only one very simple example of cases where courts of one country would be said to recognize and apply the laws of another country. Unless the notion of recognition advanced above as a criterion of membership is in some way qualified, we should have to draw the conclusion that laws of one country that are recognized and applied by the courts of another country belong to the legal system of the latter country as well as of the former. It is possible to object to the language I have used in describing such cases, since it may be said that when, for example, an English court treats a marriage solemnized in, say, the Soviet Union, as valid because the formalities were those required by Soviet law, though they differ from those of English law, it does not really apply Soviet law, but applies to the parties before it, a rule similar in content to that which a Soviet court would apply to the parties if they appeared before it in a similar case but of purely domestic character.[65] This would avoid the awkwardness and possibly misleading character of the assertion that one and the same rule was applied by courts of different systems; but it still leaves us without any satisfactory distinction between the kind of recognition that courts give to foreign laws in such cases involving foreign elements, and the recognition that is to be used as a criterion of membership. We need such a distinction, for it seems plain that in some sense of recognition courts do *recognize* foreign laws in cases raising questions of private international law even if, in deference to the argument cited above, we do not say they *apply* the foreign law, but apply a law of their own with a similar content to that of the foreign law that they recognize.

Perhaps this difficulty may be met by distinguishing two

[65] See W. W. Cook, *The Logical and Legal Bases of the Conflict of Laws* (Cambridge, Mass., 1942), ch. 1.

different sorts of recognition that might be called 'original' and 'derivative' recognition. In an ordinary case where there is no foreign element, for example, where an English court simply applies an English statute, the court does not base its recognition and application of the statute on the fact that courts of some other country have recognized or would recognize it; this is original recognition. But where, as in cases raising questions of private international law, part of the court's reasons for recognizing a law is that it has been or would be originally recognized by the courts of another country, this is derivative recognition of the foreign law. Whether in such cases we should say the court applies the law that is thus derivatively recognized or only that it applies a law with similar content does not, I think, affect this distinction, though I have no doubt it needs further elaboration.

POSTSCRIPT

See for criticisms and comments: J. Raz, 'The Identity of Legal Systems', *The Authority of Law* (Oxford 1979), 78; and 'The Purity of the Pure Theory', 138 *Revue Internationale de Philosophie* 441 (1981).

Essay 16

Lon L. Fuller: *The Morality of Law*

This imaginative, original, and thought-provoking book[1] is richly stocked with a variety of themes, many of which deserve a much fuller treatment than the author accords to them. During several rereadings of the book, my interest never for one moment waned, and I am certain that I shall return to it to ponder its wisdom and to spur my ever-flagging efforts at self-criticism. But I have found and shall find rereading necessary for other reasons. For though the main positions which the author wishes to defend are clearly and frequently stated, and though they are often illustrated with suggestive examples and analogies drawn from science or economics, it is none the less often difficult amid the author's firm and clear assertions of what is right and wrong in jurisprudence to identify any equally firm and clear argument in support of these assertions. Yet in saying this I am haunted by the fear that our starting-points and interests in jurisprudence are so different that the author and I are fated never to understand each other's work. So it may be that where I find the author's thought obscure it is really profound and out of my reach. I wish that I dare hope that where he finds my thought misguided it is really, or even merely, clear.

The central theme of the book is the unique virtue of conceiving of law and even of defining 'law' as 'the [purposive] enterprise of subjecting human conduct to the governance of rules'. This large conception of law, admittedly and unashamedly, includes the rules of clubs, churches, schools, 'and a hundred and one other forms of human association'. The outer boundaries of this wide conception cannot be determined from this book with any precision, since the author does not give us any account of what 'rules' are, but speaks throughout as if the notion of a rule were unambiguous and otherwise unproblematic. Indeed, it is clear that the author would think it of little importance to determine with any

[1] Lon L. Fuller, *The Morality of Law* (New Haven 1964).

greater precision the boundaries of what is for him 'law'. One
boundary is, however, suggested by the author when he draws
attention to the word 'enterprise' and tells us that for what it
is worth an intelligible, though not precise or important, line
between morals and law is that in the latter case, but not in
the former, the enterprise of subjecting human conduct to
the governance of rules is made the sphere of 'explicit responsibility'.

The development of a number of important issues opened
by the conception of law as the purposive enterprise of subjecting men to the guidance of rules is, then, the book's main
constructive theme. Its polemical theme is the inadequacies,
indeed the vices, of traditional efforts to distinguish law from
other forms of social control by reference to its provision for
sanctions or the hierarchical structure of its rules or by reference to the notion of formal sources. Approaches such as
these, associated as they are with the names of Austin or
Kelsen, are not credited even with the virtue of partial insights.
Nor is there in this book any concession made to the view that
investigations into the structure of legal systems and inquiries
(such as the author's) designed to draw out the implications
of law as a form of purposive activity are not rivals but complementary forms of jurisprudence. So short work is made in
this short book of some very long books.

Such then in crudest outline are the author's constructive
and destructive themes. What follows here is my estimate of
some only of his leading contentions.

I. THE MORALITY OF DUTY AND THE
MORALITY OF ASPIRATION

The book opens with a contribution to moral philosophy
which certainly deserves to be assessed as such and not merely
as a casual by-product of jurisprudential thought; for the first
chapter is a protest against thinking of morality as a simple
unitary concept, and makes a detailed plea for the discrimination within morality of different, though related, dimensions
of assessment of human conduct. The distinction upon which
the author most insists is that between a morality of duty and
a morality of 'aspiration' or, as we might say, of ideals. When
we judge conduct by reference to the former we apply to it

definite, easily formulable rules: we speak in imperative or
quasi-imperative forms ('thou shalt not', or its modern equivalents), and though deviation from the rules attracts accusations and censure, conformity with them is not usually a
matter for praise. We have to do not with the heights of moral
excellence but rather with a moral minimum. By contrast,
when we consider human conduct from the point of view of
the morality of aspiration we bring to bear on it not manda-
tory rules but conceptions of the 'Good Life', of 'what be-
seems a human being functioning at his best' or 'is unbefitting
a being with human capacities'. Here we praise for attainments
but do not condemn or accuse, though we may show disdain,
for shortcomings.

The author makes many interesting comparisons between
this divided conception of morality and economics and law.
The morality of aspiration is compared to marginal utility
economics, and the morality of duty, with its hallmark of
reciprocity, to the economics of exchange. It is true that this
laudable effort to break up excessively monolithic conceptions of the nature of morality is, as the author notes, not
new. Indeed, it could hardly be missed by anyone willing to
attend to the contrast between the common use of black and
white rule-determined words such as 'right' and 'wrong', and
the use of comparative scale-determined words like 'good',
'better', 'best'. But even if the author has not discovered, he
has certainly advanced this more realistic conception of morality as comprising distinct dimensions of assessment.

None the less, there is much in this first chapter which must
puzzle any moral philosopher worth his salt. First and fore-
most there is this: the author's initial characterization of duty
ties it very closely to what is 'rationally discoverable' and objective, as contrasted with the morality of aspiration to the
higher reaches of which he finds 'subjectivism appropriate'.
Indeed, he pours scorn on those who, failing to grasp the distinction between these two moralities, speak as if 'obvious'
duties rested on 'some essentially ineffable preference'. Yet
this clear initial picture of duty as rationally discoverable and
objective is difficult to fit with other things the author says
about duty. Though for him the morality of duty lays down
the basic rules without which an ordered society is impossible,
this does not exhaust its role; for he notes that moralists may

differ as to what range of conduct should fall within the respective spheres of duty and the morality of aspiration, and
he has some fine observations on those moralists who forever
try to expand the area of duty instead of inviting us to join
them in realizing some ideal of human nature. But it is not
clear how, given these divergent conceptions of the range of
duty, the author would apply to it his initial characterization
of rationally discoverable and non-subjective. Furthermore, it
is surprising, given this initial characterization, to find the
author speaking not only of many possible moralities of aspiration but also of alternative moralities of duty. Some of these,
he says, are 'tinctured by an appeal to self-interest', others
'rest on the lofty demands of the Categorical Imperative'.

Similar difficulties arise from the hints (they are no more)
of the author's epistemology of morals, i.e., his views as to
how we know or settle what is our duty, or 'befits beings
with human capacities'. Here he says some mysterious things:
'When we are passing a judgment of moral duty, it seems absurd to say that such a duty can in some way flow directly
from knowledge of a situation of fact.' This is contrasted with
the situation when we apply to conduct a morality of aspiration. The contrast is explained by the author as due to the
fact that before we conclude 'that a duty ought to exist', however well we may understand the facts, there will still seem to
intervene an act of legislative judgment. I think I have some
glimmer of what the author means by the close connection
between understanding a person's ideals and our approval and
disapproval. But I am most perplexed by his references to
duty as involving 'legislation'. Does this mean that duties, in
spite of their initial characterization as rationally discoverable, and as obvious, are after all a matter of choice, even if
not of 'ineffable preference'? Presumably not, since when we
pass a moral judgment of duty the author speaks of us as concluding that it 'ought' to exist. But does this 'ought' come
from the morality of duty or the morality of aspiration, or
neither?

I hope that in subsequent editions of this book the author
may deal with these unclarities, since they cloud a perceptive
approach to morality.[2]

[2] In addition to the distinction between duty and aspiration, it is necessary to
distinguish between the accepted morality of a social group and the personal or

II. INNER AND EXTERNAL MORALITIES OF LAW

The author deploys his talents for the fashioning of instructive allegories in order to introduce a legislator, Rex, who fails in eight carefully distinguished ways to produce rules apt for the guidance of his subjects. Corresponding to these eight forms of failure the author then identifies eight 'demands of the inner morality of law' which a system of rules should strive to satisfy. Rules should be (1) general; (2) made known or available to the affected party (promulgation); (3) prospective, not retroactive; (4) clear and understandable; (5) free from contradictions; they should not (6) require what is impossible; (7) be too frequently changed; finally (8) there should be congruence between the law and official action.

These eight principles for carrying out the purposive activity of subjecting human conduct to rules are designated by the author 'the inner morality of law'; his other names for them include 'the morality that makes law possible', 'the special morality of law', 'procedural natural law' and 'the principles of legality'. I shall adopt the last, most conventional, designation because, as I shall argue later, the classification of these eight principles as a form of morality breeds confusion. It should be noted that the force of the word 'inner' in the author's favoured designation is to stress the fact that these forms of legal excellence are derived, not from principles of justice or other 'external' moral principles relating to the law's substantive aims or content, but are reached solely through a realistic consideration of what is necessary for the efficient execution of the purpose of guiding human conduct by rules. We see what they are by occupying the position of the conscientious legislator bent on this purpose, and they are essentially principles of good craftsmanship. Indeed, they are compared by the author to principles (he says 'natural laws') of carpentry. They are independent of the law's substantive aims just as the principles of carpentry are independent of whether the carpenter is making hospital beds or torturer's racks.

In the detailed discussion of these eight principles of legality, the author says some novel and important things.

critical morality of individuals. 'Duty' may appear in all of these. See P. F. Strawson, 'Social Morality and Individual Ideal', 36 *Philosophy* 1 (1961).

Whereas the principle requiring promulgation of the law is, for him, a peremptory requirement which can be made the subject of definite, easily formulable rules, the remaining requirements cannot be thus formalized since their satisfaction is very often a matter of degree varying from situation to situation; exceptions are necessary and so are many compromises and adjustments. The author's account of these adjustments (or 'antinomies' as he calls them) fill what are in my opinion the best pages of the book, presenting some old issues in a welcome new light. He shows, for example, how exceptions may have to be made to the principle forbidding retrospective legislation in order to cure or counter violations of other principles, as when a law is passed to validate retrospectively marriages which are invalid because of a failure to comply with formalities required by a statute which was itself insufficiently promulgated or which specified formal requirements with which it was not possible to comply at the time of the marriages. His general discussion of retroactivity discloses the vague borderlines of this concept. If *ex post facto* criminal statutes clearly violate this principle of legality, is it equally clear that tax laws violate it by imposing taxes on earnings received before the date of their enactment? The author shows how even the demand for clarity in the sense of the requirement that rules should be understandable by those who are affected by them may conflict with the need for those technical systematic elements in a legal system which enable courts to make consistent applications of the law, and which lend to the system its predictability. He also shows how the requirement that law should be free from self-contradiction needs to be given content over and above the logician's bare veto of rules commanding subjects to do both 'A' and 'not-A'; and how this content can be given by constant recourse to the consideration that rules should afford the citizen an intelligible guide as to what to do. In the discussions of the need for congruence between enacted laws and judicial or other official action the author develops a theory of interpretation of statute which makes interesting comparisons between the task of interpretation and that of completing an incomplete invention. He exhibits the co-operative nature of the task of maintaining the principles of legality in a critique of fundamentally unsound forms of legislation such as paragraph 5 of section 4 of the Statute of Frauds which, by wrongly supposing that there was some definite relationship between the time required to perform a contract and the time when a witness would be called to testify, was to produce puzzles with no possible solutions.[3]

In general, the author considers that far greater use could and should be made by courts of the principles of legality as a relatively objective undisputed part of 'the inner logic' of law. Thus, his theme at some points resembles Professor Wechsler's plea for 'neutral principles' of decision,[4] and he argues that instead of excursions into the debatable area of 'substantive justice', the Supreme Court might well have disposed of cases by reference to the law's 'inner morality'. It was a mistake in the author's view for the Court in *Robinson* v. *California*[5] to have held that a statute making the state or condition of being a drug addict a crime punishable by six months' imprisonment violated the Eighth Amendment by imposing 'a cruel and unusual punishment'. Instead, the Court should have brought the decision within the confines of due process on the footing that the criminal law ought to be presented to the citizen in such a form that he could mould his conduct by it.

So far so good. But the author's insistence on classifying these principles of legality as a 'morality' is a source of confusion both for him and his readers. The objection that the description of these principles as 'the special morality of law' is misleading because they are applicable not only to what lawyers think of as law but equally applicable to any rule-guided activity such as games (or at least those games which possess rule-making and rule-applying authorities) would no

---

[3] The author's discussion of strict liability is less felicitous. He attempts to show that strict liability in criminal law offends against the principle that laws, since their purpose is to guide the conduct of men, should not require what is impossible. But if strict liability laws are known to those to whom they apply, they can guide their conduct just as effectively as laws which make liability to punishment dependent on 'fault'. It is strange that though the author treats strict liability in tort as a justifiable way of attaching a special surcharge of legal responsibility to certain types of conduct, e.g. blasting operations, he seems to treat all strict liability in criminal law as 'commanding the impossible'. But why should it not sometimes serve to 'guide' men away from those enterprises to which it is attached if they cannot be sure of their ability to comply with 'strict' regulations?

[4] H. Wechsler, 'Toward Neutral Principles of Constitutional Law', 73 *Harv. L. Rev.* 1 (1959).

[5] 370 U.S. 660 (1962).

doubt be rejected by the author: he would simply appeal to his wide conception of law as including the rules of games. But the crucial objection to the designation of these principles of good legal craftsmanship as morality, in spite of the quali- fication 'inner', is that it perpetrates a confusion between two notions that it is vital to hold apart: the notions of purposive activity and morality. Poisoning is no doubt a purposive ac- tivity, and reflections on its purpose may show that it has its internal principles. ('Avoid poisons however lethal if they cause the victim to vomit', or 'Avoid poisons however lethal if their shape, color, or size is likely to attract notice.') But to call these principles of the poisoner's art 'the morality of poisoning' would simply blur the distinction between the notion of efficiency for a purpose and those final judgments about activities and purposes with which morality in its vari- ous forms is concerned.

It is important to observe that this criticism of the author's designation of his eight principles as a morality is not merely a verbal criticism; for his insistence upon it causes him to mis- apply to these principles the distinction worked out in his first chapter between a morality of duty and a morality of aspir- ation, and this has grotesque results. A morality of aspiration, it will be recalled, is one by which we bring to bear on human conduct not definite rules of what must and must not be done, but a conception of the Good Life and the best develop- ment of human capacities. When we criticize human conduct by reference to such a morality, we do not condemn or blame but show disdain. But the author having called the principles of legality a morality finds himself bound to discuss the ques- tion whether they constitute a morality of aspiration or of duty; he decides that, except for the peremptory principle that laws must be promulgated, the morality of law is 'largely condemned' to remain a morality of aspiration and not of duty.

But surely both the discussion of this question and the decision reached are absurd. It is perfectly true with any prin- ciple of craftsmanship that some may be formulated as per- emptory rules (in the case of the poisoner's craft, 'See that the poison is not too big to swallow'), while others may be only advanced in terms of an indication of a direction of effort ('See that the poison is not too costly'). But this distinction

between peremptory rules and merely indicative principles
has surely nothing to do with the distinction between a morality of duty, carrying with it accusation and blame, and a
morality of aspiration, carrying with it praise and disdain. If
the legislator wantonly uses retrospective laws to terrify his
subjects, has he only violated a morality of aspiration? Can
we not accuse him of a violation of moral duty? Yet the
author says that whereas a moral duty with respect to publication is readily imaginable, the primary appeal of the inner
morality of law is to 'the pride of the craftsman'. These conclusions are strange indeed, and the root of the trouble is
surely the confusion of principles guiding any form of purposive activity with morality. What makes a morality of aspiration into a morality is not the mere fact that it is guided by
non-peremptory indicative principles towards a given end, but
that the end is some ideal development of human capacities
which is taken to be of ultimate value in the conduct of life.
Only if the purpose of subjecting human conduct to the
governance of rules, no matter what their content, were itself such an ultimate value, would there be any case for class-
ing the principles of rule-making as a morality, and discussing
whether it was a morality of duty or aspiration.

I do not think the author would have fallen into this ditch
of his own digging but for his conviction that there are important, if not necessary, connections between 'external' morality concerned with human justice and welfare, and what he
terms the 'inner morality of law'. Indeed, he says in a later
chapter that the demonstration of this connection justifies
his terming these eight principles a 'morality'. He takes me
seriously to task for having said that respect for the principles
of legality is unfortunately 'compatible with very great iniquity'; but I cannot find any cogent argument in support of
his claim that these principles are not neutral as between good
and evil substantive aims. Indeed, his chief argument to this
effect appears to me to be patently fallacious. He claims that
the simple demand of the inner morality of law that it should
be expressed in intelligible terms is not, as it might appear,
'ethically neutral'. And he cites the example of racially dis-
criminatory legislation in South Africa. This legislation, according to the author, was a gross departure from the inner
morality of law because, in the absence of any uniform or

scientific basis of racial classification, statutes attaching legal consequences to race necessarily gave rise to insoluble difficulties in interpretation. But this shows nothing to the author's purpose: it shows only that the principle that laws must be clearly and intelligibly framed is incompatible with the pursuit of vaguely defined substantive aims, whether they are morally good or evil. In particular, it does not show what the author asserts — that clear rules are not 'ethically neutral' between good and evil substantive aims. There is therefore no special incompatibility between clear laws and evil. Clear laws are therefore ethically neutral though they are not equally compatible with vague and with well-defined aims.

One feature in the author's exposition of this argument is truly surprising. He actually makes reference to what he terms 'the bitter irony' that the Israeli High Court has experienced well-nigh insoluble problems in applying the Law of the Return which grants Israeli nationality to immigrant Jews. Surely this law might be credited with a morally good substantive aim even though it is too vague to be achieved through clear rules. Do not the South African and Israeli statutes taken together show the ethical neutrality both of clarity and unclarity? Indeed, in order to purge the author's argument of its fallacy, we need the additional premise that good ends are essentially or peculiarly determinate and bad ends are essentially vague and indefinable and so cannot be achieved by clear laws. I do not know whether the author would subscribe to this view, but I do not.

It may be that the author's argument proceeds as it does because he has treated my modest remark that the inner morality of law is 'compatible with very great iniquity' as if I had said that it was compatible with every sort of iniquitous aim, vague or specific.[6] I did not say this, because, of course, it is false; just as it is false that clear laws are compatible with every sort of good aim, vague or specific. It is of course perfectly true, as the author stresses throughout the book, that, for example, the Nazi government in pursuit of monstrous aims often violated the principles of legality, notably in order to pass secret enactments designed to give retrospective cover to

---

[6] H. L. A. Hart, *The Concept of Law* 202 (1961). He says my words are an 'explicit denial of *any possible interaction* between the internal and external moralities of law' (emphasis added).

vast illegalities. It is also quite generally true that a regime bent on monstrous policies will often want the cover of secrecy and vague, indefinable laws if it is not certain of general support for its policies or finds it necessary to conciliate external opinion. But this is a matter of the varying popularity and strength of governments, not of any necessary incompatibility between government according to the principles of legality and wicked ends.

III. POLEMICS

The author has harsh words for those writers whose theories do not centrally focus, as his does, on the purposes of those who make and administer the law. But in some cases (though not in my own) the writers whom he attacks are but his own men of straw, so it is not surprising that he knocks them down with a mere puff of wind. In particular, he treats most unfairly the theory (which is no favourite of mine) that law is most usefully distinguished from other forms of social control by its organized provision for the enforcement of its rules by sanctions. The author writes as if the only excuse for putting forward this theory were the trite facts that legal systems, since they seek to control violence, must be prepared to meet it with violence, and that the administration of the criminal law, which is most directly concerned with physical sanctions, is closely identified with legal ritual and solemn forms. But the selection of the provision for sanctions as a distinguishing mark of law by writers like Austin[7] or Kelsen[8] was plainly independent of these considerations: they were motivated by the conviction that the introduction of organized sanctions explains the peculiarly imperative character of legal as distinguished from other types of social norms, and brings with it a number of associated differences. This is why not only dry, analytical jurists but legal sociologists of the stature of Max Weber and Karl Renner, who were concerned to discriminate in order to understand diverse forms of social processes, also took the provision for sanctions as a distinguishing mark of law. But, in the author's account, this theory of law is caricatured before it is butchered: no one reading this book could

---

[7] See Austin, *The Province of Jurisprudence Determined* 1–30 (5th edn. 1885).
[8] See H. Kelsen, *General Theory of Law and State* 61 (1945).

possibly imagine that the theory could have been of the slightest use to anybody. For in an extended section on 'The Concept of Science' the author compares this theory of law to the patently absurd definition of science as simply 'the use of certain kinds of instruments' or (in another version) 'the use of apparatus for measuring and testing'. This absurdity is said to be the counterpart of the theory that treats use of force as the identifying characteristic of law. But in fact the parallel to this absurd definition of science would be a theory that defined law simply as the use of force: both Austin and Kelsen are innocent of this and no 'positivist' of whom I know is guilty of it. These writers treat the provision for sanctions not as the identifying mark of law but as the feature which distinguishes legal rules from other social rules. The counterpart to this in the case of science is not the justly ridiculed characterization of science as simply the use of measurement, but its characterization as the search for uniformities of nature distinguished from other such searches by use of measurement and testing. And this, even if not adequate, is not absurd.

The author attacks the theory which treats the hierarchical or pyramidal structure of rules as a defining feature of law. The attack is in such general terms that it is hard to see which of the many varieties of this theory he has in mind. But he attributes it simply to obsession with one desideratum of the inner morality of law, the need for a final resolution of conflicts within a legal system. Yet in the case of the most famous exponent of such theories, Kelsen, surely obsession with this single issue plays little part. Kelsen's theory of the basic norm, however unsatisfactory it may be in detail, is developed in the effort to provide a satisfactory analysis of a range of ideas that constitute the framework of legal thought: among these are the concept of a legal *system*, the idea of validity, the idea of delegation, and a critique of the conventional distinction between public and private law. That the author, preoccupied with his study of legal purpose, should be uninterested in the analysis of the structural framework within which these purposes are pursued is quite understandable; but it is regrettable that this preoccupation should bind him so completely to the character and aims of the theories which he attacks.

It is, I think, also regrettable that the author should, no

doubt without realizing it, have revived an ancient libel on positivist thinkers by imputing to them a view of moral obligation to obey law which is not theirs. He does this in a passage where he criticizes those who, unlike himself, will not see that legal systems can 'half exist' and that the existence of law is a matter of the degree to which rules satisfy the inner morality of law. Here he asserts that 'legal scholars' who make the contrary assumption were not only committed to the view that the laws made by the Nazis in breach of the principles of legality were fully laws: they were ('as a grotesque outcropping of this conviction') also committed to the notion that 'the moral obligation of the decent German citizen to obey these laws was in no way affected by the fact that they were in part kept from his knowledge, that some of them retroactively "cured" wholesale murder . . .'. But if one inquires what 'legal scholars' so conceived the moral obligation to obey law, the only answer discoverable in this book is in the references to an earlier page concerning the post-war German trials of informers. Here we are told that the post-war German courts treated the judgments of the Nazi courts as nullities not on the ground that the Nazi statutes which they applied were void but on the ground that the Nazi courts had misinterpreted them. Dr Pappe is censured by the author for making too much of this distinction, since 'with statutes of the kind involved, filled as they were with vague phrases and unrestricted delegations of power, it seems a little out of place to strain questions of their proper interpretation'. But how does this show that 'legal scholars' share the notion that 'the moral obligation' of the decent German citizen to obey the law was in no way affected by the Nazi Government's wicked deviations from the principles of legality? The question in issue before the post-war German courts was whether a grudge informer who had procured the condemnation and imprisonment of his victim by the Nazi courts for the breach of Nazi statutes could rely on those statutes in order to plead before the post-war German courts that his action was not *illegal* at the time when it was done. Some of the German post-war courts held that he could not so rely, not because the statutes were void, but because they were misinterpreted by the Nazi courts. How does the anxiety of 'legal scholars' to make this distinction betray the belief that the decent German citizen

had a moral obligation to obey Nazi statutes with all their in-
iquities of form and content? At the most it implies the belief
that those who relied on such statutes were *legally* entitled to
do so.

The author devotes some pages to my book, *The Concept
of Law*, and to the most important of his criticisms I make
what answer I can below. But there is one general condemnation in which I am involved together with all the other
writers he attacks. He claims that we are all guilty of the same
fundamental mistake of viewing law as 'a manifested fact of
social power' (or, in other versions, 'of social authority or
power'), and as a 'datum of nature' in opposition to the 'right'
view of it as a purposeful enterprise. The author is aware that
at this point his readers may find his argument difficult and
may think that in his ascription of 'purpose' not only to particular laws but to law as a whole 'the spirit of Hegel rides
again'. To me the difficulties of Hegel seems child's play compared with those presented by the author's demonstration
that a 'falsification of reality' is involved in the views which
he attacks and that his own view, because 'it corresponds most
faithfully to reality', is the right view. But one thing is clear:
the author attributes without justification his own high intolerance of other approaches to jurisprudence to those whom
he criticizes, and this is in fact part, if not the whole, of his
demonstration that they are wrong. Because he attributes this
exclusive view that there is one right way in which law may
be studied he says, astonishingly, that if we are consistent with
our premises, though 'we may bemoan some kinds of retroactive laws . . . we cannot even explain what would be wrong
with a system of laws that were wholly retroactive', and that
we cannot give any adequate explanation of why normally
legal rules are general.

What can such accusations mean? Why, to take the simplest
instances, could not writers like Bentham and Austin, who
defined law as commands, have objected to a system of laws
that were wholly retroactive on the ground that it could make
no contribution to human happiness and so far as it resulted
in punishments would inflict useless misery? Why should not
Kelsen or I, myself, who think law may be profitably viewed
as a system of rules, not also explain that the normal generality of law is desirable not only for reasons of economy but

because it will enable individuals to predict the future and that this is a powerful contribution to human liberty and happiness? Why are such writers in giving these sorts of explanation inconsistent with their analytical theories or guilty of 'falsifying reality'?

In fact, the principles of legality which the author terms 'the inner morality of law' were urged by Bentham on his contemporaries in the name of utility: Bentham devoted many pages to the discussion of the evils of obscurity and retroactivity in the law.[9] Neither he nor any of the writers of his tradition thought that their definitions of law in terms of what the author calls 'a manifested fact of social power' in any way rendered illegitimate consideration of the law from a sociological, functional, or critical standpoint. Bentham not only permitted these approaches but named and practised them, as his terms 'expository' and 'censorial' jurisprudence show.[10] The author says of those he criticizes that they 'can neither formulate nor answer the problems to which . . . [his discussion of the principles of legality] was devoted'. This is surely wrong. The difference between the author and those he criticizes in this matter is that the activity of controlling men by rules and the principles designed to maximize its efficiency are not valued by the latter for their own sake, and are not dignified by them with the title of 'a morality'. They are valued so far only as they contribute to human happiness or other substantive moral aims of the law.

IV. THE CONCEPT OF LAW

The author does me the compliment of taking from my book, *The Concept of Law*, the title for his most polemical chapter. The compliment is not wholly cancelled by his inclusion at the head of this chapter of the following quotation from Nietzsche: 'Das Vergessen der Absichten ist die häufigste Dummheit, die gemacht wird.' ('Forgetting purposes is the commonest form of stupidity.') Much of his criticism of my book accordingly consists of details of the charge that I was guilty in it of the *Dummheit* of 'forgetting purpose'. So far as this

---

[9] See Bentham, *Principles of Morals and Legislation*, in 1 *Works* I, 144–5, 146 (Bowring edn. 1838–43) (ch. XIX, 11th, 14th paras.).
[10] See ibid. at 148 (ch. XIX, 21st–22nd paras.).

charge rests on the imputation to me of the view that inquiries into law's purposes are illegitimate or unimportant, I perhaps need only say that I regarded my aim in *The Concept of Law* as complementary to and in no way exclusive of the author's investigation of 'purposes'. For in my book I tried to present improved ways of describing and a clearer view of the legal structure within which these 'purposes' are pursued. So I sought to clarify in my book many things which in his the author simply takes for granted. Among these things is the notion of a *rule* which is left unanalysed by the author, but which I found to be in need of the same kind of discrimination, subdivision, and analysis as the author in his first chapter finds needed in the case of 'morality'. Though neither I nor any other jurist have yet produced an adequate taxonomy of the different types of legal rule and of the different ways in which rules guide or otherwise relate to conduct, I made one major distinction (itself susceptible of much refinement) between rules which impose legal obligations or duties and rules which confer legal powers. The chief examples of the latter are the rules which confer upon judges their jurisdiction and on legislators their authority to legislate and those rules which enable private persons to effect changes in the legal position of themselves and others. I claimed that in the union of these two sorts of rules we had an effective tool for the analysis of much that constitutes the framework of legal thought.

My distinction between these two sorts of rules was not new: continental jurists have long distinguished 'rules of competence' from rules that impose legal duties, and others have distinguished between 'enabling rules' and 'restrictive rules'. But perhaps my claim that this distinction could throw light on many dark places in jurisprudence was novel. The author certainly professes himself sceptical of this claim. Yet I find in his book dark places which could be illumined by just this form of analysis. Thus he accuses me of not seeing that 'the structure of authority, so often glibly thought of as organizing law, is itself a product of law', or (in another version) that 'the established authority which tells us what is law is itself the product of law'. But the difference between the author and me is not that I do not see or agree with this point, but that whereas I attempt some analysis of what these quoted phrases mean and of how it can be the case that, as Kelsen says, 'law regulates its own creation', the author gives us no such explanation. In my book I insisted that behind every legislative authority (even the supreme legislature of a legal system) there must be rules specifying the identity and qualification of the legislators and what they must do in order to make laws. By contrast the author's only contribution to this problem is to use again his much repeated nostrum ('a parliament's ability to enact law is itself an achievement of purposive effort') and to warn us that what we have here is 'not simply a datum of nature'. Surely this last phrase merely darkens counsel. What is a 'datum' and what makes it one 'of nature' or not? The author's use of this opaque philosophical phrase suggests that those who, like myself, attempt to analyse the notion of legislative powers in terms of rules are committed to eliminating from their analysis any reference to anything but the inanimate.

The most important of the author's criticisms concern my discussion of what I called in my book 'the rule of recognition', and my slumbers would indeed be dogmatic if I were not stirred from them by what the author says here. I used the expression 'the rule of recognition' in expounding my version of the common theory that a municipal legal system is a structure of 'open-textured' rules which has at its foundation a rule which is legally ultimate in the sense that it provides a set of criteria by which in the last resort the validity of subordinate rules of the system is assessed. This rule itself is not to be characterized as either legally valid or invalid — though it may be the subject of moral criticism, historical or sociological explanation, and other forms of inquiry. The existence of such a rule is manifested in the acknowledgement and use of the same set of criteria of legal validity by the law-making, law-applying, and law-enforcing officials and in the general conformity to law so identified.

Some theorists prefer to call this phenomenon a political fact: to treat it as the fact that a constitution exists not as so much writing on paper but as part of the life of the community living under a legal system. In my book, I offered reasons for saying that the propriety of this latter description did not exclude the classification of this phenomenon as an ultimate legal rule providing criteria for the identification of the subordinate rules of the legal system. It is, however, certainly of the first importance that anyone who like myself wishes to speak at this point of 'rules' and in particular of 'a rule' should enter the plainest caveats showing how such a legally ultimate rule differs both from the ordinary subordinate rules of the legal system and from ordinary social conventions or customs. To this end I insisted in my book that the rule of recognition was both complex and open-textured. It is complex because in modern legal systems not one criterion but several criteria of legal validity are used. Thus even in a 'unitary' system such as English law, the law is identified both by reference to judicial precedent and by reference to the enactments of Parliament. These are distinct criteria ranked in order of relative subordination and primacy: precedent is subordinate to statute in the sense that common law rules may be deprived of their status as law by statute, though their status as law is not derived from statute. The reason for still speaking of 'a rule' at this point is that, notwithstanding their multiplicity, these distinct criteria are unified by their hierarchical arrangement. I drew attention to the fact that the feature of open-texture which affects all rules is present also in the case of the rule of recognition. This, too, has its 'penumbral' area as well as its firm, well-settled 'core'. Hence it is that there are always questions about the criteria or official sources of law to which at any given moment there is no uniquely correct answer to be given until a court has ruled upon the question. And when the courts so rule they modify or develop this most fundamental rule of the legal system.

I considered in my book whether or not insistence on the terminology of rules to describe something so complex, vague, and fluid was mistaken, and I decided that it was not. The author plainly thinks I was wrong and he accuses me of supplying 'neat juristic answers to questions which are essentially questions of sociological fact'. By this phrase he means, I think, that there is no coherent conception of a rule which could be used at this point without distorting the facts. This is indeed an important question, but the issue is not to be disposed of without a patient examination of the similarities and differences between what would ordinarily be called the existence of a rule and the ways in which the validity of legal rules is assessed. The author's only alternative to my possibly mistaken form of analysis is to say that a legal system 'derives its ultimate support from a sense of its being "right"', and that this sense, 'deriving as it does from tacit expectations and acceptances, simply cannot be expressed in such terms as obligations and capacities'. Is it really not possible, without weaving fictions, to be more specific than this?

On some points of detail[11] with which I will not weary the reader the author has misunderstood me. But on one major topic his criticism is I think misdirected because in a sense it is not fundamental enough. Thus he says that I suppose that as 'a necessity of logical thinking' my rule of recognition must be unconditional and the authority of a legislature *cannot* be the subject of an explicit or implicit provision for revocation 'for abuses'. There is, however, nothing in my theory which leads to this result. There is, for me, no logical restriction on the content of the rule of recognition: so far as 'logic' goes it could provide explicitly or implicitly that the criteria determining validity of subordinate laws should cease to be regarded as such if the laws identified in accordance with them proved to be morally objectionable. So a constitution could include in its restrictions on the legislative power even of its supreme legislature not only conformity with due process but a completely general provision that its legal power should lapse if its enactments ever conflicted with principles of morality and justice. The objection to this extraordinary arrangement would not be 'logic' but the gross indeterminacy of such criteria of legal validity. Constitutions do not invite trouble by taking this form. So normally the questions, 'Is this a valid law?' and 'Is it so morally iniquitous that I must withdraw my recognition of the authority of those who made it?', are distinct. But there is nothing in my book to suggest that the latter question is not of the greatest importance. Here, if I may say so, the author's target should have been my claim that it is both intelligible and important to distinguish the general acceptance of the legally ultimate rule of a system of law which specifies the criteria of legal validity from whatever moral principles or rules individuals act upon in deciding

---

[11] Thus he says, mistakenly, that in my view 'the rule of recognition that ascribes legal sovereignty to the Queen in Parliament can . . . summarize and absorb all the little rules that enable lawyers to recognize law'. This neglects the account of the complexity even in England of the rule of recognition given in my book and explained above.

whether and to what extent they are morally bound to obey the law. Again, I may have been wrong in making this distinction, and the author may be right in thinking that any recognition of legal authority contains implicitly moral limitations. But if this was my error it stands in need of a more frontal and detailed attack than the author mounts here.

Finally, the author claims that 'the basic error' of my methods is shown by the incompetence of my theory to explain how it is that even after a revolution often a great mass of private law enacted under the old regime still continues to be regarded as law under the new regime. In my book I discussed what I there called 'the persistence of law'. But I did not deal with this phenomenon of revolution because my concern was to exhibit the inadequacies of the Austinian theory that law was the command of the sovereign 'habitually obeyed'. I argued that this could not explain how the commands of a dead sovereign no longer habitually obeyed could still be law. I claimed that this phenomenon of the persistence of law could be explained easily enough if we think in terms not of habits of obedience but in terms of a rule of recognition, pointing generally to the office of legislator and not individually to its present occupant. On this view of the matter the legislation of a past legislator is accepted as law because it is identified as such by the presently accepted rule of recognition. This, however, does not deal with the possibility of a revolutionary break such as the author invents: Rex II succeeds Rex I under presently accepted rules of succession and then Brutus without title and in violation of these rules seizes the throne. Here, too, a mass of private law enacted under the old regime continues to be recognized as law.

Though I did not deal with this case in my book I do not think there is any great difficulty in analysing such situations in terms of a rule of recognition. My explanation will be very much the same as that given by Kelsen in his *General Theory of Law and State*.[12] After a revolutionary break such as the author has imagined it must always be uncertain for some time what criteria the courts will eventually use to ascertain the law. Some time must elapse before a sufficient uniformity in practice of courts, legislators, and other officials develops

---

[12] Kelsen, op. cit. *supra* n. 8, at 117-18.

to enable an answer to be given to this question. But when things settle down it may be apparent that as well as accepting 'enactment by Brutus' as a mark of valid law, the courts will also recognize a mass of private law enacted under the old regime. In any full description of the criteria used by the courts after the revolutionary break in ascertaining the law, the old legislation would have to be specifically mentioned *eo nomine*. Had there been no revolution, it would have been identified by reference to the general provision qualifying the unbroken succession of legislators. After the revolution, there-fore, the validity of the old legislation comes to rest on a dif-ferent rule of recognition from before.

V. CONCLUSION

There is much in this small book which I have not considered here. It ends with some admirable pages on what the author terms 'the problems of institutional design'. Here he considers the appropriateness to different types of issue of different decision-procedures, among them adjudication and majority vote. He illuminatingly shows the restrictions to which the use of these methods are 'naturally' subject and the problems of co-ordinating different procedures in a single system. In an appendix there is a splendid example of the author's mytho-poetic powers, where the problem of 'the grudge informer' and retroactive legislation are discussed by five deputies. This has all the charm and revealing power of the author's famous 'Case of the Speluncean Explorers'.[13] In conclusion I would say this: the virtues and vices of this book seem to me to spring from the same single source. The author has all his life been in love with the notion of purpose and this passion, like any other, can both inspire and blind a man. I have tried to show that I would not wish him to terminate his longstanding union with this *idée maîtresse*. But I wish that the high ro-mance would settle down to some cooler form of regard. When this happens, the author's many readers will feel the drop in temperature; but they will be amply compensated by an in-crease in light.

[13] 62 *Harv. L. Rev.* 616 (1949).

POSTSCRIPT

See for criticisms and comments:

1. P. Nicholson, 'The Internal Morality of Law: Fuller and his Critics', *Ethics* 307 (1974).
2. K. I. Winston, *The Principles of Social Order* (Selected Essays of Lon L. Fuller) 33 ff. (Durham, NC, 1981).
3. R. A. Duff, 'Legal Obligation and the Moral Nature of Law', *Juridical Review* 61 (1980) 73-9.

PART IV

Essay 17

The House of Lords on Attempting the Impossible

I

In 1973 the House of Lords in *Haughton* v. *Smith*[1] reformulated the law relating to criminal attempts, expressly overruling in the process two decisions of lower courts and disapproving of some others. The unanimous decision in the case was that one who handles goods, mistakenly believing at the time of handling that they were at that time still stolen goods, cannot be convicted of an attempt to handle stolen goods.[2] In the vast Anglo-American literature on criminal attempts, such cases, where the object on which the accused operates lacks some specific legal characteristic (like 'being stolen' or 'being the property of another') defined by reference to legal rules, which it must have if his conduct is to constitute the *actus reus* of the offence which he intends to commit, are often described as cases of 'legal impossibility'. I think for reasons which I give later, that the use in this context of the terminology of 'impossibility' is confusing, and I shall refer to such cases, for short, as 'umbrella-type' cases after the famous hypothetical case put by Baron Bramwell in 1864[3] of a man who, intending to steal an umbrella, took his own, mistakenly believing it to be another's.

---

[1] [1975] AC 476. Since this essay was written, the Law Commission has published a *Report on Attempt and Impossibility in relation to Attempt, Conspiracy and Incitement* (Law Com. no. 102, HMSO, 1980). This includes a detailed criticism of *Haughton* v. *Smith* with which I generally agree.

[2] The facts in the case were that a large quantity of corned beef was stolen from a warehouse in Liverpool. Later police officers found a van on the motorway loaded with cartons of the stolen corned beef. They decided to let the van go on its way, with two police officers aboard, to the place in London where the driver was to rendezvous with those who were to take over the stolen goods for disposal. When the van arrived the respondent took a leading part in arranging the disposal of the goods. The police then made their identity known and the respondent was arrested and charged with attempting to handle stolen goods though the Crown conceded that the goods at the time of the offence, being in the lawful custody of the police, had ceased to be stolen goods by virtue of s. 24(3) of the Theft Act 1968.

[3] In *R* v. *Collins* (1864) 9 Cox CC 497 at 498.

In 1975 the Divisional Court in *Partington* v. *Williams*,[4] conceiving that it was simply giving effect to the general principles enunciated by the House of Lords, and following in particular the strong hints dropped by the Lord Chancellor concerning cases like those before it, held that a clerk who with the intention of stealing money from it took a wallet out of a drawer in the office of her employers and opened it but found it empty, could not, on those facts, be convicted of an attempt to steal. Cases of that sort, where at the relevant time no object with the physical characteristics of the kind of object upon which the accused, bent on committing a crime, intended to operate, exists at the place where he believed such an object was or might be, are described in the literature as cases of 'factual' or 'physical' impossibility. But for the reason already mentioned I shall refer to them, for short, as 'empty-pocket' type cases, after the actual case of *R* v. *Collins*[5] where the court held that a man who, intending to steal money, put his hand into the pocket of another, cannot be convicted of an attempt to steal if the pocket was in fact empty at the time. The decision in *R* v. *Collins*, which is certainly surprising to the layman, was held to be bad law in two later cases,[6] but it seemed to be restored to full favour by the discussion of it in the House of Lords and the later decision concerning the empty wallet in *Partington* v. *Williams*[7] which the then Lord Chief Justice, loyally attempting to follow the path indicated by the House of Lords, said was a case whose facts 'are very much on all fours with those in *Collins*'.[8]

However, in 1978 the House of Lords in *Director of Public Prosecutions* v. *Nock*[9] held that an agreement to do something which it is 'physically impossible' to do (in that case, to

[4] (1975) 62 Cr App Rep 220.

[5] (1864) 9 Cox CC 497. The Court of Criminal Appeal in this case allowed an appeal from the conviction of the accused on an indictment for putting their hands into the gown pocket of a woman 'with intent the property of the said woman, in the said gown pocket then being, from the person of the said woman to steal'. The conviction was quashed because there was no finding that there was any property in the woman's pocket.

[6] *R* v. *Brown* (1889) 24 QBD 357, and *R* v. *Ring* (1892) 17 Cox CC 491. No reasons were given in either of these cases and all the judges in the House of Lords in *Haughton* v. *Smith* expressed disapproval of them at least as far as they purported to overrule *R* v. *Collins*.

[7] (1975) 62 Cr App Rep 220.

[8] Ibid. at 223.

[9] [1978] AC 979.

extract a physical substance from a compound which did not contain it) could not constitute a criminal conspiracy, and two Lords of Appeal (Lords Diplock and Scarman) made a number of strong *obiter* observations which may do something to water down the effect of *Haughton* v. *Smith*, at least as far as empty-pocket type cases are concerned. Both these judges thought that the court in *Partington* v. *Williams* was wrong in its interpretation of the principles enunciated by the House of Lords, and particularly erred in suggesting that whenever an accused, intending to steal, inserted his hand into some place where something worth stealing was likely to be found, the onus lay on the prosecution to prove that something worth stealing was actually present in that particular place. So to hold, said Lord Diplock, would 'offend common sense and common justice'[10] in relation to pick-pockets at least, and since the crime which the pick-pocket sets out to commit is usually not confined to stealing from a particular person or a particular pocket or receptacle, he could be convicted in such cases of an attempt on a suitably framed indictment. This novel and ingenious effort to limit in relation to pick-pockets the scope of *R* v. *Collins* was presumably intended to reassure prosecuting authorities reportedly alarmed at its approval, without any hint of such limitation, by the House of Lords in *Haughton* v. *Smith*. It does not however appear to offer comfort to those who find the acquittal of the accused in *R* v. *Collins*, or the dishonest clerk in *Partington* v. *Williams*, contrary to 'common sense and common justice'.[11]

II

My main motive for travelling over what academic lawyers may feel to be desperately familiar and indeed a deeply rutted territory is to do two things. The first is to express concern that the House of Lords, in a case in which it was consciously reformulating the law, overruling decisions and choosing between conflicting views, should have reached its decision

[10] Ibid. at 993.

[11] Nor is it clear from Lord Diplock's observations on what principle consistent with the decision in *R* v. *Collins* a pick-pocket, whose intention in putting his hand into one pocket which was in fact empty was to run through a number of different persons' pockets till he found money to steal, could be convicted of an attempt to steal without proof that there was money in one of them.

virtually without an attempt to show that the view of the law
which it favoured was preferable to alternative views in point
of expediency, justice, or morality, or was more consistent
with reasonable conceptions of the point or purpose of punishing attempts. I say 'virtually' without any discussion of
these matters, since one such issue was raised mainly by Lord
Reid, who argued that to hold the accused guilty of an attempt on the facts of *Haughton* v. *Smith*, or any umbrella-
type case, would amount to the abandonment of the principle
that an *actus reus* as well as *mens rea* is required to constitute
a crime. So to hold would, in his view, be tantamount to 'punishing people for their guilty intentions'.[12] Whatever may be
thought of this argument, which I consider below, it certainly
raises an issue of principle.

It is also true that all the judges in *Haughton* v. *Smith* conceded that very often the accused who on their view of the
law would have to be acquitted in empty-pocket or umbrella-
type cases was morally just as reprehensible and just as much
a social danger as those who on their view of the law could be
convicted in other circumstances of attempts to commit the
same crimes. 'It is of course true, at least in theory,' said Lord
Hailsham, 'that some villains will escape by this route'.[13] In
mentioning these matters the judges offer critics the solace
that in many cases where the accused would escape conviction
for an attempt he could, on a properly framed indictment, be
convicted of some other substantive offence. But they plainly
thought that all such matters were quite irrelevant to their
business of formulating or reformulating the law. Such a view
of what is and what is not relevant to legal decision on a disputed point of law would at least be comprehensible if the
House of Lords was so constrained by the very concept of an
attempt that they had no choice but to decide as they did.
But it cannot plausibly be maintained that the judges were
confronted by any firmly and clearly established legal doctrine which compelled their decision. Nor if, as other judges
have occasionally done, they were to ask what the word

---

[12] *Haughton* v. *Smith* [1975] AC 476 at 500. So too per Lord Morris of Borth-
y-Gest, ibid. at 511, 'to convict [the respondent] of attempting to handle stolen
goods would be to convict him not for what he did but simply because he had a
guilty intention'.
[13] Ibid. at 497.

'attempt' means in ordinary non-legal contexts, could it be pretended that the plain meaning of 'attempting' or 'making an attempt' (to do something) or 'trying' (to do or not to do something) requires the decisions which the House of Lords favoured. Indeed Lord Reid actually said that the ordinary man would say of the pick-pocket in the empty-pocket case 'of course he was attempting to steal'.[14] 'But,' Lord Reid said, 'the ordinary man would say this without stopping to think'; whereas those who stop to think (*scilicet* judges) can see what ordinary men fail to see: that 'the theory which has been evolved that there can be an attempt to commit an offence although in fact that offence could not have been committed',[15] is just wrong. So it is an erroneous 'theory' though one which 'the ordinary man' shares.

III

My second complaint occupies the rest of this article. It is that the principles put forward by the House of Lords in *Haughton* v. *Smith* as general guides for determining what conduct constitutes an attempt to commit a crime, are both inadequate and unsupported by anything that could be called reasoning as distinct from the uncritical recital of what other judges have said. They are inadequate because the principles are appropriate only to one special kind of unsuccessful attempt, namely those which fail only because of an *interruption of* a sequence of events which if not interrupted would constitute the *actus reus* of the intended crime. Simple examples of attempts which do conform to this model are those where a man who shoots to kill another is frustrated only by a gust of wind which deflects his bullet, or those where a burglar who has succeeded in opening the safe is caught and desists just as his hand is closing over the diamonds inside. Of course if the only attempts are those where failure is due to interruption, the empty-pocket and umbrella-type cases cannot constitute attempts. But this model for attempts (which I shall call the Interruption Model) in terms of which alone the general principles enunciated by the House of Lords are framed, is wholly inappropriate to account for many clear cases of criminal

---

[14] Ibid. at 499.   [15] Ibid. at 498.

attempts, quite apart from the disputed empty-pocket and umbrella-type cases which this model excludes. For there are many kinds of attempt apart from these disputed ones which fail not because of any *interruption*, but are doomed to failure from the start because the means chosen for the commission of the intended crime is misdirected or insufficient. Such cases include what surely must be one of the commonest forms of unsuccessful attempt to murder or wound, namely where a man who shoots to kill or wound another simply aims his gun at the wrong angle, so the bullet flies unimpeded but harmlessly through the air, missing the intended victim. But cases where the factor frustrating the attempt is not an 'interruption', even on the most generous interpretation of that term, include also some expressly mentioned by Lords Hailsham and Reid, such as the case where an inadequate dose of poison is given, or the case where the burglar finds his jemmy too small or himself too weak to open the safe door.[16] These are said by both Law Lords to constitute criminal attempts, but nothing is said by either to show how they can fit the favoured Interruption Model. Lord Hailsham indeed makes an unexplained reference to the need for 'casuistry'[17] and Lord Reid said that such cases are 'borderline' cases[18] as if they could be accommodated by some minor adjustment to or extension of the model which juries, applying the principles enunciated by the House of Lords, may be left to make. Yet these cases are not in the least 'borderline' cases but are among the clearest cases of criminal attempts.

It is important to appreciate precisely why the Interruption Model is inappropriate to such cases of misdirected or insufficient means. It is not because of some minor detail or some feature which could be cured by a wide interpretation of the idea of 'interruption'. It is because these cases which do not fit the model all lack its central feature, much stressed by the House of Lords, namely that the events in fact initiated by the accused's overt act are, up to the point of interruption, *actual* 'steps on the way' (to use the judicially favoured metaphor) to the commission of the crime; so that these early steps but for the interruption would have been followed by others

[16] Ibid. at 493–4 and 500.
[17] Ibid. at 494.
[18] Ibid. at 500.

which would have completed the *actus reus* of the intended crime. By contrast, in the cases of misdirected or inadequate means for which the model fails to cater, the overt act and events initiated by it are not 'steps actually on the way' to the commission of the crime but only steps intended to be on their way to the completion of the offence. The accused's misdirected shot or giving an inadequate dose of poison are not the actual early members of a series which if followed by others would constitute his killing the victim; they are only steps, doomed to failure from the start, which the accused *intended* to be and believed would or might be such members of such a series.

Accordingly what is required for the explanation of such attempts is a different model which may be called 'the Intended Steps Model'. According to this model an attempt to commit a particular crime is to be defined (apart from questions of proximity) as an act done with the intention that it should initiate a series of events or acts and events which would if completed constitute the *actus reus* of that crime. In many continental jurisdictions the contrast between these two models is drawn in the trouble-laden terms of 'objective' and 'subjective' theory; but I think that, in an English context, the terms I have chosen are clearer, and better display the defective vision of the House of Lords. But I shall defer further consideration of the Intended Steps Model, in order first to inquire what process of reasoning led the House of Lords to accept the Interruption Model which necessarily excludes the recognition of empty-pocket and umbrella-type cases as examples of criminal attempts, whereas the Intended Steps Model does not.

IV

It is I think a fair characterization of Lord Hailsham's speech in *Haughton* v. *Smith* to say that its main contribution to the statement of the law of criminal attempts is to canonize with the authority of the House of Lords two formulations of the Interruption Model which are taken over with minor verbal alterations from earlier and lower authorities. The first of these two formulations appears (apart from the question of the 'proximacy' of the overt act) to state the necessary and sufficient conditions of conduct constituting a criminal attempt: 'In addition to the intention or *mens rea* there must be an overt act of such a kind that it is intended to form part and *does form part* of a series of acts which could constitute the actual commission of the offence if it were not interrupted.'[19] This is said by Lord Hailsham to be derived from earlier 'definitions' of which the 'more modern' is given in Stephen's *Digest* of 1894, and was adopted by Parker CJ in a case of 1968.[20]

Lord Hailsham's second formulation of the Interruption Model, besides it characterization of attempts in the positive terms of 'steps on the way', identifies two sorts of conduct which cannot constitute attempts, and so makes explicit an important negative necessary condition. It consists mainly of the quotation, with approval, of the observations of Birkett J in an earlier umbrella-type case,[21] where it was alleged that the accused intended to sell pears at a price in excess of the price then legally permitted, but sold them only at the permitted price, in the mistaken belief that the price he had charged for the amount sold was in excess of the legally permitted maximum. From Birkett J's judgment in that case Lord Hailsham quoted the following:

Steps on the way to the commission of what would be a crime if the acts were completed may amount to an attempt to commit the crime to which unless interrupted they would have led. But steps on the way to doing something which is thereafter done and which is no crime cannot be regarded as attempts to commit a crime.[22]

To this Lord Hailsham added a rider of his own: 'Steps on the way to do something which is thereafter *not* completed but which if done would not constitute a crime cannot be considered an attempt to commit a crime.'[23] Of course the authorities from which Lord Hailsham took his two formulations of the Interruption Model are respectable, but it is astonishing to find that he gives no reason of his own to show why they should be accepted as adequate formulations of the law of attempts. However, he does say 'without expressing' any

[19] [1975] AC 476 at 492 (italics added).
[20] *Davey* v. *Lee* [1968] 1 QB 366 at 370.
[21] *R* v. *Percy Dalton* (1949) 33 Cr App Rep 102 at 110.
[22] *Haughton* v. *Smith* [1975] AC 476 at 497.
[23] Ibid. at 497.

concluded 'opinion' in discussing the empty-pocket type cases, 'In general I regard the reasoning in *R* v. *M'Pherson* and *R* v. *Collins* as sound.'[24] So one turns with some eagerness to search the scanty pages of these two cases of 1857 and 1864 for the 'reasoning' thus approved, more than a century later, by the House of Lords. The search is not rewarding; apart from the hypothetical cases put during the argument by Bramwell B[25] all that can be found in the judgments or judicial interventions in the argument in these cases are observations of four distinguishable kinds, none of which seem well described as 'reasoning', let alone as 'sound'.

(1) First, there is the simple unargued assertion that all attempts must conform to the Interruption Model. Thus 'we think that an attempt to commit a felony can only be made out when if no interruption had taken place the attempt could have been carried out successfully' (per Cockburn CJ in *R* v. *Collins*[26]).

(2) Secondly, there are statements about the meaning of the word 'attempt'. Thus 'the word attempt clearly conveys with it the idea that if the attempt had succeeded the offence charged would have been committed' and 'An attempt must be to do that which if successful would amount to the felony charged' (per Cockburn CJ in *M'Pherson*'s case).[27] These statements of Lord Cockburn's are true, indeed truisms, but they are of course perfectly compatible with the 'idea' that conduct may constitute an attempt to commit a crime, even if it could not, as in the empty-pocket case, have been successful in the circumstances. For these true statements say nothing about the possibility or impossibility of success and speak only about what would be the case *if* an attempt were successful and the 'if' here may be 'if *per impossibile*'. Yet Lord

[24] Ibid. at 495. In *M'Pherson* (1857) Dears and B 197, the accused was indicted for breaking and entering a dwelling house and stealing certain goods therefrom specified in the indictment. At the time of the breaking and entering the goods specified were not in the house. It was held that the accused could not be convicted of attempting to steal the goods as there was no attempt to commit the felony charged. While approving of its reasoning Lord Hailsham said in *Haughton* v. *Smith* ([1975] AC 476 at 494) that the case may be regarded as simply one where a man was charged with one thing and convicted of another.
[25] *R* v. *M'Pherson* (1857) Dears and B 197 at 281 and *R* v. *Collins* (1864) 9 Cox CC 497 at 498.
[26] *R* v. *Collins* (1864) 9 Cox CC 497 at 499.
[27] *R* v. *M'Pherson* (1857) Dears and B 197 at 202.

Cockburn in his judgment treats them as if they meant or en-
tailed that to make an attempt must be to do that which could
be successful; for after making these true statements he immediately adds: 'But here the attempt never could have succeeded'[28] as if that, in conjunction with the true statements,
proved that there could be no attempt in the case before him.
But this patently is a *non sequitur* due to the confusion of the
truism that if an attempt to do some act is successful that will
amount to the doing of the act, with the false proposition
that conduct can only constitute an attempt to do a specific
act if it is possible for it to succeed.

(3) Thirdly, there are repeated warnings in these old cases
that attempting and intending to do something are different:
'you must not confound attempt with intent' (per Coleridge
J in argument in *R* v. *M'Pherson*[29]), and 'Attempting to commit a felony is clearly distinguishable from intending to commit it' (per Cockburn CJ in the same case).[30] Taken literally,
these warnings seem quite irrelevant; as the prosecuting counsel in *R* v. *M'Pherson* urged, the argument for conviction was
not that attempting to commit a crime was the same as merely
intending to commit a crime, for it was common ground that
for an attempt an overt act done with that intention was required. What these obscure warnings therefore must mean is
that there is a difference between merely *doing* one thing *with
the intention* of doing something else or bringing about some
consequence and *doing* one thing *in the attempt* to do something else or bring about some consequence. But for all the
judges say there is nothing to show that this difference consists in anything more than that in the attempt cases but not
in the doing-with-intent cases the overt act must have gone
beyond what a jury would call 'mere preparation'. There is
nothing to show that the difference must, as the judges in *R* v.
M'Pherson assume, consist in the fact that in the attempt
cases but for an interruption the intended crime could have
been carried out, whereas in the doing-with-intent cases this
need not be so.

(4) The fourth kind of observation to be found in these

cases seems no better entitled to Lord Hailsham's description of 'reasoning' than the first three. It includes the following:

(a) 'In that case no larceny would have been committed and therefore no attempt to commit larceny could have been committed' (per Cockburn CJ in *R* v. *Collins*).[31]

(b) 'When he got there the goods specified in the indictment were not there. How then could he attempt to steal those goods? There can be no attempt *asportare* unless there is something *asportare*' (per Cockburn CJ in *R* v. *M'Pherson*).[32]

(c) 'The fallacy is that he did not and he could not attempt to steal the goods specified in the indictment because they were not there' (per Bramwell B in *R* v. *M'Pherson*).[33]

These last three quotations seem to amount to the assertion that if the accused could not have succeeded in committing the intended crime of larceny because of the absence from the relevant place of the objects which the accused intended to take from it, it follows that no attempt to commit that crime could have been committed. But why should this inference be accepted? It is of course the case that expressions of the form 'He took away goods from a place where in fact there were none', or 'He took money out of a pocket which in fact was empty at the time', cannot be used to make true statements, but only statements which are necessarily false. This is so because the *meaning* of transitive verbs like 'take from' (and many others such as 'kill', 'wound', 'attack') is such that they require, if statements in which they are the main verb are to be true, that their grammatical objects should exist at the relevant time and place. A logician would say that such verbs, in such constructions, require as a matter of their meaning an *extensional object*, that is, an actually existing object, whereas other verbs like 'hunt for' or 'look for' only require an *intensional object*, i.e. an object which the subject of the verb believes, however mistakenly, existed or might exist at the relevant time or place. Hence, 'Smith killed lions in Jones's

---

[31] *R* v. *Collins* (1864) 9 Cox CC 497 at 499.
[32] (1857) Dears and B 197 at 201.
[33] Ibid. at 203.

animal reserve' entails that there actually were lions there which he killed; but 'Smith hunted (or looked for) lions there' does not entail that there actually were lions for which he hunted, but only that Smith believed that there might be. The relevance of this brief excursus into simple semantics is the following: if the judicial observations last quoted amount to any form of reasoning, it is to an inference based on a false general principle that because verbs like 'take away from' or 'kill' require in simple constructions an extensional object, so also do all complex constructions in which these simple constructions are embedded like 'attempt to take from' or 'attempt to kill'.

It is on such a shaky inference if on any form of reasoning that statements like 'In that case no larceny could have been committed and *therefore* no attempt to commit larceny could have been committed' seem to rest. But the general principle of this inference cannot be true; for there are numerous complex constructions involving these verbs which may be true even though their grammatical object does not exist, but are satisfied with an intensional object. These include: 'He intended to take money from Smith's pocket'; 'He put his hand into Smith's pocket in order to take money from it.' After any of these statements 'But there was in fact no money in it' can be added without rendering it false or incoherent. So if 'He attempted to take money from Smith's pocket but there was in fact no money in it' cannot, as the judges think, be true but is false or incoherent, this must be because of something special about 'attempt'. But what is this special factor? Is it that though, as Lord Reid said, the plain man would unthinkingly say of the accused in the empty-pocket case 'Of course he attempted to steal', this just *sounds* wrong in the ears of thinking judges? Or is it because the word 'attempt' comes to us trailing the clouds of its etymological connection with the word 'attack', such as still survives in military contexts like 'They made an attempt on the city's defences'? Or is it simply because empty-pocket and umbrella-type cases are rareties, and most attempts are in fact directed against objects of the sort and with the characteristics required for the commission of the intended offence which actually do exist and are not merely believed to exist at the appropriate time and place? These indeed seem all very poor reasons for holding that the accused's conduct in such cases cannot constitute an attempt.

Whatever may be at work in the judges' minds there is no doubt of the strength of the hold which this picture of an attempt as directed, like an attack, at an existing thing has over their imagination. The most vivid expression of what judges apparently feel (if not think) to be the essence of an attempt was given to it by Rowlatt J in clear homely language in an umbrella-type case (R v. Osborn)[34] where he decided that a man who administered a harmless substance to a pregnant woman, believing mistakenly that it was noxious, could not be guilty of an attempt to administer a noxious substance. In that case he said that conduct cannot amount to an attempt if the accused 'is not near enough to the job to attempt it'[35] or 'when he is not on the job although he thinks he is'[36] or 'where the man is never on the thing itself at all — it is not a question of impossibility'.[37] By contrast a burglar who tries unsuccessfully to burst open a safe with a wholly insufficient tool is guilty of an attempt to steal though it was impossible that it should succeed; that constitutes an attempt in Rowlatt J's view because 'You are at it, you are at the very thing'.[38] Phrases like 'not on the job' seem to express, in rough but adequate language, the same suggested condition for conduct constituting an attempt as that which the logician would phrase in terms of the requirement of an extensional object; and the distinction drawn by Rowlatt J between the failure of that condition and 'impossibility' is, as I argue below, correct and important. But neither in his judgment, nor in the House of Lords, nor in the authorities cited there, is any reason given for holding that what can constitute an attempt is limited by this condition.

V

We have unearthed so far not *reasons*, but two dogmas on which the principles enunciated by the House of Lords are founded. One is the Interruption Model; the other is the

---

[34] (1919) 84 JP 63.
[35] Ibid. at 64.   [36] Ibid. at 64.
[37] Ibid. at 64.   [38] Ibid. at 64.

dogma that attempting to do something requires an extensional object ('being on the job'). These two dogmas are different though related. The Interruption Model presupposes that the requirement of an extensional object is satisfied, for there could not be actual 'steps on the way' to the commission of the intended offence as that model requires, if the appropriate extensional object does not exist at the appropriate time and place. But the acceptance of the condition requiring an extensional object does not entail acceptance of the Interruption Model which, as we have seen, cannot cater for attempts which fail not because of any *interruption*, but because the means chosen are insufficient or misdirected. Acceptance of that condition could be combined with the Intended Steps Model which explains those cases but it would limit its scope, and in the absence of any positive reason for accepting the requirement of an extensional object, this limitation would be quite arbitrary. The Intended Steps Model explains all the cases which the Interruption Model explains, and also the cases of insufficient or misdirected means which the latter fails to explain. If not limited by the requirement of an extensional object, the Intended Steps Model would also include the empty-pocket and umbrella-type cases as unsuccessful attempts, whereas the Interruption Model excludes them as not constituting cases of attempt at all. Hence for the unrestricted Intended Steps Model there are three main types of unsuccessful attempt, since the actual series of events initiated by the accused's overt act may diverge from the series as intended for any of three different reasons: (1) insufficiency or misdirection of the means chosen; (2) interruption; (3) absence at the relevant time and place of an object of the sort or with the characteristics required for the commission of the intended offence.

The foregoing discussion of the cases is perhaps enough to show that apart from any question of justice, morality, or penal policy (which I consider at the end of this essay) there is a strong case for adopting the unrestricted Intended Steps Model and so for recognizing the empty-pocket and umbrella-type cases as cases of criminal attempts. There are however some incidental arguments, recurrent in both the judicial and academic discussion of these cases and especially the umbrella-type cases, which require for their evaluation some

ON ATTEMPTING THE IMPOSSIBLE 381

exploration of the slippery notion of 'impossibility', and to this I now turn.

I have said that the description of empty-pocket and umbrella-type cases as cases respectively of 'factual' (or 'physical') impossibility and 'legal' impossibility is unfortunate. It is in fact doubly so. For in the first place there is a sense of 'impossible' in which it is true to say of many clear cases of attempt that it was impossible in the circumstances for it to have succeeded. A man shoots to kill but the bullet is stopped by the cigarette case in the victim's breast pocket; or a burglar attempts to open a safe with a jemmy that snaps in the door. It is impossible 'factually' or 'physically' (or perhaps, more perspicuously, 'causally') that in precisely those circumstances the shot should have killed the victim or that the burglar should have opened the safe. But when empty-pocket cases are specially singled out as cases of 'factual' or 'physical' impossibility, it is left quite unclear how this differs from the impossibility of success in these ordinary cases of attempts. It is of course true that in such ordinary cases which are directed against some actually existing person or object of the appropriate kind, the attempt on that same person or object could have succeeded given other means or other circumstances, e.g. where there was no obstructing cigarette case, or there was an adequate jemmy. So in such cases success might be described as only 'relatively' impossible; whereas if the person or object against whom or on which the accused intended to operate was not present at the appropriate time and place success may be said to be 'absolutely impossible'. Some such distinction is hinted at in the literature; but in fact it is quite arbitrary and explains nothing. For if the possibility of success in other than the actual circumstances may be invoked to show that success in the shooting case where the bullet was obstructed, or in the burglar's case where the jemmy broke, was only 'relatively impossible', why should it not be invoked in the empty-pocket case? There too 'in other circumstances' i.e. if there had been coins in the pocket, success would have been possible.

As Rowlatt J said,[39] in discussing the hypothetical case of the burglar who is plainly guilty of an attempt, though it was

[39] (1920) 84 JP 63 at 64.

impossible for him to have opened the safe with his jemmy, it is not 'factual' or 'physical' impossibility, whether 'absolute' or 'relative', which prevents success in cases where as he put it 'the man is never on the job though he thinks he is'. Indeed the terminology of 'factual' or 'physical' impossibility is misleading just because it suggests an affinity between the logical impossibility of (A1) taking money out of a pocket which is in fact empty, or (A2) killing what is in fact a corpse, and the physical or causal impossibility of (B1) a shot fired to kill at a given range reaching its target undeflected by hitting a breastplate of a given strength and construction, or (B2) a burglar opening a safe with a tool of a given size and weight. As should be obvious from the short discussion in section IV of the requirement of an appropriate extensional object in the case of some verbs of action, to demonstrate the impossibility of (A1) and (A2) only an appeal to the meaning of the constituent expressions is necessary; whereas in the case of (B1) and (B2) an appeal to well-established empirical generalizations or scientific laws is required. A second objection to the description of the empty-pocket and umbrella-type cases as respectively cases of 'factual' (or 'physical') impossibility and 'legal' impossibility, is that this contrast conceals the substantial identity of what is called 'impossibility' in the two cases. In both sorts of case the 'impossibility' arises from the absence of an object of the appropriate kind (e.g. coins) or with the appropriate characteristic (e.g. belonging to another person) required by law for the commission of the intended offence. Both in the case of 'He took money from a pocket which was empty' and 'He stole an umbrella which was his own' it is logically impossible that the actions which these statements purport to describe should have been done because as a matter of their meaning the verbs of action they contain ('take from' or 'stole') require an appropriate extensional object, and this was stated to be absent at the relevant time or place.

Though the impossibility of committing the offence is a logical one, since this depends on the meaning of expressions which are required for the description of a legal offence it could, in both cases, be said, though less perspicuously, to be a legal impossibility. Both are cases where, to use Rowlatt J's language, the accused 'was never on the job', i.e. there was no appropriate extensional object, and it is misleading, as he saw, to contrast them as cases of physical versus legal impossibility. The expression 'physical impossibility' is apt, as he said, only to describe the ordinary unsuccessful attempt like the would-be safe-breaker's attempt to open a safe with an inadequate tool.

What is true and what accounts for the misleading contrast of empty-pocket and umbrella-type cases as cases of physical versus legal impossibility is that in some cases, such as the hypothetical umbrella case and the actual case of *Haughton* v. *Smith*, the object on which the accused seeks to operate is inappropriate not because it lacks any physical property, but because it lacks some non-physical property required for the commission of the intended offence such as 'belonging to another' or 'stolen'. Because this is so, the accused who operates on such an object may achieve all the physical consequences which he intends to achieve by his action; whereas in the empty-pocket type cases, he cannot achieve all the intended physical consequences since there is no object with the appropriate physical properties present at the relevant time and place.

This difference not only accounts for the misleading contrast of physical versus legal impossibility, but also for a strange line of argument which haunts the judicial discussion of most umbrella-type cases. Though there are a number of different formulations of this argument it is most clearly expressed in the following simple form: 'The accused intended to commit a crime but he has done all he intended to and this does not constitute the *actus reus* of the intended crime though he believes it does; therefore it cannot constitute an attempt to commit the intended crime'.[40]

It is on this ground, that taking an umbrella in the mistaken belief that it belongs to someone else, or handling goods in the mistaken belief that they are stolen, are said not to constitute attempts. Of course it is true that one who has done all that he intended to do, cannot be said, in doing that, to have attempted but failed to do something; but what is most strange about the use of this argument to show that umbrella-type

---

[40] Cf. *R* v. *Donnelly* [1970] NZLR 980-7, per Turner J referring to cases where a man efficiently does 'without interruption every act which he set out to do but may be saved from criminal liability by the fact that what he has done contrary to his belief at the time does not after all amount to a crime'.

cases cannot constitute unsuccessful attempts to commit crimes is the incoherence of the statement that in such cases the accused has done *all* he intended to do. For if a man intends to take an umbrella belonging to another and what he does is to take his own umbrella plainly he has not done all that he intended to do. What is true is that he intended to take a particular umbrella and did so, but that is only one of his intentions. Why should it not be said of the accused in such cases that he had both the intention to steal an umbrella and an intention to take the particular umbrella which he did take, the latter intention being derivative from the former in combination with his mistaken belief? Alternatively it could be said that the accused had a single intention of two different but connected kinds, just as a man who shoots and thereby kills, has done an act of two different kinds (shooting and killing) rather than two different acts. Nothing much turns in the present context on which of these alternative ways of counting or individuating intentions are chosen, since in either case it is false to say that the accused has done 'all' that he intended to do.

It may be that this strange argument which the House of Lords has adopted needs for its correction attention to certain complexities in which statements of intention may be involved. The important points for present purposes are the following.

When a man mistakenly believes that an object which he intends to affect by his action has some specific property, his intention may be characterized in many different ways in both first-person and third-person statements of his intention. Some of these characterizations may incorporate a description of the object in terms of a property which he mistakenly believes it to have; others may incorporate other descriptions not including that property or, in a limiting case, a true characterization of his intention may, so far as the object is concerned, incorporate no description at all but be purely referential and be effected by pointing. Thus the accused in *Haughton* v. *Smith* could have said truly at least three things: (1) 'I intended to take the stolen corned beef brought down from the North', or (2) 'I intended to take the corned beef brought down from the North', or (3) 'I intended to take that' (pointing). Corresponding third-person statements could also have been made about the accused.

It is true that relative to the last two characterizations of his intention (i.e. those not incorporating the false belief) what the actor did brought about all that he intended; or, as the judge put it, the whole intended series of events to the completion of which his action was a step was completed: there was no interruption, no breaking off, no missing last members of the series; all the intended physical consequences were achieved. Given *that* characterization of his intention what happened included all that was intended. Still to say he did *'all'* that he intended is false; it implies that what occurred did not fall short of the actor's intention however characterized. But in fact relative to the characterization of his intention which incorporates the false belief, what occurred did fall short of the intention because it was intended to, but did not, affect an object having a specific property.

VI

There remain to be considered two arguments thought by some judges to support the view that conduct in the umbrella-type cases cannot constitute a criminal attempt. Both are most clearly presented by Lord Reid in *Haughton* v. *Smith*. According to the first of these arguments, fundamental principles of English criminal law preclude the courts from holding guilty of a criminal attempt a man who, intending to steal, takes his own property, mistakenly believing it to be another's, or the accused in *Haughton* v. *Smith* who handles goods which are not stolen, in the mistaken belief that they are. To punish them, it is said, would amount to 'punishing people for their guilty intentions' since what they intended to do and have done 'does not constitute that *actus reus* of a crime'.[41] We may waive the minor inaccuracy of the last quoted words which seem to neglect the fact pointed out by Lord Hailsham,[42] that what is done in such cases may well constitute a crime, as it did in *Haughton* v. *Smith*, though not the particular crime with attempting to commit which the accused is charged. But apart from this defect the argument presented by Lord Reid

[41] [1975] AC 476.   [42] Ibid. at 497.

seems quite mistaken. Punishing such conduct as criminal attempts would not be punishing the accused for his intentions or thoughts alone, but for doing an overt act in order to carry out his intentions to commit a crime and in the (mistaken) belief that it might or would do so. The fact that what was done would not constitute the *actus reus* of a crime if it was not done with such intention is no reason for concluding that it cannot constitute the *actus reus* of a crime if it is so done.

There are at least two different reasons for rejecting Lord Reid's conclusion. The first emerges from consideration of those clear cases of attempt which fail not because of any interruption but because the chosen means is insufficient or misdirected where what is done by the accused (the administration of an inadequate dose of poison or the firing of an ill-aimed shot which flies harmlessly past its target) does not constitute the *actus reus* of the intended crime and in some cases not of any crime, yet the accused's conduct is punishable as an attempt because it is done in order to give effect to an intention to commit the crime: that is what makes his conduct the *actus reus* of a crime. Supporters of Lord Reid's argument may seek to distinguish such cases on the ground that in them, unlike the umbrella-type cases, the accused has not 'done all he intended to do'. But the falsity and indeed the absurdity of this distinction has already been discussed; and even if such a distinction could be made out it is unclear how it would support the view that in one case but not in the other punishing the accused for an attempt would be punishing for his guilty intentions.

Secondly, Lord Reid's view appears to rest on a mistaken conception of the possible interrelationships between *actus reus* and *intention*. What is needed to dissipate confusion here is the simple observation that the criminal law has at least two different ways of identifying the *actus reus* it requires. In the cases, e.g., of murder or assault it may do this directly, describing certain outward conduct, and though for liability *mens rea* is also required, no further reference to the 'mental element' is required to identify the kind of outward conduct that constitutes the *actus reus* of such charges. In other cases however, including attempts, the *actus reus* is not thus directly identified but is indirectly identified by reference to the accused's intention. In such cases the intention plays a double role: it fixes what is to count as an *actus reus* and is also an element of *mens rea*, required for liability. If this double role were objectionable there could be no law of attempt at all.

The second and last argument to be considered raises a difficulty, or at least a point, about the requirement that an overt act to constitute a criminal attempt must be 'proximate' to the commission of the intended offence. Lord Reid states, though he does not develop the point, that where as in the empty-pocket and umbrella-type cases, when it is 'impossible' that the accused should have succeeded in committing an intended offence, 'no act could be proximate'.[43] Lord Hailsham appears to disagree; for he expressly states that the reason why conduct in the umbrella-type cases cannot constitute attempt is not because there is no sufficiently proximate act but because 'the acts are not part of a series which would constitute the commission of the offence if they were not interrupted'.[44] This of course is simply to rely on the Interruption Model as if only conduct which fitted it could constitute an attempt.

Lord Reid's point still remains therefore to be considered. The requirement of 'proximacy' is of course notoriously vague. Juries are to be told that an attempt must be more than 'mere preparation' and then left to use their common sense in judging whether what was done was sufficiently close to committing the offence. But it would be strange indeed if a jury thought that a pick-pocket putting his hand into another's pocket, or a fence handling goods which he believed were stolen, were 'merely preparing' to commit a crime. From their point of view what they were doing was the last action required and not a mere preparation to effect their plans.

In fact the only reason for the contention that such acts are not sufficiently 'proximate' for an attempt seems to be blind loyalty to the Interruption Model. This indeed does require (*pace* Lord Hailsham) that a 'proximate' overt act be a step actually on the way (not merely *intended* and *believed* by the accused to be on the way) to the commission of the offence, and of course this is not true of the overt acts in the empty-pocket and umbrella-type cases. But if this is a reason

388 THE HOUSE OF LORDS

for holding an overt act not to be sufficiently proximate, then all attempts which fail not because of interruption but because of the insufficiency or misdirection of means do not satisfy the requirement of 'proximate' act. Yet giving an intended victim an inadequate dose of poison, or firing a shot intended to kill which misses because of aberrant aim doomed to failure from the start, is certainly a sufficiently proximate act; it is so not because it would have culminated in the victim's death but for an interruption, but because within the intended scheme of things it is sufficiently close to the intended outcome to rank as more than mere preparation.[45]

VII

When is the law most an ass? Is it an ass when it adopts a narrow conception of a criminal attempt which leads to the acquittal of the pick-pocket in *Collins*, the dishonest clerk in *Partington* v. *Williams*, and the would-be handler of stolen goods in *Haughton* v. *Smith*? Would it be more of an ass, as Lord Reid thought, if it adopted the wider conception of an attempt embodied in the Intended Steps Model which would lead to a conviction in those cases, but also to the conviction of the would-be murderer who shoots at a corpse believing it to be the living body of his enemy or the would-be thief who takes his own umbrella believing it to be another's?

Two important considerations support the wider conception. The first is that if the punishment of unsuccessful attemps to commit crimes is morally justifiable at all, exactly the same deterrent and retributive justifications are available in the cases of impossibility as in the ordinary cases of attempt. The accused in the impossibility case having done his best to implement his intention to commit a crime is just as much deserving of punishment as the accused in the ordinary case;

[45] Cf. the ALI Model Penal Code, Proposed Official Draft, art. 5, s. 501, which provides as a condition of criminal liability for attempts that the person 'purposely does or omits to do anything which under the circumstances as he believes them to be is an act or omission constituting a substantial step in a course of conduct planned to culminate in his commission of the crime'. The scheme of the Model Penal Code is to eliminate altogether from the law of criminal attempts what it terms 'the defence of impossibility', and in effect it adopts what I have called the Intended Steps Model. In many United States jurisdictions the law of attempts is already in accordance with that model. In New York the legislature amended the law in 1967.

and the same considerations of general and individual deterrence apply with equal force, whether or not at the relevant time and place the object on which the accused intends to operate exists and has the properties required for the commission of the intended offence.

Secondly, both the narrow conception of an attempt favoured by the House of Lords and the wider conception embodied in the Intended Steps Model have attendant but contrasting disadvantages. If the narrower conception is adopted some 'villains' may, as Lord Hailsham said, escape conviction for an attempt; whereas if the wider conception is adopted, this may lead to the conviction of possibly harmless persons like the love-sick girl who tries to kill or disfigure her rival by sticking pins into her wax image. Such persons, entertaining false and possibly superstitious general beliefs about causal laws and physical processes, may often be unlikely to resort to any more dangerous means to accomplish their ends and may be thought harmless. Of these two contrasting disadvantages the second seems to me the less serious and the most amenable to rational legal control. For reasonable provision can be made for such harmless offenders by the exercise of judicial discretion at the sentencing stage, when there will be an opportunity to investigate and assess both the firmness of their intention to harm and the likelihood of their resorting to dangerous means.

By contrast the only consideration that mitigates the disadvantage of the narrower conception is the possibility that the accused in the impossibility cases, who will be acquitted of an attempt, may be convicted of some other offence. But to rely on that is to rely on something entirely haphazard. In many cases there will be no other available charge and even when other charges are available they may be for minor offences not matching the seriousness of the attempts. In any case to rely on the possibility of bringing other charges is to take far too optimistic a view of the resourcefulness of our prosecuting authorities, who in *Haughton* v. *Smith* failed to see that the accused who was acquitted could with his accomplices certainly have been convicted of theft and conspiracy to handle stolen goods and possibly of other offences.

Against these two considerations supporting the wider conception, the only support for the narrower conception consists of a highly selective appeal to the alleged intuitions of 'common sense' uncorrupted by any consideration of reasonable social aims or penal policy, as if we can just see without thinking that it is 'absurd' to convict a would-be thief who takes his own umbrella (however many he has stolen in the past and is likely to steal in the future) and 'asinine' to convict the would-be murderer who mistakes a corpse for a living body, however likely he is to get his victim next time. The capricious as well as the unreliable nature of this appeal to 'common sense' is made painfully obvious when we are told by judges that the ordinary man's view, that a would-be pick-pocket who puts his hand into an empty pocket has attempted to steal, must be rejected because the ordinary man 'has not stopped to think'.

Finally, English law as stated by the House of Lords in *Haughton* v. *Smith* is now in a position of virtual and, as it seems to me, unsplendid isolation. It is out of line with the law of the major European countries and with most countries of the Commonwealth. It is also out of line with the codes and main trends of decision in the United States. The New York case of *The People* v. *Jaffé*[46] in which the facts and grounds of decision were similar to those in *Haughton* v. *Smith*, and which was approved by Lord Hailsham in that case as supporting his view of the law,[47] had already been rejected when the legislature of New York amended the law in 1967. The provisions of the American Law Institute Model Penal Code[48] in effect approximates very closely to what I have called the Intended Steps Model. In this country, since the decision in *Haughton* v. *Smith* there have been judicial attempts,[49] one of them in the House of Lords, to water down, qualify, or to treat as *obiter* some of the general principles enunciated by the House of Lords, but these seem only to have added complexity, confusion, and artificiality to the law. It is very much to be hoped that legislation may be

---

[46] *People* v. *Jaffé* 185 NY 497 (1906).
[47] [1975] AC 476 at 497
[48] See n. 5 above.
[49] See *DPP* v. *Nock* [1978] AC 979 discussed above at n. 9. See also *Re A-G's References (Nos. 1 and 2 of 1979)* [1979] 3 All ER 143 and *R* v. *Bayley and Easterbrook* [1980] Crim LR 503, and comment thereon.

speedily introduced to eliminate the doctrine of 'impossi-bility', so called, from the law of criminal attempt.[50]

[50] This has been recommended by the Law Commission and their report (n. 1 *supra*) includes a draft bill designed to secure this. A bill (no. 21 of 1980) was introduced into the House of Commons by the Home Secretary purporting to implement many of the Law Commission recommendations. As originally drafted the bill appeared to preserve the decision in *Haughton* v. *Smith*. (See Glanville Williams, 'The Government's Proposals on Criminal Attempts' (1981) NLJ 80 ff and 104ff.) But the whole doctrine of 'impossibility' has now been eliminated by The Criminal Attempts Act 1981.

Index of Names

Index of Subjects

America, United States of, Constitution 155-7, 175-8, 183; Declaration of Independence 133, 145-6, 149-50, 181, 183; sovereign in 60; Supreme Court, powers of 124-7; *and see* jurisprudence; realism

attempts, criminal 389-91; *actus reus* of 385-8; and punishment 389-91

command, law as 57-62, 147, 271-2, 273

conceptualism 104, 268, 270-1

constitutional law, existence of 259; self-entrenched clauses of 173-5, 178

contract, will theory of 94-6, 279

corporate personality 23-5, 30-43; and criminal liability 43-7

definition 3, 32-3, 272; and analytical jurisprudence 288; and theory 22-48; Bentham on 26-7, 31; of law 89-91

democracy 193, 217, 234; *and see* utilitarianism

discretion, judicial 107-8; *and see* judges

duty, legal analysis of 91-3; natural 240-3; relation of legal to moral 280-99; and ideals 344-50; and basis of society 354-6; *and see* obligation

equality, of concern and respect 198, 208, 211; and utilitarianism 200-1, 210; and external preferences 212-31

fiction, corporate personality and 23-5, 32-3; rights as 23-5, 32-3

formalism 64-70

intention, analysis of 97-8

internal vs. external, aspect of rules 14-15, 166; statements 166-7

judges, and law-making 75, 65-71, 86-7, 124-32, 134-42, 152-4, 273

jurisprudence, analytical 57, 65, 109, 111, 271; American 121-59; 'Begriffsjurisprudenz' 267-8; expository vs. censorial 272; 'mechanical' 268; Pure Theory of Law and 288-9; Scandinavian 159-78; sociological 142-3

justice, and general legal rules 18, 81, 163; and utility 116-18, 188-9; and liberty 223-47

Kelsen, H., doctrines of: rules of law in a descriptive sense 287-95, 328-30; juristic definition 289, 295-9, 301; normative science of law 290-6; delict and sanction 295-301; 330; international and municipal law 309, 311-24; legal system, membership of 313, 321-3, 334-42; basic norm 338-9, 354

language, open texture of 4, 274-5; operative or performative use of 4, 94-6, 275-7; *and see* meaning; rules

law, definition of 89-91; criticism of 109-19; economic theory of 143-4; international 22 n, 309, 311-24; *and see* command; judges; Natural Law; sanction; sovereign

laws, self-referring 170-8; individuation of 273, 336-8; *and see* rules

liability, objective 282-4

liberties, basic 226-32, 241-3; and rights 209-21

liberty, and equality 217-18; restrictions of 204, 206, 209, 232-41; priority of 223-47; right to 209

logic, and legal reasoning 99-103, 129-31, 260-9, 280-1; of the will 273

morality, enforcement of 248-62; inner, of law 347-53; and purpose 350-3, 356, 363; separation of and law 6-12, 40-87, 146-8

meaning, and force 2, 5, 93-4; core and penumbra 63-8, 71-2; and